THE EMPIRE STATE OF THE SOUTH

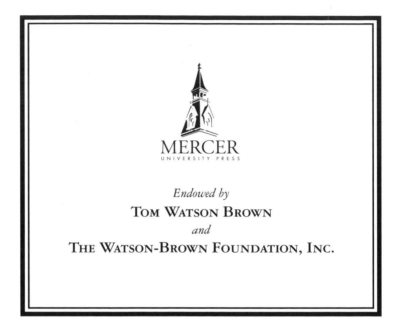

THE EMPIRE STATE OF THE SOUTH

GEORGIA HISTORY IN DOCUMENTS AND ESSAYS

Edited by

Christopher C. Meyers

Mercer University Press
Macon, Georgia

MUP/H758
P377

© 2008 Mercer University Press
1400 Coleman Avenue
Macon, Georgia 31207

First Edition.

Library of Congress Cataloging-in-Publication Data

The empire state of the South : Georgia history in documents and essays /
edited by Christopher C. Meyers. -- 1st ed.
p. cm.
Includes bibliographical references and index.
ISBN-13: 978-0-88146-110-7 (hardback : alk. paper)
ISBN-10: 0-88146-110-5 (hardback : alk. paper)
ISBN-13: 978-0-88146-111-4 (pbk. : alk. paper)
ISBN-10: 0-88146-111-3 (pbk. : alk. paper)
1. Georgia—History. 2. Georgia—History—Sources.
I. Meyers, Christopher C.
F286.E52 2008
975.8--dc22
2008008050

Dedicated to my wife Tracy

CONTENTS

PREFACE

History teachers, no matter the particular discipline, are always looking for ways to improve their classes. One way is through the use of original documents. Primary sources can make the history of an era, an individual, a movement, and even a state come alive. Through original documents students can read history rather than read about history; instead of reading an historian's interpretation, students can draw their own conclusions.

Primary sources are documents that were created by participants in history and can be any kind of written document. This volume contains numerous types of documents including speeches, newspaper columns, letters, treaties, laws, proclamations, state constitutions, court decisions, and many others. Some are excerpts while others are entire documents. Many of these documents are simply too long to be reprinted in their entirety, and in those cases only that part of the document that is most significant (in my estimation) is used. These documents do not exist in a vacuum; it is expected that history teachers will place the documents in their proper historical context. Writing practices, styles, and spellings have varied throughout Georgia's history; in order to retain the flavor of the document and the time period, this volume retains the original grammar and spelling. In addition, the use of "[sic]" to indicate misspellings has been avoided as it only clutters the volume and interrupts the flow of the document.

The documents contained in this volume were chosen carefully. Some outline general themes or movements in Georgia History while others address narrower issues. The documents themselves range from the usual—state constitutions, laws, and speeches—to the inordinate—plans for constructing what is regarded as the state's first concrete home, a corny campaign song, and a reward for the apprehension of a man who proposed that Georgia and South Carolina unite. Georgia has indeed had a colorful history, and these documents narrate that history.

Except for the introduction, each chapter consists of several parts. In the first, a brief narrative introduces the chapter. The documents themselves comprise the second part. Following the documents, two essays written by historians discuss some topic relevant to the chapter; these essays do not always relate directly to the documents. At the end of each chapter is a short list of suggested readings. Some of the recommended books are standard works on Georgia history, but most are volumes that have been published in the last fifteen years. The introduction describes Georgia's geography. At the end of this volume are several appendices that list Georgia's population, governors, counties, and symbols.

A project of this type cannot be completed alone and I had a great deal of assistance. The archivists and librarians at the various repositories I visited were always helpful and accommodating in locating the material and information I requested; they are the lifeline for any historian conducting research. I would like to thank the staffs at the Georgia Archives, MARBL at the Emory University Library, the Hargrett Rare Book and Manuscript Library and the Richard B. Russell Library for Political Research and Studies at the University of Georgia, the Atlanta History Center, the Georgia Historical Society, and the Valdosta State University Archives. Susan Newton at the Winterthur Museum was particularly helpful in locating a photograph. All of the presses and journals were accommodating in agreeing to my requests to reprint excerpts, and I would especially like to thank Stan Deaton at the Georgia Historical Society.

Financial and moral support came from many places. The Watson-Brown Foundation awarded a grant for the completion of this project and I would especially like to thank the foundation's president, Tad Brown. Valdosta State University awarded a grant for this project from the Graduate School Faculty Development Fund. The dean of the College of Arts and Sciences, Linda Callendrillo, generously granted my request for reassigned time to complete this volume. Everyone in the History Department lent encouragement and support, and I would like to particularly thank David Williams, Mary Block, Dixie Haggard, and David Carlson for assistance in locating documents. Paul Riggs, head of the History Department, continuously offered support. I owe Marc Jolley of Mercer University Press a great debt of gratitude for agreeing to publish this book.

My family was always a source of encouragement and support. My parents, Charles and Jill Meyers, always had encouraging words, as did my brother and sisters, Carl, Caren, Nancy, and Julie. My wife Tracy and son Jacob were incredibly tolerant of my preoccupation with this project. My wife's support, encouragement, love, and confidence in me are immeasurable. I could not have done this without her, and for her support and understanding I dedicate this book to her.

James Oglethorpe is considered the founder of the Georgia colony. *Courtesy of Hargrett Rare Book & Manuscript Library, University of Georgia, Athens.*

The Trustees of Georgia meet a delegation of Yamacraw Indians in this 1734 or 1735 oil painting by William Verelst titled "Trustees of Georgia." James Oglethorpe is in the center standing next to the Indian boy. Tomochichi stands to the right of the boy with an outstretched arm. *Courtesy of Winterthur Museum, Winterthur DE.*

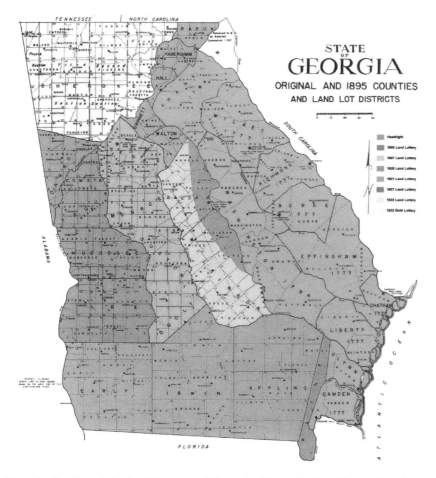

Georgia distributed the land it acquired from the Native Indian Nations in a lottery system. The state held six lotteries, in 1805, 1807, 1820, 1821, 1827, and 1832.

Courtesy of Georgia Archives, Morrow.

Georgia's capitol was located in Milledgeville from 1806 to 1868. The old capitol is now part of Georgia Military College. *Courtesy of Hargrett Rare Book & Manuscript Library, University of Georgia, Athens.*

Sequoyah was the creator of the Cherokee syllabary, completed in 1825. *Courtesy of Prints & Photographs Division, reproduction number LC-USZC4-2566, Library of Congress, Washington, DC.*

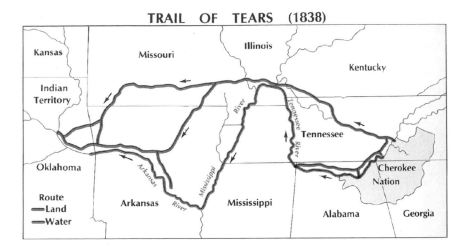

TRAIL OF TEARS (1838)

This map shows the routes of the 1838 Cherokee Trail of Tears. Thomas W. Hodler and Howard A. Schretter, eds., *The Atlas of Georgia* (Athens: University of Georgia, 1986). *Courtesy of the Institute of Community and Area Development, University of Georgia. Used with permission.*

This plantation home was built in Augusta in 1854 by Dennis Redmond (see chapter 5, document 4). It was later the home of Fruitlands Nursery and is currently the clubhouse of the Augusta National Golf Club. *Courtesy of Vanishing Georgia Collection, image number ric035, Georgia Archives, Morrow.*

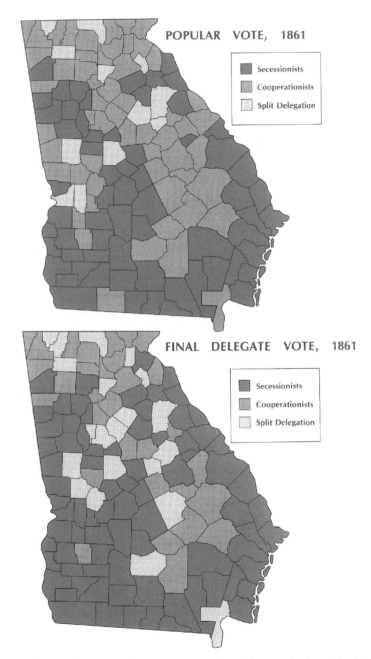

POPULAR VOTE, 1861

Secessionists
Cooperationists
Split Delegation

FINAL DELEGATE VOTE, 1861

Secessionists
Cooperationists
Split Delegation

This map depicts the support for secession in Georgia's counties in 1861. Thomas W. Hodler and Howard A. Schretter, eds., *The Atlas of Georgia* (Athens: University of Georgia, 1986). *Courtesy of the Institute of Community and Area Development, University of Georgia. Used with permission.*

Georgia's state capitol building was moved to Atlanta in 1868. The gold dome on top of the capitol contains 43 ounces of Georgia gold. 2006. *Courtesy of Jacob W. Meyers, Valdosta, GA.*

Joseph E. Brown was a consummate politician. He was elected governor of Georgia in 1857, 1859, 1861, and 1863. He also served in the U.S. Senate from 1880 to 1891. *Courtesy of Hargrett Rare Book & Manuscript Library, University of Georgia, Athens.*

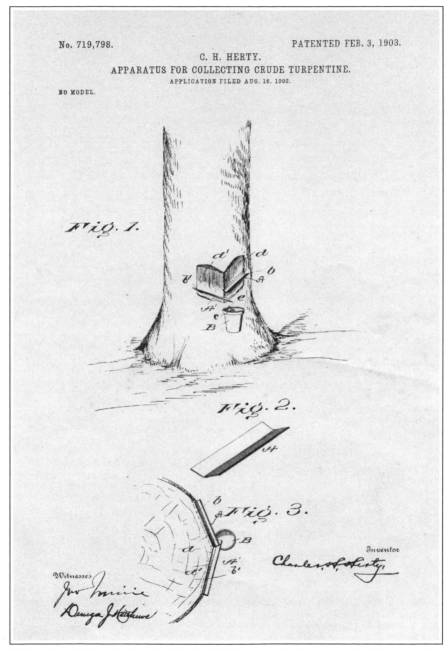

University of Georgia chemist Charles H. Herty received a patent for his cup-and-gutter system of collecting pine resin. This 1903 drawing accompanied Herty's patent application. *Courtesy of Charles H. Herty Papers, box 46, folder 9, Manuscript, Archives, and Rare Book Library, Emory University, Atlanta, Georgia.*

Tom Watson, in this photo taken about 1904, was Georgia's most renowned
Populist. He ran for President on the Populist ticket in 1904. *Courtesy of Vanishing
Georgia Collection, image number mcd051, Georgia Archives, Morrow.*

SPREAD OF BOLL WEEVIL, 1892 - 1922

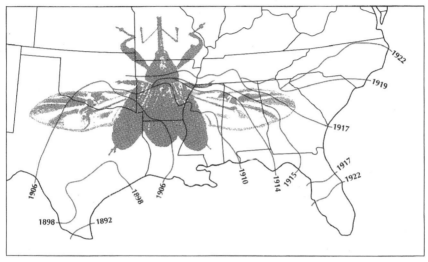

This map traces the progress of the boll weevil from Texas; the vermin arrived in Georgia in the 1910s. Thomas W. Hodler and Howard A. Schretter, eds., *The Atlas of Georgia* (Athens: University of Georgia, 1986). *Courtesy of the Institute of Community and Area Development, University of Georgia. Used with permission.*

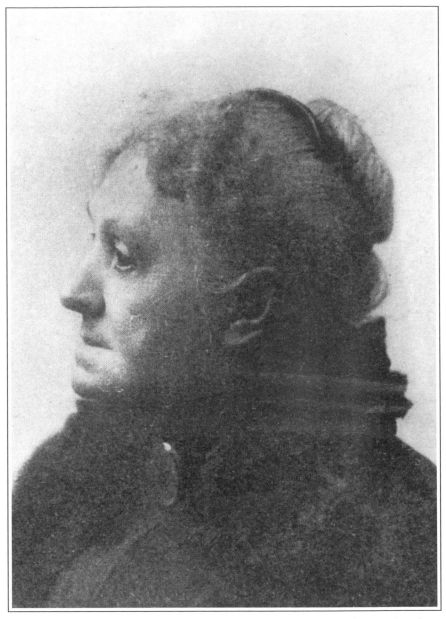

Rebecca Latimer Felton was Georgia's most renowned champion of women's rights and the first woman to serve in the U.S. Senate, in 1922. *Courtesy of Hargrett Rare Book & Manuscript Library, University of Georgia, Athens.*

PERCENTAGE TENANCY BY COUNTY, 1930

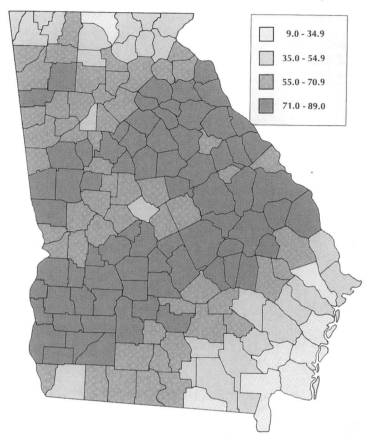

☐	9.0 - 34.9
☐	35.0 - 54.9
▦	55.0 - 70.9
▦	71.0 - 89.0

This map depicts the rate of tenancy in Georgia's counties in 1930. Thomas W. Hodler and Howard A. Schretter, eds., *The Atlas of Georgia* (Athens: University of Georgia, 1986). *Courtesy of the Institute of Community and Area Development, University of Georgia, Athens. Used with permission.*

German prisoners of war were incarcerated in Georgia during World War II. The POWs pictured here were held at Camp Fargo. Note the "P" and "W" on their pants. 1945. *Courtesy of Renate Milner, Valdosta, GA.*

Franklin D. Roosevelt's Little White House in Warm Springs, Georgia. 2002. Roosevelt visited 41 times for a total of 797 days (see chapter 13, document 4) and died there on April 12, 1945. *Courtesy of Carl Vinson Institute of Government, University of Georgia, Athens.*

Dr. Martin Luther King, Jr., Rev. Ralph Abernathy, and Dr. William Anderson are arrested in Albany in July 1962. At left is police chief Laurie Pritchett. *Courtesy of Prints & Photographs Division, NYWT&S Collection, reproduction number LC-USZ62-135511, Library of Congress, Washington, DC.*

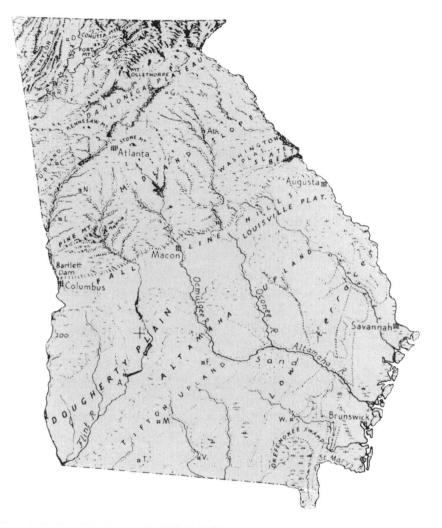

Georgia's Natural Environment. Thomas W. Hodler and Howard A. Schretter, eds., *The Atlas of Georgia* (Athens: University of Georgia, 1986). *Courtesy of the Institute of Community and Area Development, University of Georgia. Used with permission.*

GEORGIA

Georgia has 159 counties, more than any state except Texas. *Courtesy of Carl Vinson Institute of Government, University of Georgia, Athens.*

INTRODUCTION

Georgia:
The Natural Setting[1]

Max E. White

Georgia's natural environment has undergone many changes over the past 12,000 years as climatic events affected world or regional climates. But not all changes in the environment have been wrought by ice ages or other climatic phenomena. Human beings too have changed the landscape, even before Europeans appeared on the scene to reshape it forever. Native peoples cleared areas for their settlements and agricultural fields; they set fire to the forests to drive out game or to clear undergrowth; they made trails; they made fish traps in the creeks and rivers of the Piedmont and mountains; and they quarried rocks and minerals to make tools and weapons and to trade with people in areas where these materials did not occur....

The northwest corner of Georgia—Dade County and parts of Walker and Chattooga Counties—is part of the Cumberland Plateau geographic province, which extends through several states. Typical of this area are hills and steep-sided valleys. The flat tops of Lookout Mountain, Sand Mountain, and Pigeon Mountain overlook this part of Georgia. Underlain by limestone and other sedimentary rocks, the region, except for the valleys, has rather thin and poor soil. Its northern portion is drained by tributaries of the Tennessee River, while its southern portion lies in the watershed of the Coosa River.

The Cumberland Plateau province in Georgia was originally covered by a forest where several varieties of oak predominated, along with poplar and American chestnut.

The parallel ridges and valleys of the northwestern corner of Georgia that lie between the Cumberland Plateau and the Appalachians form part of the Great Valley. This geographic feature extends through several states along the western side of the Appalachian Mountains. A region of sedimentary rocks, it is

---

[1] Reprinted from Max White, *The Archaeology and History of the Native Georgia Tribes* (Gainesville: University Press of Florida, 2002) 1–8. Reprinted with permission of the University Press of Florida.

the location of several types of chert, highly prized by native peoples, for it is easily chipped into tools with a sharp cutting edge. The boundary between the Ridge and Valley province and the Appalachians is obvious, frequently marked by precipitous cliffs on the mountains that tower above the valleys on the eastern side.

The valleys of this province are mostly covered in forest dominated by white oak; along the ridges an oak and pine forest is most common. In some areas oak and hickory varieties more often occur, and in former times the American chestnut grew here. Red cedar dominates the low, flat limestone ridges, forming a unique environment called a cedar glade, a feature that appears in a few places in the Chickamauga Valley.

Most of the Ridge and Valley province is drained by the Coosa River and its main tributary, the Oostanaula. The northern portion of the Chickamauga Valley, however, is drained by the Chickamauga Creek, which empties into the Tennessee River near Chattanooga.

The Blue Ridge Mountains in Georgia mark the southernmost extension of the Appalachian Mountains. This area includes the highest point in Georgia (Brasstown Bald, 4,768 feet above sea level), as well as the most rugged terrain. That the Appalachians form one of the earth's oldest mountain ranges explains their rounded and heavily eroded features. Ancient igneous and metamorphic rocks occur throughout. Quartzite and steatite (soapstone), both used by prehistoric inhabitants, are found widely, and marble occurs in a few locations. Mica, gold, and copper are also present in some areas.

Originally, this entire region was covered in forest, as it mostly is today. The type of forest, however, varied with such factors as elevation, soil type, and moisture. Cool, moist slopes on the north side of mountains often host northern hardwood species that represent relict communities, for these locations remained cool enough for northern tree varieties to survive after the Ice Age. The hardwood forest of the lower elevations is generally dominated by hemlock, poplar, beech, hickory, and oak varieties. The American chestnut was once a dominant species in the mountain forest, but it was virtually eliminated by blight early in the twentieth century.

The Blue Ridge province is included in several watersheds. To the northwest, the area is drained by the Little Tennessee, Hiawassee, and Toccoa Rivers and their tributaries, which flow in to the Tennessee River or its major tributaries. Elsewhere, the mountains are the point of origin for the Coosawattee and Etowah Rivers, which form the Coosa River; the Chattahoochee, which empties into the Gulf of Mexico; and the Tugalo, one of the main tributaries of the Savannah River.

The Piedmont Plateau is one of the larger geographic features of the state. Its high inner edge, known as the Dahlonega Plateau, reaches elevations of up to 1,800 feet above sea level where it meets the Appalachians. Typified by hills and stream valleys with steep sides, the Dahlonega Plateau merges in the south with the Atlanta Plateau, which has lower hills and broader stream valleys. Both of these portions of the Piedmont contain monadnocks, isolated mountains of a very rocky nature. Currahee Mountain in Stephens County, Yonah Mountain in White County, and Stone Mountain near Atlanta are examples. The remainder of the Piedmont is typified by low hills or almost level land. Igneous and metamorphic rocks underlie the entire region. Quartzite is most common, steatite (soapstone) is locally present, and there are isolated outcrops of basalt.

Almost the entire Piedmont was covered in forest dominated by various species of oak and hickory, as well as poplar, pine, and other tree varieties. The American chestnut once grew in the upper Piedmont. River bottoms were often covered in vast canebrakes—thickets of native river cane.

Streams flowing into the Coosa, Chattahoochee, and Tallapoosa Rivers drain the western portion of the Piedmont Plateau. The remainder is drained by the Ocmulgee, Flint, Oconee, and Savannah Rivers and their tributaries.

All of Georgia south of the Fall Line, more than half of the state, lies in the Coastal Plain province. The Fall Line marks the boundary between the Coastal Plain and the Piedmont, and it extends roughly from Augusta through Macon to Columbus. It is an obvious geologic feature, as the ancient granitic rocks of the Piedmont end and the younger sedimentary rocks of the Coastal Plain begin. The Fall Line gets its name from the numerous waterfalls formed as streams pour across the hard, granitic rocks of the Piedmont onto the softer sedimentary rocks of the Coastal Plain. Visually, the Fall Line is harder to identify, for the low, rolling hills of the Piedmont extend into the Coastal Plain for a few miles.

At times in the past, the Coastal Plain has been under water, a phenomenon explained best by Charles Wharton:

> The Coastal Plain has been covered by successive inundations of the sea. Numerous fossil localities yield whale bones, shark teeth, and marine shells across the breadth of it. The greatest of these inundations occurred during the last epoch of the age of Dinosaurs, the Cretaceous, which left great quantities of marine sands and clays that we now call the Fall Line Sand Hills. The seashore has withdrawn further during each successive inundation, so that as we drive from Macon to Brunswick we cross younger and younger sea floors and, sometimes, the remnants of old beaches and dune systems.

Although one might not think so, the Coastal Plain is a varied landscape. Along the coast, saltwater marshes and tidal rivers are typical. Barrier islands, often bordered on the mainland side by saltwater marsh, form some of the most picturesque places in Georgia. Inland from the coast, swamps are common. Included is the Okefenokee, the second-largest swamp in the United States. In some areas of the Coastal Plain, gently rolling hills replace the flatlands. Sinks and springs dot the landscape, and each microenvironment hosts unique plant and animal species.

The Coastal Plain is underlain by sedimentary rocks, chiefly sandstone and limestone. Several types of chert occur here.

Apparently, the Coastal Plain was originally covered in a mixed hardwood forest whose main species included beech, several varieties of oak, cypress, pine, and varieties of hickory. Along the coast, tree species include red bay, sweet bay, red cedar, slash pine, and others.

This region of Georgia is drained primarily by streams that flow into the Savannah, Ogeechee, Oconee, Ocmulgee, Flint, and Chattahoochee Rivers.

Additional Sources

Bartley, Numan V. *The Creation of Modern Georgia.* Second Edition. Athens: University of Georgia Press, 1990.

Coleman, Kenneth, editor. *A History of Georgia.* Second Edition. Athens: University of Georgia Press, 1991.

Cook, James F. *The Governors of Georgia.* Third Edition. Macon GA: Mercer University Press, 2005.

Hill, Melvin B., Jr. *The Georgia State Constitution: A Reference Guide.* Westport CT: Greenwood Press, 1994.

Saye, Albert. *A Constitutional History of Georgia, 1732–1945.* Athens: University of Georgia Press, 1948.

Chapter 1

COLONIAL BEGINNINGS TO 1764

The period of Georgia History to 1764 was marked by control of the region by native Indian nations, the advent of European contact, the clashing of cultures, the European powers vying for control of the "debatable land," and finally successful colonization by England. For centuries the area was inhabited by numerous native Indian nations, including the Creeks, Cherokees, Yamacraw, Yamassee, and other associated groups. The natives' legacy lives on in the names of many of the state's rivers: Chattahoochee, Oostanaula, Coosa, Oconee, Ocmulgee, and Ogeechee. The native nations covered Georgia like dew, but their territorial possessions would gradually dwindle until they were completely driven from the state. Beginning in the early 1500s a veritable tidal wave of European explorers and settlers initiated the decline in the natives' fortunes.

Three European nations attempted to colonize Georgia—Spain, France, and England. When Ponce de Leon's expedition arrived on the coast in 1513, the Spanish became the first European nation to set foot on Georgia soil. Focusing on the region south of Georgia, the Spanish established a colony in 1565 at St. Augustine and from there expanded northward into Georgia. In their effort to colonize Georgia, the Spanish established missions and presidios. Missions were inhabited by one or two Catholic friars and had the objective of converting the natives to Christianity. The presidio was established for defense and housed some number of soldiers. Until 1670 the Spanish retained almost unchallenged control over the region.

Spain's domination ended when England established a permanent colony in the Carolinas. With the Spanish in Florida and the British in Carolina, the land between them was claimed by both and became "the debatable land." It remained that way until the British established a permanent colony in 1733. Led by James Oglethorpe, a group of twenty-one men petitioned King George II in 1730 for permission to establish a colony in what is now Georgia. The petition was granted in 1732 and these twenty-one men, called the Trustees, began recruiting colonists. In all, 125 hand-picked men made the voyage across the Atlantic and established the colony of Georgia between the Savannah and Altamaha rivers. Oglethorpe accompanied the first settlers, and although he did not hold an official post he exercised control. The Trustees tried several social experiments, all of which failed—neither slavery nor liquor was permitted; Catholics and lawyers were also banned.

The establishment of a British colony on the Savannah River heightened tensions with Spain. These pressures were exacerbated when Oglethorpe established several forts close to Spanish Florida, one of which was at the mouth of the St. John's River. Animosities exploded into open warfare in 1739 with a conflict known as the War of Jenkins's Ear. The most well-known engagement was the Battle of Bloody Marsh, fought on July 7, 1742. The conflict resolved none of the disagreements. In the meantime the British settlers expanded their colony, including the establishment of Frederica on St. Simons Island.

The terms of the charter from King George II stipulated that the Trustees would turn over control of the colony to the king in 1753. By the 1750s the Trustees began to lose interest in the colony, which was not at all profitable. In 1752, a year early, the Trustees turned over the colony to the king, making Georgia a royal colony, the thirteenth and final colony.

Documents

In the first document below, a shipwrecked Spanish sailor describes a ball game the Guale played and a ceremony the sailor calls a "fiesta." The second document is the charter King George II issued in 1732 for the Georgia colony. In the third document, a report dated January 10, 1733, James Oglethorpe describes the progress made in establishing the colony. Document 4 is James Oglethorpe's initial agreement with the Lower Creek Indians made May 21, 1733. The fifth and sixth documents outline the positions of both the Spanish and English governments on possession and ownership of Georgia; these comprise the crux of the "debatable land" argument. Document 7 is a British plan for fighting the Spanish in 1740, outlining offensive and defensive measures during the conflict known as the War of Jenkins's Ear. The eighth and final document, dated July 3, 1752, is a memorandum in which the Trustees advise on the future of the Georgia colony.

1. Guale Game and Ceremony[1]
ca. 1595

...They received us with happy faces and affable expressions and words that we did not understand just as they did not understand us. They soon attempted to entertain us with a certain game. To start it off, they all assembled together in one section of the plaza together with their cacique, each one with a pole or a piece of a sharp-pointed lance of the shape and size of a dart. One of them did not resemble them. The chief had a stone in his hand of the shape and size of a half-real bread roll. On beginning the game, the one who held it threw it rolling with all his strength, and they threw their poles after the stone all at one time and without any order. They took off after them at a run at the same time. I did not understand the game very well. But it appeared to me that the one who ran the best and arrived first took his pole and the stone and, without hesitating for a moment, threw it back again in the direction from whence it came. They spent a great deal of time in this exercise and became so involved in the chase that the sweat ran from all over their bodies. Once the entertainment had ended, we all entered into the council house together and we all sat down,

---

[1] From Fray Andres de San Miguel, *An Early Florida Adventure Story* (Gainesville: University Press of Florida).

Spaniards, chiefs, and leading men, on the bed made of tree branches, which was raised more than a yard from the ground. In the council house and close to the door on its right side, there was a little idol or human figure badly carved. For ears it had those of a coyote and for a tail that of the coyote as well. The rest of the body was painted with red ochre. Close to the idol's feet there was a wide-mouthed jar full of a drink that they call *cacina* and around the jar and the idol was a great number of two-liter pots, also full of *cacina*. Each Indian took one of these in his hand, and with reverence they went about giving it to those who had played, who were each seated on a bench. Each one took and drank his. As a result of this their bellies became like a drum and as they went on drinking, their bellies kept on growing and swelling. They carried this on calmly for awhile, and we [were] waiting to see how the fiesta would come to an end, when we saw that, on opening their mouths with very great calmness, each one began ejecting by way of them [their mouths] a great stream of water as clear as it was when they drank it, and others, on their knees on the ground with their hands, went about spreading the water that they ejected to one side and the other. All those who did this were leading men. That solemn fiesta ended in this fashion.

2. Colonial Charter[2]

George the Second by the Grace of God To all To Whom these presents shall come Greetings Whereas wee are Credibly Informed that many of our Poor Subjects are through misfortunes and want of Employment reduced to great necessities insomuch as by their labour they are not able to provide a maintenance for themselves and Families and if they had means to defray the Charge of Passage and other Expenses incident to new Settlements they would be Glad to be Settled in any of our Provinces in America whereby Cultivating the lands at present wast and desolate they might not only gain a Comfortable Subsistence for themselves and Families but also Strengthen our Colonies and Encrease the trade Navigation and wealth of these our Realms And whereas our Provinces in North America have been frequently Ravaged by Indian Enemies more Especially that of South Carolina which in the late war by the neighbouring Savages was laid wast with Fire and Sword and great numbers of the English Inhabitants miserably Massacred And our Loving Subjects who now Inhabit these by reason of the Smallness of their numbers will in case of any new war be Exposed to the like Calamities in as much as their whole Southern

---

[2] Courtesy of the Georgia Archives.

Frontier continueth unsettled and lieth open to the said Savages And whereas wee think it highly becoming Our Crown and Royal Dignity to protect all our Loving Subjects be they never so distant from us to Extend our Fatherly Compassion even to the meanest an most unfortunate of our people and to relieve the wants of our abovementioned poor Subjects And that it will be highly Conducive for the accomplishing those Ends that a Regular Colony of the said poor people be Settled and Established in the Southern Frontiers of Carolina and whereas wee have been well Assured that if wee would be Graciously pleased to Erect and Settle a Corporation for the receiving managing and Disposing of the Contributions of our Loving Subject divers persons would be Induced to Contribute to the uses and purposes aforesaid Know yee therefore that wee have for the Considerations aforesaid and for the better and more Orderly Carrying on the said good purposes of our Especial Grace certain Knowledge and Meer Motion Willed Ordained Constituted and Appointed And by these Presents for us our Heirs and Successors Do Will Ordain Constitute Declare and Grant that our Right Trusty and Wellbeloved John Lord Viscount Percival of our Kingdom of Ireland Our trusty and Wellbeloved Edward Digby George Carpenter James Oglethorpe George Heathcote Thomas Tower Robert More Robert Hucks Rogers Holland William Sloper Francis Eyles John Laroche James Vernon William Belitha Esquires Stephen Hales Master of Arts John Burton Batchelor in Divinity Richard Bundy Master of Arts Arthur Bedford Master of Arts Samuel Smith Master of Arts Adam Anderson and Thomas Coram Gentlemen and Such other persons as shall be Elected in the manner hereinafter mentioned and their Successors to be Elected in manner as hereinafter is directed be and shall be one Body Politick and Corporate in Deed and in name by the Name of The Trustees for Establishing the Colony of Georgia in America....

By Writt of Privy Seal

3. James Oglethorpe Reports on the Settlement of Georgia[3]

From the Camp near Savannah,
10th of February 1733

I gave you an Account, in my last, of our Arrival at Charles Town; the Governor and Assembly have given us all possible Encouragement. Our People arrived at Beaufort on the 20th of January, where I lodged them in some new Barracks built for the Soldiers, whilst I went myself to view the Savannah River. I fixed upon a healthy Situation, about Ten Miles from the Sea. The River here forms an Half-moon, along the South side of which the Banks are about Forty Feet high, and on the Top a Flat, which they call a Bluff. The plain High ground extends into the Country Five or Six Miles, and along the River-side about a Mile. Ships that draw Twelve Feet Water can ride within Ten Yards of the Bank. Upon the River-side, in the Centre of this Plain, I have laid out the Town, opposite to which is an Island of very rich Pasturage, which I think should be kept for the Trustees Cattle. The River is pretty wide, the Water fresh, and from the Key of the Town you see its whole Course to the Sea, with the Island of Tybee, which forms the Mouth of the River, for about Six Miles up into the Country. The Landskip is very agreeable, the Streams being wide, and bordered with high Woods on both Sides. The whole People arrived here on the First of February; at Night their Tents were got up. 'Till the 7th we were taken up in unloading and making a Crane, which I then could not get finished, so took off the Hands, and set some to the Fortification, and began to fell the Woods. I have marked out the Town and Common; half of the former is already cleared, and the first House was begun Yesterday in the Afternoon. A little Indian nation, the only one within Fifty Miles, is not only at Amity, but desirous to be Subjects to his Majesty King George, to have Lands given them among us, and to breed their Children at our Schools. Their Chief and his beloved Man, who is the Second Man in the Nation, desire to be instructed in the Christian religion.

---

[3] From Allen D. Candler, ed., *The Colonial Records of the State of Georgia*, vol. 3 (Atlanta: Franklin Printing and Publishing Company, 1905).

4. Oglethorpe's First Treaty with the Lower Creeks[4]

May 21, 1733

Articles of Friendship and Commerce between the Trustees for Establishing the Colony of Georgia in America and the Chief Men of the Nation of the Lower Creeks.

First. The Trustees bearing in their hearts great Love and Friendship to you the said Head Men of the Lower Creek Nation do engage to let their people carry up into your Towns all kinds of Goods fitting to trade in the said Towns at the Rates and Prices settled and agreed upon before you the said Head Men and annexed to this Treaty of Trade and Friendship.

Secondly. The Trustees do by these Articles promise to see Restitution done to any the People of your Towns by the People they shall send among you upon Proof made to the Beloved Man they shall at any time send among you That they who have either committed Murder, Robbery, or have beat or wounded any of your People or any ways injured them in their Crops by their Horses or any other ways whatever and upon such proof the said People shall be tryed and punished according to the English law.

...Fourthly. We the Head Men of the Coweta and Cussita Towns in behalf of all the Lower Creek Nation being firmly persuaded that He who lives in Heaven and is the occasion of all good things has moved the hearts of the Trustees to send their Beloved men among us for the good of us our Wives and Children and to Instruct us and them in what is Streight do therefore declare that we are glad that their People are come here, and though this Land belongs to us the Lower Creeks yet we that we may be instructed by them do consent and agree that they shall make use of and possess all those Lands which our Nation hath not occasion for to use and we make over unto them their Successors and Assigns all such Lands and Territories as we shall have no occasion to use, Provided always that they upon Settling every New Town shall set out for the use of ourselves and the People of our Nation such Lands as shall be agreed upon between their Beloved Men and the head men of our Nation and that those Lands shall remain to us forever.

...Sixthly. And we the Head Men for ourselves and People do promise to apprehend and secure any negro or other slave which shall run away from any of the English Settlements to our Nation and carry them either to this Town or the Savannah or Pallachuckala Garrison and there to deliver him up to the

---

[4] From John T. Juricek, ed., *Early American Indian Documents: Treaties and laws, 1607–1789*, vol. 11, Georgia Treaties, 1733–1763 (Washington, DC: University Publications of America, 1989).

Commander of such Garrison and to be paid by him four Blankets or two Guns or the value thereof in other goods Provided such runaway Negro or other slave shall be taken by us or any of our People on the further side of Ocony River, and in case such Negro or runaway Slave shall be taken on the hither side of the said River and delivered to the Commander as aforesaid then we understand the pay to be one Gun or the Value thereof. And in case we or our People should kill any such slave for resistance or Running away from us in apprehending him then we are to be paid One Blanket for his head by any Trader we shall carry such Slaves head unto.

Lastly. We promise with streight Hearts and Love to our Brothers the English to give no encouragement to any other White People but themselves to settle among us, and that we will not have any correspondence with the Spaniards or French. And to shew that we, both for the good of ourselves our Wives and Children do firmly promise to keep this Talk in our Hearts as long as the Sun shall shine or the waters run in the Rivers we have each of us set the marks of our Families.

5. James Oglethorpe on English Ownership of Georgia[5]

April 1736

The first Discovery of this Country was made by Sebastian Cabbat who was fitted out by Henry the 7th and 8th and Possession then taken in the Name of the King of England, and Sir Francis Drake did in the Reign of Queen Elizabeth upon the Spaniards settling there take and burn the Fortress of Augustine and thereby maintained the English Right.

The Spaniards some years after the burning of Augustine by Sir Francis Drake retook possession of that Place, but the Crown of England looked upon the same as an Intrusion, and continued asserting their rights to these Countrys as far as the 29th Degree of Northern Latitude. And King Charles the First made a Grant upon that Right of this Province then called Carolana. Afterwards King Charles the Second, still presuming upon the same right, did upon the former Patent being for Non use forfeited, grant all the Lands from 36 to 29 Degrees of Northern Latitude, to the Lords Proprietors of Carolina, and thereby asserted his right to these Countrys.

But the Spaniards say that they have always continued in possession of Augustine under the Pope's Grant, and that they have supported that Grant by

---

[5] From John T. Juricek, ed., *Early American Indian Documents: Treaties and Laws, 1607–1763*, vol. 11, Georgia Treaties, 1733–1763 (Washington, DC: University Publications of America, 1989).

Conquest, that when my Lord Cardross came and settled at Port Royal under a Grant from the Lords Proprietors, they Dislodged him by force of Arms, as being an Intruder upon their Dominions, and that the Crown of England sat down contented therewith.

In answer to which we do allow that they did dislodge my Lord Cardross by treachery, and murdered several Families, which was an Infraction of the Peace then subsisting with the Crown of Spain. And the said Injury was afterwards fully revenged by the Crown of Great Britain, for the Creek Indians being in Alliance with the Crown of Great Britain did in the year 1705 attack the Spaniards and Appellachee Indians took the Appellachee's Towns and the Spanish Forts. And that the same Indians being in Alliance with the English did soon after take the Town of Augustine, besiege the Fort, but not having Artillery for to take the Fort, they at last raised the Siege, and came back over the Rivers, but would never suffer the Spaniards to pass the River St. Johns. That in that Expedition which was during an open War between the French and Spaniard on one Side and the Queen of England and her Allies on the other, the Creek Indians being of the Number of her Allies, did by force of Arms beat the Spaniards out of all the Islands and Lands from Port Royal to Augustine.

That after the raising of the Siege at Augustine, the Creek Indians still kept Possession of the River St. Johns, and would never suffer the Spaniards to resettle either on the Islands or Continent on this Side of the River, and that, during that Possession, the Treaty of Utrecht was made, by which her Majesty and her Allies were to keep all that they were then possessed of, except such places as in that Treaty were stipulated to be Delivered up.

And that since that Treaty the Creek Indians have continued in Possession to the very Hour that they delivered the Possession thereof to James Oglethorpe for the use of his Britannick Majesty, pursuant to a Treaty Concluded between his said Majesty and that Nation. Therefore it appears that the Lands as far as St. John's River doth belong unto his Majesty by the same Right, that any other Lands in America do belong unto him, which is by being in possession thereof under Treaties of Peace, and whatsoever can be urged against his Majesty's Right to these his Dominions may as well be urged against his right to Nova Scotia, Jamaica, or any other part of America, since the Pope's Grant reaches to all America, and the Spaniards never gave up their Rights in form to any Part, only that each Party should hold what they stood possessed of at the time of concluding the Treaty. And the Crown of Britain by their Allies and Creeks, were in possession of the same at the time of the Treaty of Utrecht, and have continued in Possession thereof to this hour, as appears by the Affidavits hereunto annexed. And the Spaniards have acquiesced in that

Possession since they never pretended to keep any Guard beyond St. John's River, but have always kept one, and sometimes two Guards on the South side of St. John's River.

6. Antonio de Arredondo on Spanish Ownership of Georgia[6] Ca. 1742

At the cost of much Christian blood and the vast expanse of labor, the Spaniards were in possession, as has been seen in the preceding chapters, of the country included between Santa Elena in the north latitude 32° 30', and 25°, where the Continent of Florida terminates on the east. They had settlements and missions on nearly all the islands and mainland of the coast, and in the interior in the provinces of Guale, Coava, Orista, Timucua, Santa Fe, San Martin, San Pedro, Azile, Vitachuco, Apalache, Caueta, Apalachicolo, Talapuses, and others; while the English were undoubtedly owners from the cape and bay of Santa Maria as far as South Carolina or South Charleston. Then the Most Serene and Powerful King Charles II, King of Great Britain, and the Most Serene and Powerful Carlos II, Catholic King of Spain, solemnly concluded a treaty and amicable agreements for the purpose of restoring and establishing peace in the Western Indies and renewing the friendly intercourse which had been interrupted by various and mutual injuries and depredations which had occurred.

By article 7 of this treaty [Treaty of Madrid of 1670] it was agreed that...the Most Serene King of Great Britain, and his heirs and successors, should hold forever in plenary right of sovereignty, dominion and possession "all the lands, regions, islands, colonies, and dominions in the Western Indies or in any part of America which the said King of Great Britain and his subjects hold and possess at present, so that under his name or title, or under pretext of any other claim, there cannot be, and ought never to be, any force used or any controversy started in the future."

This clearly implies that the English are and will be owners of all the lands which they possessed and held at the time when the treaty was signed, and that they are not and cannot be owners of what they did not hold or possess at that

---

[6] From Herbert Bolton, ed., *Arredondo's Historical Proof of Spain's Title to Georgia* (Berkeley: University of California Press, 1925).

time. And although in the year 1670 they only held and possessed the territory as far as South Charleston, on the east coast of Florida, it follows that up to this place they ought legally to hold and possess, and no contention should be made against them....

It follows then by necessary inference, that Great Britain has legal ownership (permissive and only by force of the treaty) over all the lands held by it in the year named, and no others; and since it is clearly proved in the paragraphs concerning the discoveries, conquests, and possessions, that in the year specified the English were not owners of the territory comprised between latitude 32° 30' inclusive (that is, San Felipe in Santa Elena) and 29°, which region for the past ten years they have called Georgia, it naturally follows that such an establishment is a usurpation, and beyond dispute calls for another treaty like that in the year 1670, in which another article like number 7 the Catholic King may grant to Great Britain plenary right of sovereignty, etc., such as he granted in the former, over the rest of the regions and islands that he possessed at the time. But without this requisite, the Spaniards justly claim and ought to claim all the country from 32° 30' to 30° 26', where the San Juan River is situated, the point to which during the last ten years the British nation has extended itself under the name of Georgia; for from that river toward the south the Spaniards are now living, as is well known.

7. Proposals Relating to the War in Georgia and Florida[7] Ca. 1740

Offensive. If I had one Batalion of Land Forces more with a small Train of Artillery, Engineers & Gunners from Europe & an Allowance for Pioneers whom I could raise in America & for the two Troops of Rangers, the Highland Company for Indians & for One hundred Boat Men, and to buy such Craft here as might oppose the half Gallies. I think the place might be reduced this Winter, we ought to begin any time after September, when the heats are over in this Country, the Winters are so temperate that we can keep the Field all the Season and as our Partys have hindered them from Planting this Year, they will be greatly distressed for provisions, besides our Experience in the last Siege will give us great Advantage.

---

[7] Courtesy of the Georgia Archives.

Defensive. The above may be done if His Majesty thinks we should act upon the Offensive. If we are to act upon the Defensive the two Troops of Rangers, One hundred Boat Men with proper craft, & the Two Sloops that are now here, the small Garrisons that are in the Country, & the Highland Company will be necessary to be continued, as also some Artillery Ammunition to be sent for the Defence of the Town & Harbour and the Fortifications of Fort St. Andrew & Fort William to be improved, and orders for me to continue the fortifying this Town, the Barracks &c.

8. Pro Memoria from the Late Trustees of the Colony of Georgia[8]

July 3, 1752

As the Georgia Trustees have surrendered their Trust into the Hands of his Majesty, they flatter themselves that the following Observations, which They take the Liberty of offering to your Lordship, will be ascribed to no other Motive, but a Sense of their Duty to his Majesty, and a Regard for the Honour of his Administration, and for the Rights of the People, who have gone to Georgia in an absolute confidence in the Privileges granted them in his Majesty's Charter.

1st. It is expressly declared therein that Georgia shall be a Separate and Independent province, and that the Inhabitants shall not be bound to obey and Laws or Orders of South Carolina.

2. Notwithstanding this, the People of Georgia are apprehensive of the Colony's being put under the Government of South Carolina, and have been even lately alarmed with Threats from some Inhabitants of this Province, that on the Alteration of Government They Shall be Ousted from their Settlements, cultivated at a great Expense, under pretense of old Grants, which were totally neglected, and indeed forfeited before the Georgia Charter, and absolutely set aside by it....

The Trustees are sensible how great an Attention is given to your Lordship to the Rights of the most distant of his Majesty's Subjects; They will not therefore add to his Trouble by making any Apology for it; But, They take Leave to Submit to your Lordship's Consideration, whether a Speedy Resolution as to the Form of Government to be Established in Georgia might not be expedient, in order to quiet the Minds of the People there, and to

---

[8] Courtesy of the Georgia Archives.

prevent or at least to silence any idle Disputes or Jealousies between the Inhabitants of the two Provinces.

ESSAYS

The Yamassee Revolt of 1597[9]

J. G. Johnson

In 1597 a young chief of the province of Guale, annoyed by the reprimands of Father Corpa, apostasized from the faith and instigated the Indians to revolt. Gathering a group of malcontents, he advised them to go with him into the interior where they could enjoy the liberty to which they had been accustomed before the coming of the missionaries. This they did, but after a few days of contemplation over their grievances, real and imaginary, they decided to return and kill Father Corpa. As an argument in favor of this step, the chief predicted that if they did not kill the missionaries, the Spaniards would come in force and deprive them of their liberty and lands, the first step to which was the coming of the Franciscans, who, while talking of peace, were preparing to make themselves their masters. He further told them that after the missionaries were dead, it would be an easy matter to kill the soldiers, and only in that way could their liberty be preserved. Following this advice the horde of hostile warriors, armed with bows and arrows and wearing large head-dresses of feathers, returned to the Christian Indians.

Going to Tolomato at night, the rebels concealed themselves in the church. At daybreak, when Father Corpa opened the door of his house, they killed him, cut off his head, and placed it on a stick, which in turn was tied to a post. Several of the natives of the settlement now joined the party of the rebellious chief. On the following day the young Indian collected his followers, and according to the chronicler of the affair, harangued them thus:

"Now the father is dead, but he would not have been if he had allowed us to live as we did before we became Christians. Let us return to our former customs, and prepare to defend ourselves against the punishment which the

---

[9] Reprinted from "The Yamassee Revolt of 1597 and the Destruction of the Georgia Missions," *Georgia Historical Quarterly* 7/1 (March 1923). Courtesy of the Georgia Historical Society.

governor of Florida will try to inflict upon us, for if he succeeds in it, he will be as rigorous for this one father as though we had made an end of them all, for he will surely persecute us for the father we have killed the same as for all."

The suggestion that the surviving Franciscans be put to death was approved, and the leader continued:

"They take away our women, leaving us only one in perpetuity, and prevent us from trading her; they interfere with our dances, banquets, foods, ceremonies, fires, and wars, in order that, by not practicing them we shall lose our ancient valor and skill, inherited from our ancestors; they persecute our old men, calling them magicians; even our work troubles them, for they try to order us to lay it aside on some days; and even when we do everything that they say, they are not satisfied; all they do is to reprimand us, oppress us, preach to us, insult us, call us bad Christians, and take away from us all the happiness that our forefathers enjoyed, in the hope that they will give us heaven."

Fired by their hatred for the Spaniards, the murderers went to Father Rodriguez's mission at Torpiqui [on Ossabaw]. Entering his house suddenly and stealthily, they told him that they had come to kill him. The priest attempted to dissuade them, but they told him not "to weary himself preaching to them, but to call on God to help him." Whereupon Rodriguez begged to be allowed to say mass, and requested that after his death they bury his body. He then divided the few things that he possessed among the poor Indians of the town, after which he knelt before his executioners. While in this posture he was slain, and his body thrown out in the open for the birds and beasts to eat. However, none approached it but a dog, "which ventured to touch it and fell dead."

The Indians now sent a messenger to the chief of Guale Island, ordering him to kill the priests on that island, warning him that they were coming to see if it had been done, and if not, he and all his people would die with the missionaries. The chief, being friendly toward the Spaniards and unable to prevent the threatened invasion, secretly sent a supposedly faithful native to Assopo, where Aunon and Badajoz had their mission. He hoped that, when apprised of the danger, they would retire to the Spanish presidio, some distance away on the same island, until the danger was past. In that way he would not only save the Franciscans but would also clear himself.

The messenger, however, through treachery or fear, did not deliver the message but returned to his master with a fictitious reply. The chief, who was well informed of the danger, again sent him to Assopo. This he did for three consecutive days, even offering the priests a boat to cross over to the mainland, but the warning never reached them. At the end of three or four days the rebels appeared, and such was their anger toward the Guale chief that he would have been killed had he not been able to offer plausible excuses. Wishing to be absolved from all blame he went to the mission, where he spoke to Father Aunon as follows:

"It would have been better if you had believed me, and had put yourself in safety; but you did not wish to take my advice, and it will not be possible to defend you from these people who have come to kill you."

The missionaries replied that they had been ignorant of all that, and that he should not be troubled, as they were willing to die. The chief then bade them farewell, saying that he was going away to weep for them, and that he would return and bury their bodies.

Upon their arrival at Assopo, the Indians first sacked the mission, after which they fell upon the priests with sticks and *macanas* (wooden knives edged with flint). Father Aunon was held in such high esteem that, at the first blow given to him, many of the Indians were moved to compassion and wished to spare him. As he knelt before the savages, a dispute arose among them until one, stealing up behind, slew him. They left the bodies where they fell, but some Christian Indians buried them at the foot of a large cross which had been erected by Father Aunon.

The murderous band now crossed over in great haste to Asao, on St. Simon Island, in search of Father Velascola. They learned in town that the missionary was in St. Augustine, but, ascertaining the day he would return, they hid themselves in the reeds near the place at which he would disembark. As he was a man of immense physical strength they feared to attack him openly. When he landed they slyly approached him and he fell under the blows of the *macanas* and tomahawks.

Continuing on their way southward, the Indians stopped at Jekyl Island and surprised Father Davilla at his mission at Ospo. Hearing the clamor without, and understanding the danger, he refused to open the door. The invaders prepared to break it down, whereupon Father Davilla opened it and slipped past in the darkness while they sacked the building. They were as anxious to plunder as to kill, and occupied themselves first in seizing the spoils.

While this was taking place the priest had time to conceal himself in a dense thicket near by. When the looting was finished, the rebels went out to look for Father Davilla, and upon discovering him began to shoot arrows at him. After having both shoulders pierced he was captured by the savages, who prepared to put him to death, but his life was spared when one of the enemy, desiring the poor clothing he wore, interceded for him. When they had deprived him of his clothing they sent him to one of their towns in the interior to serve as a slave.

Elated at their success, the natives, being reinforced by other malcontents, provided themselves with a good supply of arrows and embarked in more than forty canoes, with the intention of investing San Pedro Island and killing the missionaries and Spanish soldiers there. They especially desired to put to death the chief of that island, since he was an ally of the Spaniards and therefore their enemy. When they neared the harbor, likewise known as San Pedro, they saw a brigantine lying at anchor near the place where they would have to land. This boat had already remained in the harbor thirty days on account of contrary winds, and now its presence prevented the massacre of the inhabitants and the destruction of the important establishments maintained there.

The boat contained only one soldier and a few sailors, but the sight of it was sufficient to throw the hostile natives into confusion. Perceiving this confusion, the chief of the island sallied forth with more boats than his opponents possessed and attacked them. The invaders fought doggedly at first, but, seeing defeat before them, became panic-stricken and fled. Many of them leaped to the shore of the island, and having no means of escape were either killed or died of starvation in the woods. The leader escaped to the mainland with the survivors and fled to the north.

When Governor Canco of Florida heard of the insurrection, he led overland a force of infantry to the Peninsula of Guale [Ossabaw], while a number of ships proceeded to the same destination. The Indians, however, hid themselves in the swamps, and the governor was able to capture but one live Indian, an interpreter, from whom he secured no information other than that the missionaries had been killed. In retaliation the soldiers burned the corn in the fields, in consequence of which famine completed the punishment which the Spaniards found themselves unable to inflict....

Frederica in 1742[10]

J. T. Scott

During the first decade after its founding in 1736, Frederica housed over one hundred civilians, several hundred soldiers, and several hundred more sutlers and soldiers' relatives. General James Oglethorpe made Frederica his base of operations during the early stages of King George's War, and Mary Musgrove Bosomworth, the so-called Queen of the Creeks, lived there for a time in the early 1740s. Both John and Charles Wesley briefly inhabited the town, and

---

[10] Reprinted from "The Frederica Homefront in 1742," *Georgia Historical Quarterly* 78/3 (Fall 1994). Courtesy of the Georgia Historical Society.

George Whitefield held for a short time the appointment of the town's Anglican priest. As the southernmost outpost of the British North American empire, Frederica possessed immense strategic and symbolic importance, and for a brief moment in July 1742 it found itself on the front-line of the War of Jenkins' Ear....

The population of Frederica in 1742 is an appropriate place to begin an analysis of the town. That year it ranged from 100 to 150 men, women, and children, excluding the military and their camp followers. The number of residents of Frederica during its first decade was stable and quite fluid. Approximately half of the town lots changed hands between 1736 and 1743, though new settlers normally replaced those that left. Most of those who left headed for South Carolina, while new arrivals came primarily from South Carolina or from London. Curiously enough, none of the sources report a population exodus in the face of the Spanish invasion in 1742. Indeed, John Terry, the one person reported as having left the colony for fear of the Spanish, received a fair bit of ridicule from the townspeople for his cowardly retreat.

Frederica in 1742 enjoyed as much demographic variety as any settlement in the New World and certainly more than earlier colonial outposts such as Jamestown, Virginia, an all-male enterprise. The sexes in Frederica had been fairly well balanced from the initial settlement and remained so in 1743. The numerous marriages between 1736 and 1743 indicate an adequate, if not plentiful, supply of potential spouses. An abundance of children flowed naturally from most colonial marriages, and Fredericans were no exception. Almost fifty children, ranging from infancy to near adulthood, inhabited Frederica in 1742, forming roughly a third of the population. Henry and Katherine Myers possessed the largest documented brood—seven children ranging from seventeen to a newborn. Not all couples were newlyweds or even at childbearing years. Several couples over sixty years old settled in Frederica.

For young and old alike, death was a constant pall. Men, women, and children all fell prey to disease, malnutrition, or accidental death without respect for station or influence. Several townsmen lost their wives to the traumas of childbirth and raised their children on their own. Numerous women lost husbands, leaving them to fend for themselves, sometimes with no estate and with no marketable skill. Economically as well as emotionally devastating, a husband's death meant that a middle-class wife could and did easily become a pauper widow. Nevertheless, many continued with their lives and quickly remarried neighbors, friends, and even servants.

Along with the population, the variety of buildings in the town most explicitly defined Frederica in 1742. Along Broad Street, especially on the riparian side of town, stood a series of reasonably impressive houses, at least by

Frederica standards. Samuel Davison and Benjamin Hawkins both resided in multi-story brick dwellings on the southern side of Broad Street. Across the street stood the large houses of Samuel Perkins and David Calwell, the latter's considered the "best in Town." His three-story dwelling had a huge basement with tile flooring, two hearths and an oven, and two staircases. Behind Perkins's house stood the twin houses of Francis Moore, one of brick and one of wood, which Moore claimed together cost him 400 pounds. Farther down Broad Street and on scattered outer lots were less imposing houses, many built of tabby, logs, or clapboards, or some combination thereof. While often sufficient and even comfortable by eighteenth-century colonial standards, these dwellings were neither visually impressive nor archaeologically long-standing. The outer reaches of the settled part of the town contained a series of huts and shacks which were not substantial by any definition. These housed the unfortunates of Frederica, many of whom had been forced into poverty by death, desertion, or disaster. The last row of lots on the south side of town was never occupied and presumably remained unimproved.

Fredericans, for the most part, seemed to be a hard-working lot. There were very few gold-seekers and no criminals or previously imprisoned debtors in early Frederica, despite Georgia's reputation as a debtor colony. The townsfolk came mostly from working-class London and pursued virtually every trade imaginable: cordwainers, vintners, wheelwrights, carpenters, shoemakers, pilots, bricklayers, tavernkeepers, fishermen, painters, an accountant, a hatter, merchants, blacksmiths, a locksmith, a bedsteadmaker, a mantuamaker, a dyer, and for that matter, a butcher, a baker, and a candlestick maker. These laborers, craftsmen, and shopkeepers enabled Frederica to provide for itself many of the services and products needed in a colonial village.

Besides the trades these townspeople undertook, most also pursued gardening or farming of some sort, and at least one settler seriously tried his hand at pig herding. In addition to their small town lots, settlers generally received middle-sized garden plots adjacent to the village and larger farm plots further away. While none of these lots were large enough to generate a fortune, records indicate that several settlers made a comfortable living as husbandmen and planters. The crops they grew ranged from foodstuffs to more exotic endeavors like grape vineyards. Like many others in colonial Georgia, Thomas Hird attempted silk production. He obtained mulberry plants and silkworm eggs, but again like many others, his efforts proved futile. Thomas Walker undertook a more successful endeavor: by 1742 he tended thirty-five beehives which produced 77 gallons of honey in 1742 and 180 gallons in 1743. Daniel Cannon's efforts at pig ranching suffered a setback in 1741 when James

Oglethorpe ordered fifty of his stock slaughtered because Cannon had violated Oglethorpe's ban on pigs in the town area.

Frederica's diverse economic structure stood her well in wartime when supplies and especially manufactured products were harder to obtain. Part of Frederica's attractiveness to Oglethorpe in the face of Spanish invasion threats came from her diversified, well-balanced occupational makeup. Had Frederica not been able to provide Oglethorpe with much of what he needed to fight a war, he may well have given up on the St. Simons settlement and fallen back to Savannah....

Frederica was neither the best nor the worst place to live in the English world in 1742. Its location on the Altamaha River made it at the same time accessible to British seagoing merchant ships and vulnerable to Spanish war ships. Although—or perhaps because—it possessed a relatively stable, even prosperous village economy, thanks to the presence of an English regiment, Frederica had not yet developed (and ultimately never did develop) the agricultural hinterlands needed for long-term urban growth. The town could boast some fine homes, but it was by no means architecturally advanced. In terms of sheer numbers, huts significantly outnumbered houses in the civilian portion of the town. This situation, its abundant modest housing and stable level of population, meant that Frederica provided many of the qualities Oglethorpe needed in a town to serve as his base of operations during King George's War. Unfortunately, it had none of the qualities necessary to sustain a vibrant colonial port. With war looming in the early 1740s, one would assume that the needs and the future of the town and its people would have been subverted by the much more pressing concern of Spanish invasion and conquest. The records suggest otherwise.

For a brief moment Frederica found itself on the front line of the War of Jenkins's Ear. As inhabitants of the southernmost coastal outpost of the British empire in North America, Fredericans were under constant threat of invasion or attack from sea or land. The Spanish had a well-worn reputation among the English for practicing "more than Turkish cruelties" on its enemies, and the distant memories and knowledge of General Pedro Menendez de Avile's relentless attack on the interloping French settlement at La Caroline and the merciless execution of the men of Rene Laudonnierre in 1564 would no doubt have colored their attitudes and feelings toward the Spanish once the war began. One would expect in such an exposed setting to see some manifestation of war fever, or war hysteria, or town unity in the face of this Iberian menace. Although the records are unfortunately silent about Frederica in July 1742, the primary attention of the colonists between 1739 and 1745 (after which the records become exceedingly scarce) appears to have been focused on far more mundane problems....

By the time of the Revolution, Frederica was little more than a dot on a map. With the Spanish gone, Savannah thriving, and the regiment withdrawn, Frederica quickly fell from disrepair into disuse. Indeed, by the mid-1750s the town-lot numbering system had become confused and altered to the point that the ownership of specific lots could not be ascertained. Without either the regiment or the necessary agricultural infrastructure, the Frederica economy quickly deteriorated. By that time, however, it had served its primary purpose. The garrison at Frederica, if not the townspeople, had turned back the last serious Spanish attack on the Atlantic coast of Britain's North American empire, and both Savannah and Charleston had been spared attack and invasion. Frederica is remembered now not for its residents but for its military role in King George's War. And yet, on a hot summer day in 1742, Fredericans and their problems, and not the global affairs of His Royal Majesty, George II, dominated the town's attention.

Additional Sources

Baine, Rodney. *Creating Georgia: Minutes of the Bray Associates 1730–1732 & Supplementary Documents.* Athens: University of Georgia Press, 1995.

Cashin, Edward J., editor. *"Key of the Indian Countrey."* Macon GA: Mercer University Press, 1986.

———. *Governor Henry Ellis and the Transformation of British North America.* Athens: University of Georgia Press, 1994.

Hahn, Steven C. *The Invention of the Creek Nation, 1670–1763.* Lincoln: University of Nebraska Press, 2004.

Hudson, Charles. *Knights of Spain, Warriors of the Sun: Hernando de Soto and the South's Ancient Chiefdoms.* Athens: University of Georgia Press, 1997.

Ivers, Larry. *British Drums on the Southern Frontier: The Military Colonization of Georgia, 1733–1749.* Chapel Hill: University of North Carolina Press, 2005.

Lanning, John T. *The Spanish Missions of Georgia.* Chapel Hill: University of North Carolina Press, 1935.

Parker, Anthony W. *Scottish Highlanders in Colonial Georgia: The Recruitment, Emigration, and Settlement at Darien, 1735–1748.* Athens: University of Georgia Press, 1997.

Smith, Marvin T. *Coosa: The Rise and Fall of a Southeastern Mississippian Chiefdom.* Gainesville: University Press of Florida, 2000.

Sweet, Julie A. *Negotiating for Georgia: British-Creek Relations in the Trustee Era, 1733–1752.* Athens: University of Georgia Press, 2005.

Thomas, David H. *The Archaeology of Mission Santa Catalina de Guale*. New York: American Museum of Natural History, 1987.

White, Max E. *The Archaeology and History of the Native Georgia Tribes*. Gainesville: University Press of Florida, 2002.

Worth, John E. *The Struggle for the Georgia Coast: An 18th-Century Spanish Retrospective on Guale and Mocama*. New York: American Museum of Natural History, 1995.

Chapter 2

THE REVOLUTIONARY ERA, 1765–1787

Georgia was a divided colony in the years immediately preceding the Revolution and during the conflict itself. As the newest British colony, Georgia relied more heavily on aid from England than the twelve other colonies. Because it was closer to England than the other colonies, Georgia was slow in accepting the Revolutionary movement; it was a colony of divided loyalties. One of the first serious crises, and perhaps the best example of a divided colony and Georgia's lingering loyalty to England, concerned the Stamp Act. In January 1766 Georgia governor James Wright permitted some sixty ships to enter the port of Savannah with stamps in place. This is generally regarded as the only instance of the stamps being sold in the thirteen colonies and was considered so serious that Carolina threatened to invade Georgia.

Over the next few years opposition to British policies developed in Georgia but had not yet hardened into radicalism as in other colonies. By 1773 a committee of correspondence had been created and in the summer of 1774 two meetings were held in a Savannah tavern to consider the state of affairs. These meetings, especially the second during which a series of resolutions was written, were the first indication that some in Georgia had joined the revolutionary movement. Later in 1774 Georgia was not represented at the First Continental Congress, an indication that the colony was still divided. By 1775 more Georgians opposed British policies and in February 1776 Governor Wright felt it prudent to leave the colony.

In the absence of royal authority Georgia revolutionaries moved to create a state government to fight the British. Georgians took the first step in April 1776 by writing the first state constitution, called Rules and Regulations. The Rules and Regulations created a government with three departments: legislative, executive, and judicial; most of the power rested in the legislative department. The document was designed to be temporary and lasted only until February 1777, when the permanent Constitution of 1777 was adopted. This document again assigned the legislative branch most of the power; a unique feature of this constitution was the inclusion of a bill of rights. In the meantime Georgia was represented at the Second Continental Congress by Button Gwinnett, George Walton, and Lyman Hall, who signed the Declaration of Independence.

Georgia did not experience anything resembling large-scale military campaigns until the end of 1778. On December 29, 1778, a 3,000-man force of British, Loyalist, and German troops under Lieutenant Colonel Archibald Campbell marched into Savannah largely unopposed. The city remained in enemy hands for the remainder of the war. In early 1779 Georgians began a series of campaigns to recapture the city, which resulted in a couple of relatively small engagements between Augusta and Savannah. In February colonials defeated a force at Kettle Creek, and the following month at Briar Creek the British claimed victory. Later in September 1779 Georgians' hopes rose when a French fleet arrived off the coast of Savannah and began siege operations. The French commander, Count d'Estaing, grew impatient and assaulted the city on October 9, an attack that failed miserably. The French fleet gave up and sailed away. The British eventually evacuated Savannah in July 1782.

In the aftermath of the war Georgia assumed unfettered autonomy over its government and land. In 1786 the assembly moved the capital from Savannah to Louisville, but Augusta would serve as the capital until 1795 when Louisville was ready. Lastly, Georgia rewarded its war veterans with land grants.

DOCUMENTS

The first document that follows is a series of reports from Governor Wright on the 1766 Stamp Act crisis. The second document lists the set of resolutions the revolutionaries passed in Savannah in 1774. The third document is Georgia's first state constitution, written in 1776. Document 4 is the Constitution of 1777. The fifth document is correspondence related to the proposal from South Carolina to unite the two colonies and Georgia's response to that proposal. Document 6 is the legislation that granted land to Georgia's Revolutionary War veterans.

1. Stamp Act Crisis[1]

Governor James Wright to Board of Trade, January 15, 1766
My Lords
The beginning of last Month I did my Self the Honor of writing your Lordships two letters which I sent to Charles Town in South Carolina to go by the Grenville Packet, in which I acquainted your Lordships of the Perplexed Situation I was then in, with Respect to the Stamp Duty, and in the last Mentioned that the Papers &c were brought here by His Majesties Ship Speedwell, and has been Landed & Lodged in the Kings Store in Fort Halifax under the Care and Commissary without any appearance of Mob or Tumult, but that I had great reason to apprehend there was a design, when the distributor Should arrive to Compell him to resign or Promise not to act, as has been done in every other Colony to the Northward of this....

...Notwithstanding my Lords I have been so far Successful in Supporting His Majesties Authority in this Case. Yet my Lords I must not Conceal from His Majesty, that Several Public Insults have been offered, & abuses Committed, and that I have very nearly seen the Power & Authority His Most Sacred Majesty has been graciously Pleased to Vest in me, wrested out of my Hands, a Matter my Lords too Cutting for a good Subject & Servant to Bear. No Pains my Lords has been Spared in the Northern Colonies to Spirit up and inflame the People here, and a Spirit of Faction & Sedition has been Stirred up throughout this Province....

---

[1] From Kenneth Coleman and Milton Ready, eds., *Colonial Records of the State of Georgia*, vol. 28, pt. 2 (Athens: University of Georgia Press, 1979).

...The People in general my Lords I think not ill disposed, but have been Misled & Influenced to a degree of Madness, by the Seditious & Rebellious acts & Publications of the other Colonies. And I humbly hope the whole Province will not suffer in your Lordships Opinion for the Rashness of Some. At the Same time my Lords it Seems very Clear that the Executive Part of Government requires Some further degree of Strength & Support....

Governor James Wright to Board of Trade, February 1, 1766
My Lords
...Some Incendiaries were Sent here from Charles Town in South Carolina, full Fraught with Sedition, and have been about the Country and Inflamed the People to Such a degree, that they were assembling together in all Parts of the Province, & to the Number of about 600 were to have come here as yesterday, all armed, and as I have been Informed were to have Surrounded my House & Endeavoured to extort a Promise from me, that no Papers Should be issued till His Majesties Pleasure is known on the Petitions Sent from the Colonies. And if I did not Immediately Comply, they were to Seize upon & destroy the Papers & Commit many acts of Violence against the Persons & property of those Gentn. who have declared themselves Friends to Government. On this last alarm I thought it advisable to Remove the Papers to a Place of greater Security, and accordingly ordered them to be Carried to Fort George on Cockspur Island, where they are Protected by a Captain 2 Subalterns & 50 Private Men of Rangers.... My task is rendered much more difficult by the Carolinians going the Lengths they have done, & Still do, & Spiriting up the People here to follow their Example....

2. Tondee's Tavern Resolutions[2]

August 10, 1774
Resolved, nemine contradicente, That his Majesty's subjects in America owe the same allegiance, and are entitled to the same privileges, and immunities with their fellow subjects in Great Britain.
Resolved, nemine contradicente, That as protection and allegiance are reciprocal, and under the British Constitution, correlative terms, his Majesty's subjects in America have a clear and indisputable right, as well as from the

---

[2] From George White, ed., *Historical Collections of Georgia* (New York: Pudney & Russell, Publishers, 1855).

general laws of mankind, as from the ancient and established customs of the land so often recognized, to petition the Throne upon every emergency.

Resolved nemine contradicents, That an Act of Parliament lately passed, for blockading the port and harbour of Boston, is contrary to our idea of the British Constitution: First, for that in effect deprives good and lawful men of the use of their property without judgment of their peers; and secondly, for that it is in nature of an *ex post facto* law, and indiscriminately blends as objects of punishment the innocent with the guilty; neither do we conceive the same justified upon a principle of necessity, for that numerous instances evince that the laws and executive power of Boston have made sufficient provision for the punishment of all offenders against persons and property.

Resolved, nemine contradicente, That the Act for abolishing the Charter of Massachusetts Bay tends to the subversion of *American* rights; for besides those general liberties, the original settlers brought over with them as their birthright, particular immunities granted by each charter, as an inducement and means of settling the Province; and we apprehend the said Charter cannot be dissolved but by a voluntary surrender of the people, representatively declared.

Resolved, nemine contradicente, That we apprehend the Parliament of Great Britain hath not, nor ever had, any right to tax his Majesty's American subjects; for it is evident beyond contradiction, the constitution admits of no taxation without representation; that they are coeval and inseparable; and every demand for the support of government should be by requisition made to the several houses of representatives.

Resolved, nemine contradicente, That it is contrary to natural justice and the established law of the land, to transport any person to Great Britain or elsewhere, to be tried under indictment for a crime committed in any of the colonies, as the party prosecuted would there be deprived of the privilege of trial by his peers from the vicinage, the injured perhaps prevented from legal reparation, and both lose the full benefit of their witnesses.

Resolved, nemine contradicente, That we concur with our sister colonies in every constitutional measure to obtain redress of *American* grievances, and will by every lawful means in our power, maintain those inestimable blessings for which we are indebted to God and the Constitution of our country—a Constitution founded upon reason and justice, and the indelible rights of mankind.

Resolved, nemine contradicente, That the Committee appointed by the meeting of the inhabitants of this Province, on Wednesday, the 27th of July last, together with the deputies who have appeared here on this day from the different parishes, by a General Committee to act; and that any eleven or more of them shall have full power to correspond with the Committees of the several

Provinces upon the continent; and that copies of these resolutions, as well as all other proceedings, be transmitted without delay to the Committees of Correspondence in the respective Provinces.

3. Rules and Regulations[3]

Whereas, the unwise and iniquitous system of administration obstinately persisted in by the British Parliament and Ministry against the good people of America hath at length driven the latter to take up arms as their last resource for the preservation of their rights and liberties which God and the Constitution gave them;

And whereas an armed force, with hostile intentions against the people of this province, having lately arrived at Cockspur, his Excellency Sir James Wright, Baronet, and King's Governor of Georgia, in aid of the views of the administration and with a design to add to those inconveniences which necessarily result from a state of confusion, suddenly and unexpectedly carried off the great seal of the Province with him;

And whereas, in consequence of this and other events, doubts have arisen with the several magistrates how far they are authorized to act under the former appointments, and the greatest part of them have absolutely refused to do so, whereby all judicial powers are become totally suspended to the great danger of persons and property;

And whereas, before any general system of government can be concluded upon, it is necessary that application be made to the Continental Congress for their advice and directions upon the same; but nevertheless, in the present state of things, it is indispensably requisite that some temporary expedient be fallen upon to curb the lawless and protect the peaceable;

This Congress, therefore, as the representatives of the people, with whom all power originates, and for whose benefit all government is intended, deeply impressed with a sense of duty to their constituents, of love to their country, and inviolable attachment to the liberties of America, and seeing how much it will tend to their advantage of each to preserve rule, justice and order, do take upon them for the present, and until the further order of the Continental Congress, or of this, or any future provincial Congress, to declare, and they

---

[3] From Walter McElreath, *A Treatise on the Constitution of Georgia* (Atlanta: Harrison Co., 1912).

accordingly do declare, order, and direct that the following rules and regulations be adopted in this Province—that is to say—

1st. There shall be a President and Commander-in-Chief appointed by ballot in this Congress, for six months, or during the time specified above.

2d. There shall be, in like manner, and for the like time, also a Council of Safety, consisting of thirteen persons, besides the five delegates to the General Congress, appointed to act in the name of a Privy Council to the said President or Commander-in-Chief.

3d. That the President shall be invested with all the executive powers of government not inconsistent with what is hereafter mentioned, but shall be bound to consult and follow the advise of the said Council in all cases whatsoever, and any seven of the said Committee shall be a quorum for the purpose of advising.

4th. That all laws, whether common or statute, and the acts of Assembly which have formerly been acknowledged to be of force in this Province, and which do not interfere with the proceedings of the Continental or our Provincial Congresses, and also all and singular the resolves and recommendations of the said Continental and Provincial Congress, shall be of full force, validity, and effect until otherwise ordered.

5th. That there shall be a Chief-Justice, and two assistant Judges, an Attorney-General, a Provost-Marshal, and Clerk of the Court of Sessions, appointed by ballot, to serve during the pleasure of the Congress. The Court of Sessions, or Oyer and Terminer, shall be opened and held on the second Tuesday in June and December, and the former rules and methods of proceedings, as nearly as may be, shall be observed in regard to summoning of juries and all other cases whatsoever.

6th. That the President or Commander-in-Chief, with the advise of the Council as before mentioned, shall appoint magistrates to act during pleasure in the several Parishes throughout this Province, and such magistrates shall conform themselves, as nearly as may be, to the old established forms and methods of proceedings.

7th. That all legislative powers shall be reserved to the Congress, and no person who holds any place of profit, civil or military, shall be eligible as a member either of the Congress or of the Council of Safety.

4. Constitution of 1777[4]

Whereas the conduct of the Legislature of Great Britain for many years past has been so oppressive on the people of America that of late years they have plainly declared and asserted a right to raise taxes upon the people of America, and to make laws to bind them in all cases whatsoever, without their consent; which conduct being repugnant to the common rights of mankind, hath obliged the Americans, as freemen, to oppose such oppressive measures, and to assert the rights and privileges they are entitled to by the laws of nature and reason;...

And whereas it hath been recommended...to the respective assembles and conventions of the United States, where no government, sufficient to the exigencies of their affairs, hath been hitherto established, to adopt such government as may, in the opinion of the representatives of the people, best conduce to the happiness and safety of their constituents in particular and America in general;...

We, therefore, the representatives of the people, from whom all power originates, and for whose benefit all government is intended, by virtue of the power delegated to us, do ordain and declare, and it is hereby ordained and declared, that the following rules and regulations be adopted for the future government of this State:

Article I. The legislative, executive, and judiciary departments shall be separate and distinct, so that neither exercise the powers properly belonging to the other.

Article II. The legislature of this State shall be composed of the representatives of the people, as is hereinafter pointed out; and the representatives shall be elected yearly, on the first Tuesday in December; and the representatives so elected shall meet the first Tuesday; in January following, at Savannah, or any other place or places where the house of assembly for the time being shall direct.

On the first day of the meeting of the representatives so chosen they shall proceed to the choice of a governor, who shall be styled "honorable;" and of an executive council, by ballot out of their body....

Article IV. The representation shall be divided in the following manner: ten members from each county....

Article VI. The representatives shall be chosen out of the residents in each county, who shall have resided at least twelve months in this State, and three months in the county where they shall be elected...and they shall be of the

---

[4] From Robert and George Watkins, eds., *A Digest of the Laws of the State of Georgia* (Philadelphia: R. Aitken, 1800).

Protestant on, and of the age of twenty-one years, and shall be possessed in their own right of two hundred and fifty acres of land, or some property to the amount of two hundred and fifty pounds.

Article VII. The house of assembly shall have power to make such laws and regulations as may be conducive to the good and wellbeing of the State; provided such laws and regulations be not repugnant to the true intent and meaning of any rule or regulation contained in this constitution....

Article IX. All male white inhabitants, of the age of twenty-one years, and possessed in his own right of ten pounds value, and liable to pay tax in this State, or being of any mechanic trade, and shall have been resident six months in this State, shall have a right to vote at all elections for representatives, or any other officers, herein agreed to be chosen by the people at large; and every person having a right to vote at any election shall vote by ballot personally....

Article XII. Every person absenting himself from an election, and shall neglect to give in his or their ballot at such election, shall be subject to a penalty not exceeding five pounds....

Article XIX. The governor shall, with the advice of the executive council, exercise the executive powers of government, according to the laws of this State and the constitution thereof, save only in the case of pardons and remission of fines, which he shall in no instance grant; but he may reprieve a criminal, or suspend a fine, until the meeting of the assembly, who may determine therein as they shall judge fit.

Article XX. The governor, with the advice of the executive council, shall have power to call the house of assembly together, upon any emergency, before the time which they stand adjourned to....

Article XXIII. The governor shall be chosen annually by ballot, and shall not be eligible to the said office for more than one year out of three, nor shall he hold any military commission under any other State or States....

Article XXIX. The president of the executive council, in the absence or sickness of the governor, shall exercise all the powers of governor....

Article XXXIII. The governor for the time being shall be captain-general, and commander-in-chief over all the militia, and other military and naval forces belonging to this State....

Article LI. Estates shall not be entailed; and when a person dies intestate, his or her estate shall be divided equally among their children; the widow shall have a child's share, or her dower, at her option....

Article LIV. Schools shall be erected in each county and supported at the general expense of the State, as the legislature shall hereafter point out....

Article LVI. All persons whatever shall have the free exercise of their religion; provided it be not repugnant to the peace and safety of the State; and shall not, unless by consent, support any teacher or teachers except those of their own profession.

Article LVII. The great seal of this State shall have the following device: on one side of a scroll, whereon shall be engraved "The Constitution of the State of Georgia;" and the motto "Pro bono publico." On the other side, an elegant house, and other buildings, fields of corn, and meadows covered with sheep and cattle; a river running through the same, with a ship under full sail, and the motto, "Deus nobis haec otia fecit."

…Article LX. The principles of the habeas-corpus act shall be a part of this constitution.

Article LXI. Freedom of the press and trial by jury to remain forever inviolate forever….

Article LXIII. No alteration shall be made in this constitution without petitions from a majority of the counties, and the petitions from each county to be signed by a majority of voters in each county within this State; at which time the assembly shall order a convention to be called for that purpose, specifying the alterations to be made, according to the petitions preferred to the assembly by the majority of the counties aforesaid.

5. Proposed Union of Georgia and South Carolina[5]

William Drayton to Humphrey Wells

June 8, 1777

Sir,—In compliance with your request, I do myself the pleasure of committing to paper some of the principal circumstances and arguments relative to the late proposition of an union between South Carolina and Georgia.

By our General Assembly, which is a pretty numerous body, it was unanimously resolved, that an union between the two States would tend effectually to promote their strength, wealth, and dignity, and to secure their liberty, independence, and safety. Commissioners were sent to Savannah to treat of an union, and I was honoured by being upon this business….

Being admitted to an audience in Convention, after a short introduction of what I had to say, I stated, that chance had originally placed the present districts of South Carolina and Georgia under one government at Charlestown; and

---

[5] From George White, ed., *Historical Collections of Georgia* (New York: Pudney & Russell, Publishers, 1855).

although these districts, then forming but one, had been separated and placed under two governments, yet nature pointed out that two should again form but one; for their climate, soil, productions, and interests were the same. That if they continued two States, we had only to recollect the history of mankind, and the nature of things, to foresee that from such causes their counsels and conduct would clash; and of course jealousies and rivalship would daily increase between them, to the natural prejudice of their internal improvement, common production, and foreign commerce. That there might be dangerous disputes about boundaries, and the property of Savannah River; since on these subjects many people in Carolina and Georgia thought very differently; a natural and great obstruction to the rise of the value of property. But that, on the other hand, by an union, all such jealousies, rivalship, prejudice, danger, and obstruction, would be removed. Improvements of every kind, especially in agriculture, inland navigation, and foreign commerce, would be studied and advanced with rapidity. The expense of Government would be lessened, to the great ease of the people, because only one establishment of civil officers would be paid in the room of two. The public defence would be more powerful, and at less expense, under one government than under two, which might be jealous of, and, therefore, often desirous to thwart each other, and at any rate certainly liable, undesignedly, to defeat each other's plans, to the ruin of the people concerned. And thus, sir, you see many important advantages that would be common to the two States by an union. But there are others which would be peculiar to Georgia.

By an union, the land in Georgia would rise in value, because the Carolina planters would be encouraged to extend their improvements into Georgia, and the merchants carry that trade immediately to Georgia, which otherwise must continue to be carried on as it always has been, and especially of late, through Carolina. The Georgia currency, always hitherto of inferior value to that of Carolina, (some more than 20 per cent.,) would be put upon an equal footing with that of South Carolina. The town of Savannah, in particular, and the adjacent lands, would be of much more importance and value, because Savannah River would be immediately cleared, a measure that would encourage and occasion an immediate increase of agriculture upon all the land within reach of its navigation, and hence an amazing increase of produce and river navigation, all of which would centre in Savannah. Thus, in a state of separation from South Carolina, Savannah could reasonably expect, and that but by slow degrees, and at a distant day, only the one-half of the produce of a well-improved cultivation of the lands on that river, but by an union she would, in a very short time, receive the whole of that improved cultivation and trade; and her own commerce would be increased almost beyond imagination, although she would lose the seat of government. Finally, I may add, that in a state of separation, in all probability Savannah will be ruined, because it will be our interest to preserve our trade for our own people....

Having discoursed upon such topics about an hour, I delivered a written proposition as a groundwork to proceed upon, and then departed....

A Proclamation

WHEREAS it hath been represented unto me, that WILLIAM HENRY DRAYTON, of the State of South Carolina, Esq., and divers other persons, whose names are yet unknown, are UNLAWFULLY endeavouring to POISON the minds of the good people of this State against the Government thereof, and for that purpose are, by letters, petitions, and otherwise, daily exciting animosities among the inhabitants, under the pretense of redressing imaginary grievances, which by the said WILLIAM HENRY DRAYTON it is said this state labours under, the better to effect, under such specious pretences, an union between the States of Georgia and South Carolina, all which are contrary to the Articles of Confederation, entered into, ratified, and confirmed by this State as a cement of union between the same and the other United and Independent States of America, and also against the resolution of the Convention of this State, in that case made and entered into: THEREFORE, that such pernicious practices may be put an end to, and which, if not in due time prevented, may be of the most dangerous consequences, I HAVE, by and with the advice and consent of the Executive Council of this State, thought fit to issue this Proclamation, hereby offering a reward of ONE HUNDRED POUNDS, lawful money of the said State, to be paid to any person or persons who shall apprehend the said WILLIAM HENRY DRAYTON, or any other person or persons aiding and abetting him in such unlawful practices, upon his or their conviction: And I DO hereby strictly charge and require all magistrates and other persons to be vigilant and active in SUPPRESSING THE SAME, and to take all lawful ways and means for the discovering and apprehending of such offender or offenders, so that he or they may be brought to condign punishment.

GIVEN under my Hand and Seal in the Council Chamber at Savannah, this fifteenth day of July, one thousand seven hundred and seventy-seven.

JOHN ADAM TREUTLEN

6. Land Grants to Georgia's Revolutionary Soldiers[6]

Be it enacted by the authorities aforesaid, That any person or persons who shall produce a certificate from their commanding officer of the district to which he belongs, to have the legislature of this State (on the total expulsion of the enemy from it) of his having stedfastly done his duty from the time of passing of this act, shall be entitled to two hundred and fifty acres of good land (which shall be exempt from taxes for the space of ten years thereafter;) *Provided* such person or persons cannot be convicted of plundering or distressing the country.

Savannah, August 20, 1781.

ESSAYS

The British Capture of Savannah[7]

David K. Wilson

In 1778 Savannah was surrounded by a series of dilapidated, twenty-year-old fortifications built to defend the city from the Spanish during the Seven Years' War. General Howe and the civilian government should have shored up the fortifications much earlier, but it was too late for that now. Howe correctly concluded that it would be futile to defend the town from within the city's decrepit "walls," which would only serve to trap the American forces when the British arrived.

Howe assumed that he would be heavily outnumbered, given that he had so few troops at his disposal. Indeed, his numbers were so anemic that he considered giving up Savannah without a fight and withdrawing his troops to fight another day. The American commander called a council of war on Christmas Eve 1778 to solicit the opinions of his senior officers. These officers, many of whom lived in the city or in other parts of Georgia, thought that Savannah ought to be defended. They argued that if Savannah could be

---

[6] From *Acts of the General Assembly of the State of Georgia*, 1781.

[7] From David K. Wilson, *The Southern Strategy: Britain's Conquest of South Carolina and Georgia, 1775–1780* (Columbia: University of South Carolina Press, 2005) 72–77. Used with permission of the University of South Carolina Press.

defended even for a few days, General Lincoln might arrive in time to relieve the town with the forces he was known to be gathering at Charlestown. Howe found this argument compelling. He resolved to attempt a defense of Savannah, or at least to fight a delaying action there before falling back to South Carolina.

As the Americans planned their defenses, Lieutenant Colonel Campbell's expedition arrived off Tybee Island at the mouth of the Savannah River on December 23, 1778. Campbell immediately sent a light infantry company of the 71st ashore to capture some locals and procure intelligence. A black slave and his taskmaster were captured and interrogated. The slave, named Peter, told Campbell that Howe's army had 1,800 men (roughly twice its actual size) and was disposed to defend Savannah. Acting on this information, Campbell decided to disembark his troops about 2 miles from the city at Girardeau's plantation, "the first practicable landing-place on the Savannah River." The fleet took two days to navigate the muddy river. Two small American galleys fired on the lumbering column in a futile attempt to delay its advance upriver, but a single shot from a British man-of-war sent the little American boats running. The fleet reached the landing at Girardeau's plantation early in the morning of December 29, 1778, and Campbell ordered his officers to begin landing their troops at first light.

Colonel Samuel Elbert, commander of Georgia's Continentals, purportedly told General Howe that he thought the American army should make a stand at Brewton's Hill, the bluff that overlooked the rice fields of the plantation where the British troops were landing. From that vantage point the Americans would be able to pour artillery and musket fare down on the disembarking British troops; the steep bluff would also give the defending Americans the advantage in close combat. Howe rejected Colonel Elbert's advice, however, because he thought the landings at Girardeau's might be a feint. Instead, Howe sent just one company of South Carolina Continentals to occupy Brewton's Hill with orders to delay the British advance off the beachhead. The American commander then deployed the rest of his army in an open field about one-half mile southwest of Savannah.

Lieutenant Colonel Campbell designated the two light infantry companies of the 71st Regiment, led by Sir James Baird and Captain Charles Cameron, to act as the vanguard to the army. The boats of Baird's company grounded before they could reach shore, so Captain Cameron's light company went ashore by themselves. Cameron moved immediately to execute his orders to "take Possession of the Commanding Grounds in Front of the Disembarkation."

...Campbell accompanied Cameron's men as they waded ashore. The lieutenant colonel personally dressed the troops' battle line and began them marching toward Brewton's Hill, which was about 600 yards from the river.

The bluff rose about 40 feet above the rice swamps, and the view from buildings that dotted its crest dominated the landing area. The British could not safely disembark the rest of their troops and supplies without possession of the bluff. Cameron ordered his troops to advance in three lines: leading the way was a "forlorn hope" of 5 men, about 50 yards behind were 13 men acting as skirmishers, with the rest of the 120-man company in battle order following close behind.

Captain John Carraway Smith commanded the company of fifty South Carolina Continentals on the bluff. His men occupied a series of buildings on the bluff and "knocked out Planks for their Firelocks to look through." When the British light infantry came within about 100 yards of the buildings, Smith's company fired a volley. The British did not fire back but instead advanced rapidly to attack with their bayonets. The rapid charge left no time for a second volley by the Americans, and in less than three minutes Cameron's men were in possession of the bluff. "The Rebels retreated with precipitation by the back Doors and Windows," Campbell reported. Captain Smith's Continentals withdrew in good order and suffered no casualties, but they had yielded an important piece of ground. The British suffered four killed and five wounded, including Captain Cameron, who was mortally injured leading the attack. Campbell lamented the loss of Cameron, calling him "an Officer of Distinguished Merit and Bravery."

Campbell thought it foolish of the Americans not to have invested more in the defense of the bluff (exactly as Colonel Elbert had argued). "Had the Rebels stationed four Pieces of Cannon on this Bluff with 500 men for its Defense," Campbell wrote later, "it is more than probable, they would have destroyed the greatest part of this Division of our little Army."

After hearing of Captain Smith's retreat from Brewton's Hill, General Howe held another council of war at ten o'clock that morning. The enemy had landed in force, and the Americans were heavily outnumbered. The question Howe put before the council was whether they should abandon the town. Howe's senior officers decided that, considering the proximity of the enemy (only a few miles distant), they should stand and fight, and retreat if necessary. The British landing, meanwhile, proceeded at a slow pace. It was only at midday, five or six hours after the first men had waded onto the banks, that the majority of the British made it ashore. During this critical time the Americans did not attempt to counterattack or otherwise hinder the disembarkation. Howe later claimed that the scout he had assigned to watch the British disembarkation had run off on a "private errand," leaving him ignorant of the situation there.

Shortly after noon, elements of the British army proceeded carefully down the road toward Savannah. At about two o'clock they finally arrived at the plantation of former governor James Wright, near the main American battle line. Clambering up a tall tree, the energetic Lieutenant Colonel Campbell surveyed the situation. From his new perspective Campbell was able to discover the American dispositions: "The Rebel Army were formed on a level Piece of Ground, across the Savannah Road with their Front towards the West, their Right to Tatnel's House joining a thick Wood...Their left was nearly extended to the Rice Swamps on the South east Quarter."

Howe's deployment was just as Campbell had observed. The American battle line was roughly one-half mile southeast of Savannah in a shallow "V" shape, with the open end facing the British line and both ends anchored by woods and swamps. Owing to the lay of the land and the defensive works the Americans had made, the "V" shape was a good defensive formation. If the British charged the American center, Howe's entire line would have a good angle from which to shoot. A small trench had been dug across the American front, behind which Howe arrayed his troops. On his left, Howe had placed Colonel Samuel Elbert's Georgia Brigade, a mix of about 200 Georgia militia and Continentals. Howe's right consisted of approximately 464 South Carolina Continentals composed of Colonel Isaac Huger's 5th South Carolina Regiment and Lieutenant Colonel William Thompson's 3rd South Carolina Rangers. The 4th South Carolina Regiment of Artillery supported the line with four fieldpieces; one piece was deployed on either end of the main line and two pieces together in the center behind a small breastwork. To guard his flanks, Howe detached troops from the line companies to act as light infantry—Georgians on the left and South Carolinians on the right.

About 100 yards in front of the American line was a small, marshy rivulet. While not a significant water barrier, the marshy stream would slow down anyone passing through it—and just when they were coming within musket range of the Americans. Spanning the stream at the road was a bridge, which the Americans had set on fire. A line of riflemen acted as skirmishers ahead of the main American line.

Baird's light infantry led the British column as it filed down the road toward Savannah. About 800 yards from the American position the light troops deployed along a rail fence that extended perpendicular to the road. About this time the American artillery began to fire at the British light troops, but with little effect. Meanwhile, the rest of the British column held up behind the plantation, out of sight of the American guns.

Howe had chosen a strong defensive position. If Campbell attempted a frontal assault, there is little doubt that the British would have met stiff resistance. The British were saved from this necessity through the cooperation of a slave found on Wright's plantation. The man, whom some have identified as "Quamino Dolly," told Campbell that "he could lead the Troops without Artillery through the Swamp upon the Enemy's Right."

Campbell ordered Sir James Baird to take the Light Infantry Corps, follow the slave through the wooded swamp on the Patriots' right, and attack the American army in the flank. Campbell then redeployed his forces: "I ordered the first battalion of the 71st to form on our right of the road and move up to the rear of the light-infantry, whilst I drew off that corps to the right as if I meant to extend my front to that quarter, where a happy fall of ground favored the concealment of this maneuver [sic], and increased the jealously of the enemy with regard to their left."

Baird's 350 light infantry filed off to their right and circled around the rear of the British army, following their guide down a narrow path through the swamp on the British left (the American right). The New York Volunteers followed the light infantry in a supporting role, bringing the total strength of the flanking column to 588 men. Campbell placed one of his officers—one Major Skelly—in a tall tree to observe the movement of the light infantry. Skelly was ordered to signal when he saw that Baird had begun his attack. Campbell then arranged his main battle line. He formed his artillery and the Wollwarth Regiment behind a "swell of ground" on the left of the road, while the 1st Battalion of the 71st Regiment held the ground to the right at the rail fence. Thus deployed, nearly the entire British line was hidden from the Americans' view by the small bluff to its front.

Baird's corps quickly and quietly followed their black scout through the quagmire that formed the right flank of the American line. The trail eventually terminated just where the slave said it would: at the barracks in the American rear. Howe had placed no pickets in the area, and so the Americans were completely unaware they were being flanked. Colonel George Walton, a signer of the Declaration of Independence, attempted to warn Howe to guard the side path around the American right flank before the battle began. This warning was apparently ignored out of belief that the British would never find the obscure route.

Baird's men charged out of the overgrown morass and furiously fell on the unsuspecting Georgians. Sitting high in his tree, Major Skelly saw the powder smoke in the American rear. He waved his hat to alert Lieutenant Colonel Campbell that Baird's attack had begun. On that signal, Campbell ordered the British artillery to the hilltop to his front. When these guns opened fire on the American line, 437 men of the 71st Highlanders and another 442 troops of the Wollwarth Regiment were ordered to advance across 800 yards of no-man's land. They did so, according to Campbell, with "alacrity."

Near the center of the American line, General Howe heard the unexpected sound of musket shots coming from the direction of the barracks to his rear. At the same time British cannonballs began to crash about him, causing casualties. The American line had been standing to their arms for the better part of the day. Suddenly cannonballs were flying about them, and the inexperienced American troops began to shift and twitch nervously under the British bombardment. Then came the sight of the red-coated British and blue-uniformed German troops surging over the hill in front of the American position. Howe suddenly realized that he was caught between the hammer and the anvil. He immediately ordered a general retreat. The American troops began an orderly march to the rear, but as the king's forces crossed the marshy rivulet and charged with their bayonets, the retreat turned into a rout. Few Americans, regulars or militia, bothered to fire a shot. Many flung their weapons aside in their desperation to escape. "It was scarcely possible to come up with them," Campbell later wrote, "their Retreat was rapid beyond Conception."

As the main American line crumbled, Baird's light infantry drove into George Walton's militia who were guarding the barracks in the rear. The heavily outnumbered militia ran, and Walton took a bullet in the thigh and fell from his horse. Walton was captured by the advancing British, who apparently never found out that he was a signer of the Declaration of Independence (an act that in the British eyes made him a certified traitor, punishable by death).

Sweeping past the barracks, the light infantry took control of the Augusta road, an act that sealed the main escape route out of the city. The trap had been closed. The redcoats and Hessians, particularly the 1st Battalion of the 71st Regiment, kept a close pursuit of the Americans. Howe's troops fled the battlefield and made a mad scramble into the city. Hundreds of soldiers from both sides charged through the lovely streets and squares of Savannah. As the Highlanders tore through the town, many terrified Patriot citizens who had taken up arms in the city militia grounded their weapons and surrendered....

Colonel Huger mounted a desperate rearguard action, aided by the American artillery under Colonel Owen Roberts. They were able to hold off the pursuing British long enough for many American soldiers to get out of the city. Colonel Roberts was able to bring off three fieldpieces before all the roads out of the city were closed off. Despite Colonel Huger's valiant efforts, he was forced to fall back before the tide of British troops. Many Patriot soldiers attempted to swim Yamacraw Creek to escape. Tossing their weapons aside, soldiers and officers alike leaped into the water and made for the safety of the opposite shore. Campbell estimated that thirty men drowned trying to cross, but there is no way of knowing the true number. General Howe, along with

Colonels Thompson and Huger, were forced to abandon their horses and brave the dangerous waters. Once on the other side, Howe fled with what was left of his army and regrouped 8 miles away at Cherokee Hill. From there he fell back to Zubly's Ferry, crossed the Savannah River into South Carolina, and made camp at Purrysburg. Only about 342 men remained of Howe's army, less than half the force he had at the start of the day. Colonel Elbert's Georgia brigade had suffered particularly badly, with only 30 soldiers escaping capture out of 200.

In one quick stroke Campbell had taken the capital of Georgia. The spoils of war included 48 cannons in the city's defensive works, 23 mortars and howitzers, 817 muskets, a number of ships, and large quantities of goods and foodstuffs. The loss of small arms was a particularly hard-felt loss for the Patriots, as military-grade weapons were difficult to come by for the Americans. The British captured 453 men of all ranks and found 83 Americans dead on the field. There were at least eleven, and probably many more, Americans wounded. The British sustained negligible losses: seven killed and seventeen wounded. A contemporary American officer, Colonel Henry "Light Horse Harry" Lee, said of the battle: "Never was a victory of such magnitude so completely gained with so little loss."

Land and Allegiance in Revolutionary Georgia[8]

Leslie Hall

The story of the Revolutionary War in Georgia can be told in terms of rebels and loyalists or winners and losers, but a more complex and informative story reveals itself when one takes into account those Georgians who did not fall readily into these broad categories. Georgia alone of all the colonies in rebellion had British civil government reestablished during the war, and as a result inhabitants came under unique pressures regarding the pledging of their allegiance. The rival governors, legislative bodies, judiciary systems, and militia and regular troops, as well as the lack of a decisive military victory, motivated many to view the giving of their allegiance with ambiguity and pragmatism. As the war progressed, military and civilian authorities on both sides came to

---

[8] From Leslie Hall, *Land and Allegiance in Revolutionary Georgia* (Athens: University of Georgia Press, 2001). Used with permission of the University of Georgia Press.

recognize that civilians would give their allegiance if their property rights were protected.

Rebel and loyal governments were desperate to earn civilian support, and a flexible loyalty gave civilians some control over the powers of government, control they did not have before or after the war. Yeoman farmers, determined not to give up their land, had the opportunity to acquire additional property through booty, plunder, and reward. Many of the more prosperous took the opportunity of wartime to assume ownership of "enemy" estates, sometimes through purchase, other times through plunder, and also through lawsuits. Others, however, lost much, if not all, of their property through debt, plundering, or evacuation.

The various civil governments that operated in Georgia between 1775 and 1782 received help from London and Philadelphia, but they had to rely on themselves for raising much of the needed resources and for developing strategies to secure their position and gain popular support. These civil governments understood that securing civilian property, above all else, provided the key for maintaining their power. During the war these governments sought to maintain orderly property records and allow for the collection of debts and the retrieval of property, all the while confiscating "enemy" property themselves. Both royal and state governments established commissions to administer abandoned property in order to raise money through rental and sale and later to use the property as barter. Although civil authority remained unstable because neither government could maintain law and order, it was resilient. Calls for elections went out numerous times, enjoyed wide participation, and signified civilian desires for a return to stability. Although the settlers may appear inconsistent in their allegiance and fickle in their politics, they were steadfast in their support of civil authority. Throughout the war civil government operated somewhere in Georgia at all times.

Obtaining citizen loyalty was of utmost concern for the competing governments. The state government required oaths of allegiance and forced many loyalists and neutrals to leave the state between 1776 and 1778. After the British reoccupation of lower Georgia, both governments found requiring loyalty from civilians both difficult and unproductive. They shared a desperate need to keep the resident population on the land: without a civilian presence, neither competing government could claim political ownership of Georgia, and without civilian provender, neither government's military forces could remain for any length of time. Government weakness left large areas of Georgia essentially lawless, and citizens took matters into their own hands. Forced by circumstances to respond to revolution in political but nonideological terms, they operated in a practical way and switched allegiance or attempted to remain nonpartisan. In the backcountry area of Georgia, for example, many settlers may have switched their allegiance as many as seven times between January 1779 and October 1780. In the end, pragmatic considerations influenced rebel leaders to offer people what they wanted, land, in exchange for their timely allegiance. Had the royal governor been able to offer land for allegiance, he no doubt would have been as successful as the rebels in attracting recruits....

The August 1781 assembly had defined the category of property owners whose land could be confiscated by the state as those already behind enemy lines, those who had fought or died in the service of the king, or both, and it had also set up committees to prevent internal conspiracies. The January 1782 assembly went further. Anyone named in the 1778 Confiscation Act, anyone who had ever been within the British lines, anyone who had not joined the militia by October 1, 1781, or those "who are not at this time looked on and respected as Citizens of this State" could expect to have their property confiscated. Loyalists who had fled the backcountry at the height of the partisan fighting before passage of this legislation certainly had no hope of returning to claim their property.

The legislature also passed various requisition acts to use the confiscated property as a means of payment for a variety of debts: to pay for war materials, provide special bounties and bonuses to soldiers, pay the salaries and expenses of government officials, and pay for public service. These requisitions took the form of certificates of indebtedness or special scrip to be cashed in confiscated property or out of the receipts therefrom, orders against particular property, and requests for special sales. The Georgia rebel government offered what it had in abundance, confiscated property and public domain land, and people took it in payment for goods and services.

The state offered confiscated loyalist property in the form of slaves and plantations as payment for services. Officers of the Georgia line received certificates for 100 guineas each, payable in confiscated property. Colonel James Jackson received a house in Savannah and his dragoons one slave each. Colonel Elijah Clarke received a plantation and his troops one slave to each three men or a certificate of twenty guineas each. The state later acknowledged these certificates, known as "Gratuitous Certificates," as a part of the state debt if they had not been exchanged. The state awarded a plantation and a 5,000-guinea certificate to General Nathanael Greene and a plantation and a 4,000-guinea certificate to General Anthony Wayne in gratitude for their services to the state....

The legislation passed by the restored rebel government secured the neutrality, if not the allegiance, of the backcountry population. While the last of the targeted loyalists fled to Savannah, those who remained kept their land by joining the rebel militia and thus received easy amnesty and land bounties. In essence, the rebel civil and military authorities offered land and citizenship in exchange for passive support. This support (or promised lack of aggression) allowed the rebel forces to move out of the backcountry toward Savannah between January and June 1782.

In contrast, British civil government offered no bounties to those who pledged their allegiance. Had Governor Wright been able to offer land in return for militia duty, more men, particularly poor settlers, may have joined the loyalist units. Unable to rely on the support of the British military and perfectly aware of the deteriorating situation of the civilians, Wright understood their choice in accepting rebel amnesty and bounties in order to retain their land and plant their crops.

Many Georgians responded to the exigencies of war in such a way as to keep their families alive and their land and possessions safe. British and rebel civil and military authorities vied simultaneously for the loyalty of Georgians between 1779 and 1782 and eventually were compelled to modify the ancient concept of allegiance as a formal bond between themselves and the civilian population. Neither the rebels nor the British could protect the civilian population, yet both needed the peoples' support; without settlers to farm and join the militia, famine and anarchy would overcome all civil claim to Georgia held by either country. When the traditional taking of an oath or declaration of allegiance remained a requirement of citizenship, the continual pattern of oath taking, oath breaking, and renewal of allegiance broke down the symbolic authority of the oath. The loyalty oath had once been a political tool wielded by civil and military authorities to control the civilian population; by the end of the Revolutionary War in Georgia the loyalty oath had become a pliant tool of survival manipulated by the settlers to remain in their land.

Additional Sources

Coleman, Kenneth. *The American Revolution in Georgia, 1763–1789*. Athens: University of Georgia Press, 1958.

Hall, Leslie. *Land and Allegiance in Revolutionary Georgia*. Athens: University of Georgia Press, 2001.

Killion, Ronald G., and Charles T. Waller. *Georgia and the Revolution*. Atlanta: Cherokee Publishing Company, 1975.

Searcy, Martha. *The Georgia-Florida Contest in the American Revolution, 1776–1778*. Tuscaloosa: University of Alabama Press, 1985.

Wilson, David K. *The Southern Strategy: Britain's Conquest of South Carolina and Georgia, 1775–1780*. Columbia: University of South Carolina Press, 2005.

Chapter 3

GEORGIA IN THE NEW NATION, 1787–1845

Following the Revolution, Georgia helped establish a permanent government for the new independent nation. Georgians attended the Constitutional Convention in Philadelphia and two, William Few and Abraham Baldwin, signed the document when it was completed. Upon completion of the Federal Constitution, Georgia revised its state constitution in 1789. This document provided for a two-house legislature and a governor, without a council, who was chosen by the legislature. This constitution was in place for only a few years before the state's biggest land scandal occurred, the Yazoo Land Fraud. In 1795 four Yazoo land companies succeeded in passing legislation through the General Assembly that permitted them to purchase between 35 and 50 million acres of Georgia's western lands. In order to get the bill passed, legislators were bribed and received stock in the land companies. This was clearly a fraudulent transaction, and Georgians were just a little angry when they learned the details. In 1796 the General Assembly witnessed wholesale turnover. The legislature rescinded the sale and burned all documents related to the incident. Largely as a result of the land fraud, Georgia revised the state constitution in 1798 and one provision specifically declared the Yazoo land sale null and void. The constitution was amended only infrequently and lasted until 1861.

James Jackson established himself as a political leader in his opposition to the Yazoo land sales. He resigned his seat in the US Senate to return to Georgia and was elected first to the General Assembly and then in 1798 as governor. In 1801 he was returned to the US Senate, where he remained until his death in 1806. Jackson was the undisputed leader of Georgia politicians. When Jackson died, his considerable following turned to William H. Crawford and George M. Troup. Their political opposition was led by John Clark. The Troup and Clark factions dominated Georgia politics for almost thirty years. They alternated in controlling the state's government until a realignment of Georgia politics occurred over the tariff issue in the 1830s. Most of Clark's followers opposed the tariff and supported the policies of President Andrew Jackson; Troup's followers tended to support the tariff and fell under the spell of John C. Calhoun. The General Assembly rejected nullification in 1832, helping to stem the spread of the doctrine and confine it to South Carolina. Following the nullification controversy, Troup men largely joined the Georgia Whig Party while Clark supporters were Democrats.

An important element of Georgia's history was the discovery of gold in the late 1820s. Although there were numerous "first" discoveries of gold in Georgia, the earliest documented discovery took place in August 1829. By autumn Georgia newspapers were widely reporting the story, and by the following summer there were some 4,000 miners in Georgia. In all, approximately 10,000 miners searched the state for the mother load, with the center of mining operations headquartered in Dahlonega. Between 1830 and 1837, miners poured $1,798,900 of Georgia gold into the federal mint at Philadelphia. In 1838 a mint opened in Dahlonega. Of Georgia's bounty the mint produced 1.5 million gold coins of varying denominations with a face value of over $6 million. The capitol dome in Atlanta is gilded in 43 ounces of Georgia gold.

DOCUMENTS

The first document below is Georgia's ordinance ratifying the US Constitution. Document 2 details important provisions of the Constitution of 1789. The third document is a report by a General Assembly committee on the Yazoo Land Fraud. Document 4 contains important provisions of the Constitution of 1798. The fifth document is an 1824 law that changed how the state's governors would be chosen—by popular vote. Document 6 is an 1830 request from Governor George Gilmer to President Andrew Jackson for the removal of federal troops from the state. The seventh document is a resolution by the General Assembly calling for a meeting of Southern states to address the 1832 nullification issue. Document 8 is the initial report on the survey for the construction of the state-owned Western and Atlantic Railroad.

1. Ordinance Ratifying the U.S. Constitution[1]

Wednesday, January the second, one thousand seven hundred and eighty-eight

To all to whom these presents shall come, Greeting:

---

[1] Courtesy of the Georgia Archives.

Whereas the form of a Constitution for the Government of the United States of America, was, on the seventeenth day of September, one thousand seven hundred and eighty-seven, agreed upon and reported to Congress by the Deputies of the said United States convened in Philadelphia; which said Constitution is written in the words following, to wit;...

And whereas the United States in Congress assembled did, on the twenty-eighth day of September, one thousand seven hundred and eighty-seven, Resolve, unanimously, That the said Report, with the Resolutions and Letter accompanying the same, be transmitted to the several Legislatures, in order to be submitted to a Convention of Delegates chosen in each state by the People thereof, in conformity to the Resolves of the Convention made and provided in that Case:

And Whereas the Legislature of the State of Georgia did, on the twenty-sixth day of October, one thousand seven hundred and eighty-seven, in pursuance of the above recited resolution of Congress, resolve, That a Convention be elected on the day of the next General Election, and in the same manner as Representatives are elected; and that the said Convention consist of not more than three members from each County: And that the said Convention should meet at Augusta on the fourth Tuesday in December the next, and as soon thereafter as convenient, proceed to consider the said Report, Resolutions and Letter, and to adopt or reject any part of the whole thereof.

Now Know Ye, that We, the Delegates of the People of the State of Georgia, in Convention met, pursuant to the Resolutions of the Legislature aforesaid, having taken into our serious consideration the said Constitution, Have assented to, ratified and adopted, and by these presents Do, in virtue of the powers and authority to Us given by the People of the said State for that purpose, for, and in behalf of ourselves and our Constitution, fully and entirely assent to, ratify and adopt the said Constitution.

Done in Convention, at Augusta in the said State, on the second day of January, in the year of our Lord one thousand seven hundred and eighty-eight, and of the Independence of the United States the twelfth.

2. Constitution of 1789[2]

We, the underwritten delegates from the people, in convention met, do declare that the following articles shall form the constitution for the

---

[2] From *Acts of the General Assembly of the State of Georgia*, 1789.

government of this State; and, by virtue of the powers in us vested for that purpose, do hereby ratify and confirm the same.

ARTICLE I.

Section 1. The legislative power shall be vested in two separate and distinct branches, to wit, a senate and house of representatives, to be styled "The General Assembly."

Section 2. The senate shall be elected on the first Monday in October in every third year, until such day of election be altered by law; and shall be composed of one member from each county, chosen by the electors thereof, and shall continue for the term of three years.

Section 3. No person shall be a member of the Senate who shall not have attained to the age of twenty-eight years, and who shall not have been nine years an inhabitant of the United States, and three years a citizen of this State; and shall be an inhabitant of that county for which he shall be elected, and have resided therein six months immediately preceding his election, and shall be possessed in his own right of two hundred and fifty acres of land, or some property to the amount of two hundred and fifty pounds.

...Section 6. The election of members for the house of representatives shall be annual, on the first Monday in October, until such day of election be altered by law, and shall be composed of members from each county, in the following proportions: Camden, two; Glynn, two; Liberty, four; Chatham, five; Effingham, two; Burke, four; Richmond, four; Washington, two; Green, two; and Franklin, two.

Section 7. No person shall be a member of the House of representatives who shall not have attained to the age of twenty-one years, and have been seven years a citizen of the United States, and two years an inhabitant of this State; and shall be an inhabitant of that county for which he shall be elected, and have resided therein three months immediately preceding his election; and shall be possessed in his own right of two hundred acres of land, or other property to the amount of one hundred and fifty pounds.

...Section 11. The meeting of the General Assembly shall be annual, on the first Monday in November, until such day of meeting be altered by law.

...Section 16. The General Assembly shall have powers to make all laws and ordinances which they shall deem necessary and proper for the good of the State, which shall not be repugnant to this constitution.

...Section 18. No clergyman of any denomination shall be a member of the General Assembly.

ARTICLE II.

Section 1. The executive power shall be vested in a governor, who shall hold his office during the term of two years, and shall be elected in the following manner:

Section 2. The house of representatives shall, on the second day of their making a house, in the first, and in every second year thereafter, vote by ballot for three persons; and shall make a list containing the names of the persons voted for, and the number of votes for each person; which list the speaker shall sign in the presence of the house, and deliver it in person to the senate; and the senate shall, on the same day, proceed, by ballot, to elect one of the three persons having the highest number of votes; and the person having a majority of the votes of the senators present shall be governor.

Section 3. No person shall be eligible to the office of governor who shall not have been a citizen of the United States twelve years, and an inhabitant of this State six years, and who hath not attained to the age of thirty years, and who does not possess five hundred acres of land, in his own right, within this State, and other species of property to the amount of one thousand pounds sterling.

Section 4. In case of death, resignation, or disability of the governor, the president of the senate shall exercise the executive powers of government until such disability be removed, or until the next meeting of the General Assembly.

...Section 6. He shall be commander-in-chief in and over the State of Georgia and of the militia thereof.

...Section 10. He shall have the revision of all bills passed by both houses, before the same shall become laws; but two-thirds of both houses may pass a law, notwithstanding his dissent, and, if any bill should not be returned by the governor within five days after it hath been presented to him, the same shall be a law, unless the General Assembly, by their adjournment, shall prevent its return.

ARTICLE IV.

Section 1. The electors of the members of both branches of the General Assembly shall be citizens and inhabitants of this State, and shall have attained to the age of twenty-one years, and have paid tax for the year preceding the election, and shall have resided six months within the county.

...Section 3. Freedom of the press and trial by jury shall remain inviolate.

Section 4. All persons shall be entitled to the benefit of the writ of habeas corpus.

Section 5. All persons shall have the free exercise of religion, without being obligated to contribute to the support of any religious profession but their own.

...Section 8. This constitution shall take effect, and be in full force, on the first Monday in October next, after the adoption of the same; and the executive shall be authorized to alter the time for the sitting of the superior courts, so that the same may not interfere with the annual elections in the respective counties, or the meeting of the General Assembly.

Done at Augusta, in convention, the sixth day of May, in the year of our Lord one thousand seven hundred and eighty-nine and in the year of the Sovereignty and Independence of the United States the thirteenth.

3. Legislative Committee Report on Yazoo Land Fraud[3]

In the House of Representatives
Friday January 22nd 1796

James Jackson from the committee to whom was referred the consideration of the constitutionality and validity of a certain Act of the last session of the Legislature passed at Augusta on the 7th day of January 1795 and divers petitions preferred to the late Convention and to the present Legislature, touching the act for appropriating a part of the western territory of this State made a report which being read was agreed to by the House and is as follows to wit. - -

The committee to whom the consideration of the constitutionality and validity of a certain act of the last session of the Legislature passed at Augusta on the 7th day of January 1795 entitled an Act supplementary to an Act for appropriating a part of the unlocated territory of this State to the payment of the late State troops & as well as the various petitions and remonstrances of the good people of this State against the said Act, presented to the late convention and present legislature were referred, Report, that they have had the same under their serious consideration, and lament that they are compelled to declare that the Fraud, corruption and collusion by which the said Act was obtained, and the unconstitutionality of the same, evinces the utmost depravity in the majority of the late Legislature. It appears to your committee that public good was placed entirely out of view, and private interest alone consulted, and the rights of the present generation were violated and the rights of Posterity bartered by the said Act—that by it the mounds of equal rights were broken down and the principles of Aristocracy established in their stead. The committee whilst they thus with shame and confusion acknowledge that such a

---

[3] From Abraham Baldwin Papers, courtesy of Hargrett Rare Book & Manuscript Library/University of Georgia Libraries.

Legislature entrusted with the rights of their constituents should have existed in Georgia, cannot however forbear to congratulate the present Legislature and the community at large that there are sufficient grounds as well with respect to the unconstitutionality of the Act as from the testimony before the committee of the Fraud, practised to obtain it, to pronounce that the same is a nullity of itself and not binding or obligatory on the people of this State, and they flatter themselves that a declaration to that purport, by a Legislative Act will check that rapacious and avaricious spirit of speculation which has in this State over leaped all decent bounds, and which if it were to continue would totally Annihilate morality and good faith from among the citizens of this State. The committee for this purpose beg leave to report "An Act for declaring the said usurped Act void and for expunging the same from the face of the public records," and they also herewith report in part testimony before them fifteen affidavits taken on the subject of the fraud practised to obtain it.

4. Constitution of 1798[4]

ARTICLE I.

Section 1. The legislative, executive, and judiciary departments of government shall be distinct, and each department shall be confined to a separate body of magistracy; and no person or collection of persons, being of one of these departments, shall exercise any power properly attached to either of the others, except in the instances herein expressly permitted.

Section 4. No person shall be a senator who shall not have attained the age of twenty-five years, and have been nine years a citizen of the United States, and three years an inhabitant of this State, and shall have usually resided within the county for which he shall be returned, at least one year immediately preceding his election, (except persons who may have been absent on public business of this State or of the United States,) and is and shall have been possessed, in his own right, of a settled freehold estate of the value of five hundred dollars, or taxable property to the amount of one thousand dollars, within the county, for one year preceding his election, and whose estate shall, on a reasonable estimation, be fully competent to the discharge of his just debts over and above that sum.

Section 7. The house of representatives shall be composed of members from all the counties which now are, or hereafter may be, included within this State,

---

[4] From *Acts of the General Assembly of the State of Georgia*, 1798.

according to their respective numbers of free white persons, and including three fifths of all persons of color. The actual enumeration shall be made within two years, and within every subsequent term of seven years thereafter, at such time and in such manner as this convention may direct. Each county containing three thousand persons, agreeably to the foregoing plan of enumeration, shall be entitled to two members; seven thousand to three members; and twelve thousand to four members; but each county shall have at least one and not more than four members. The representatives shall be chosen annually, on the first Monday in November, until such day of election be altered by law....

Section 8. No person shall be a representative who shall not have attained to the age of twenty-one years, and have been seven years a citizen of the United States, three years an inhabitant of this State, and have usually resided in the county in which he shall be chosen one year immediately preceding his election, (unless he shall have been absent on public business of this State or of the United States,) and shall be possessed in his own right of a settled freehold property of the value of two hundred and fifty dollars, or of taxable property to the amount of five hundred dollars within the county, or one year preceding his election, and whose estate shall, on a reasonable estimation, be competent to the discharge of his just debts, over and above that sum.

Section 12. The meeting of the General Assembly shall be annually, on the second Tuesday in January, until such day of meeting be altered by law; a majority of each branch shall be authorized to proceed to business; but a smaller number may adjourn from day to day, and compel the attendance of their members in such manner as each house may prescribe.

Section 16. All bills for raising revenue or appropriating moneys shall originate in the house of representatives, but the Senate shall propose or concur with amendments, as in other bills.

ARTICLE II.

Section 1. The executive power shall be vested in a governor, who shall hold his office during the term of two years, and until such time as a successor shall be chosen and qualified. He shall have a competent salary, established by law, which shall not be increased or diminished during the period for which he shall have been elected; neither shall he receive, within that period, any other emolument from the United States, or either of them, or from any foreign power.

Section 2. The governor shall be elected by the general assembly, at their second annual session after the rising of this convention, and at every second annual session thereafter, on the second day after the two houses shall be organized and competent to proceed to business.

Section 3. No person shall be eligible to the office of governor who shall not have been a citizen of the United States twelve years, and an inhabitant of this State six years, and who hath not attained to the age of thirty years, and who does not possess five hundred acres of land, in his own right, within this State, and other property to the amount of four thousand dollars, and whose estate shall, on a reasonable estimation be competent to the discharge of his debts, over and above that sum.

ARTICLE III.

Section 1. The judicial power of this State shall be vested in a superior court, and in such inferior jurisdictions as the legislature shall, from time to time, ordain and establish. The judges of the superior court shall be elected for the term of three years, removable by the governor, on the address of two-thirds of both houses for that purpose, or by impeachment and conviction thereon. The superior court shall have exclusive and final jurisdiction in all criminal cases which shall be tried in the county wherein the crime was committed and in all cases respecting titles to land, which shall be tried in the county where the land lies....

ARTICLE IV.

Section 1. The electors of members of the general assembly shall be citizens and inhabitants of this State, and shall have attained the age of twenty-one years, and have paid all taxes which have been required of them, and which they may have had an opportunity of paying, agreeably to law, for the year preceding the election, and shall have resided six months within the county....

Section 5. Freedom of the press, and trial by jury, as heretofore used in this State, shall remain inviolate; and no ex post facto law shall be passed.

Section 9. The writ of habeas corpus shall not be suspended, unless when in case of rebellion or invasion the public safety may require it.

Section 11. There shall be no future importation of slaves into this State, from Africa or any foreign place, after the first day of October next. The legislature shall have no power to pass laws for the emancipation of slaves without the consent of each of the representative owners, previous to such emancipation....

Section 12. Any person who shall maliciously dismember or deprive a slave of life shall suffer such punishment as would be inflicted in case the like offence had been committed on a free white person, and on the like proof, except in case of insurrection by such slave, and unless such death should happen by accident in giving such slave moderate correction.

In testimony thereof we, and each of us, respectively, have hereunto set our hands, at Louisville, the seat of government, this thirteenth day of May, in the year of our Lord one thousand seven hundred and ninety-eight, and in the twenty-second year of the Independence of the United States of America; and have caused the great seal of the State to be affixed thereto.

5. Governor to Be Chosen by Popular Vote[5]

Whereas, the second section of the second article of the constitution of the state of Georgia is in the following words:

"The Governor shall be elected by the General Assembly, at their second annual session after the rising of this Convention, and at every second session thereafter, on the second day after the two houses shall be organized and competent to proceed to business."

And as the said second section requires amendment,

Be it therefore enacted by the Senate and House of Representatives of the State of Georgia, in General Assembly met, and it is hereby enacted by the authority of the same, That as soon as this act shall have passed, agreeably to the requisition of the constitution, the following amendment shall be adopted in lieu of the said section: "The Governor shall be elected by persons qualified to vote for members of the General Assembly, on the first Monday in October, in the year of our Lord one thousand eight hundred and twenty-five, and on the first Monday in October, in every second year thereafter, until such time be altered by law, which election shall be held at the place of holding general elections in the several counties of this state, in the same manner as is prescribed for the election of members of the General Assembly.... The members of each branch of the General Assembly shall convene in the Representative chamber, and the President of the Senate, and the Speaker of the House of Representatives shall open and publish the returns in presence of the General Assembly, and the person having the majority of the whole number of votes given in, shall be declared duly elected Governor of this state: but if no person have such a majority, then from the persons having the two highest number of votes who shall be in life, and shall not decline an election at the time appointed for the legislature to elect, the General Assembly shall elect immediately a Governor by joint ballot: and in all cases of election of a Governor by the General Assembly, a majority of the votes of the members present shall be necessary for a choice...."

---

[5] From *Acts of the General Assembly of the State of Georgia*, 1824.

Assented to, November 17, 1824.

6. Request for Removal of Federal Troops from Georgia[6]

Executive Department, Georgia
Milledgeville 29 October 1830

Sir:

By an Act of the Legislature of Georgia passed at the last session, all the Cherokee territory and the persons occupying it were subjected to the ordinary Jurisdiction of the State after the first of June then next ensuing. This Act has gone into operation. The acknowledgement of the President of the right of the State to pass such an Act renders it unnecessary to say any thing in its justification. The object of this letter is to request the President that the U. States troops may be withdrawn from the Indian territory within Georgia. The enforcement of the non intercourse law within the limits of the State, is considered inconsistent with the right of the Jurisdiction which is now exercised by its Authorities and must if continued lead to difficulties between the officers of the U. States and State governments which it is very desirable should be avoided. No doubt is entertained that the object of the President in ordering the U. States troops into the Cherokee territory, was the preservation of the peace of the Union. The motive is duly appreciated. The Legislature of the State is now in session. The special object of its meeting is the enforcement of the laws of the State, within the Cherokee Country, and the punishment of intrusion into it by persons searching for gold. Its powers are amply sufficient for that purpose. As it is expected that the law for the punishment of trespassery upon the public lands will go into operation within a few days, the President is therefore requested to withdraw the troops as soon as it can be conveniently done. The conduct of Maj. Wager has been very severe to the gold diggers. In some instances unoffending citizens have been made the subjects of punishment, in violation of their rights and the authority of the State. Complaints have been made to this Department and redress asked for is the removal of the troops is believed to be the most effectual means of preventing the repetition of such injuries. Information has been also received at this

---

[6] From Governor George Gilmer to President Andrew Jackson, October 29, 1830, Governor's Letterbooks, Georgia Archives.

Department, that the digging for gold is still carried on in various parts of the Cherokee territory, and that the extent of country containing mines is so great, that it is wholly impossible to prevent it by the use of military force alone. It is said that the Indians are even more extensively employed in taking gold than before the arrival of the troops. This proceeds from their residence within the country, intimate acquaintance with it, and other means of avoiding the operation of the troops. The fear of the whites had restrained them formerly.

The President is assured, that whatever measures may be adopted by the State of Georgia in relation to the Cherokees the strongest desire will be felt to make them accord with the policy which has been adopted by the present Administration of the General Government upon the same subject.

The President   Very Respectfully Yours & c.
of the U. States   George Gilmer

7. Nullification Resolves[7]

House of Representatives.

Whereas, The Tariff Law of the last session of Congress has not satisfied the just expectation of the people of the Southern States: *whereas,* the recent attempt to provide a remedy for the evils which we suffer from the protective system, by a State Convention, not only will probably be abortive, but is likely, if persisted in, materially to disturb the public harmony, and lessen the moral force of the State:…

Therefore,

Resolved, That if a Southern Convention be desirable, it is expedient for the State of Georgia, to invite the States of Virginia, North Carolina, South Carolina, Alabama, Tennessee, and Mississippi, to concur with her in electing Delegates to a Convention, which shall take into consideration the Tariff system of the General Government, and devise and recommend the most effectual and proper mode of obtaining relief from the evils of that system.

Resolved, That in order to ascertain the sense of the people of Georgia, on this subject, the following plan of a Southern Convention, be submitted to them.…

---

[7] From *Journal of the House of Representatives of the State of Georgia, 1832* (Milledgeville: Prince & Ragland, Printers, 1833).

Plan of a Southern Convention

Art. 1. The State of Georgia invites the States of Virginia, North Carolina, South Carolina, Alabama, Tennessee, and Mississippi, to concur with her in electing Delegates to a Convention, which shall take into consideration the Tariff system of the General Government, and devise and recommend the most effectual and proper mode of obtaining relief from the evils of that system.

Art. 3. The Convention shall not take place, unless (five) States of the six, which it proposed to invite, assent to the proposal.

Art. 7. If the delegates assembled in a Southern Convention, according to the above plan, shall agree on a course of proceeding which they recommend to the States represented, the Governor of this State is authorized and desired to issue a proclamation, with timely notice, for an election of delegates to a State Convention.... To the State Convention thus elected, the recommendations of the Southern Convention shall be submitted. If the same are approved by the State Convention, they shall then be referred to the people for final ratification, in such manner as may be prescribed by said Convention; and if they are ratified by the majority of those persons entitled to vote for members of the General Assembly, the State Convention shall proclaim that the said recommendations being regularly adopted, express the will of the people of Georgia....

Resolved, That if the above plan of a Southern Convention is adopted by the votes of a majority of the citizens of this State, given in the manner therein described, it will be the right and duty of the different functionaries of the State Government, to afford all necessary aid in facilitating its execution.

Resolved, That we abhor the doctrine of Nullification as neither a peaceful, nor a constitutional remedy, but on the contrary, as tending to civil commotion and disunion; and while we deplore the rash and revolutionary measures, recently adopted by a Convention of the people of South Carolina, we deem it a paramount duty to warn our fellow citizens against the danger of adopting her mischievous policy.

Agreed to, November 29, 1832.

In Senate, concurred in, December 12, 1832.

Approved, December 14, 1832.

8. Western and Atlantic Railroad Surveys[8]

Col. Long's First Report
Athens, July 1st, 1837

Sir,

In accordance with the requisitions of the act of your Legislature, authorizing the survey, location and construction of the Western and Atlantic Rail Road of the State of Georgia, I have the honor to submit my first quarterly Report....

I forthwith engaged in a reconnaissance of the country likely to be traversed by the contemplated Rail Road, and in the course of my examinations, had my attention directed to the following general routes, which from the best information I have been able to obtain of the country, both from observation and enquiry, appear to have the strongest claim to consideration. The several routes are of course comprised within the limits specified in the act before mentioned.

1st. The most northerly route examined commences on the Chattahoochie river, near Winn's Ferry, and proceeds N. Westerly between Coal & Sawney Mountains, and downward in the valley of Setting-down Creek, to the mouth of this Stream on the Etowah. The continuation of this route by the valley of the Long Swamp and Talking Rock Creek to the Coosawattie, and thence to the Tennessee Line, near McNair's Boat Yard, has been partially surveyed by General Brisbane and found objectionable on account of the unavoidable abruptness of the gradations, especially in the valley of the two Creeks just mentioned.

2nd. A route crossing the Chattahoochie at or near Collin's Ferry or in the vicinity of Warsaw. This route crosses the grounds dividing between the waters of the Chattahoochie and Etowah, at the source of the Little River, and proceeds downward in the valley of the latter to its mouth. It thence passes in a direction to strike Wasfords Trace, leading from the Etowah to the head of the Pine Log Valley, whence it descends either by the valley of Pine Log Creek, or by that of Sillacoe to the Coosawattie and thence across the grounds dividing between this river and the Connasawga, and up the valley of the latter to the Tennessee Line, or upward in the valley of the Coogehulley, to Red Clay. This route is deemed too devious and the aspect traversed by it too numerous, and in places too much broken to justify a survey.

---

[8] From Georgia Western and Atlantic Railroad Correspondence and Reports, Georgia Archives.

3rd. A road leading from the vicinity of Pitman's Ferry, crossing the high ground between the Chattahoochie and Etowah, near Young's Store, and proceeding thence to a point near the mouth of the Noon Day Creek, and thence by Allatoona to Pitner's Ferry on the Etowah. This route then pursues a course leading toward Hargraves Mill on Two Run Creek, and thence down the valley of this Creek and across a low summit into the valley of Connaseens Creek. It then ascends in the valley of the latter, and descends in the valley of the Oothealoga to the Oostanolla, which it crosses a few miles below New Echota. It then passes upward in the valley of the Connasawga and Coogehully, either in a direction for Red Clay or in a direction for Chatoogela Gap, and from the latter proceeds northwardly to the Tennessee Line.

Within a few miles before reaching the Tennessee Line, this route may be deflected westward in a direction towards Taylor's Gap, from which it may bend northwestwardly to the Tennessee Line.

From Taylor's Gap, a route leading in a direction towards Rossville, has been deemed worthy of a survey in order to determine the features of the most feasible pass to that point within the limits of the State.

4th. A route leading from Montgomery's ferry on the Chattahoochie, to Marietta and thence northwardly of Kennesaw mountains and by the flats of the Alatoona and Pumpkin Pine Creeks to the Etowah, at or near May's Ferry, or at the mouth of the Pimpkin Pine. This route proceeds thence as in the preceding to Hargraves Mills and thence in coincidence with route No. 3, to the Tennessee Line.

In addition to the examinations made at the localities mentioned in reference to routes No. 3 & No. 4, numerous explorations were made on the right and left of these routes with the view of discovering the most favorable passes for the road....

To his Excellency   S.H. Long,
William Schley   Chief Engineer,
Governor of Georgia   W. & A. R. Road of Georgia

ESSAYS

The Georgia Gold Rush[9]

David Williams

Human beings were not the first to extract gold from the Georgia hills. For millions of years the forces of erosion have mined gold in the southern Appalachians. Over the eons wind, rain, freezing, thaw, and plant growth slowly chiseled tons of earth, including gold-bearing quartz veins, from these mountains. As erosion wore the mountains down, new streams containing gold sediments were created, leaving the older, dry creek bottoms behind to form gold-bearing layers embedded in the hills. Early Georgia miners distinguished between these two types by referring to gold found in and along streams as "deposits" and to the older sediments found along the hillsides as "surfaces." These loose particles of gold, whether found along streams or hillsides, are collectively called placers….

When the miners found a spot that showed good color, they set up camp and began working the area in earnest. A variety of crude devices were used to wash these deposits in an effort to extract the fine gold particles. By far the simplest method was panning for gold. Pans varied in size, thought the average was around 14 inches in diameter. A promising scoop of dirt was laid in the pan along with an equal amount of water. The miner then jostled the mixture as the heavy gold flakes worked their way to the bottom. The top layers of soil were periodically allowed to wash over the side, with the miner adding water as needed. Finally, after all the lighter material was washed off, a thin layer of black sand was left at the bottom of the pan. If the gold hunter was lucky, a few brilliant specks of gold could be seen highlighted against the dark surroundings. A skilled miner could go through this process in just a minute or two.

Though the popular image of an early gold miner calls to mind a bearded figure stooped beside a mountain stream looking intently at his pan, the scene was not as typical as one might expect in gold rush Georgia. This method was far too time consuming since only a handful of dirt could be processed at a time. Panning was primarily used in testing soil for gold content and as a final step in more elaborate methods of gold hunting. Panning was also used when it was inconvenient to set up regular equipment at a particular location, especially if

---

[9] From David Williams, *The Georgia Gold Rush* (Columbia: University of South Carolina Press, 1993). Used with permission of the University of South Carolina Press.

the site belonged to someone else. But even with its limitations, the gold pan remained the single most widely used extracting device during the gold rush.

Next to the gold pan, the most popular device in early placer mining was the cradle rocker. The first crude rockers, small half-cylinder wooden troughs into which water and gravel were dumped, were little more than oversized gold pans. A miner would rock the trough back and forth while agitating the mixture by hand, allowing the heavier gold flakes to settle to the bottom. As the gold worked its way down, the miner scraped off the top layers. Eventually, as with the panning process, only a thin layer of black sand, which the miner hoped contained gold, was left at the bottom.

An improved version of the cradle was a wooden box about 3 feet in length mounted on rockers. Water was poured into the upper end, or hopper, washing gold-bearing gravel through perforations and onto a canvas apron. This apron deflected the gravel to one end of the rocker's lower compartment. Small wooden bars nailed to the bottom of the cradle's open end, called riffle bars, caught sediments containing gold as the gravel washed through.

Another popular device was the sluice box, sometimes called a rippler. This was a simple contraption that consisted of a water flume between 10 and 20 feet long containing riffle bars. A continuous flow of water ran through the sluice as miners shoveled in dirt. The flow of water was stopped occasionally, and the gold-bearing sediments were collected and panned out....

Placer mining was the most popular type among the early gold diggers because it required very little capital. But as more people moved into the gold region and towns began to grow, money became available for investment in vein mining. It was evident to the miners all along that the gold they were panning had been washed down from gold-bearing quartz veins embedded in the surrounding hills. When the land lottery ended in 1833 and land ownership became more settled, miners began prospecting for the rich gold veins in earnest.

The first vein discoveries were more a result of accident than of intention, but miners soon became adept at locating gold veins. Beginning from a spot on a creek or river known to contain placer deposits, a miner would work his way upstream, testing the soil as he went. When the soil's gold content dropped abruptly, the miner knew that there was a vein somewhere in the surrounding hills. Soil testing would continue until a trail of gold was found that led up to the vein. It was difficult to tell from these initial tests how productive a particular vein might turn out to be. The thickness of veins containing gold ore varied from a few inches to more than 20 feet in some places. These "pinches and swells" occurred with some regularity at a few mines, such as the Franklin, but this was the exception rather than the rule.

The equipment required to conduct vein mining was considerably more complex than that involved in washing placers. Some of the first attempts involved open-pit operations, but most vein mining required the digging of shafts and tunnels. Seven square feet was the recommended size for these tunnels, but most, smaller tunnels operated by one or two miners, were no more than 3 to 4 feet in diameter—just large enough for a person to crawl through. Once tunnels were dug, timbers had to be put in places to avert cave-ins. This was particularly important in the Georgia mines because the surrounding rock was riddled with fissures....

Where tunnels were dug into the mountainsides, the gold ore was usually hauled out in wheelbarrows. A few of the larger operations laid rail tracks into the mines and brought the ore out in heavy wooden carts. When vertical shafts were sunk, equipment had to be set up to hoist ore to the surface. Rope or cable was run through a pulley suspended over the shaft, and a large bucket or tub was attached and lowered into the hole. Miners working deep in the earth filled these containers with ore, and they were then pulled to the surface by human or horse power. Predictably, the miners generally preferred the use of horses for such work.

Once the gold ore was brought out of the mines, it was crushed almost to powder in a small mortar-and-pestle operation or a larger stamp mill. Stamp mills ranged in size and complexity from a single stamp suspended from a bent-over sapling to mills consisting often or twelve stamps driven by a water wheel. The simplest stamp mill was no more than a 6-foot oak log between 6 and 8 inches in diameter suspended from a bent-over hickory tree. Using handles attached to either side of the log, one or two men could bring it down with considerable force. When the log was pulled down, a metal plate fastened over its lower end broke up the gold ore. The hickory tree provided enough spring action to lift the log for another descent. Repeated pounding reduced the ore to a fine sand, and the gold was then panned out....

Once this gold was panned out or separated from its ore, it was often used as a direct medium of exchange. Miners carried gold dust in goose quills and small pouches or simply loose in their vest pockets. On Saturday afternoons they took their gold into town and sold it to the storekeepers or traded it for merchandise. Taverns were very popular among the miners, and they spent much of their gold in these establishments. Some of the gold made its way to Tennessee and Kentucky in exchange for livestock brought to the gold region by drovers from those states. Gold was also sold to individuals and bankers at very low rates. Because of its fineness, Georgia gold was popular for making jewelry and was also in demand as an export commodity.

A substantial portion of the gold was sent to the federal mint in Philadelphia. Between 1830 and 1837 the mint received $1,798,900 in gold from the Georgia mines. When gold was brought to the mint, the treasurer issued a certificate testifying to its value and stating the amount in gold coin to be paid for it. If the owner wished, he could present the certificate at the Bank of the United States in Philadelphia and receive the amount of gold stated thereon or he could wait for his own gold to be minted. The former option was usually preferred since it could take as long as three months for raw gold to be returned as coin. If the owner did not want to make the trip to Philadelphia, he could deposit his bullion at branch banks in Charleston or Savannah. However, he would be paid no more than two-thirds of the gold's estimated value at the time of deposit. The balance would be paid when the bullion's value was fixed by the mint, a process which sometimes took several months.

Political Parties in the Jacksonian Era[10]

Anthony G. Carey

Early Georgia politics revolved around personalities. The state's most important political figure at the turn of the century was James Jackson, a headstrong Revolutionary War hero from Savannah who served as governor, congressman, and United States senator. A personal faction composed of Jackson and his friends first organized during the furor over the Yazoo land frauds in the mid–1790s subsequently dominated state politics. Following Jackson's death in 1806, leadership of the faction passed to William H. Crawford and George M. Troup. Crawford was a native Virginian whose family had moved to Georgia in 1783 and had settled along the Broad River in the neighborhood of other Virginia emigrants. He rose quickly in politics and, after an apprenticeship in the state legislature, in 1807 took a seat in the United States Senate. Troup meanwhile focused on managing the state's affairs. Born in 1780 along the frontier in what became Alabama, Troup graduated from Princeton before beginning a career as a Savannah lawyer, gentleman planter, and political chieftain. Opposition to the Jackson-Crawford-Troup faction came from the allies of John Clark, the son of a Revolutionary War general and no stranger to dueling grounds and military camps. One opponent remembered

---

[10] From Anthony Gene Carey, *Parties, Slavery, and the Union in Antebellum Georgia* (Athens: University of Georgia Press,1997). Used with permission of the University of Georgia Press.

Clark as a rowdy with "the temper of a clansman," who demanded that every man "be for or against him" and "suffered no one of any consequence to occupy middle ground."

The animosities that divided Troupites and Clarkites were obscurely rooted in rivalries between Piedmont settlers in the era immediately following the American Revolution. The area along the Broad River in Elbert and Wilkes Counties was settled chiefly by emigrants from Virginia and North Carolina, respectively, and each group developed its own network of personal alliances and kin relationships. Leaders of the Virginians, who were perhaps slightly wealthier and possessed greater pretensions to distinguished ancestry, looked down on North Carolinians generally and particularly detested John Clark. Over the years, contests for political offices and militia appointments, disputes over the Yazoo sales and other western land schemes, and numerous personal altercations deepened and widened the divisions between the two factions. Troupites, in general, amassed strength in the Low Country and in the easternmost counties of the developing Black Belt, while John Clark and his allies appealed to settlers on the expanding frontier. If Troupites and Clarkites were not always sure what they differed over, they did differ violently, as exemplified by the 1806 duel between John Clark and William Crawford in which the latter received a pistol ball that shattered his left wrist....

Factional divisions remained inchoate until a series of contests between 1819 and 1825 extended the Troup-Clark alignment throughout the state. George Troup lost the governorship to John Clark in both 1819 and 1821 before finally beating Clarkite Matthew Talbot in the 1823 election. Along with consolidating factional lines in the legislature, these battles heightened public interest in state politics and led to an 1824 constitutional amendment that provided for the popular election of governors. That same year, Troupite leader William H. Crawford's candidacy shattered Georgia's heretofore monolithic front in presidential politics. Clarkites, unwilling to back an ancient enemy, turned to General Andrew Jackson, a legendary Indian fighter, the hero of the Battle of New Orleans, and a sometime Republican politician from Tennessee. Jackson's warm friendship with John Clark and his enmity for Crawford placed the presidential race within the familiar personal context of the Troup and Clark factions. The legislature decided the contest, giving Georgia's electoral votes to Crawford, but a constitutional amendment adopted soon thereafter turned the selection of presidential electors over to the voters. Procedural changes that placed elections directly in the hands of the mass of white men compelled leaders to conduct statewide, popular campaigns for gubernatorial and presidential candidates and propelled them toward creating political organizations that united allies across county borders.

The cohesive power of the Troup and Clark factions peaked in 1825, when the two leaders clashed for the last time. An observer remembered that the "virulence of party...pervaded every family, creating animosities which neither time nor reflection ever healed." The campaign combined personal enmity with concerns about Indian removal, an issue of considerable importance to white men who coveted tribal lands. Governor Troup was engaged in a controversy with President John Quincy Adams over the dubious Treaty of Indian Springs, which had supposedly ceded the remainder of the Creek lands in Georgia. Troup's vehement insistence that Adams honor the treaty threatened to embroil Georgia in hostilities with the federal government. Clarkites, while wholeheartedly endorsing Creek removal, made criticism of Troup's impulsiveness their key issue. More than four-fifths of the eligible voters came to the polls and narrowly reelected Troup; a disappointed John Clark soon moved to Florida.

The waning of the Troup-Clark rivalry after 1825 coincided with the rise of Andrew Jackson as an overshadowing figure. With William Crawford sidelined by illness and defeat, the 1826 legislature almost unanimously endorsed Jackson for the presidency. The formation of two Jackson electoral tickets in 1828—the Troupite slate won—further demonstrated Old Hickory's appeal. Jackson's forceful personality, obsessive concern with honor, fabled military career, and status as a slaveholding planter made him a model of Southern white manhood and brought him victory in Georgia. His championing of Cherokee removal then cemented a popularity that long forbade opposition; state political movements for the next eight years hinged on reactions to Jackson's conduct....

The question in Georgia was *how*, not *whether*, to oppose the 1828 tariff, and debates centered on problems of political tactics and constitutional theory surrounding John C. Calhoun's doctrine of nullification. Calhoun's ideas rested on familiar premises: the original sovereignty of the states, the formation of the Union as a compact, the necessity for strict construction of the Constitution, and the reserved rights of the states. From these first principles, Calhoun arrived at one conclusion that few white men in Georgia doubted in 1828: protective tariffs represented a congressional abuse of the limited grant of power to raise revenue and were therefore unconstitutional. Calhoun's proposed method for handling disputes regarding the rightful powers of the federal government, however, aroused vast controversy. The states, Calhoun declared, were the final arbiters of the constitutionality of federal laws. States, acting individually through state conventions, could interpose their authority, nullify unconstitutional federal acts, and prevent the execution of the offensive laws within their borders. If negotiation or constitutional amendments failed to resolve the conflict, the offended states could resort to secession.

By mid-1831 it appeared likely that South Carolina might act on Calhoun's theories and attempt to nullify the 1828 tariff. Since Andrew Jackson loathed Calhoun and had publicly condemned nullification, any clash between South Carolina and the federal government portended a crisis of the Union. By bringing into conflict concerns over the protective tariff, allegiance to states' rights, love for the Union, and loyalty to Andrew Jackson, the nullification controversy sparked a realignment in which new political parties organized along ideological lines superseded the archaic Troup-Clark factions.

The Clarkites, who had faltered badly in recent state elections, moved first and decisively to embrace the cause of Andrew Jackson and the Union. One of Calhoun's erstwhile Clarkite friends, Milledgeville physician Tomlinson Fort, informed him that many citizens sensed a "powerful passion of disloyalty" behind nullification and were concerned that the doctrine amounted to a "virtual dissolution of the Union." State defiance of federal laws, Fort warned, could bring only anarchy and civil war. Quickly adding "union" to the Clark name, Clark-Unionists caucused at Athens and nominated Wilson Lumpkin as their standard-bearer in the 1831 gubernatorial election.

The Clark-Unionist critique of nullification emphasized the distinctions between Calhoun's doctrine and traditional states' rights principles. Insisting that only two parties, "the *Troup*, or *disunion* party, and the *Clark*, or *union* party," existed in Georgia, the *Milledgeville Federal Union* declared that Clark-Unionists were "the true State Rights party" that stood for "the *limited sovereignty* of the states and the *limited sovereignty* of the General Government." Under the federal system, Clarkites contended, the state and federal governments had separate and distinct powers and were sovereign within their respective spheres. Strict limitations on the power of the federal government, enshrined in the Constitution, protected minority interests while still allowing majority rule. The doctrine of nullification, in contrast, tolerated state defiance of federal laws, negated majority rule, and weakened the bonds of the Union. Tomlinson Fort admonished Calhoun that to "object to a majority passing a law to favor their own interests is to object to our system altogether." Clark-Unionists accordingly denounced South Carolinians and strove to link Troupite antitariff protesters such as John Berrien with disunionist radicalism.

The Clark-Unionist challenge overpowered the staggering Troupites. George Gilmer secured the Troupite caucus nomination for governor, but Thomas Haynes briefly entered the race as the candidate of John Forsyth's dissident faction. John Berrien and other Troupites meanwhile continued to stir up antitariff feeling, although they disavowed any connection with nullification. Clark-Unionists persuaded enough voters that Troupites were nullifying disunionists and enemies of Andrew Jackson to give Wilson Lumpkin a narrow triumph. The continued growth of frontier counties, where Andrew Jackson's appeal was strongest, aided the Clark-Unionists, as did their trumpeting of Unionist themes. Troupites fared best in old middle Georgia, their traditional stronghold, where antitariff feelings ran high among planters.

The disintegration of the Troup faction continued apace following the 1831 defeat. A few Troupite leaders, along with scattered Clarkites such as John H. Howard of Columbus, openly embraced nullification. South Carolina nullifiers courted Georgians, and dinners at Hamburg, South Carolina, and Augusta in the spring of 1832 promoted antitariff cooperation. The most prominent Georgia nullifier was Congressman Augustin S. Clayton, a Troupite from Athens, who angrily charged that unconstitutional protective tariffs were impoverishing the staple-producing South; he and other hotspurs talked of secession as a legitimate response if their grievances remained unredressed. The Troupite *Columbus Enquirer* declared that the "tariff is now considered a question of rights, and the [protective] system must be abandoned or the Union must and will be dissolved. The south will no longer submit."...

The climax of the nullification crisis came in March 1833, when Congress passed a compromise tariff bill that gradually reduced duties over a nine-year period and seemingly abandoned the principle of protection. Along with the tariff, Congress enacted a Force Bill, which granted the president the power to use the army and navy to enforce federal laws. South Carolinians, disgruntled but partially victorious, thereafter rescinded their original nullification ordinance and symbolically nullified the Force Bill. Clark-Unionists congratulated themselves for backing Jackson, while most Troupites, who execrated the "bloody force bill" and deplored the president's conduct, still remained reluctant to break completely with Jackson. Congressman James M. Wayne and Senator John Forsyth had already deserted over nullification, and many more of the rank and file would surely follow if the Troupites abandoned Old Hickory.

Short on options, the Troupites tried relying an a familiar name in 1833 and nominated William Crawford's son, Joel, for the governorship. His candidacy promptly aroused criticism. Extreme states' rights men and a few nullifiers, including some former Clarkites, complained that Crawford "was nominated merely as a Troup man," without regard to principle. Others, usually called Troup-Unionists, worried that the younger Crawford might secretly be a nullifier. Crawford's ambiguous public statements scarcely clarified his views on nullification, Andrew Jackson, or anything else. Enthusiastic Clark-Unionists reprised familiar antinullification themes, exploited Troupite dissension, and returned Governor Wilson Lumpkin to office by a handsome majority.

The defeat finished the Troup faction as such and led to an overhaul of the state's political organizations. William Crawford, Augustin Clayton, Seaborn Jones, Richard W. Habersham, Absalom H. Chappell, and other prominent Troupites met in Milledgeville on November 13, 1833 and formed the State Rights party in opposition to Andrew Jackson. Focusing totally on national issues, they enumerated the consolidationist errors of Jackson's proclamation, urged Georgians to sustain Jeffersonian principles, and demanded the immediate repeal of the Force Bill. The Meeting also appointed a state central committee of thirteen that included such diverse figures as Joel Crawford and old Clarkite nullifier John H. Howard, and asked State Rights supporters to organize similar county organizations. Except for a smattering of Clarkite converts, the State Rights party consisted of Troup men.

Clark-Unionists gathered a week later and established the Union-Democratic Republic Party—the Georgia branch of the national Democracy. Unionists attacked nullification, outlined their understanding of states' rights principles, and proclaimed unswerving allegiance to Andrew Jackson. A subsequent meeting selected a state central committee composed of Clarkite stalwarts such as Tomlinson Fort, John A. Cuthbert, Augustus H. Kenan, and Charles J. McDonald. The Unionists called for the creation of county organizations and recommended that the party prepare to send delegates to the 1836 national Democratic convention. The mass of Clarkites—along with such Troup leaders as James Wayne, John Forsyth, Seaton Grantland, and a relatively small, scattered, yet important contingent of Troupite voters—formed the core of the Union party.

Additional Sources

Carey, Anthony G. *Parties, Slavery, and the Union in Antebellum Georgia.* Athens: University of Georgia Press, 1997.

Foster, William O. *James Jackson: Duelist and Militant Statesman, 1757–1806.* Athens: University of Georgia Press, 1960.

Lamplugh, George R. *Politics on the Periphery: Factions and Parties in Georgia, 1783–1806.* Cranbury NJ: University of Delaware Press, 1986.

Murray, Paul. *The Whig Party in Georgia, 1825–1853.* Chapel Hill: University of North Carolina Press, 1948.

Williams, David. *The Georgia Gold Rush: Twenty-Niners, Cherokees, and Gold Fever.* Columbia: University of South Carolina Press, 1993.

Chapter 4

THE NATIVE AMERICAN NATIONS

Georgia has had a long relationship with the Native Americans, some of it cooperative and some of it stormy. Initial contact between natives and Europeans tended to be more cooperative but turned antagonistic as Georgians coveted Indian lands. One theme stands out in the Georgia-Native relationship—the Indian nations ceded more and more of their land to Georgia. Almost from the minute James Oglethorpe and his settlers landed in Georgia, native Indian lands were vulnerable. A century later virtually all Indian land claims had been extinguished.

Before the Revolution, Georgians had secured land cessions from the natives in 1733, 1739, 1758, 1763, and 1773. The concerted effort to acquire Indian lands came after the end of the war. In the 1790s the US government appointed Indian agents to deal with Indian affairs, and in some cases these agents paved the way for more land cessions. One of the most well known, or infamous, agents was Benjamin Hawkins, who in 1796 was appointed as agent to the Creeks. By the turn of the nineteenth century Georgia was adamant about acquiring all Indian lands in the state and in 1802 reached an agreement with the federal government for that specific purpose. The Compact of 1802 was an agreement by which the US government agreed to remove all of the native nations in the state of Georgia as soon as possible. By 1838 that mission was accomplished.

Of the two major Indian nations in Georgia, the Creeks and the Cherokees, the Creeks lost all of their land first, an effort that predated the Compact of 1802. Among the larger Creek cessions were the Treaty of New York in 1790, the Treaty of Fort Jackson in 1814, and the Treaty of Indian Springs in 1821 and 1825. Georgia acquired the final small parcels of Creek land in 1827 and the remaining Creeks were removed to Oklahoma. The Cherokee land became even more desirable when gold was discovered in 1829. The Cherokees held out until 1835 when they agreed to the Treaty of New Echota, which extinguished the last Cherokee land claims in Georgia. By 1838 the Indian nations in Georgia were physically removed from the state.

The Cherokees in Georgia struggled mightily to keep their lands, even to the point of changing their entire social structure. In the hopes of keeping their land the Cherokees pursued a policy of adaptation—adapting to white Anglo society. The idea was that if the Cherokees completely made over their society they might be able to keep their lands. Accordingly, the Cherokees largely abandoned the nomadic lifestyle and created a more fixed agrarian society. They herded farm animals, completed a syllabary for the Cherokee language in 1825, published a newspaper, the *Cherokee Phoenix*, in 1828 in both Cherokee and English, and in 1827 wrote a constitution based on the US Constitution. The Cherokees established a capital at New Echota and adopted the institution of slavery. And when the state of Georgia extended its authority over Cherokee land in June 1830, the Cherokees turned to the courts. With William Wirt as their lead attorney, the Cherokee Nation pursued two cases to the US Supreme Court. In the second case, *Worcester v. Georgia* (1832), the Supreme Court held that Georgia's laws were invalid in the Cherokee Nation. Although the Cherokees had ostensibly won the case, the chances of it being enforced were slim; President Jackson allegedly commented, "John Marshall has made his decision; let him enforce it." Three years later the Treaty of New Echota ceded the last of the Cherokee lands to the United States, and three years after that the last of the Cherokees were removed to Oklahoma.

The distribution of Indian lands to Georgians merits some attention. In part because of the Yazoo land fraud of the 1790s, the state of Georgia distributed ceded Indian lands through a lottery system. Georgia citizens could receive land free through the lotteries. The state held six lotteries, in 1805, 1807, 1820, 1821, 1827, and 1832. To enter the lottery one needed to be a citizen and resident of the state; veterans of the Revolution and widows of veterans received additional chances to win land. Most notably, the 1832 lottery included land that contained gold.

Documents

The first document below is the Compact of 1802, the agreement by which the US government agreed to remove the Indians from Georgia. Document 2 is the 1814 Treaty of Fort Jackson with the Creeks. In the third document, an 1826 speech, Elias Boudinot describes how the Cherokees adapted to white society. Document 4 is the 1827 Cherokee Constitution. The fifth document is the first edition of the Cherokee newspaper Cherokee Phoenix. Document 6 is the 1828 law the General Assembly passed that extended the state's control over Cherokee land, which took effect on June 1, 1830. The seventh document is the US Supreme Court's decision in the 1832 Worcester v. Georgia case. Document 8 is the 1835 Treaty of New Echota.

1. Compact of 1802[1]

Georgia: Cession of Western Land Claims
April 24, 1802

The State of Georgia cedes to the United States all the Right, Title, and Claim, which the said State has to the Jurisdiction and Soil of the Lands situated within the Boundaries of the United States, South of the State of Tennessee and West of a Line beginning on the western Bank of the Chatahochie River, where the same crosses the boundary Line between the United States and Spain; running thence up the said River Chatahochie and along the western Bank thereof to the great Bend thereof next above the Place where a certain Creek or River called Uchee (being the first considerable Stream, on the western side, above the Cussetas and Coweta Towns) empties into the said Chatahochie River; thence in a direct Line to Nickajack on the Tennessee River; then crossing the said last mentioned River, and thence running up the said Tennessee River and along the western Bank thereof to the southern boundary Line of the State of Tennessee: upon the following express conditions, and subject thereto, that is to say:

First,—That out of the first nett Proceeds of the Sales of the Lands thus ceded, which nett Proceeds shall be estimated by deducting from the gross Amount of Sales the Expenses incurred in surveying, and incident to the Sale, the United States shall pay, at their Treasury, One million two hundred and fifty thousand Dollars, to the State of Georgia....

Fourthly,—That the United States shall, at their own expense, extinguish for the Use of Georgia, as early as the same can be peacefully obtained on reasonable terms, the Indian Title to the County of Talassee, to the Lands left out by the line drawn with the Creeks in the Year one thousand seven hundred and ninety eight, which had been previously granted by the State of Georgia; both which Tracts had formerly been yielded by the Indians; and to the lands within the Forks of Oconee and Oakmulgee rivers; for which several Objects the President of the United States has directed that a Treaty should be immediately held with the Creeks: and that the United States shall, in the same manner, also extinguish the Indian Title to all the other Lands within the State of Georgia....

---

[1] From Clarence E. Carter, ed., *The Territory of Mississippi, 1798–1817,* vol. 5 of *The Territorial Papers of the United States* (Washington, DC: Government Printing Office, 1937).

In faith thereof the respective Commissioners have signed these Presents, and affixed hereunto their seals. Done at the City of Washington, in the district of Columbia, this twenty fourth day of April One thousand eight hundred and two.

2. Treaty of Fort Jackson[2]

Articles of agreement and capitulation, made and concluded this ninth day of August, one thousand eight hundred and fourteen, between major general Andrew Jackson, on behalf of the President of the United States of America, and the chiefs, deputies, and warriors of the Creek Nation.

Whereas an unprovoked, inhuman, and sanguinary war, waged by the hostile Creeks against the United States, hath been repelled, prosecuted, and determined, successfully, on the part of the said States, in conformity with principles of national justice and honorable warfare— And whereas consideration is due to the rectitude of proceedings dictated by instructions relating to the re-establishment of peace.... Wherefore,

1st—The United States demand an equivalent for all expenses incurred in prosecuting the war to its termination, by a cession of all the territory belonging to the Creek nation within the territories of the United States, lying west, south, and south-eastwardly, of a line to be run and described by persons duly authorized and appointed by the President of the United States....

2nd—The United States will guarantee to the Creek nation, the integrity of all their territory eastwardly and northwardly of the said line to be run and described as mentioned in the first article.

3rd—The United States demand, that the Creek nation abandon all communication, and cease to hold any intercourse with any British or Spanish post, garrison, or town; and that they shall not admit among them, any agent or trader, who shall not derive authority to hold commercial, or other intercourse with them, by license from the President or authorized agent of the United States.

4th—The United States demand an acknowledgment of the right to establish military posts and trading houses, and to open roads within the territory, guaranteed to the Creek nation by the second article, and a right to the free navigation of all its waters.

---

[2] From Charles J. Kappler, ed., *Indian Affairs. Laws and Treaties*, vol. 2 (Washington, DC: Government Printing Office, 1904).

5th—The United States demand, that a surrender be immediately made, of all the persons and property, taken from the citizens of the United States, the friendly part of the Creek nation, the Cherokee, Chickasaw, and Choctaw nations, to the respective owners; and the United States will cause to be immediately restored to the formerly hostile Creeks, all the property taken from them since their submission, either by the United States, or by any Indian nation in amity with the United States, together with all the prisoners taken from them during the war.

6th—The United States demand the caption and surrender of all the prophets and instigators of the war, whether foreigners or natives, who have not submitted to the arms of the United States, and become parties to these articles of capitulation, if ever they shall be found within the territory guaranteed to the Creek nation by the second article.

7th—The Creek nation being reduced to extreme want, and not at present having the means of subsistence, the United States, from motives of humanity, will continue to furnish gratuitously the necessaries of life, until the crops of corn can be considered competent to yield the nation a supply, and will establish trading houses in the nation, at the discretion of the President of the United States, and at such places as he shall direct, to enable the nation, by industry and economy, to procure clothing.

8th—A permanent peace shall ensue from the date of these presents forever, between the Creek nation and the United States, and between the Creek nation and the Cherokee, Chickasaw, and Choctaw nations.

The parties to these presents, after due consideration, for themselves and their constituents, agree to ratify and confirm the preceding articles, and constitute them the basis of a permanent peace between the two nations; and they do hereby solemnly bind themselves, and all the parties concerned and interested, to a faithful performance of every stipulation contained therein.

In testimony whereof, they have thereunto, interchangeably, set their hands and affixed their seals, the day and date above written.

3. An Address to the Whites by Elias Boudinot[3]

To those who are unacquainted with the manners, habits, and improvements of the Aborigines of this country, the term *Indian* is pregnant with ideas the most repelling and degrading. But such impressions, originating as they

---

[3] From "An Address to the Whites Delivered in the First Presbyterian Church, on the 26th of May, 1826, by Elias Boudinott, A Cherokee Indian" (Philadelphia: Printed by William F. Geddes, 1826).

frequently do, from infant prejudices, although they hold too true when applied to some, do great injustice to many of this race of beings....

What is an Indian? Is he not formed of the same materials with yourself? For "of one blood God created all the nations that dwell on the face of the earth." Though it be true that he is ignorant, that he is a heathen, that he is a savage; yet he is no more than all others have been under similar circumstances. Eighteen centuries ago what were the inhabitants of Great Britain?

You here behold an *Indian*, my kindred are *Indians*, and my fathers sleeping in the wilderness grave—they too were *Indians*....

The Cherokee nation lies within the charted limits of the states of Georgia, Tennessee, and Alabama. Its extent as defined by treaties is about 200 miles in length from East to West, and about 120 in breadth. This country which is supposed to contain about 10,000,000 of acres exhibits great varieties of surface, the most part being hilly and mountainous, affording soil of no value. The vallies, however, are well watered and afford excellent land, in many parts particularly on the large streams, that of the first quality. The climate is temperate and healthy, indeed I would not be guilty of exaggeration were I to say, that the advantages which this country possesses to render it salubrious, are many and superior....

The rise of these people in their movement towards civilization, may be traced as far back as the relinquishment of their towns; when game became incompetent to their support, by reason of the surrounding white population. They then betook themselves to the woods, commenced the opening of small clearings, and the raising of stock; still however following the chase....

It is a matter of surprise to me, and must be to all those who are properly acquainted with the condition of the Aborigines of this country, that the Cherokees have advanced so far and so rapidly in civilization.... To give you a further view of their condition, I will here repeat some of the articles of the two statistical tables taken at different periods.

In 1810 there were 19,500 cattle; 6,100 horses; 19,600 swine; 1,037 sheep; 467 looms; 1,600 spinning wheels; 30 waggons; 500 ploughs; 3 saw-mills; 13 grist-mills &c. At this time there are 22,000 cattle; 7,600 horses; 46,000 swine; 2,500 sheep; 762 looms; 2,488 spinning wheels; 172 waggons; 2,943 ploughs; 10 saw-mills; 31 grist-mills; 62 Blacksmith-shops; 8 cotton machines; 18 schools; 18 ferries; and a number of public roads....

There are three things of late occurance, which must certainly place the Cherokee Nation in a fair light, and act as a powerful argument in favor of Indian improvement.

First. The invention of letters.

Second. The translation of the New Testament into Cherokee.

And third. The organization of a Government.

When before did a nation of Indians step forward and ask for the means of civilization? The Cherokee authorities have adopted the measures already stated, and with a sincere desire to make their nation an intelligent and virtuous people....

4. Constitution of the Cherokee Nation[4]

We, the representatives of the people of the Cherokee Nation, in Convention assembled, in order to establish justice, ensure tranquility, promote our common welfare, and secure to ourselves and our posterity the blessings of liberty; acknowledging with humility and gratitude the goodness of the sovereign Ruler of the Universe, in offering us an opportunity so favorable to the design, and imploring His aid and direction in its accomplishment, do ordain and establish this Constitution for the Government of the Cherokee Nation.

ARTICLE I.

...Section 2. The sovereignty and Jurisdiction of this Government shall extend over the country within the boundaries above described, and the lands therein are, and shall remain, the common property of the nation; but improvements made thereon, and in the possession of the citizens of the Nation, are the exclusive and indefeasible property of the citizens respectively who made; or may rightfully be in possession of them....

ARTICLE II.

Section 1. The power of this Government shall be divided into three distinct departments; the Legislative, the Executive, and Judicial....

ARTICLE III.

Section 1. The legislative power shall be vested in two distinct branches; a Committee and a Council, each to have a negative on the other, and both to be styled the General Council of the Cherokee Nation....

Section 2. The Cherokee nation, as laid off into eight Districts, shall so remain.

---

[4] From *Laws of the Cherokee Nation: Adopted by the Council at Various Periods. Printed for the Benefit of the Nation* (Tahlequah, Cherokee Nation: Cherokee Advocate printing Office, 1852).

Section 3. The Committee shall consist of two members from each District, and the Council shall consist of three members from each District, to be chosen by the qualified electors of their respective Districts, for two years....

Section 4. No person shall be eligible to a seat in the General Council, but a free Cherokee male citizen, who shall have attained to the age of twenty-five years. The descendants of Cherokee men by all free women, except the African race, whose parents may have been living together as man and wife, according to the customs and laws of this Nation, shall be entitled to all the rights and privileges of this Nation, as well as the posterity of Cherokee women by all free men....

Section 7. All free male citizens (excepting negroes and descendants of white and Indian men by negro women who may have been set free,) who shall have attained to the age of eighteen years, shall be equally entitled to vote at all public elections.

...Section 15. The General Council shall have power to make all laws and regulations, which they shall deem necessary and proper for the good of the Nation, which shall not be contrary to this Constitution.

...Section 23. The General Council shall have the sole power of deciding on the construction of all Treaty stipulations.

ARTICLE IV.

Section 1. The Supreme Executive Power of this Nation shall be vested in a Principal Chief, who shall be chosen by the General Council, and shall hold his office four years; to be elected as follows,—The General Council by a joint vote, shall, at their second annual session, after the rising of this Convention, and at every fourth annual session thereafter, on the second day after the Houses shall be organized, and competent to proceed to business, elect a principal Chief.

Section 2. No person, except a natural born citizen, shall be eligible to the office of Principal Chief; neither shall any person be eligible to that office, who shall not have attained to the age of thirty-five years.

Section 3. There shall also be chosen at the same time, by the General Council, in the same manner for four years, an assistant Principal Chief.

Section 4. In case of the removal of the Principal Chief from office, or of his death, resignation, or inability to discharge the powers and duties of the said office, the same shall devolve on the assistant Principal Chief, until the inability be removed, or the vacancy filled by the General Council.

...Section 14. Every Bill which shall have passed both Houses of the General Council, shall before it becomes a law, be presented to the Principal Chief of the Cherokee Nation. If he approve, he shall sign it, but if not, he shall return it, with his objections, to that house in which it shall have originated, who shall enter the objections at large on their journals, and proceed to reconsider it. If, after such consideration, two thirds of that House shall agree to pass the bill, it shall be sent, together with the objections, to the other house, by which it shall likewise be reconsidered, and if approved by two thirds of that house, it shall become a law. If any bill shall not be returned by the Prin'l Chief within five days (Sundays excepted) after it shall have been presented to him, the same shall be a law, in like manner as if he had signed it; unless the General Council by their adjournment prevent its return, in which case it shall be a law, unless sent back within three days after their next meeting.

ARTICLE V.

Section 1. The Judicial Powers shall be vested in a Supreme Court, and such Circuit and Inferior Courts, as the General Council may, from time to time ordain and establish.

Section 2. The Supreme Court shall consist of three Judges, any two of whom shall be a quorum.

Done in Convention at New Echota, this twenty-sixth day of July, in the year of our Lord, one thousand eight hundred and twenty-seven.

5. *Cherokee Phoenix*[5]

February 21, 1828 [Volume 1, Number 1]

To the Public

We are happy in being able, at length, to issue the first number of our paper, although after a longer delay than we anticipated....

In the commencement of our labours, it is due to our readers that we should acquaint them with the general principles, which we have prescribed to ourselves as rules in conducting this paper. These principles we shall accordingly state briefly....

As the Phoenix is a national paper, we shall feel ourselves bound to devote it to national purposes. "The laws and public documents of the Nation," and matters relating to the welfare and conditions of the Cherokees as a people, will be faithfully published in English and Cherokee....

We will not unnecessarily intermeddle with the politics and affairs of our neighbors. As we have no particular interest in the concerns of the surrounding

---

[5] From *Cherokee Phoenix*, February 21, 1828.

states, we shall only expose ourselves to contempt and ridicule by improper intrusion. And though at times, we should do ourselves injustice, to be silent, on matters of great interest to the Cherokees, yet we will not return railing for railing, but consult mildness, for we have been taught to believe, that "A soft answer turneth away wrath; but grievous words stir up anger." The unpleasant controversy existing with the state of Georgia, of which many of our readers are aware, will frequently make our situation trying, by having hard sayings and threatenings thrown out against us, a specimen of which will be found in our next. We pray God that we may be delivered from such spirit....

We would now commit our feeble efforts to the good will and indulgence of the public, praying that God will attend them with his blessings, and hoping for that happy period, when all the Indian tribes of America shall arise, Phoenix like, from their ashes, and when the terms, "Indian depredation," "war whoop," "scalping knife," and the like, shall become obsolete, and for ever be "buried deep under the ground."

6. Georgia Assumes Control over Cherokee Land[6]

Be it enacted by the Senate and House of Representatives of the State of Georgia, in General Assembly met, and it is hereby enacted by the authority of the same, That from and after the passing of this act, all that part of the territory, within the limits of this state, and which lies between the Alabama line, and the old path leading from the Buzzard Roost, on the Chattahoochee river, to Sally Huse's, where the said path strikes the Alabama road, thence with said road, to the boundary line of Georgia, be and the same is hereby added to, and shall become a part of the county of Carroll.

Sec. 2. *And be it enacted by the authority aforesaid,* That all that part of the said territory, lying and being north of the last mentioned line, and south of the road, running from Charles Gates ferry, on Chattahoochee river, to Dick Roes, to where it intersects with the path aforesaid be, and the same is hereby added, and shall become a part of the county of DeKalb.

Sec. 3. *And be it further enacted,* That all that part of said territory lying north of the last mentioned line, and south of the old federal road be, and the same is hereby added, and shall become a part of the county of Gwinnett.

Sec. 4. *And be it further enacted,* That all that part of the said territory, lying north of the last mentioned line, and south of a line to begin on the Chestertee river, at the mouth of Yoholo creek, thence up said creek, to the top of the Blue

---

[6] From *Acts of the General Assembly of the State of Georgia*, 1828.

ridge, thence to the head waters of Notley river, thence down said river, to the boundary line of Georgia be, and the same is hereby added to, and shall become a part of the county of Hall.

Sec. 5. *And be it further enacted*, That all that part of the said territory, lying north of the last mentioned line, within the limits of Georgia be, and the same is hereby added to, and shall become a part of the county of Habersham.

Sec. 6. *And be it further enacted*, That the laws of this State be, and the same are hereby extended over said territory, and all white persons residing within the same, shall immediately after the passage of this act, be subject and liable to the operation of the said laws, in the same manner as other citizens of the state, or the citizens of said counties respectively.

Sec. 7. *And be it further enacted*, That after the first day of June, 1830, all Indians then, and at that time, residing in said territory, and within any one of the counties as aforesaid, shall be liable and subject to such laws and regulations, as the legislature may hereafter prescribe.

Sec. 8. *And be it further enacted*, That all laws usages, and customs made, established and in force, in the said territory, by the said Cherokee Indians be, and the same are hereby on, and after the first day of June, 1830, declared null and void.

Sec. 9. *And be it further enacted*, That no Indian, or decendant of Indian, residing within the Creek or Cherokee nations of Indians, shall be deemed a competent witness, or a party to any suit, in any court created by the constitution, or laws of this state, to which a white man may be a party.

Assented to, December 20, 1828.

7. *Worcester v. State of Georgia*[7]

January Term, 1832

This was a writ of error to the superior court for the county of Gwinnett, in the state of Georgia.

...The Indian nations had always been considered as distinct, independent political communities, retaining their original natural rights, as the undisputed possessors of the soil, from time immemorial, with the single exception of that imposed by irresistible power, which excluded them from intercourse with any European potentate than the first discoverer of the coast of that particular region claimed: and this was a restriction which those European potentates

---

[7] From *Worcester v. State of Georgia*, 31 US 515.

imposed on themselves, as well as the Indians. The very term "nation," so generally applied to them, means "a people distinct from others"....

The Cherokee nation, then, is a distinct community occupying its own territory, with boundaries accurately described, in which the laws of Georgia can have no force, and which the citizens of Georgia have no right to enter, but with the assent of the Cherokees themselves, or in conformity with treaties, and with the acts of congress. The whole intercourse between the United States and this nation, is, by our constitution and laws, vested in the government of the United States.

The act of the state of Georgia, under which the plaintiff in error was prosecuted, is consequently void, and the judgment a nullity....

If the review which has been taken be correct, and we think it is, the acts of Georgia are repugnant to the constitution, laws, and treaties of the United States.

They interfere forcibly with the relations established between the United States and the Cherokee nation, the regulation of which, according to the settled principles of our constitution, are committed exclusively to the government of the union.

They are in direct hostility with treaties, repeated in a succession of years, which mark out the boundary that separates the Cherokee country from Georgia; guaranty to them all the land within their boundary; solemnly pledge the faith of the United States to restrain their citizens from trespassing on it; and recognize the pre-existing power of the nation to govern itself.

They are in equal hostility with the acts of congress for regulating the intercourse, and giving effect to the treaties.

The forcible seizure and abduction of the plaintiff in error, who was residing in the nation with its permission, and by authority of the president of the United States, is also a violation of the acts which authorize the chief magistrate to exercise this authority....

It is the opinion of this court that the judgment of the superior court for the county of Gwinnett, in the state of Georgia, condemning Samuel A. Worcester to hard labour, in the penitentiary of the state of Georgia, for four years, was pronounced by that court under the colour of a law which is void, as being repugnant to the constitution, treaties, and laws of the United States, and ought, therefore, to be reversed and annulled.

Mr. Justice McLean

8. Treaty of New Echota[8]

Whereas the Cherokees are anxious to make some arrangements with the Government of the United States whereby the difficulties they have experienced by a residence within the settled part of the United States under the jurisdiction and laws of the State Governments may be terminated and adjusted; and with a view to reuniting their people in one body and securing a permanent home for themselves and their posterity in the country selected by their forefathers without the territorial limits of the State sovereignties, and where they can establish and enjoy a government of their choice and perpetuate such a state of society as may be most consonant with their views, habits and condition; and as may tend to their individual comfort and their advancement in civilization....

Therefore the following articles of a treaty are agreed upon and concluded between William Carroll and John F. Schermerhorn commissioners on the part of the United States and the chiefs and head men and people of the Cherokee nation in general council assembled this 29th day of Decr 1835.

Article 1. The Cherokee nation hereby cede relinquish and convey to the United States all the lands owned claimed or possessed by them east of the Mississippi river, and hereby release all their claims upon the United States for spoliations of every kind for and in consideration of the sum of five millions of dollars to be expended paid and invested in the manner stipulated and agreed upon in the following articles....

Article 2. Whereas the treaty of May 6th 1828 and the supplementary treaty thereto of Feb. 14th 1833 with the Cherokees west of the Mississippi the United States guarantied and secured to be conveyed by patent, to the Cherokee nation of Indians the following tract of country.... In addition to the seven millions of acres of land thus provided for and bounded, the United States further guaranty to the Cherokee nation a perpetual outlet west, and a free and unmolested use of all the country west of the western boundary of said seven millions of acres, as far west as the sovereignty of the United States and their right of soil extend.

Article 4. The United States also stipulate and agree to extinguish for the benefit of the Cherokees the titles to the reservations within their country made in the Osage treaty of 1825....

Article 5. The United States hereby covenant and agree that the lands ceded to the Cherokee nation in the forgoing article shall, in no future time without

---

[8] From Charles J. Kappler, ed., *Indian Affairs: Laws and Treaties*, vol. 2 (Washington, DC: Government Printing Office, 1904).

their consent, be included within the territorial limits or jurisdiction of any State or Territory....

Article 6. Perpetual peace and friendship shall exist between the citizens of the United States and the Cherokee Indians. The United States agree to protect the Cherokee nation from domestic strife and foreign enemies and against intestine wars between the several tribes....

Article 7. The Cherokee nation having already made great progress in civilization and deeming it important that every proper and laudable inducement shall be offered to their people to improve their condition as well as to guard and secure in the most effectual manner the rights guarantied to them in this treaty, and with a view to illustrate the liberal and enlarged policy of the Government of the United States towards the Indians in their removal beyond the territorial limits of the States, it is stipulated that they shall be entitled to a delegate in the House of Representatives of the United States whenever Congress shall make provision for the same.

Article 8. The United States also agree and stipulate to remove the Cherokees to their new homes and to subsist them one year after their arrival there and that a sufficient number of steamboats and baggagewagons shall be furnished to remove them comfortably, and so as not to endanger their health, and that a physician well supplied with medicines shall accompany each detachment of emigrants removed by the Government....

Article 19. This treaty after the same shall be ratified by the President and Senate of the United States shall be obligatory on the contracting parties.

In testimony whereof, the commissioners and the chiefs, head men, and people whose names are hereunto annexed, have affixed their hands and seals for themselves, and in behalf of the Cherokee nation.

ESSAYS

Georgia and Muscogee/Creek Treaties[9]

Grace M. Schwartzman and Susan K. Barnard

Prior to the arrival of General James Oglethorpe in Georgia in 1733, the Muscogee/Creek Nation, described by Alan Gallay as "the most powerful Indian nation on the southern frontier," inhabited land from the Atlantic ocean to the Mississippi River. Through a series of negotiations, first with the English and then with the new American government, these vast holdings were quickly reduced, with river banks serving as dividing lines. Needing a word to describe these diplomatic maneuverings, the white men turned to the French word "traite" which was derived from the Latin "tractare," meaning to handle, or discuss. From 1733 until 1826, "treaty" became the mechanism for "peaceful" usurpation of Indian land while establishing control in the yet unacquired territory. By 1796 the eastern boundary of this Native American nation extended eastward only as far as the Oconee River.

In the early colonial period many Europeans viewed the Indians as people who could be dealt with and assimilated into their culture. However, as Alden T. Vaughan has noted, when the Indians rejected Christianity and the European way of life, white attitudes toward them changed; they were relegated to a less than equal status. The English even anglicized the name Muscogee (also spelled Muskogee), an Algonquin word meaning "people of the lowland," by referring to them as Creeks since they lived along waterways.

Following the Revolutionary War and the ratification of the Constitution on July 26, 1788, the new federal government urged the states to define their western boundaries. The unoccupied land was to be established as new territories. Georgia, the last state to comply, offered a compromise: it would relinquish a portion of its land along the southern boundaries of present-day Alabama and Mississippi to Congress if it could retain the remainder. This offer was rejected.

The Georgia legislature, looking at its western lands as a means of retiring the state's Revolutionary War debt, passed the Yazoo Act on January 7, 1795, which enabled four companies of land speculators to purchase over 35 million

---

[9] Reprinted from "A Trail of Broken Promises: Georgians and Muscogee/Creek Treaties, 1796–1826," *Georgia Historical Quarterly* 75/4 (Winter 1991). Courtesy of the Georgia Historical Society.

acres of Indian land stretching from the Alabama and Coosa rivers to the Mississippi for 1 1/2 cents per acre. This became known as the Yazoo Land Fraud. Many Georgians protested, arguing that they had been robbed of the opportunity to purchase land when there was no necessity to sacrifice such a huge parcel of territory to outside investors. This discontent, coupled with the involvement of a number of legislators in the scheme, led to the seating of a reform legislature on January 14, 1796, which succeeded in rescinding the fraudulent Yazoo Act.

The federal government, angered by Georgia's blunder, devised an alternative method to legally obtain land still in the hands of the Indians. This entailed imposing its civilization on the red man on the grounds that farming and husbandry required less territory than the vast hunting areas. The unused hunting tracts would then be available for cession. To facilitate this process, Benjamin Hawkins was appointed Indian agent in 1796 and placed his agency on the eastern side of the Flint River. His job was to accelerate the acquisition of more land and to teach the Indians new farming techniques.

Hawkins organized two distinct governments within the Muscogee/Creek Nation: Little Prince became leader of the Lower Towns' capital at Coweta and Tustennuggee Thlocco/Big Warrior was declared head of the Upper Towns at Tuckabatchee. Hawkins helped erode an ancient tradition of clan power by convincing the National Council to establish law menders to enforce laws while exempting them from clan punishment for violations. Much of what Hawkins did widened an already developing rift between Upper Towns, which pursued ancient ways of hunting and fishing, and Lower Towns, which adopted the settlers' lifestyle.

The federal government's boundary negotiations with Georgia concluded with the 1802 Compact, signed on April 24, in which Georgia granted to the United States about 86 million acres of Indian land from her present-day Alabama line to the Mississippi River. For this agreement, Georgia received $1,250,000 and a promise "that the United States shall, at their own expense, extinguish for the use of Georgia, as early as the same can be peaceably obtained, on reasonable terms, the Indian title" *to all* Indian land east of the present-day boundary line within Georgia.

The ink was barely dry on this compact when the Treaty of Fort Wilkinson was negotiated. This document, signed on June 16, 1802, ceded a strip of Muscogee/Creek land between the Oconee and Ocmulgee rivers to the United States. In payment, the Nation was to receive $3,000 annually for an unspecified number of years and the chiefs were to receive $1,000 for ten years. Another $25,000 was to be doled out in goods and merchandise, satisfying Indian debts at trading posts and payment for stolen slaves and horses.

Honoring its agreement with Georgia, Secretary of War Henry Dearborn directed Hawkins in 1804 to meet with the Muscogee/Creek National Council and use every reasonable method at his command to obtain further land cessions. These persuasions resulted in a treaty signed in Washington on November 14, 1805. It picked up where the Treaty of Wilkinson left off, ceding a tract of land between the Oconee and Ocmulgee rivers, and allowed the federal government to run a horse path through Muscogee/Creek country from the Ocmulgee River to the Mobile River....

Under the terms of the Treaty of Fort Jackson, signed on August 9, 1814, the Muscogee/Creek Nation surrendered over 20 million acres of land in payment for expenses incurred by the United States for the war; the value was determined by President James Madison. Once again the Muscogee/Creeks were guaranteed all their unceded territory. One square mile of land was reserved within the newly ceded territory for any chief or warrior who had supported the United States during the war. Once the occupant or his descendants abandoned the property, it was to revert to the United States.

After signing the "Treaty of Conquest" (Fort Jackson), the Muscogee/Creek Nation was reduced to a confederacy of starving people bereft of honor, dignity, and the basic necessities for survival. To help alleviate their suffering, President Madison offered to furnish the "necessaries of life" until their next crop of corn ripened. Trading houses were established within the Nation to enable the Indians to procure clothing. The president then assured the Indians that their remaining lands would never be taken from them without their consent and suitable payment....

After further debate, the Muscogee/Creek Indians signed a treaty in Washington on January 24, 1826. The 1825 treaty boundaries were expanded, leaving more land in the Muscogee/Creek Nation's hands. They were to receive $217,600 following ratification and $20,000 annually in a perpetual annuity. They had twenty-four months to vacate. Finally on November 15, 1827 the United States succeeded in acquiring the last acre of Georgia land held by the Muscogee/Creeks.

Forced from their homeland into Oklahoma territory, the Muscogee/Creeks became a captive nation. This status restricted the tribal leaders' powers, further impoverished the people, and made them heavily dependent upon federal assistance. Later, with the discovery of natural resources, further exploitation of the Indians created an internal colony. Matthew Snipp stated, "As internal colonies, Indian lands are being developed primarily for the benefit of the outside, non-Indian economy."

In less than fifty years the federal government managed to fulfill its obligation under the Compact of 1802 to extinguish the Muscogee/Creeks from

Georgia. This once powerful nation was broken and moved westward river by river with treaties being used a leverage, despite President George Washington's promise to the Muscogee/Creek Indians that they would retain their ancestral lands "until the Great Spirit saw cause to destroy the world." The proud Muscogee/Creek Indians are gone; they took a rich civilization with them. What Georgia gained materially ~~they~~it lost culturally.

The Cherokee Trail of Tears[10]

Ronald N. Satz

In March 1837, Martin Van Buren, the sagacious and consummate politician who was the architect of the political coalition that captured the White House for Jackson in 1828, assumed the presidency. During his first year in office, relations between Cherokees and whites in Georgia were at a crisis level as Treaty Party leaders had feared. The growing prospect of federal-state conflict if the Cherokees remained in Georgia beyond the date specified for their removal prompted Van Buren to send General Winfield Scott to the Cherokee country in April 1838 to ensure compliance with the removal provisions of the Treaty of New Echota.

Although the official military records of the Cherokee removal reveal that there was a conscientious effort to minimize hostilities and to complete the task as quickly and efficiently as possible, there was little understanding of the extent of the suffering of the Indians. General Scott ordered his troops, as well as the state militia and the less disciplined volunteers who assisted them, to treat the Cherokees humanely. Nevertheless, Scott authorized the taking of women and children as hostages to encourage removal, and some soldiers, especially the volunteers, were cruel as they herded the Indians together into wooden stockades in preparation for their removal. Forced to abandon their homes, crops, livestock, and other belongings at a moment's notice, many Indians lacked sufficient clothing, bedding, and cooking utensils, among other items, when their exodus began under military escort in June of 1838. As a result of their poor preparation for removal, the physical hardships of the long journey, and such factors as disease, exposure, and fatigue along the way, many Indians died en route to the West.

News of the suffering of the emigrant Cherokees led General Scott to suspend further operations until the autumn. Meanwhile, Chief Ross, convinced

---

[10] Reprinted from "The Cherokee Trail of Tears: A Sesquicentennial Perspective," *Georgia Historical Quarterly* 73/3 (Fall 1989). Courtesy of the Georgia Historical Society.

that there was now no alternative to removal, urged Scott to allow the Cherokee Nation to supervise its own removal to the West. When Andrew Jackson learned that Scott had persuaded the Van Buren administration to turn the removal of the Cherokees over to Ross, he protested. The United States was suffering from the strains of a severe depression, and the former president privately warned his hand-picked successor that "the scamp Ross" would never follow "principles of economy" and that the expenses of removal would therefore "shake the popularity of the administration to its center."

President Van Buren, however, followed General Scott's advice rather than that of former President Jackson. Chief Ross was permitted to serve as superintendent of Cherokee Removal and Subsistence even though his estimates of the cost of removal greatly exceeded the actual congressional appropriation. Van Buren allowed Ross to take over supervision of the removal operations because he was anxious to minimize any political damage that might come to his administration from carrying out the forced removal of the Cherokees. In addition to the controversial Treaty of 1835, Van Buren had inherited from the Jackson administration a bloody war in Florida with the Seminoles and a corrupt Commissioner of Indian Affairs. Cognizant of the Whigs capitalizing on the situation in Florida and concerned about rumors of speculation in Indian land allotments and other alleged "treachery" by Commissioner Carey Allen Harris, Van Buren found it expedient to follow the recommendation of General Scott, a Whig, and turn the removal operations over to the Cherokee leadership.

Ross and the tribal committee he worked with divided the Cherokee Nation into thirteen detachments of about 1,000 people each. Emigration began the first week in October, and the last of the detachments was underway by mid-November. Some federal officials complained that the Cherokees were spending too much money on transportation and supplies. In fact, the Cherokees did exceed the allocation for removal. This occurred, however, not because Chief Ross "lined his pockets" at the expense of his people as some of his detractors asserted, but, rather, because of the greed of white merchants, traders, ferry operators, and toll road keepers with whom the Indians had to deal along the route.

The westward trek was fatiguing, and disease was rampant. Among the Indians who never reached present-day Oklahoma was Quatie Ross, the wife of Chief Ross, who died en route and was buried at Little Rock, Arkansas. An army private who accompanied the Cherokees on the Trail of Tears recalled the event years later as follows:

I was sent as an interpreter…and witnessed the execution of the most brutal order in the History of American warfare. I saw the helpless Cherokees arrested and dragged from their homes, and driven at the bayonet point into the stockades. And in the chill of a drizzling rain on an October morning I saw them loaded like cattle or sheep into six hundred and forty-five wagons and started toward the west.

One can never forget the sadness and solemnity of that morning. Chief John Ross led in prayer and when the bugle sounded and the wagons started rolling many of the children rose to their feet and waved their little hands good-by to their mountain homes, knowing they were leaving them forever. Many of these helpless people did not have blankets and many of them had been driven from their home barefooted.

…The sufferings of the Cherokees were awful. The trail of the exiles was a trail of death. They had to sleep in the wagons and on the ground without fire. And I have known as many as twenty-two of them to die in one night of pneumonia due to ill treatment, cold, and exposure.

By late March 1839, the Cherokees emigrating under the direction of tribal leaders had completed the exodus from their homeland.

Only about 1,400 Cherokees managed to avoid removal. They accomplished this either by hiding out in the mountains or by taking advantage of a provision in the Treaty of New Echota (and two earlier treaties) allowing certain Indians to become citizens of the states in which they resided. About 1,100 of the Indians who stayed behind were unacculturated full bloods in the Great Smoky Mountains in North Carolina. Another 300, generally more acculturated than their North Carolina kinfolk, remained in Georgia, Tennessee, and Alabama. Anxious to finalize his role in the removal process and to convince Georgia officials that all was going well, General Scott assured Governor George Gilmer in October of 1838 that "in your State, I am confident there are not left a dozen Indian families, and at the head of each is a citizen of the United States."

The Trail of Tears was both a Cherokee tragedy and an American tragedy. The forced removal of the Cherokees shocked many contemporaries because of the significant progress that these Indians had made in what Americans often referred to as "the great principles of civilization." Geologist George Featherstonhaugh, who visited the Cherokee country in 1837, reported that he had seen signs of progress everywhere—the presence of Christian missionaries and churches, books printed in the native language, a tribal government based on written laws, and fields under cultivation. Featherstonhaugh lamented that the Cherokees were being forced out of Georgia "not because they cannot be civilized, but because a pseudo set of civilized beings [namely, white Georgians], who are too strong for them, want their possessions!" Forced from their ancestral homeland after accepting many of the ways of the white people who were encircling them, confronted with numerous indignities and much suffering as a result of their capture, detention, and exodus, the Cherokee tragedy continued in their new location.

Additional Sources

Anderson, William, editor. *Cherokee Removal: Before and After*. Athens: University of Georgia Press, 1991.

Ehle, John. *Trail of Tears: The Rise and Fall of the Cherokee Nation*. New York: Doubleday, 1988.

Ethridge, Robbie. *Creek Country: The Creek Indians and Their World*. Chapel Hill: University of North Carolina Press, 2003.

McLoughlin, William G. *Cherokee Renascence in the New Republic*. Princeton: Princeton University Press, 1987.

Perdue, Theda. *Slavery and the Evolution of Cherokee Society, 1540–1866*. Knoxville: University of Tennessee Press, 1979.

Perdue, Theda. *Cherokee Women: Gender and Culture Change, 1700–1835*. Lincoln: University of Nebraska Press, 1998.

Williams, David. *The Georgia Gold Rush: Twenty-Niners, Cherokees, and Gold Fever*. Columbia: University of South Carolina Press, 1993.

Chapter 5

ANTEBELLUM ECONOMICS

The antebellum Georgia economy was decidedly agricultural in nature with only a little industry or manufacturing. The Georgia Trustees had some definite ideas about what would drive the colony's economy; these included the production of citrus fruits, wine, and silk. Unfortunately for the Trustees, none of these products became staples. Instead, the first staples of the Georgia economy were tobacco, rice, and cotton. Along the coast, or Low Country, rice was the predominant crop while tobacco and later cotton featured in the Upcountry, or interior. Other crops such as potatoes, corn, wheat, oats, and other grains were grown for home consumption. Cotton became the most important cash crop in antebellum Georgia, especially after Eli Whitney developed the cotton gin in 1793 on a Georgia plantation. Georgia cotton farmers grew Sea Island cotton and short staple cotton. By the 1820s Georgia was producing more cotton than any other state in the union.

Manufacturing in the early antebellum period was limited to handicraft-type operations for local sale. More accurately, Georgians were artisans or craftsmen and included blacksmiths, silversmiths, tanners, weavers, millers, bakers, tailors, and the like. By the 1830s cotton had grown to be so important to the state's economy that textile mills were introduced to Georgia. Centered along the Fall Line where water power was available, over forty textile mills were in operation by the time of the Civil War. Lumbering became established in the late antebellum period with Savannah as the center of the industry; the city was one of the country's busiest lumber markets. Savannah was notable as the state's industrial center and the primary port for Georgia's exports. All told, the 1860 census counted 1,890 manufacturing establishments with 11,575 workers in Georgia.

Regardless of what drove the state's economy, an efficient transportation system was essential. In the years after the Revolution, this meant the construction of a road system and the development of river transportation. River improvements were made to the Savannah River in the 1790s, and in 1798 a canal from the Altamaha River southward was approved although it was never completed. It was not until after the War of 1812 that Georgia embarked on a comprehensive internal improvements program. By the 1830s the construction of railroad lines dominated transportation and Georgia laid its share of track. By the time of the Civil War, the state had expended $26 million on railroad construction; of the entire South, Georgia's railroad system was second only to Virginia.

Cotton remained central to Georgia's economy up to the outbreak of the Civil War in 1861; cotton was definitely king. Production increased from 150,000 bales in 1826 to 326,000 in 1839 and 701,000 in 1860. At the time of the Civil War, only Alabama, Mississippi, and Louisiana produced more cotton than Georgia.

Documents

Document 1 below is an excerpt from the first issue of the agricultural journal *Southern Cultivator*, which originated in Georgia. The second document reports on the possible cultivation of indigo in the state. Document 3 is an 1850 article on Georgia's economic resources. The fourth document is a description of the construction of a plantation house in Augusta. Documents 5 and 6 are charts of agricultural and industrial production in Georgia in 1850 and 1860. The seventh document is a description of agriculture in the Confederacy.

1. *Southern Cultivator*[1]

March 1, 1843
Augusta, Georgia

To Southern Planters

In obedience to a promise made some time since, we have entered upon a new enterprise, and to-day send forth for your inspection, and we fondly hope, your approval, the first number of the "Southern Cultivator." In commencing a work of such importance to the cultivators of the soil, we have been influenced by no other motives than to contribute our humble but zealous efforts to the restoration of the exhausted lands of the country, to introduce an enlightened system of agriculture, and to afford an acceptable medium for the interchange of views between planters, upon a subject in which all classes of society are so deeply interested. We have seen and felt the blighting effects upon the interests and independence of Southern planters, which have been produced by the too

---

[1] From *The Southern Cultivator*, March 1, 1843.

common and fatal system of Agriculture almost universally adopted, and it has long been to us a source of deep anxiety. To correct the evils of a system so long established and practised upon, and to introduce one better adapted to the wants and comforts of the whole population, we are fully aware, is a work of no ordinary labor, both physical and mental; but when we reflect upon the important advantages which a proper direction of our energies promises to develope to the great agricultural interests of the South, we enter upon the duties with the highest confidence of success, relying for aid upon those who have embarked in this valuable and interesting pursuit. To the Planters, therefore, of Georgia and the surrounding Southern States, do we appeal for aid in this enterprise—we ask not only their influence in circulating the work among all the tillers of the soil, but as we hope and believe that it will derive its chief interest from an interchange of their views upon all subjects pertaining to agriculture and the general business of the farm, we invite their cordial and sincere co-operation in forwarding to us their views, and the result of experiments in every department of this deeply interesting branch of industry....

2. Cultivation of Indigo in Georgia?[2]

Agricultural Association of the State of Georgia
Report of the Committee on Indigo

The opinion has been entertained, and sentiments expressed within two or three years in agricultural essays, that Indigo might be cultivated in the Southern States advantageously, and that by diverting a part of the labor from this country from the great staple (cotton) it might be rendered more valuable and uniform in price, and we should add another important article to our agriculture. This opinion was strengthened by the known fact that in former times both Carolina and Georgia made the article in question for exportation, as well as for domestic use; and here it may be remarked, that for the latter purpose it is still produced, by the small planters, of pretty good quality, without any difficulty. The serious objection to the cultivation of indigo upon a large scale, or in other words as we cultivate cotton for exportation, is the unhealthiness of the process used to extract the coloring matter from the plant, and to such an extent was this believed to be true, that it is said to have been the

---

[2] From *The Southern Cultivator*, January 1848.

main cause of its discontinuance in Carolina. Under this view of the subject, the chief object of the committee has been to determine if it was practicable to obviate this great objection by a different process of manufacture....

There are four varieties of the indigo plant, one of which is a native of Georgia, and is now found in great abundance in the newly settled part of southwestern Georgia; it is the *indigojera orgentia* or wild indigo; it is a perennial plant, much improved by cultivation, may be cut twice a year, and it is said by those who cultivate it for domestic use to improve for 10 or 12 years in the quantity of the weed annually produced; it is considered next to the best variety in the quality of the coloring matter.

If the sulphate of indigo is valuable for dying, it can be abundantly made in Georgia. The subject may be worth further consideration.

3. Georgia's Economic Resources[3]

It is an undeniable fact, that no State in the Union possesses, in so great a degree, the elements of national and individual wealth as Georgia. All that we need, is legislation looking to their development and the enterprise of a few public-spirited individuals to give direction to our energies....

A wise economy, therefore, says to our people, keep these dividends and interest at home to enrich yourselves. This can be done by increasing our banking capital. New banks should be established, and located at such points as their capital was needed. Macon, Columbus, Atlanta and Griffin, four of the most important interior commercial points in the State, have not a dollar of banking capital of their own....

The completion of the Georgia, Central and Macon railroads, the partial completion of the Western and Atlantic road, has thus far stimulated the enterprise of our State, far beyond the most sanguine expectations of the advocates of those works. The completion of the State road to Chattanooga, the construction of a branch to Rome, and the improvement of the navigation of the Coosa river, will pour the produce of Tennessee and north Alabama into our State. The construction of the South western railroad will give us the control of the entire products of our own State in that direction, that of western Florida and of all southern Alabama. The construction of the railroad from Columbus eastward will give us the control of middle Alabama. Through all

---

[3] From *DeBow's Review*, January–June 1850.

these channels an immense amount of commerce must pour itself to enrich our State....

Georgia is the greatest cotton *growing* State in the Union, and she is destined to be the largest cotton *manufacturing* State, because she can manufacture cheaper and as well as any other State. It costs at least twenty-per cent upon the price of the raw material to transport it from Macon, Ga., to Lowell, Mass. This is no small advantage to start with. Then, a given number of spindles can be put in operation *here*, with all necessary appendages, for much less cost than a like number can be put in operation in any of the northern States, because of the difference in the value of land, water power and buildings. They can be put in operation for much less, because of the difference in the price of labor, provision, clothing and fuel. This must necessarily give us the advantage in the markets of the whole world; and this advantage will soon cause factories to spring up in almost every county—not to supply alone the local demand, but that of foreign markets....

Georgia has minerals of vast amount and value; and her Legislature should appoint a geologist to explore and develop them. Our mountains are filled with inexhaustible beds of the very best iron ore, sufficient to supply ourselves and a large portion of our Union. In the May number of the "Merchant's Magazine" there is an article on the subject of Manufacture of iron in Georgia, by the geologist of the State of New York; and, after speaking of its inexhaustible supply, says: "The iron is of superior quality, resembling that made of the best hematiles in other localities. It is suitable both for foundry and forge purposes, inclining particularly to the best No. 1 iron. From the abundance both of ore and charcoal, cheapness of living and labor, and great profits in this region on stone goods, the expenses of manufacture are extremely low, while the price of iron, both that made into castings for the supply of the country around and of the bar, are what would be considered, at northern works, remarkably high." This is sufficient inducement to capitalists to embark in this most lucrative business. Lime, coal and marble, all abound throughout our mountain regions, and would prove sources of great wealth when developed, as they must be in a few years....

Georgia has the resources—she must develop them slowly, but yet they will surely be developed. All that our people need, is to be told what they can do, and how it should be done; and as knowledge pours in upon them, so will their energies be stimulated and aroused.

4. Augusta Plantation House[4]

"Fruitland": The Residence of Dennis Redmond
By Dennis Redmond

The most obvious requirements of a Southern country house are: *ample space; convenient arrangement of rooms; shade, and ventilation.* To these should be added, if possible, a reasonable share of architectural style—an outward appearance in keeping and harmony with the interior and surrounding scenery...It was, therefore, after a very careful study of the requirements of our climate, and a familiarity with the various popular works on architecture, that the writer adopted the plan here given, which he trusts will be found to possess some commendable features, and to admit of such modifications as will adapt it to the tastes and necessities of others.

The site of this house is a dry and gravely knoll, in the orchard, at "Fruitland." It is on the dividing ridge between Rae's Creek and the Savannah River, and from the peculiar formation of the locality, commands a very beautiful prospect of the city of Augusta, the opposite hills of South Carolina, and the surrounding country, for many miles. The walls are of concrete, or artificial block—a material which possesses many and striking advantages over the *perishable* and *combustible* wood generally used for outside walls, and, if properly put up, is superior to brick in many respects....

By reference to the elevation and accompanying plans, it will be seen that the house is a nearly square structure of two-stories, fifty by fifty-five feet, entirely surrounded and shielded from sun and storm, by an ample verandah, ten feet wide. The lower story, or basement, contains the dining room, pantry, store-room, office, bathing room, fruit room, and ice-house—in short, all the *working rooms*, or apartments for every day practical use; while the second story contains the library, parlor, bedrooms, closets, etc. Two large halls, fifty-three by ten feet, run directly through the building, securing perfect ventilation, especially to the second-story, where transom-lights, over each door and opposite the outer windows, admit the freest possible circulation of pure air. The basement floor is raised several inches above the surface, filled in with pounded rock and gravel and laid in cement, which adheres firmly to the walls, thus affording perfect security against fires, dampness, and the depredations of ants and other vermin. By a very simple arrangement, the stairs leading from the basement to the second floor, and thence to the observatory or cupola, are removed from their usual position in the halls, leaving the latter entirely free

---

[4] From *The Southern Cultivator*, August 1857.

and unobstructed...The lower division walls, separating the hall from the dining room, office, etc., are built of concrete, one foot thick, but all the partitions, above and below, are lathed and plastered....

Advantages. A house of this description is admirably adapted to our Southern climate. Being a non-conductor, it is cool in summer and warm in winter—the walls do not absorb moisture from the atmosphere, like a brick house—with a cement floor, it is proof against every description of vermin—it is not near as liable to burn and decay as a wooden house, its walls becoming harder and harder, with age, until it is almost a solid mass of rock; and it possesses an *enduring* and *permanent* character, superior in many respects, to either wood or brick. Its most striking advantages over brick are, that it can be built in many locations where brick cannot be readily obtained—that it costs much less than brick, in almost all cases—and that the erection of the walls only needs the superintendance of one good mechanic, (mason or bricklayer) all the heavy labor being done by common field hands. The walls of our dwelling at "Fruitland," enclose an area of over 50 feet square—they are 20 feet high; 18 inches thick in the basement (9 ft.) and 12 inches in the upper story (11 ft.) with two lower partition walls, 9 feet high, 1 foot thick, and 52 feet long each....

5. General Agricultural Statistics[5]

	1850	1860
Number of farms	51,759	62,003
Acres in farms	22,821,379	26,650,490
Average acres per farm	440.9	429.8
Value of farms (dollars)	$95,753,445	$157,072,803
Cotton (bales)	499,091	701,840
Tobacco (pounds)	423,924	919,318
Rice (pounds)	38,950,691	52,507,652
Corn (bushels)	30,080,099	30,776,293
Wheat (bushels)	1,088,534	2,544,913
Oats (bushels)	3,820,044	1,231,817

[5] US Bureau of the Census, 1850, 1860.

6. General Industrial Statistics[6]

	1850	1860
Number of establishments	1,522	1,890
Number of workers	8,368	11,575
Value of products (dollars)	$7,082,075	$16,925,564

7. Agriculture in the Confederate States[7]

It should be one of the main objects of our new Confederacy to foster and develope, in the most direct and practical way, the highest Agricultural improvement among our people. How to do this is a question which admits of (and will probably receive) much discussion, but we are sorry to see that, thus far, our Representatives at Montgomery, have not found opportunity to give the subject the attention it demands. It is time, therefore, for the *people* themselves to urge it upon the attention of their servants, and to demand the establishment of a Board of Agricultural Commissioners, or a similar body, whose duty it shall be to devise some proper plan for the diffusion of correct Agricultural facts and general information, and the spread of real, progressive Agricultural *improvement* among the people of these States.

Depending, as we of the South do, almost wholly upon *Agriculture*, and possessing, without question, some of the best lands and the very finest climate of the world for all the various pursuits of rural life, we are still far in the rear of other less highly-favored regions, and much less perfect than we should be in all the essentials of good husbandry.

We do not advocate or recommend any "royal road" to Agricultural perfection; but we do advise that our leading Planters and Farmers everywhere, through public meetings or otherwise, give expression to their views on the true wants of our Agricultural system and the proper modes of inaugurating a reform that shall be radical and thorough.

Immediate and prompt action in this matter is necessary, if we wish the matter to obtain proper recognition and attention from our new Government; for we should know by this time that if Agricultural people do not look to their own best interests, the Politicians will be sure to overlook them.

---

[6] US Bureau of the Census, 1850, 1860.
[7] From *The Southern Cultivator*, March 1861.

Let the great and powerful Planting Interest of the South be properly represented in our new Confederacy of Planting States; and let all the laws of trade and commerce be so regulated that our most vital pursuit—that which is the basis of all our prosperity and power—shall have all the legitimate and proper aid that belongs to it. We ask nothing more, and we will be content with nothing less than this; and we trust our readers will aid us in the development and advocacy of the proper policy to be pursued in attaining the objects we desire.

ESSAYS

Rice Culture in Low Country Georgia[8]

Julia Floyd Smith

It was customary along the rice coast to perform all work by tasks. In the extremely laborious field work required in growing rice, the task system offered a more realistic method for work assignments than the gang system; the task system was also adopted on Sea Island cotton plantations. Task assignments were designed to produce effective performance and served as a convenient measurement of labor requirements on various projects. The standard measurement (daily assignment) was one-quarter of an acre, a square 105 feet on a side. The equivalent of this measurement was expected whether the work was planting, cultivating, harvesting, or preparing rice for market. Variations in this standard occurred when more strenuous assignments were performed, like clearing and preparing new land for cultivation, or when lighter tasks were given, which justified more extensive work. When rice was being planted, the task of a full hand was from 1 to 2 acres; when hoeing was being done, the task was a half-acre or less, depending upon the density of the soil and weeds. When rice was being harvested, the task was three-quarters of an acre; threshing with a flailing stick, 600 sheaves for the men and 500 for the women.

---

[8] From Julia Floyd Smith, *Slavery and Rice Culture in Low Country Georgia, 1750–1860* (Knoxville: University of Tennessee Press, 1985). Used with permission of the University of Tennessee Press.

Clearing swamp land to create rice plantations was a tremendous undertaking, and gangs of slave laborers performed such work. The area to be developed was first measured off and then cleared of all growth like Cyprus and gum trees, including a jungle-like maze of undergrowth. When the swamp was cleared, an outside bank, or levee, was constructed to surround the proposed rice fields completely. This bank was built of mud and dirt thrown up while digging an inside ditch about 20 feet from it. The ditch created was approximately 5 feet deep and wide; later, when the fields were flooded, this ditch served as a canal along which flatboats traveled during harvesting. The outside bank had to be higher than the highest tides to insure protection against both salt water flood tides from the ocean side and high tides or freshets from fresh water rivers. It took several years to rejuvenate fields after the soil had been inundated with salt water pushed over the outside bank by hurricane winds or exceptionally high flood tides.

The level of the land inside the outer bank had to be low enough to be flooded from fresh water rivers at high tide, yet high enough to drain properly at low tide. Before the enclosed area was ready for planting, floodgates were installed in the outer bank, all tree stumps removed, and the land drained and leveled off as evenly as possible. This area within the outside bank to be cultivated in rice was, on average, from 200 to 500 acres. It was now divided into rice fields, the size of the fields varying from 10 to 20 acres. Each field was subdivided into 1-acre plots by drains called force ditches that were 4 feet wide and deep, sloping to 2 feet at the bottom. Each drain had shorter outlets called quarter-drains that ran through each acre. The quarter-drains were 2 feet wide, 3 feet deep, sloping to 1 foot at the bottom. This arrangement insured an adequate and consistent flow of water to and from each acre when fields were being flooded and drained. Trunks were installed in the larger inside banks (created by ditching) to control the flow to each field. The trunks provided individual irrigation at various stages of culture.

The main floodgates, installed in the outside bank to connect with the river or a canal that led to the river, were constructed of heavy timbers strong enough to withstand the pressure of tidal flow. These gates were composed of two facing doors, 15 to 20 feet apart, built on and bolted to a heavy wooden frame foundation. At high tide, if the fields were to be flooded, the outer door was raised by the trunk-minder, the slave responsible for that particular task, and the pressure of the water from the river or outside canal constructed to connect with it pushed the inside door open, filling the ditches and flowing into the rice fields. The water continued to flow until it reached the level of the river or canal. As the tide receded, the pressure of the water that flowed from the ditches forced the inside door to close and allowed the water to remain in the fields for the desired time.

Rice fields were prepared for planting in March. Oxen and mules were used to plow and harrow the soft, boggy soil. The mules were sometimes equipped with shoes or boots, placed on their hind hoofs to prevent bogging while they pulled the implements. The boots were made of leather, padded on the inside with straw, reinforced with soles of wood or iron, and tied to the animal's hoofs with leather thongs. Prior to planting, parallel trenches from 12 to 15 inches apart were dug the total length of the field. Seed rice, which had been threshed by hand with a flailing stick, was used for planting—never mill rice, which might have been injured during the milling process. The rice was placed in the trenches and the water was let into the fields. This first flooding, the "sprout flow," remained from two to five days until the grain pipped [germinated]. The fields were then drained and allowed to dry.

When the seedling plants appeared, the fields were again flooded. During this second stage of irrigation, the "point" or "stretch" flow, the water again remained on the plants from two to five days; it was then drained off and the plants grew for about two weeks, during which time they were lightly hoed. The third irrigation, the "long" or "deep flow," occurred at mid-season and for several days completely submerged the rice. Dead weeds and other trash floated to the surface, to be raked off into the banks. The water also killed any insects that may have infested the plants. It then was drained off gradually to a level of 6 inches and remained from two to three weeks before being drained completely from the fields. For several weeks the fields remained dry while the plants were given two vigorous hoeings. The rice plants were now ready for the fourth and last irrigation, the "lay-by" or "harvest" flow. The fields were flooded and the water remained in the trenches from seven to eight weeks, supporting the rice plants as they grew and the heads of their stalks became heavy and ripened. The water was then drained off and the rice was ready to harvest, usually late in August and in September....

When the rice was harvested, all available hands were engaged in this important task. The stalks were cut with sickles (rice hooks) and were left on the bank for one or two days to dry. They were then tied together in sheaves and loaded onto flatboats and taken to the plantation yard to be stacked. Sheaves were stacked together on top of each other to a height of 15 feet, tapering like a haystack so as to shed rainwater. The outside measurement of the stacked sheaves was 45 feet by 12 feet. Bundles of sheaves stacked in these measurements produced about a thousand bushels of rough rice when threshed. Stacking was done with great care; any wet sheaves were opened and dried before stacking to protect the stalks against moisture. The sheaves remained stacked for several weeks or longer while food crops were harvested.

In November and December the rice was threshed, winnowed, and prepared for market. When rice was threshed by hand, slaves used flailing sticks (while the sheaves were still tied) to beat the grain from the stalks onto the clean hard ground or a threshing floor especially designed for that purpose. After the seeds were threshed, they were taken to the winnowing house to be separated from the chaff (husks of the grain and grasses). The winnowing house was a room 10 feet square, elevated from the ground about 15 feet by supports, with an outside stairway leading up to the room. When the wind was sufficiently strong, the rice was thrown through a grating in the middle of the floor of the room to the surface below while the chaff was blown away. The rice was still in its outer shell and was called rough rice. Pounding or grinding was the next process used to separate the seed from the outer shell. Before pounding mills were perfected for this purpose, mortars made of hollowed out logs held the rice and a wooden pestle was used to pound it. Pounding produced the clean white rice and a residue known as rice flour. Rice was shipped to market as either rough rice or white rice. Plantations like Gowrie and the Hermitage on the Savannah River, Wild Heron on the Ogeechee, and Hopeton on the Altamaha had mills where machines threshed, winnowed, and pounded the rice to prepare it for market. The entire process of growing, harvesting, and preparing rice for market was more intricate and demanding than the process involved in producing cotton, and capital investment in land, labor, and machinery was certainly greater....

Cotton Textiles in Georgia, 1810–1865[9]

Richard W. Griffin

For two decades after the War of 1812, little interest was evinced in cotton manufacture in this or any of the other Southern states; it being a period of great agricultural prosperity, men of wealth were not disposed to risk capital in such speculative investments. In the 1820s, however, a growing agricultural prostration was evidenced by a rapid decline in the price of cotton, and planters and their associates—cotton factors, bankers, shippers, and other

---

[9] From Richard W. Griffin, "The Origin of the Industrial Revolution in Georgia: Cotton Textiles, 1810–1865," *Georgia Historical Quarterly* 42/4 (December 1958). Courtesy of the Georgia Historical Society.

businessmen—viewed the declining prosperity with increasing alarm. Symptomatic of the conditions was the rapid emigration of planters and farmers from the older Southeastern states to the rich cotton lands of Alabama, Mississippi, Louisiana, Arkansas, and Texas. The growing instability forced more thoughtful Georgians to seek a means of keeping their citizens and wealth at home. Offering new investment opportunities and new ways of earning a livelihood seemed to be the only way of preserving some part of their accustomed way of life.

In 1827–1828 definite signs were shown that both individuals and state governments were displaying heightened interest in a diversified economy. Groups of interested citizens in both Georgia and North Carolina were asking their respective legislatures to investigate the opportunities for the establishment of cotton manufactures. In Georgia the aim was to enlist the aid of the state in proving the utility of slave labor in industrial enterprises, and a memorial requesting such action did not fall on deaf ears.

The desire to find profitable employment for surplus capital, as well as the controversy over the Tariff of 1828, stimulated much debate as to the propriety of Georgia becoming an industrial state. Many Georgians of wealth and property, who were soon to form the nucleus of the Whig Party, encouraged and supported entrepreneurs in their plans to start cotton factories. At the same time newspapers in Savannah, Augusta, Milledgeville, and other Georgia towns noted with great interest the advance of the cotton mill campaign.

It was reported that a competent judge found the falls above Augusta eminently suitable to furnish water power for cotton mills and other types of manufactures, his estimate of the cost of building a cotton factory there being about $40,000. Such evidence provided sufficient indication that Georgians should turn from unprofitable cotton culture, as "the road to prosperity and wealth lies plain and direct before us!" The view was current that the introduction of the manufacture of cotton bagging alone would retain $250,000 annually in circulation in the state, an amount which at that time was being spent in other states for hemp bagging.

The manufacturing spirit caught on quickly, notices of projected cotton mills appearing with growing frequency. Even in the state capital, there were in the process of organization two mills designed to make bagging, negro cloth [a coarse, unrefined blend of cotton and wool used for making slave clothing], and sheeting. A Savannah mercantile house had an agent buy a site at Indian Springs for the erection of a cotton mill, while in 1828 John Schley—already noted for his part in Georgia's second cotton factory—went north to examine and purchase the latest machinery for a factory in Jefferson County. He made the long and arduous journey by stage coach on the "Alligator Line" from Augusta to Philadelphia. Here he secured the necessary equipment, which was sent by sea and land transport, and which was immediately put to work making 30-inch negro osnaburgs [a heavy, coarse cotton fabric used for making gain sacks, upholstery, drapery, and sometimes slave clothing]. The factory operated for many years under various names and at several locations before it was finally called Belleville Factory and situated on Butler's Creek near Augusta. The later addition of a dye-house enabled the company to manufacture stripes, plaids, and blue and brown denims.

The excitement over cotton mills inspired nearly all of the newspapers of Georgia to a discussion of the problems and efforts involved. Many editors felt that such enterprises were no longer experimental, having been proven practicable by experience of cotton manufactures in other Southern states. It was generally agreed that the many advantages of the whole region—excellent water power, suitable white and slave labor, cheap cotton, inexpensive food, and labor stability—gave it a clear superiority over the North....

The growth and advancement of Georgia's cotton industry was such that by 1834 a factory at Augusta was manufacturing its own spindle frames in its machine shop. In many parts of the state where there was plentiful water power, more and more men were experimenting with the manufacture of the staple. Near Atlanta, Roswell King and other local citizens built a spinning and weaving factory.

The growth of industry was all but phenomenal in the twelve years after 1828. The census of 1840 listed nineteen cotton mills with 42,589 spindles, 779 employees, and two dye-houses; these were capitalized at $573,835, with an annual product value of $304,342....

Throughout the state there were many new cotton factories of varied sizes, and as each new one was built more interest was stimulated in the industry. In 1845 Savannah lost by fire Dr. Poullain's factory, which had been capitalized at over $60,000 and had given employment to 300 of the city's poor. Although fire and flood took their toll on such enterprises, groups of citizens throughout the central counties remained undaunted in their attempts to establish similar businesses.

This was especially true throughout the 1840s, when the price of cotton barely covered the cost of its cultivation. Planters were urged to sell part of their lands to pay their debts, investing surplus capital in manufactories. A definite movement toward greater investment in such enterprises was seen in all states from Virginia to Louisiana. Every state south of the Potomac was turning increasing attention to the fabrication of iron, wool, and especially cotton....

In 1848 there were thirty-two cotton mills in the state, representing a total investment of $2,000,000 and giving direct support to over 6,000 operatives and their families. These mills were consuming annually nearly 20,000 bales of cotton, which was made into yarn and cloth; over one-third of this was sold out of state, some going as far as China....

The period from 1851–1857 was not particularly propitious for the manufacturers of cotton. Within these years the price of cotton increased so rapidly that the mills were forced to shut their doors, while the depression of 1857 also took its toll. In the last few years of the decade the mounting sectional crisis consumed the attention of all the leading men of the South, and the castigation of New Englanders as factory slave drivers caused many Southern editors to refrain from any mention of the rising mills in Georgia.

Although they shared the reversals of fortune that affected all of the South, the two most prominent centers for the cotton industry in Georgia were Augusta and Columbus. Considerable interest was early developed in building a large cotton mill in Augusta as a means of rehabilitating the declining economy of the town. Sufficient interest was aroused so that the citizens raised $500,000 for the construction of a canal to convey to the city water power from the shoals of the Savannah River. On the side of this canal the Augusta Company built its first mill in 1847. Jabez Smith, who was noted for his part in making Petersburg, Virginia, a great textile center, and for similar efforts in North Carolina, expertly supervised the construction.

This mill, despite the feeling of many residents that sufficient labor could never be secured, enjoyed almost immediate success. When the foreboding was proved unjustified the supporters of the enterprise rejoiced.

The management reported that there were more applications for employment than they could hire, and also that Georgia girls were showing a great deal of ability in learning the various activities around the factory. The prosperity of this mill was so great that Augustans were clamoring to take stock at above-par prices. In spring 1849 stockholders voted to increase the capital of the company from $160,000 to $360,000 to enable those who wished stock to satisfy their desire. The first mill was manufacturing 32,000 yards of cloth per week, and the directors planned to use the additional capital to build a second and large mill....

Columbus was cited as one of the leading and most progressive cities in Georgia. It had outstanding business and professional men with much civic pride, and it was said to be unparalleled for its enterprising citizens. With its many factories in addition to four cotton mills and a machine shop for making cotton mill machinery, Columbus was for some the leading manufacturing city of the state. The total capital invested in manufactures was over half a million dollars, and the industry gave employment to citizens, business to local merchants, and a market for the food crops of planters in the area—all of which added much to the prosperity of the entire region.

An 1850 record of the cotton mills sheds some light on the manufacturing enterprise of the town and its effect on the working classes. The Coweta Falls Mill operated 2,500 spindles and 44 looms, which produced 1,800 pounds of thread and 1,800 yards of cloth daily. The company employed 120 boys and girls over the age of twelve. The superintendent of the mill earned $1,000 annually, while the wages of ordinary hands ran from $7.50 for a spinner to $60 a month for overseers. Carter's Factory, in the process of erection, was valued at $100,000. The plans called for 10,000 spindles and 200 looms, which were to require 800 hands to operate.

The Howard Manufacturing Company was, at the time, the largest mill in operation, having 5,000 spindles and 103 looms. This mill wove 15,000 yards of osnaburgs, sheetings, and shirtings weekly. The wages of common hands ranged from 12 to 75 cents a day, earnings of supervisors went as high as $2.50 a day, and the superintendent's pay was $900 a year. The annual profits of these mills varied from each other as much as 10 to 20 percent. Their labor costs were not entirely based on the wages paid, as they furnished schools and churches for the edification of their help....

Additional Sources

Bode, Frederick A., and Donald E. Ginter. *Farm Tenancy and the Census in Antebellum Georgia.* Athens: University of Georgia Press, 1986.

Bonner, James C. *A History of Georgia Agriculture, 1732–1860.* Athens: University of Georgia Press, 1964.

Gilespie, Michele. *Free Labor in an Unfree World: White Artisans in Slaveholding Georgia, 1789–1860.* Athens: University of Georgia Press, 2000.

Reidy, Joseph P. *From Slavery to Agrarian Capitalism in the Cotton Plantation South: Central Georgia, 1800–1880.* Chapel Hill: University of North Carolina Press, 1992.

Smith, Julia Floyd. *Slavery and Rice Culture in Low Country Georgia, 1750–1860.* Knoxville: University of Tennessee Press, 1985.

Chapter 6

SLAVERY AND FREE AFRICAN AMERICANS

Slavery in Georgia has had an unusual existence, from being prohibited at its founding to slaves making up over 40 percent of the state's population in 1861. When the Georgia colony was founded the Trustees embarked on a number of social experiments, one of which was the prohibition of slavery. This experiment lasted only until 1750, when the Trustees relented and allowed the institution to enter the colony. From that time the number of slaves in the state continually increased. Although many in Georgia opposed the institution during the eighteenth century on economic grounds, they tolerated it as a "necessary evil." With the invention of the cotton gin and the increasing need for labor, by the 1820s and 1830s slavery was accepted by most as a "positive good."

The slaves' lives were, to say the least, difficult. Owners punished their slaves as they saw fit, which usually meant harsh punishments for minor indiscretions. More serious transgressions often resulted in death. Georgia passed a variety of laws that governed the lives of the slaves; the Slave Code of 1833 was probably the most complete codification of these laws. Slaves lived in a rather structured environment, and within the institution there were different categories, or classes, of slaves. At the bottom of slave society were the field workers, who, as their name suggests, worked in the fields. They were the most numerous of the various classes of slaves. The next step up in this social pyramid consisted of house servants. There were fewer house servants than field workers, and they performed domestic roles such as cook, butler, and similar occupations. House servants rarely, if ever, worked in the fields. A step higher was the slave artisan, who knew a trade such as carpentry. The highest class in slave society was the body servant, who worked more closely with the owner family than any other class of slaves.

Free African Americans never made up a significant segment of Georgia's population; in 1860 there were only 3,500, which made up less than 1 percent of the state's black population. The largest number of free blacks resided in Savannah, which boasted 705 in 1860, roughly 20 percent of all free blacks in Georgia. Like slaves, free African Americans' lives were heavily governed by Georgia law. The General Assembly passed laws in 1818, 1829, and 1859 that restricted the activities of free blacks. Although limited in what they could do, Georgia's free African American communities survived and provided a small glimpse of what black life would be like following the Civil War.

DOCUMENTS

The first document to follow is the original law that prohibited slavery in the Georgia colony. Document 2 is a 1739 petition to continue the prohibition of slavery. The third document is the 1750 law that legalized slavery in colonial Georgia. Document 4 is a 1786 law that manumitted two Georgia slaves. The fifth document enumerates the population of slaves and free African Americans in the state between 1790 and 1860. Document 6 is an 1829 law by which the state of Georgia purchased slaves. The seventh document is an 1833 law that placed restrictions on the activities of free African Americans. Document 8 contains slave songs from the Georgia Sea Islands. The ninth document, an 1850 article from the Liberator, describes the ordeal of William and Ellen Craft, two fugitive slaves from Macon.

1. Law Prohibiting Slavery in Georgia[1]

Whereas Experience hath Shewn that the manner of Settling Colonys and Plantations with Black Slaves or Negroes hath Obstructed the Increase of English and Christian Inhabitants therein who alone can in case of a War be relyed on for the Defence and Security of the same, and hath Exposed the Colonys so settled to the Insurrections Tumults and Rebellions of such Slaves & negroes and in Case of a Rupture with any Foreign State who should Encourage and Support such Rebellions might Occasion the utter Ruin and loss of such Colonys, For the preventing therefore of so great inconveniences in the said Colony of Georgia We the Trustees for Establishing the Colony of Georgia in America humbly beseech Your Majesty That it may be Enacted And be it Enacted that from and after the four and twentieth day of June which shall be in the Year of Our Lord One thousand Seven hundred and thirty five if any Person or Persons whatsoever shall import or bring or shall cause to be imported or brought or shall sell or Barter or cause in any manner or way

---

[1] From Allen D. Candler, *The Colonial Records of the State of Georgia*, vol. 1 (Atlanta: Franklin Printing and Publishing Company, 1904).

whatsoever in the said Province or in any Part of Place therein any Black or Blacks Negroe or Negroes such Person or Persons for every such Black or Blacks Negroe or Negroes so imported or brought or caused to be imported or brought or sold bartered or used within the said Province Contrary to the intent and meaning of this Act shall forfeit and lose the Sum of fifty pounds Sterling Money of Great Britain....

And be it further Enacted that from and after the said four and twentieth day of June in the Year of Our Lord One thousand Seven hundred and thirty five all and every the Black or Blacks Negroe or Negroes which shall at any time then after be found in the said Province of Georgia or with any Part or Place thereof in the Custody house or Possession of whomsoever the same may be shall and may be Seized and taken by such person or persons as for that purpose shall be authorized and Impowered by the said Common Council of the said Trustees or the Major part of them who shall for that purpose be present and Assembled and the said Black or Blacks Negroe or Negroes so seized and taken shall be deemed and adjudged and are hereby declared to be the Sole property of and to belong only to the said Trustees and their Successors and shall and may be Exported Sold and disposed of in such manner as the said Common Council of the said Trustees or the Major part of them for that purpose present and Assembled shall think most for the benefit and good of the said Colony....

To which the Common Seal was affixed the Ninth day of January 1734.

2. Darien Antislavery Petition (1739)[2]

To his Excellency General Oglethorpe.

The Petition of the Inhabitants of New Inverness.

We are informed, that our neighbors of Savannah have petitioned your Excellency for the Liberty of having Slaves: We hope, and earnestly intreat, that before such Proposals are hearkened unto, your Excellency will consider our Situation, and of what dangerous and bad Consequence such Liberty would be of to us, for many Reasons.

1. The Nearness of the *Spaniards*, who have proclaimed Freedom to all Slaves, who run away from their Masters, making it impossible for us to keep

---

[2] From Trevor Reese, ed., *The Clamorous Malcontents: Criticisms & Defenses of the Colony of Georgia, 1741–1743* (Savannah: The Beehive Press, 1973).

them, without more Labour in guarding them, than what we would be at to do their Work.

2. We are laborious, and know a white Man may be, by the Year, more usefully employed than a Negroe.

3. We are not rich, and becoming debtors for Slaves, in Case of their running away or dying, would inevitably ruin the poor Master, and he become a greater Slave to the Negro-Merchant, than the Slave he bought could be to him.

4. It would oblige us to keep a Guard Duty at least as severe, as when we expected a daily Invasion: And if that was the Case, how miserable would it be to us, and our Wives and Families, to have one enemy without, and a more dangerous one in our Bosoms!

5. It is shocking to human Nature, that any Race of Mankind and their Posterity should be sentence'd to perpetual Slavery; nor in Justice can we think otherwise of it, than that they are thrown amongst us to be our Scourge one Day or other for our Sins: And as Freedom must be as dear to them as to us, what a Scene of Horror must it bring about! And the longer it is unexecuted, the bloody Scene must be the greater. We therefore for our own Sakes, our Wives and Children, and our Posterity, beg your Consideration, and intreat, that instead of introducing Slaves, you'll put us in the way to get us some of our Countrymen, who, with their Labour in Time of Peace, and our Vigilance, if we are invaded, with the Help of those, will render it a difficult Thing to hurt us, or that Part of the Province we possess. We will for ever pray for your Excellency, and are will all Submission, etc.

Signed by eighteen freeholders of New Inverness, in the District of Darien.

3. Law Permitting Slavery in Georgia[3]

Whereas an Act was passed by his Majesty in Council in the Eighth Year of his Reign Intituled (an Act for rendering the Colony of Georgia more defensible by prohibiting the Importation and Use of Black Slaves or Negroes into the same) by which Act the Importation and Use of Black Slaves or Negroes in the said Colony was absolutely prohibited and forbid under the Penalty therein mentioned And Whereas at the time of passing the said Act the said Colony of Georgia being in its Infancy the Introduction of Black Slaves or

---

[3] From Allen D. Candler, ed., *The Colonial Records of the State of Georgia*, vol. 1 (Atlanta: Franklin Printing and Publishing Company, 1904).

Negroes would have been of dangerous Consequence but at present it may be a Benefit to the said Colony and a Convenience and Encouragement to the Inhabitants thereof to permit the Importation and Use of them into the said Colony as the late War hath been happily concluded and a general peace established. Therefore We the Trustees for establishing the Colony of Georgia in America humbly beseech Your Majesty that it may be Enacted And be it Enacted That the said Act and every Clause and Article therein contained be from henceforth repealed and made void and of none Effect And be it Further Enacted that from and after the first day of January in the Year of Our Lord One thousand seven hundred and fifty it shall and may be lawful to import or bring Black Slaves or Negroes into the Province of Georgia in America and to keep and to use the same therein under the Restrictions and Regulations hereinafter mentioned and directed to be observed concerning the same....

To which the Common Seal was affixed the Eighth day of August 1750.

4. Emancipating Two Georgia Slaves[4]

Whereas Austin a mulatto man at present the property of the Estate of Richard Aycock, Esquire, during the late revolution instead of advantaging himself of the times to withdraw himself from the American lines and enter with the majority of his colour and fellow slaves in the service of his Brittainick Majesty and his officers and vassals, did voluntarily enroll himself in some one of the Corps under the command of Col. Elijah Clark, and in several actions and engagements behaved against the common Enemy with a bravery and fortitude which would have honored a freeman, and in one of which engagements he was severely wounded, and rendered incapable of hard servitude, and policy as well as gratitude demand a return for such service and behavior from the Commonwealth.

Be it Enacted that the said Austin be, and he is hereby emancipated and made free, and he is and shall be hereby entitled to all the liberties, privileges and immunities of a free citizen of this State so far as free negroes and mulattos are allowed, and is, and shall be, entitled to annuity allowed by this State to wounded and disabled soldiers.

And be it further Enacted that Colonel Elijah Clark, Lachariah Lamar, and John Talbot shall be and they are hereby appointed agents for the State, to contract and agree with the heirs Executors or administrators of the said Richard Aycock for the value of the said Austin, provided the same does not

---

[4] From *Acts of the General Assembly of the State of Georgia*, 1786.

exceed the sum of seventy pounds, and that they give a certificate for such sum to the proper owner of the said Austin for which sum his Honor the Governor is hereby empowered to draw on the Treasury of the State.

And be it also Enacted that, negro Harry late the property of William Sherrill for his meritorious service to this State, be also emancipated and made free and entitled to the rights of citizenship so far as free negroes and mulattos are entitled as aforesaid.

By order of the House
Augusta, 14th August 1786

5. Population of Slaves and Free African Americans in Georgia, 1790–1860[5]

Year	# of Slaves	# of Free Blacks	Total
1790	29,264	398	29,662
1800	59,406	1,019	60,425
1810	105,218	1,801	107,019
1820	149,656	1,763	151,419
1830	217,531	2,486	220,017
1840	280,944	2,753	283,697
1850	381,682	2,931	384,613
1860	462,198	3,500	465,698

6. The State of Georgia Becomes a Slave Owner[6]

Be it enacted by the Senate and House of Representatives of the State of Georgia, in General Assembly met, and is so hereby enacted by the authority of the same, That so soon after the passage of this act as circumstances may require, it shall be the duty of his excellency the Governor to appoint two fit and proper persons to superintend the improvement of the public roads and the rivers of this State, who shall be removable from office at the pleasure of the Governor, who, in case of such removal, may appoint others in their stead.

---

[5] US Bureau of the Census, 1790, 1810, 1820, 1830, 1840, 1850, 1860.
[6] From *Acts of the General Assembly of the State of Georgia*, 1829.

Section 2. And be it further enacted by the authority aforesaid, That the sum of fifty thousand dollars, including the twenty thousand dollars heretofore appropriated for the improvement of the Savannah river above Augusta, be, and the same is hereby appropriated, out of any funds in the treasury not otherwise pledged, to and for the purchase of such a number of able-bodies negroes within the State of Georgia, and who have been in Georgia twelve months, as will, in addition to the number now owned by the State, amount to the number of one hundred ninety....

Assented to, December 18, 1829.

7. Restrictions on Free Persons of Color[7]

Be it enacted by the Senate and House of Representatives of the state of Georgia, in General Assembly met, and it is hereby enacted by the authority of the same, That each and every guardian of a free person of colour, shall, on or before the first day of May in each year, make a return in the clerk's office of the superior court of the county in which he lives, stating the name of such free person of colour, the date of his letters of guardianship, the occupation of his ward, and shall specify the means by which he obtained his or her freedom, and such return shall be sworn to by such guardian.

Sec. 2. *And be it enacted by the authority aforesaid,* That each guardian failing to make such return, shall be liable to a penalty not exceeding one thousand dollars for each such failure, to be levied upon his proper goods and chattels, lands and tenements, if these shall be insufficient, on the goods, chattels, lands and tenements of the ward or wards of such guardian, as he shall have failed to make a return of, as required in the first section of this act....

Sec. 3. *And be it enacted, by the authority of the aforesaid,* That it shall not be lawful for any person to give credit to any free person of colour, but on a written order of the guardian.

...Sec. 5. *And be it enacted by the authority aforesaid,* That no person of colour, whether free or slave, shall be allowed to preach to, exhort or join in any religious exercise, with any persons of colour, either free or slave, there being more than seven persons of colour present. They shall first obtain a written certificate from three ordained ministers of the gospel of their own order, in which certificate shall be set forth the good, moral character of the applicant, his pious deportment, and his ability to teach the gospel; having a due respect of

---

[7] From *Acts of the General Assembly of the State of Georgia,* 1833.

the character of those persons to whom he is to be licensed to preach, said ministers to be members of the Conference, Presbytery, Synod, or Associations to which the Churches belongs in which said coloured preachers may be so licensed to preach, and also the written permission of the justices of the inferior court of the county, and in counties in which the county town is incorporated, in addition thereto, the permission of the mayor, or chief officer, or commissioners of such incorporation, such license not to be for a longer term than six months, and to be revocable at any time by the persons granting it....

Sec. 7. *And be it enacted by the authority aforesaid*, That from and after the passage of this act, it shall not be lawful for any free person of colour in this state, to own, use, or carry fire arms of any description whatever.

8. Slave Songs of the Georgia Sea Islands[8]

I Gwine T' Beat Dis Rice

I gwine t' beat dis rice
Gwine t' beat 'um so
Gwine t' beat 'um until the hu'ks come off
Ah hanh hanh [nasal]
Ah hanh hanh
Gwine t' cook dis rice when I get through
Gwine t' cook 'um so
Ah hanh hanh
Ah hanh hanh
Gwine f' eat mh belly full
Ah hanh hanh.

Peas an' the Rice
Peas an' the rice, peas an' the rice
Peas an' the rice done done done done
Peas an' the rice, peas an' the rice done done done done
New rice an' okra, eat some an' lef' some
Peas an' the rice, peas an' the rice done done done done.

---

[8] From Lydia Parrish, *Slave Songs of the Georgia Sea Islands* (Athens: University of Georgia Press, 1942).

Five Fingers in the Boll

Way down in the bottom—whah the cotton boll's a rotten
Won' get my hundud[9] all day
Way down in the bottom—whah the cotton boll's a rotten
Won' get my hundud all day.
Befo'e I'll be beated—befo'e I'll be cheated
I'll leave five finguhs in the boll
Befo'e I'll be beated—befo'e I'll be cheated
I'll leave five finguhs in the boll.
Black man beat me—white man cheat me
Won' get my hundud all day
Black man beat me—white man cheat me
Won' get my hundud all day.

9. William and Ellen Craft in Boston[10]

Our city, for a week past, has been thrown into a state of intense excitement by the appearance of two prowling villains, named Hughes and Knights, from Macon, Georgia, for the purpose of seizing William and Ellen Crafts, under the infernal Fugitive Slave Bill, and carrying them back to the hell of slavery. Since the days of '76, there has not been such a popular demonstration on the side of human freedom in this region. The humane and patriotic contagion has infected all classes. Scarcely any other subject has been talked about in the streets, or in the social circle. On Thursday, of last week, warrants for the arrest of William and Ellen were issued by Judge Levi Woodbury, but no officer has yet been found ready or bold enough to serve them. In the mean time, the Vigilance Committee, appointed at the Faneuil Hall meeting, have not been idle. Their number has been increased to upwards of a hundred 'good men and true,' including some thirty or forty members of the bar; and they have been in constant session, devising every legal method to baffle the pursuing bloodhounds, and relieve the city of their hateful presence. On Saturday, placards were posted up in all directions, announcing the arrival of these slave-hunters, and describing their persons. On the same day, Hughes and Knights were arrested on the charge of slander against William Crafts....

---

[9] "Hundud," or hundred, refers to the daily picking quota of 100 pounds.
[10] From *The Liberator*, November 1, 1850.

Hughes and Knights have since been twice arrested and put under bonds of $10,000, charged with a conspiracy to kidnap and abduct William Crafts....

The following is a *verbatim et literatim* copy of the letter sent by Knight to Crafts to entice him to the U.S. Hotel, in order to kidnap him...:

Boston Oct 22 1850 11 oclk P.M.

Wm Craft—Sir—I have to leave so Eirley in the morning that I could not call according to promise, so if you want me to carry a letter home with me, you must bring it to the United States Hotel to morrow and leave it in Box 44 or come your self to morro Eavening after tea and bring it. Let me no if you come your self by sending a note to Box 44 U.S. Hotel so that I may no whether to wate after tea or not by the Bearer. If your wif wants to se me you cold bring her with you if you come your self.

JOHN KNIGHT

ESSAYS

Slavery in Georgia[11]

Betty Wood

...The decision to exclude slavery had been taken without regard to advice from America; the formal ending of the prohibition came only after protracted discussions between the Trustees and their officials in Georgia. The Trustees' initial approach to [William] Stephens and his assistants took the form of a series of questions regarding such fundamental points as the most appropriate size, distribution, and employment of any slave work force introduced into the colony. The questions asked and the answers given indicate that the Trustees and their officials were in broad agreement on one crucial point: slavery in Georgia must be made subject to rigid controls. Both sides in the slavery debate acknowledged that slaves would threaten the physical, if not the psychological, security of Georgia's white inhabitants and, down to the late 1740s, the Trustees had insisted that the Georgians' security could be guaranteed only by the total exclusion of slaves. Their opponents had argued that the colony's and their own personal security would not be jeopardized but that economic growth might be achieved by the limited importation of slaves and the imposition of a

---

[11] From Betty Wood, *Slavery in Colonial Georgia, 1750–1775* (Athens: University of Georgia Press, 1984). Used with permission of the University of Georgia Press.

clearly defined ratio between the races. Although the Georgia Board would not contemplate such a proposal as long as Spain challenged the very existence of Georgia, it was one they were keen to incorporate into their slave code.

The Trustees asked their officials whether any limits ought to be imposed on the size of individual slaveholdings. Although such a restriction would have served the purpose of establishing a rough numerical balance between the races, it is possible to place a different interpretation on the Trustees' question. Since the inception of the Georgia project, they had been highly critical of the "luxury" and "idleness" of America's plantation societies and at the same time had pointed to the unenviable lot of landless, nonslaveholding whites in such societies. Apparently they still held out the hope that the emergence of a planter elite in Georgia might be prevented while safeguarding the interests of those whites who were unwilling or unable to invest in slave labor.

Stephens and his assistants suggested that any limitations on the size of individual slaveholdings would pose "many and great inconveniences," not for masters but for Georgia's slaves. If, for example, an owner was restricted to a maximum holding of ten slaves, it was likely that sooner or later he would have to dispose of some of his bondsmen and possibly split black families. For this reason the colonial officials declared themselves opposed to the restriction proposed by the Trustees. They agreed, however, that there ought to be a fixed, and low, ratio between the races and proposed that of one white man for every five "Working Negroes." Mainly for the reasons outlined by William Stephens in 1742, they agreed that slaves ought to be confined to "the necessary Work of Plantations and for Exporting the Manufactures of the Colony."

The Trustees' next question focused on the relationship between master and slave. More specifically, they asked whether "it is just and Equitable that the Proprietors of Negroes should have an unlimited power over them?" Stephens and his assistants declared emphatically that they should not. In their opinion, any owner who "willfully and maliciously Murders Dismembers or Cruelly and Barbarously uses a Negro" should be dealt with in precisely the same way and made subject to precisely the same penalties as if the offense had been committed against a white person. They did not discuss, perhaps because they had not been asked to, the legal rights, if any, to be enjoyed by the slave.

Finally, the Trustees inquired whether slaves ought to be made to work on Sundays. The colonial officials endorsed the theory, if not always the practice, operative in the other plantation colonies by saying that they should not. They added that they wished to "make the condition of Slavery as easy as may be consistent with the Safety of His Majesty's Subjects" and hoped that their proposals would shame the other colonies into following Georgia's humane example.

Although some of the Trustees' supporters were skeptical of the malcontents' willingness to abide by any rules and regulations governing the employment of slaves, the Trustees were persuaded of the settlers' good intentions and, in May 1749, they agreed to press for the repeal of the Act of 1735. Events moved forward in rapid order. In July of that year, replying to the proposals submitted from Georgia, the Trustees suggested that one white man, aged between twenty and fifty-five, would be needed to superintend every four, rather than every five, working blacks. They also argued that slaves must be exposed to all the spiritual benefits of Christianity; that miscegenation ought to be forbidden; that the silk industry would benefit were slave women trained in the techniques of silk production; and, finally, that a duty ought to be levied on slave imports. Although in close agreement with the Trustees, Georgia's officials asked that the lower age limit on white males be reduced from twenty to sixteen years because slightly younger men made "better Servants": they were "more docile, healthier, and sooner reconciled to this Climate as well as more alert in Arms than those of more advanced Years." Otherwise they merely repeated their request that coopers and sawyers be allowed to take on black apprentices.

The Trustees received these comments in spring 1750 and referred them to the relevant committee of their Common Council for consideration. By August they were ready to submit proposals to the Lords Justice in Council. They began by explaining why they wished the Act of 1735 to be rescinded. In 1735 there had been every reason to "apprehend a Rupture with the Spaniards," but since "a general Peace" now obtained there was no longer any pressing military need for them to persevere with their prohibitory policy. The Trustees declared themselves satisfied that the introduction of slaves would be consistent with the "safety" of Georgia and, moreover, finally admitted that the institution of slavery would "conduce to the Prosperity" of the colony. They therefore wished to permit the Georgia settlers to employ slaves from January 1, 1751. They included with their petition a draft copy of an act that not only lifted the ban on slavery but also stipulated the conditions under which the institution would be permitted in Georgia. As Benjamin Martyn remarked to William Stephens, the Trustees' slave code was virtually identical to that proposed by the Georgians.

The Trustees did not limit the size of individual slaveholdings but imposed a ratio between adult male slaves and white men aged between sixteen and sixty-five of four to one. But it was one thing to formulate such a ratio and another to enforce it. The Trustees believed that the desired racial balance could be maintained through a system of fines of up to £10 sterling for every slave held in excess of the permitted number and £5 sterling per month for as long as the offense continued. There were readily apparent reasons for wishing to ascertain the size and distribution of Georgia's blacks and, in order that this might be done regularly, the Trustees incorporated a census mechanism into their slave code. They were also concerned to ensure the health of the black, and thereby the white, population, and to prevent the introduction of "contagious Distempers (particularly the Yellow Fever)" by the opening of the slave trade, they devised a comprehensive set of quarantine regulations for slave ships.

The remainder of the code was concerned with the employment, religious welfare, and treatment of Georgia's slaves. On the matter of employment the Trustees followed the advice given by their officials: coopers and sawyers could take on black apprentices, but otherwise slaves were to be used only for unskilled plantation work. Two other regulations formulated by the Trustees suggested that they still held out high hopes for silk culture in Georgia. They decreed that at least 500 mulberry trees must be planted on each 500-acre land grant "and so in proportion" and that slave women must be sent to Savannah "at the proper Season in every Year" to learn the techniques of reeling and winding silk.

The Trustees did not deal with the punishment of slave offenders; their main concern was with whites who maltreated their black workers. They emphasized the duties and responsibilities of the white community, and, in effect, their slave code amounted to a rigorous code of behavior for Georgia's whites. The Trustees' humanitarianism now found an important expression in a concern for the welfare of Georgia's black element. It is important to emphasize that their proposals were very similar to those submitted by the colony's local officials. Any white who inflicted physical punishment "endangering the Limb of a Negro" would be fined "not less" than £5 sterling for the first offense and at least £10 for any subsequent infringement. No mention was made of the judicial procedures that would obtain in such cases. For example, could blacks be allowed to testify against whites? The Trustees gave no guidance, although they included a regulation in their code to cover the murder of a slave by a white person. Any white so accused would "be tried according to the Laws of Great Britain" and, one assumes, if found guilty be liable to the same penalty as that which obtained in the home country.

The only detailed reference in the slave code to the punishment of slaves was in the brief section dealing with miscegenation. The Trustees' thoughts on this subject were in keeping with those reflected in the slave codes of the other plantation colonies: interracial marriage was forbidden, and any such unions already entered into were declared "absolutely null and void." In cases of interracial fornication the Georgia Board drew no distinction between male and female offenders. Blacks would be subject to "Corporal Punishment" of a type and amount left to the discretion of the courts; whites would be fined £10 sterling and might also receive such corporal punishment as the courts deemed appropriate....

The sum total of the Trustees' deliberations and consultations with the Georgia settlers was a slave code that in some respects, for example those sections dealing with religion and miscegenation, was not dissimilar to those of the other Southern colonies. But in other respects, and most notably in the absence of regulations that sought to govern the behavior of slaves, it was unlike any other colonial slave code. It had two primary aims: to permit slavery and to attempt to curb white behavior....

Free African-American Women in Savannah[12]

Whittington B. Johnson

For most Savannahians, the dawning of the nineteenth century brought few changes of any substance. But for a very small minority of African-American women who had only recently gained their freedom, the new century marked the dawn of a new life. They knew only too well the customary roles that had been assigned to the city's black women since Africans accompanied Georgia's first settlers in the 1730s.

Very early in their lives, female slaves were trained to meet the needs of their masters, mistresses, and their families; little consideration, if any, was given to their own personal needs. They often suffered under oppressive taskmasters, worked long arduous hours, were sexually abused, were whipped for the slightest provocation, and witnessed the sale and subsequent separation of their children and husbands.

The experiences of slave women have in recent years been the focus of increased scholarly attention. But still largely unexplored are chronicles of their non-enslaved sisters, those black women who, for a variety of reasons, obtained their freedom yet continued to live and work in the midst of a slaveholding society that made aberrations of their newly won status. Free black females generally pursued the same vocations and suffered much of the same exploitations they had known under bondage. But at the same time, they enjoyed considerable advantages and escaped much of the oppression suffered by their enslaved counterparts. Taking advantage of the legal rights, and social

---

[12] From Whittington B. Johnson, "Free African-American Women in Savannah, 1800–1806: Autonomy and Affluence Amid Adversity," *Georgia Historical Quarterly* 76/2 (Summer 1992). Courtesy of the Georgia Historical Society.

and economic opportunities available to them in an urban environment, the free black women of Savannah made substantial contributions to their community, which maintained its position as Georgia's most progressive black community throughout the antebellum period.

Savannah also boasted the state's largest free black populace. The city's free African-American population increased by nearly 50 percent between 1800 and 1810 (from 224 to 329) and continued to grow, although less spectacularly, until 1860, when it reached 705, or 20 percent of the state's total number of free blacks.

The lone black religious institution in Savannah at the turn of the century, the First African Baptist Church, founded in 1788, quickly felt the impact of the population increase as the number of worshipers (including a huge slave following) outgrew the edifice, causing Andrew Bryan, its founder, to consider organizing another black Baptist church. This was accomplished in December 1802 under the leadership of Henry Cunningham, a former slave and McIntosh County native, who had moved to Savannah and joined the First African Baptist Church. Joining Cunningham in organizing the new church were nine other free African-Americans, including five women: Elizabeth (Betsy) Cunningham (his wife), Susan Jackson, Silva Monnox, Leah Simpson, and Charlotte Walls. These women were among the more affluent free blacks in the community and they contributed to the spiritual life of their new church, the Second African Baptist Church. Other free women were active in the First African Baptist Church, and later Third African Baptist Church, while still others attended biracial churches—Christ Episcopal Church, the Independent Presbyterian Church, and St. John the Baptist Catholic Church—where they had less important roles than in the African churches. When the Andrew Methodist and St. Stephen's Episcopal churches established chapels for blacks, respectively, free African American women became active in those congregations.

It was in the Baptist church, Savannah's only autonomous black religious institution, however, where free women were most visible, valuable, and influential. They were church mothers, a position that may have carried as much influence and respect as its male counterpart, the deacons; they formed their own benevolent and temperance societies, sang in the choir, and taught Sunday School. Although men dominated offices in the black Baptist churches, females enjoyed voice and vote in the monthly business conferences, the governing body of each Baptist congregation. Since majority rule prevailed, and there were no distinctions between males and females, or clergy and laity, females exercised influence commensurate with their considerable numbers, thus partially overcoming the male dominance of church offices....

The list of free black female occupations in 1823 indicates that washerwoman (30) and seamstress (26) were the most common vocations; they were followed by seventeen cooks, eleven sellers of small wares, five housekeepers, and four nurses. No more than two persons were employed in the remaining occupations. The 1860 census, however, reveals significant changes in vocational preferences (which probably resulted from the law of supply and demand): seamstress/dressmaker (121) far outnumbered washerwoman as the most common, with the latter a distant second (44); domestic servants (32) and pastry cooks (20) emerged as popular vocations; and the number of nurses (10) more than doubled. Teaching, prostitution, and selling milk still were not listed....

In spite of the disadvantages encountered in the job market, women were well represented among real estate owners in the black community. As Loren Schweninger maintained in his study of Southern black property owners, African Americans placed great importance upon owning property, which they perceived as an indicator of prosperity and an important way to gain the respect of whites. The high visibility of black females among the propertied class is thus positive evidence of their prosperity, which, in turn, was a key factor in the economic growth of their community.

Over the years, black women acquired a numerical advantage among real estate owners in all categories, but especially those in the most highly assessed property. In 1820, thirty-six free blacks in Savannah owned homes that were assessed at a minimum of $200 each, for a total of $31,250. Women home owners (21) comprised a majority of this group, their holdings totaling $17,700 or 56 percent of the total. In 1820, a majority of the home owners (5 of the 9) in the $1,000 and higher category also were women. After 1830, when the number of free (male and female) home owners decreased, females still retained their lead and actually increased their proportion of higher-priced real estate ($1,000 and higher). In 1858, seventeen of the nineteen home owners in that category were women who, combined, owned property valued at $37,750, nearly 90 percent of the total ($41,950) owned by this group. Schweninger offered a sound reason for the large presence of women among property owners: "free women sought to acquire property as a means of protection, economic independence, and self-sufficiency."

Home ownership made free African-Americans taxpayers, rather than taxable personal property, another major and meaningful distinction between free and slave status. In the nineteenth century, real estate taxes were the primary source of revenue for state and local governments. Since women owned the majority of, and the most valuable, property in the black community, they paid more taxes than free black males, propertyless whites (males and females), and slaves, who were ineligible to own land. The tax digests reveal that free African American women acted responsibly in discharging this important civic responsibility....

Perhaps the most successful free African American female of her generation (pre-1850) was Susan Jackson, owner of valuable real estate in the city and a thriving business. She was evidently a very astute person, for in 1812 her husband Simon, a successful tailor and community leader, entrusted her with the responsibility of going to Charleston, South Carolina, to close the deal on their house and lot in Reynolds Ward, which they were able to purchase for $1,500 with a loan secured from Richard Stites, a prominent Savannah lawyer who handled Simon Jackson's legal matters. After her husband's death, Susan Jackson paid both the balance on the mortgage (about $600) and a long-standing debt of $200 that Simon Jackson had secured by using their real estate as collateral. This allowed her to gain clear title to the property. She earned the money to meet these obligations by operating a pastry shop and renting property. Susan Jackson died of heart disease on January 12, 1862 at the age of eighty-two.

Ann H. Gibbons was the most successful of the post-1850 women, but her life is something of a mystery. Although she had a daughter, Claudia, in 1820, and she owned the most valuable real estate among African Americans in 1860, neither the father of her child nor the source of her income is known. After appearing on the tax digest in 1833 as propertyless, she started her climb up the economic ladder in the 1840s and, by 1850, she declared two lots containing dwellings and four slaves. In 1852, her slaves were assessed at $2,200, placing her second to Anthony Odingsell (whose nine slaves were assessed at $2,700) among the small group of black slaveholders in the Chatham-Savannah area. In 1860, Gibbons owned two lots in North Oglethorpe Ward, one in Middle Oglethorpe (with a total value of $9,000) and three prime slaves....

It is very clear that free African American women in Savannah often prospered in spite of the hostile environment in which free status was not an inalienable right. Because women usually outlived their mates, the responsibility for preserving their gains, however meager, fell upon their shoulders. After 1830, when circumstances tightened and manumissions declined precipitously, the blood of free African American women flowing through the veins of their newborn infants assured freedom, regardless of their father's status. This factor contributed significantly to the continued growth of the free black population in Savannah, despite legislation to effect just the opposite. Free women defied bans on teaching blacks how to read, thus breaking barriers and, in the process, instilling a desire among blacks to obtain an education after the Civil War.

Furthermore, they met their civic responsibility by paying their share of real estate taxes.

Free women, therefore, enjoyed certain privileges that were denied slave females and one that was even denied other African-Americans, whether free or slave; these women, moreover, served as role models for their daughters, showed slave females and others a different role black women could perform, helped build the black church, and generally contributed to the growth, progress, and prosperity of the black community. Thus, free status created opportunities for African American women in Savannah, 1800–1860, to live distinctly different from slave females.

Additional Sources

Alexander, Adele L. *Ambiguous Lives: Free Women of Color in Rural Georgia, 1789–1879.* Fayetteville: University of Arkansas Press, 1991.

Craft, William. *Running a Thousand Miles for Freedom: The Escape of William and Ellen Craft.* Edited by R. J. M. Blackett. Baton Rouge: Louisiana State University Press, 1999.

Dusinberre, William. *Them Dark Days: Slavery in the American Rice Swamps.* New York: Oxford University Press, 1996.

Lockley, Timothy J. *Lines in the Sand: Race and Class in Low Country Georgia, 1750–1860.* Athens: University of Georgia Press, 2001.

Reidy, Joseph P. *From Slavery to Agrarian Capitalism in the Cotton Plantation South: Central Georgia, 1800–1880.* Chapel Hill: University of North Carolina Press, 1992.

Smith, Julia F. *Slavery and Rice Culture in Low Country Georgia, 1750–1860.* Knoxville: University of Tennessee Press, 1985.

Wallenstein, Peter. *From Slave South to New South: Public Policy in Nineteenth-Century Georgia.* Chapel Hill: University of North Carolina Press, 1987.

Wood, Betty. *Slavery in Colonial Georgia, 1730–1775.* Athens: University of Georgia Press, 1984.

Wood, Betty. *Women's Work, Men's Work: The Informal Slave Economies of Lowcountry Georgia.* Athens: University of Georgia Press, 1995.

Young, Jeffrey R. *Domesticating Slavery: The Master Class in Georgia and South Carolina, 1670–1837.* Chapel Hill: University of North Carolina Press, 1999.

Chapter 7

THE CIVIL WAR ERA, 1845–1865

The Civil War Era, here defined as 1845–1865, was a tumultuous period for Georgia and its citizens, as it was for the rest of the country. The sectional controversies, already in existence, became much more serious and ultimately led to outright conflict. The Mexican War (1846–1848) and its consequences started America on this downhill slide to civil war. As a state, Georgia generally supported the war with Mexico, but Georgia Whigs, following the national party sentiment, opposed it. As a result of the war the United States acquired a great deal of territory; between 1846 and 1861, the issues surrounding slavery in these territories became the most important political issue in America. Pennsylvania representative David Wilmot set off the controversy with the introduction of his proviso in August 1846. Georgians generally opposed the Wilmot Proviso, which prohibited the introduction of slavery into the new territories. Georgia's response was to call for a convention of Southern states to draft a response in the event the proviso passed. The measure never passed, but Georgia showed it was prepared to stand with the rest of the South in opposing the expansion of slavery.

Georgia and its political leaders were a calming influence in the next sectional crisis, the admission of California into the Union. California's application kicked off another round of crises, which were resolved by the Compromise of 1850. Authored by Henry Clay, the compromise was shepherded through the Senate by Illinoisan Stephen A. Douglas and through the House by Georgians Howell Cobb, Alexander H. Stephens, and Robert Toombs. Following the passage of the compromise measures, the General Assembly passed the Georgia Platform, a series of resolutions that urged acceptance of the compromise. The remainder of the decade of the 1850s witnessed a series of sectional controversies, many of which originated over the question of slavery in the territories. The Whig party in Georgia was in a state of turmoil, a condition illustrated in the 1852 election when over 5,000 Georgia Whigs cast votes for Daniel Webster even though he was dead. The state's two-party system was in jeopardy. Some Georgia Whigs joined the Know-Nothings while most became Democrats. Between 1854 and 1856 Georgia experienced a political realignment much like the rest of the country. Georgia's realignment, however, resulted in a one-party system with the Democrats in control. The Democrats would remain in power in the state through the Civil War.

The sectional crisis grew more serious as the presidential election of 1860 approached and the national Democratic party was divided. A divided Democratic party almost assured the six-year-old Republican party of winning the election, thereby setting off yet another crisis. The split in the Democratic party became formalized when it nominated two separate candidates, one representing the North (Stephen A. Douglas) and one representing the South (John C. Breckinridge). Georgia cast all of its ten electoral votes for Breckinridge even though he received less than 50 percent of the popular vote. Georgia seemed to be a divided state, a condition even more evident in the debate over secession. Following South Carolina's lead, Georgia called for a special secession convention to meet in January 1861, with Georgia voters choosing delegates in a special election. The results of this election, as released by Governor Joseph E. Brown in April 1861, indicate a large majority of delegates who favored immediate secession over those who were against immediate secession (50,243 to 37,123). Recent research, particularly that conducted by historian Michael P. Johnson, seems to indicate that the vote was much closer than the figures Governor Brown released. In the secession convention, Georgia's delegates voted on January 19, 1861 to secede by a vote of 208 to 89. Georgia was the fifth Southern state to secede.

There was not much significant military activity in Georgia during the first couple years of the war. Georgians first had to tend to their coastal defenses and the defense of Savannah. The Savannah River was defended by a small "fleet" of river boats and tugs under the command of Commodore Josiah Tattnall while the city's defenses was commanded by General Robert E. Lee. The key to the river defenses was Fort Pulaski, which the Federals captured on April 11, 1862. The loss of Pulaski made Savannah and its port all but useless. Later, on September 19–20, 1863, the Confederate Army of Tennessee engaged the Federal Army of the Cumberland in Northwest Georgia in the Battle of Chickamauga. The battle was fought in a tangle of woods, and the Confederate army emerged with a much-needed victory.

The most spectacular campaigns in Georgia during the war were General William T. Sherman's Atlanta Campaign and his 1864 March to the Sea. Sherman embarked on his campaign to capture Atlanta, which was important as a rail junction, in May 1864. By July the federal forces had maneuvered their way to the city's defenses. After several hard-fought battles on the outskirts of the city, the Confederate army was besieged inside Atlanta. By September 1, 1864, the Confederate position in Atlanta was untenable and the city was abandoned; Sherman's troops moved in the next day. Before evacuating the city,

Confederate authorities ordered everything of military value burned, which started a conflagration. After two-and-a-half months in Atlanta, Sherman's troops left the city and marched toward the coast, reaching Savannah on December 20, 1864. Sherman spared the city, offering it to President Lincoln as a Christmas gift. One final campaign in Georgia was Union general James H. Wilson's 1865 cavalry raid. With 15,000 cavalrymen, the largest cavalry force ever assembled in the Western Hemisphere, Wilson destroyed factories in Columbus and Macon, thereby destroying the Confederate ability to continue the war. On May 10, 1865, Wilson's cavalrymen captured Confederate president Jefferson Davis in Irwinville, Georgia. One last military aspect of the war in Georgia that merits attention is the prisoner of war camp at Andersonville. Federal prisoners began arriving in February 1864, and by May 1865, 45,613 US prisoners had been held there. Nearly 13,000 prisoners died at Andersonville, a figure that earned prison commander Henry Wirz a trial for war crimes. Wirz, hanged on November 10, 1865, was the only Confederate official executed for war crimes.

On the home front, enthusiasm for the war quickly turned to open opposition as the hardships increased throughout the war. Confederate government policies created much of the opposition. Among the most hated were impressments, conscription, and the exemption provisions of the draft law. These provisions led to the charge that the conflict was "a rich man's war and a poor man's fight." Inflation and a worthless currency only added to the problems at home, forcing many women to take drastic actions to feed their families. Slaves in Georgia also took action during the war years, resisting their bondage; this resistance was surprisingly overt. Slaves were willing to take considerable risks to secure their freedom during the war.

DOCUMENTS

The first document below is the 1850 Georgia Platform, the state's response to the Compromise of 1850. Documents 2 and 3 are speeches made in 1860 by Robert Toombs and Alexander H. Stephens, respectively, to the General Assembly concerning the looming secession crisis. The fourth document is Georgia's Ordinance of Secession. Document 5 is Alexander H. Stephens's 1861 Cornerstone Speech, which he delivered in Savannah. The sixth document is the state's Constitution of 1861. Document 7 presents two different views on class voting patterns in 1863 Columbus. The eighth document is the 1865 criminal indictment of Henry Wirz, the commander of Andersonville Prison during the Civil War.

1. Georgia Platform[1]

Be it Resolved by the People of Georgia in Convention assembled,

1st, That we hold the American Union, secondary in importance only to the rights and principles it was designed to perpetuate. That past associations, present fruition, and future prospects, will bind us to it so long as it continues to be the safeguard of those rights and principles.

Secondly, That if the thirteen original parties to the contract, bordering the Atlantic in a narrow belt, while their separate interests were in embryo their peculiar tendencies scarcely developed, their revolutionary trials and triumphs, still green in memory, found Union impossible without Compromise, the thirty-one of this day, may well yield somewhat, in the conflict of opinion and policy, to preserve that Union which has extended the sway of republican government over a vast wilderness to another ocean, and proportionally advanced their civilization and national greatness.

Thirdly, That in this spirit, the State of Georgia has maturely considered the action of Congress embracing a series of measures for the admission of California into the Union, the organization of territorial Governments for Utah and New Mexico, the establishment of a boundary between the latter and the State of Texas, the suppression of the slave trade in the District of Columbia, and the extradition of fugitive slaves, and (connected with them) the rejection of propositions to exclude slavery from the Mexican territories and to abolish it in the District of Columbia; and whilst she does not wholly approve, will abide by it as a permanent adjustment of this sectional controversy.

Fourthly, That the State of Georgia in the judgment of this Convention, will and ought to resist even (as a last resort,) to a disruption of every tie which binds her to the Union, any action of Congress upon the subject of slavery in the District of Columbia, or in any places subject to the jurisdiction of Congress incompatible with the safety, domestic tranquility, the rights and honor of the slave-holding States, or any act suppressing the slave trade between the slave-holding States, or any refusal to admit as a State any territory hereafter applying, because of the existence of slavery therein, or any act prohibiting the introduction of slaves into the territories of New Mexico and Utah, or any act repealing or materially modifying the laws now in force for the recovery of fugitive slaves.

Fifthly, That it is the deliberate opinion of this Convention, that upon the faithful execution of the *Fugitive Slave Bill* by the proper authorities depends the preservation of our much loved Union.

---

[1] From *Georgia Telegraph*, December 17, 1850.

2. Robert Toombs on the
Sectional Conflict and Secession[2]

November 13, 1860

Gentlemen of the General Assembly: I very much regret, in appearing before you at your request, to address you on the present state of the country, and the prospect before us, that I can bring you no good tidings. The stern steady march of events has brought us in conflict with our non-slaveholding confederates upon the fundamental principles of our compact of Union. We have not sought this conflict; we have sought too long to avoid it; our forbearance has been construed into weakness, our magnanimity into fear, until the vindication of our manhood, as well as the defense of our rights, is required at our hands. The door of conciliation and compromise is finally closed by our adversaries, and it remains only to us to meet the conflict with the dignity and firmness of men worthy of freedom....

The South at all times demanded nothing but equality in the common territories, equal enjoyment of them with their property, to that extended to Northern citizens and their property—nothing more.... Give us equality of enjoyment, equal right to expansion—it is as necessary to our prosperity as yours. In 1790 we had less than eight hundred thousand slaves. Under our mild and humane administration of the system they have increased above four millions...before the end of this century, at precisely the same rate of increase, the Africans among us in a subordinate condition will amount to eleven millions of persons. What shall be done with them? We must expand or perish. We are constrained by an inexorable necessity to accept expansion or extermination....

The North...have told us for twenty years that their object was to pen up slavery within its present limits—surround it with a border of free States, and like the scorpion surrounded with fire, they will make it sting itself to death. One thing at least is certain, that whatever may be the effect of your exclusion from the Territories, there is no dispute but that the North mean it, and adopt it as a measure hostile to slavery upon this point. They all agree, they are all unanimous in Congress, in the States, on the rostrum, in the sanctuary—everywhere they declare that slavery shall not go into the Territories. ...every Abolitionist in the Union, in or out of place, is openly pledged, in some manner, to drive us from the common Territories. This conflict, at least, is irrepressible—it is easily understood—we demand the equal

---

[2] From Frank Moore, ed., *The Rebellion Record: A Diary of American Events*, supplement to vol. 1 (New York: G. P. Putnam, 1861–1863).

right with the North to go into the common Territories with all of our property, slaves included, and to be there protected in its peaceable enjoyment by the Federal Government, until such Territories may come into the Union as equal States—then we admit them with or without slavery, as the people themselves may decide for themselves. Will you surrender this principle? The day you do this base, unmanly deed, you embrace political degradation and death....

I can go anywhere except in my own country, whilom [formerly] called "the glorious Union;" here alone am I stigmatized as a felon; here alone am I an outlaw; here alone am I under the ban of the empire; here alone I have neither security nor tranquility; here alone are organized governments ready to protect the incendiary, the assassin who burns my dwelling or takes my life or those of my wife and children; here alone are hired emissaries paid by brethren to glide through the domestic circle and intrigue insurrection with all of its nameless horrors. My countrymen, "if you have nature in you, bear it not." Withdraw yourselves from such a confederacy; it is your right to do so—your duty to do so. I know not why the abolitionists should object to it, unless they want to torture and plunder you. If they resist this great sovereign right, make another war for independence, for that then will be the question; fight its battles over again—reconquer liberty and independence. As for me, I will take any place in the great conflict for rights which you may assign. I will take none in the Federal Government during Mr. Lincoln's administration.

3. Alexander H. Stephens on the Sectional Conflict and Secession[3]

November 14, 1860

Fellow Citizens: I appear before you tonight at the request of Members of the Legislature and others, to speak of matters of the deepest interest that can possibly concern us all, of an earthly character. There is nothing, no question or subject connected with this life, that concerns a free people so intimately as that of the Government under which they live....

My object is not to stir up strife, but to allay it; not to appeal to your passions, but to your reason. Let us, therefore, reason together....

The first question that presents itself is, shall the people of Georgia secede from the Union in consequence of the election of Mr. Lincoln to the

---

[3] From Richard Johnston and William Brownlee, *Life of Alexander H. Stephens* (Philadelphia: J. B. Lippincott & Co., 1878).

Presidency of the United States? My countrymen, I tell you frankly, candidly, and earnestly, that I do not think that they ought. In my judgment, the election of no man, constitutionally chosen to that high office, is sufficient cause to justify any State to separate from the Union. It ought to stand by and aid still in maintaining the Constitution of the country. To make a point of resistance to the Government, to withdraw from it because any man has been elected, would put us in the wrong. We are pledged to maintain the Constitution. Many of us have sworn to support it. Can we, therefore, for the mere election of any man to the Presidency, and that, too, in accordance with the prescribed forms of the Constitution, make a point of resistance to the Government, without becoming the breakers of that sacred instrument ourselves, by withdrawing ourselves from it? Would we not be in the wrong? Whatever fate is to befall this country, let it never be laid to the charge of the people of the South, and especially the people of Georgia, that we were untrue to our national engagements. Let the fault and the wrong rest upon others....

My honorable friend who addressed you last night [Robert Toombs], and to whom I listened with the profoundest attention, asks if we would submit to Black Republican rule? I say to you and to him, as a Georgian, I would never submit to any Black Republican aggression upon our Constitutional rights....

I am for exhausting all that patriotism demands, before taking the last step. I would invite, therefore, South Carolina to a conference. I would ask the same of all the other Southern States, so that if the evil has got beyond our control, which God in his mercy grant may not be the case, we may not be divided among ourselves; but if possible, secure the united cooperation of all the Southern States, and then in the face of the civilized world, we may justify our action, and, with the wrong all on the other side, we can appeal to the God of Battles, if it comes to that, to aid us in our cause. But do nothing, in which any portion of our people, may charge you with rash or hasty action. It is certainly a matter of great importance to tear this government asunder. You were not sent here for that purpose. I would wish the whole South to be united, if this is to be done; and I believe if we pursue the policy which I have indicated, this can be effected.

4. Ordinance of Secession[4]

An Ordinance

To dissolve the Union between the State of Georgia, and other States united with her under a compact of government, entitled the Constitution of the United States of America:

We, the people of the State of Georgia, in Convention assembled, do declare and ordain, and it is hereby declared and ordained, that the Ordinance adopted by the people of the State of Georgia, in Convention on the second day of January in the year of our Lord Seventeen hundred and eighty-eight, whereby the Constitution of the United States of America was assented to, ratified and adopted; and also all acts and parts of acts of the General Assembly of this State ratifying and adopting amendments of the said Constitution are hereby repealed, rescinded and abrogated.

We do further declare and ordain, that the union now subsisting between the State of Georgia and other States under the name of the United States of America is hereby dissolved, and that the State of Georgia is in full possession and exercise of all those rights of Sovereignty which belong and appertain to a Free and Independent State.

5. Alexander H. Stephens's Cornerstone Speech[5]

Savannah, Georgia, March 21,1861

Mr. Mayor, and Gentlemen of the Committee, and Fellow Citizens:

For this reception you will please accept my most profound and sincere thanks....

I was remarking, that we are passing through one of the greatest revolutions in the annals of the world. Seven States have within the last three months thrown off an old government and formed a new. This revolution has been signally marked, up to this time, by the fact of its having been accomplished without the loss of a single drop of blood.

This new constitution [Confederate Constitution], or form of government, constitutes the subject to which your attention will be partly invited. In reference to it, I make this first general remark. It amply secures all our ancient rights, franchises, and liberties....

---

[4] Courtesy of the Georgia Archives.
[5] From *Savannah Republican*, March 23, 1861.

...The new constitution has put at rest, *forever*, all the agitating questions relating to our peculiar institution—African slavery as it exists amongst us—the proper *status* of the negro in our form of civilization. This was the immediate cause of the late rupture and present revolution. Jefferson in his forecast, had anticipated this, as the "rock upon which the old Union would split." He was right. What was conjecture with him, is now a realized fact. But whether he fully comprehended the great truth upon which that rock *stood* and *stands*, may be doubted. The prevailing ideas entertained by him and most of the leading statesmen at the time of the formation of the old constitution, were that the enslavement of the African was in violation of the laws of nature; that it was wrong in *principle*, socially, morally, and politically....

Our new government is founded upon exactly the opposite idea; its foundations are laid, its corner-stone rests upon the great truth, that the negro is not equal to the white man; that slavery—subordination to the superior race—is his natural and normal condition.

This, our new government, is the first, in the history of the world, based upon this great physical, philosophical, and moral truth....

6. Constitution of 1861[6]

ARTICLE I

Declaration of Fundamental Principles
...3. Protection to person and property is the duty of Government....

4. No citizen shall be deprived of life, liberty or property, except by due process of law; and of life or liberty, only by the judgment of his peers.

5. The writ of "Habeas Corpus" shall not be suspended unless in case of rebellion or invasion, the public safety may require it.

6. The right of the people to keep and bear arms shall not be infringed.

7. No religious test shall be required for the tenure of any office; and no religion shall be established by law; and no citizen shall be deprived of any right or privilege by reason of his religious belief.

8. Freedom of thought and opinion, freedom of speech, and freedom of the press, are inherent elements of political liberty. But while every citizen may freely speak, write and print, on any subject, he shall be responsible for the abuse of the liberty.

---

[6] From *Acts of the General Assembly of the State of Georgia*, 1861.

ARTICLE II

Section I

1. The Legislative, Executive and Judicial departments, shall be distinct; and each department shall be confided to a separate body of magistracy....

2. The Legislative powers shall be vested in a General Assembly, which shall consist of a Senate and House of Representatives.

3. The meeting of the General Assembly shall be annual, and on the first Wednesday in November, until such day of meeting shall be altered by law.... No session of the General Assembly continue for more than forty days, unless the same shall be done by a vote of two-thirds of each branch thereof.

Section II

1. The Senate shall consist of forty-four members, one to be chosen from each senatorial district, which district shall be composed of three contiguous counties.

2. No person shall be a Senator who shall not have attained to the age of twenty-five years, and be a citizen of the Confederate States, and have been for three years an inhabitant of this State, and for one year a resident of the district from which he is chosen.

Section III

1. The House of Representatives shall be composed as follows: The thirty-seven counties having the largest representative population shall have two representatives each. Every other county shall have one Representative.

2. No person shall be a Representative who shall not have attained to the age of twenty-one years, and be a citizen of the Confederate States, and have been for three years an inhabitant of this State, and for one year a resident of the county which he represents.

Section IV

...8. Every Senator and Representative, before taking his seat, shall take an oath or affirmation to support the Constitution of the Confederate States and of this State....

Section V

1. The General Assembly shall have power to make all laws and ordinances, consistent with this Constitution and not repugnant to the Constitution of the Confederate States, which they shall deem necessary and proper for the welfare of the State....

Section VII

1. The importation or introduction of negroes from any foreign country, other than the slave-holding States or Territories of the United States of America, is forever prohibited.

2. The General Assembly may prohibit the introduction of negroes from any State; but they shall have no power to prevent immigrants from bringing their slaves with them.

3. The General Assembly shall have no power to pass laws for the emancipation of slaves.

4. Any person who shall maliciously kill or maim a slave, shall suffer such punishment as would be inflicted in case the like offense had been committed on a free white person.

ARTICLE III

Section I

1. The executive power shall be vested in a Governor, who shall hold his office during the term of two years, and until such time as a successor shall be chosen and qualified....

2. The Governor shall be elected by the persons qualified to vote for members of the General Assembly, on the first Wednesday in October, in the year of our Lord 1861....

3. No person shall be eligible to the office of Governor who shall not have been a citizen of the Confederate States twelve years, and an inhabitant of this State six years, and who hath not attained the age of thirty years.

ARTICLE V

1. The electors of members of the General Assembly shall be free white male citizens of this State; and shall have attained the age of twenty-one years; and have paid all taxes which may have been required of them, and which they have had an opportunity of paying, agreeably to law, for the year preceding the election; and shall have resided six months within the district or county.

...6. This Constitution shall be amended only by a Convention of the people called for that purpose.

7. This Constitution shall not take effect until the same is ratified by the people....

Done in Convention of the Delegates of the people of the State of Georgia, at Savannah, on the 23rd of March, in the year of our Lord, eighteen hundred and sixty-one.

7. Two Views of Class Voting Patterns[7]

Columbus Enquirer
October 9, 1863
Voting by Classes
Our election on Wednesday developed an organization or opposition of classes, which we trust is only temporary, and will be obliterated before another election is held. A ticket headed "Mechanics and Working Men's Ticket" was very extensively voted by the workmen employed in the Government and other shops and it prevailed by a very large majority. We have heard it said that the resident citizens engaged in other than mechanical pursuits voted about as generally for other candidates as the "mechanics and working men" did for the names on their ticket.

There is certainly no good ground for any antagonism in this city between the mechanics and other classes of our citizens. If we believed that there was, we should zealously and earnestly advocate the healing of the breach by the removal of the evils that produced it; but we are totally ignorant of any cause for the state of opposition developed by this election. Nothing can be more mischievous in any society than antagonistic organizations of its classes. Such divisions are more bitter in their alienations than any other political parties and are far more apt to produce hurtful collisions. The beauty and healthfulness of free communities consists in the *equality* of all their citizens in political and social rights, and the *harmony* of their classes in the discharge of public duties....

We do not wish to be understood as disparaging the choice, as to men, made by either party in this unfortunate division of classes.... But we do deprecate any causeless divisions of our citizens into classes or clans, and entreat them to discourage all organizations of a character so mischievous. The very fact that there is no good reason for such divisions of our citizens almost assures us that the condition of things exhibited on Monday has no permanent foothold, and that in a short time no unpleasant trace of its existence will be discovered.

Columbus Daily Sun
October 13, 1863
Voting by Classes
I notice in the Enquirer of Friday evening, an article complaining bitterly of the people voting by classes, in which both classes are accused of clannishness, but the burden of his complaint seems to rest on mechanics and working men.

---

[7] From *Columbus Enquirer*, October 9, 1863; and *Columbus Daily Sun*, October 13, 1863.

He says "there is certainly no ground for any antagonism in the city." In this the Enquirer is mistaken; for any man, woman or child can see that the people are dividing into two classes, just as fast as the pressure of the time can force them on....

The men know well enough that their helpless families are not cared for, as they were promised at the beginning of the war. They know that the depreciation of our currency is only a trick of our enemies at home, else why would they strive so hard to secure it all? They know, too, that every day they remain from home, reduces them more and more in circumstances, and that by the close of the war a large majority of the soldiery will be unable to live; in fact, many of them are ruined now, as many of their homes and other effects are passing into the hands of speculators and extortioners, for subsistence to their families....

In view of these things, is it not time that our class should awake to a sense of their danger, and in the mildest possible manner begin the work of self-defence, and endeavor to escape a bondage more servile than that imposed by the Aristocracy of England on their peer peasantry? Then we claim the right, as the first alternative, to try and avert the great calamity, by electing such men to the councils of the nation as we think best represent our interests. If this should fail, we must then try more potent remedies....

Let us compare a few figures before we close, and you can see that we have justified cause of complaint. I once could get 75 pounds of flour for a day's work. What do I get now? I once got 25 pounds of bacon for a day's work. What do I get now? *Only two.* I once could get 50 pounds of beef for a day's work. What do I get now? *Only six.* I once could get eight bushels of sweet potatoes for a day's work. What can I get now? *Not one.* And at the same rate through the whole catalogue of family supplies.

But, notwithstanding the mechanics and working men can barely sustain animal life, their condition is much better than the poor soldiers who are fighting the rich man's fight....

8. Indictment of Henry Wirz[8]

General Court Martial Orders, No. 607

Washington, November 6, 1865

I. Before a military commission which convened at Washington, D.C., August 23, 1865, pursuant to paragraph 3, Special Orders, No. 453, dated August 23, 1865, and paragraph 13, Special Orders, No. 524, dated October 2, 1865, War Department, Adjutant-General's Office, Washington, and of which Maj. Gen. Lewis Wallace, U.S. Volunteers, is president, was arraigned and tried—

Henry Wirz.

Charge I: Maliciously, willfully, and traitorously, and in aid of the then existing armed rebellion against the United States of America, on or before the 1st day of March, A.D. 1864, and on divers other days between that day and the 10th day of April, 1865, combining, confederating, and conspiring, together with John H. Winder, Richard B. Winder, Joseph [Isaiah H.] White, W. S. Winder, R. R. Stevenson, and others unknown, to injure the health and destroy the lives of soldiers in the military service of the United States, then held and being prisoners of war within the lines of the so-called Confederate States, and in the military prisons thereof, to the end that the armies of the United States might be weakened and impaired, in violation of the laws and customs of war.

Specification.—In this, that he, the said Henry Wirz...maliciously, traitorously, and in violation of the laws of war, to impair and injure the health and to destroy the lives—by subjecting to torture and great suffering; by confining in unhealthy and unwholesome quarters; by exposing to the inclemency of winter and to the dews and burning sun of summer; by compelling the use of impure water; and by furnishing insufficient and unwholesome food—of large numbers of Federal prisoners, to wit, the number of 30,000 soldiers in the military service of the United States of America, held as prisoners of war at Andersonville, in the State of Georgia, within the lines of the so-called Confederate States did...maliciously, wickedly, and traitorously confine a large number of such prisoners of war, soldiers in the military service of the United States, to the amount of 30,000 men, in unhealthy and unwholesome quarters, in a close and small area of ground wholly inadequate to their wants and destructive to their health, which he well knew and intended; and, while there so confined during the time aforesaid, did, in furtherance of his

---

[8] From *War of the Rebellion: A Compilation of the Official Records of the Union and Confederate Armies*, ser. 2, vol. 8 (Washington, DC: Government Printing Office, 1880–1901).

evil design, and in aid of the said conspiracy, willfully and maliciously neglect to furnish tents, barracks, or other shelter sufficient for their protection from the inclemency of winter and the dews and burning sun of summer; and with such evil intent did take, and cause to be taken, from them their clothing, blankets, camp equipage, and other property of which they were possessed at the time of being placed in his custody; and, with like malice and evil intent, did refuse to furnish, or cause to be furnished, food either of a quality or quantity sufficient to preserve health and sustain life; and did refuse and neglect to furnish wood sufficient for cooking in summer and to keep the said prisoners warm in winter; and did compel the said prisoners to subsist upon unwholesome food, and that in limited quantities entirely inadequate to sustain health, which he well knew; and did compel the said prisoners to use unwholesome water, reeking with the filth and garbage of the prison and prison guard, and the offal and drainage of the cookhouse of said prison, whereby the prisoners became greatly reduced in their bodily strength, and emaciated and injured in their bodily health; their minds impaired and their intellects broken; and many of them, to wit, the number of 10,000, whose names are unknown, sickened and died by reason thereof, which he, the said Henry Wirz, then and there well knew and intended....

ESSAYS

The Georgia Homefront during the Civil War[9]

David Williams

In April 1862, the Confederate Congress passed the first national conscription act in American history. Like the North's later draft, men of wealth could avoid military service by hiring a substitute or paying an exemption fee. And slaveholders who owned twenty or more slaves were automatically excused from the draft. This twenty-slave law was perhaps the most widely hated act ever imposed by the Confederacy, especially for poor soldiers already in the ranks. Said one Southern private, "It gave us the blues; we wanted twenty negroes.

---

[9] From David Williams, *Johnny Reb's War: Battlefield and Homefront* (Abilene TX: McWhiney Foundation Press, 2000). Used with permission from the McWhiney Foundation Press.

Negro property suddenly became very valuable, and there was raised the howl of 'rich man's war, poor man's fight....'"

Another practice that helped turn thousands of Johnny Rebs against the Richmond government was the confiscation of private property, or "impressments." Soldiers resented the fact that their families back home were forced to give up a portion, sometimes a major portion, of their meager produce, while the more politically influential planters were left alone. That they had to sell at prices set by the government was even more galling. But it usually did not matter what the prices were. All farm families got in exchange were promissory notes, usually unredeemable, or inflated paper currency that was nearly as worthless. Very often they got nothing at all....

The Confederate government could not survive without support from its own people, and that fact was widely acknowledged during the war. "If we are defeated," announced one Atlanta newspaper, "it will be by the people at home." And so the Confederacy was defeated: by arrogant planters, greedy capitalists, corrupt officials, and most of all by disillusioned Johnny Rebs.

Perhaps nowhere could the divisive role of the Southern class system be viewed more clearly than in the South's keystone state of Georgia. Primarily an agricultural region, its population ran the socioeconomic scale from planters and lesser slaveholders down through landed yeoman farmers to landless tenant farmers and slaves. In addition to the rural farming folk, there were merchants, factory workers, skilled artisans and craftsmen, urban professionals, and industrial entrepreneurs....

One of the most severe hardships to confront families back home was excessive inflation. At first, few thought it would be a problem, since the war was expected to end quickly. Even after First Manassas, some scoffed at the blockade and its economic threat. Others, however, were more farsighted. John B. Lamar, Howell Cobb's brother-in-law, wrote to the politician-general in November of 1861, "we can laugh at the blockade for a while if salt is $12 a sack," but he wondered what the impact would be if the blockade lasted another year: "It makes me hold my breath when I think of it." Less than a year later the blockade grew even tighter, and salt was selling for $125 a sack when it was available at all. It had been only 2 dollars before the war.

Such dramatic price increases for even the most basic commodities were not uncommon. Butter went from 12 cents a pound in 1861 to 75 cents two years later. By the end of the war it was 5 dollars or more. Corn that was 2 dollars a bushel in 1863 sold for 14 by February 1865. Bacon went from 12 cents to 50 cents a pound in the war's first year. By the end of the war a pound of bacon was 4 dollars. Flour that sold for 9 dollars a barrel before the war was going for 400 by war's end. Coffee went to 30 dollars a pound shortly after the war began and from there to 60 and 70 dollars. The cost of more potent beverages was on the rise as well. Rum that was purchased for just 17 cents a gallon in Cuba sold for 25 dollars after being run through the blockade. That was an increase of nearly 15,000 percent....

For many women laboring under the burdens of inflation, impressments, sick children, and absent husbands, their best was simply not good enough. Thousands of petitions from women all across the South describing their desperate situation and begging for relief flooded into Richmond....

Abandoned and starving, thousands of women became beggars just to keep their families alive. Leaving children at home for days or weeks at a time, they roamed the countryside pleading for food. Sympathetic railroad conductors and steamboat captains occasionally provided transportation, but most often the women made their way on foot. Some planters gave what they could to the women; others did not. But even the more generous viewed these unfortunates with contempt. One planter called the starving women "perfect nuisances."

Impressment, taxation, inflation, starvation, and no help from callous government officials or planters—it was all too much for many women. Hundreds took matters into their own hands and turned to stealing rather than see their children starve. After all, so much had been taken from them, they saw themselves as taking back only what was theirs in the first place. Many women took food from plantations whether the planters offered it or not. Women in Miller County were known to steal livestock on a regular basis. At one point, a group of about fifty soldier's wives raided the government depot in Colquitt and took a hundred bushels of corn....

By 1863 food riots were breaking out in major cities all across the South, including the Confederate capital of Richmond. In Georgia, a band of women attacked a wagon near Thomasville and made off with three sacks of corn. Another group broke into the government warehouse in Valdosta and stole a wagonload of bacon. When an Atlanta merchant told one of his customers that bacon was $1.10 a pound, she drew a pistol and took what she needed, prompting other women in the store to do the same. From there, they moved on to nearby stores, paying whatever prices they wanted or nothing at all. Similar riots broke out in Macon, Augusta, Marietta, Forsyth, Cartersville, Hartwell, and Blackshear. A crowd of starving women numbering perhaps a hundred rioted in Savannah, looting several stores on Whitaker Street. And on April 10, 1863, a mob of about sixty-five Columbus women, some armed with pistols and knives, marched down Broad Street "to raid the stores of speculators."

In April 1862 the Confederate Congress passed an Enrollment Act that gave the president authority to force young men into the military with or without their consent. Under the terms of this act, commonly known as conscription or the draft, white males between the ages of eighteen and thirty-five became subject to involuntary military service. As an inducement to enlist before the draft went into effect, the government offered a cash bonus to those who volunteered and allowed them to serve with the units of their choice. Fearing they would be drafted anyway, hundreds of reluctant men volunteered in March and early April 1862....

Resentment toward conscription was evident throughout Georgia. A report from Franklin County made it clear that there were so many deserters and draft dodgers in the county that conscription efforts were useless. One conscript officer was nearly killed when he tried to enforce the draft law at Fort Gaines. Threats to his life became so serious that he fled the state. Resistance to the draft was rampant all across the South. Howell Cobb thought it would take the whole Confederate army to enforce conscription. The law, he said, threatened the Confederacy "as fatally as...the armies of the United States."

But conscription was an established fact and thousands of letters poured into both state and Confederate offices requesting exemptions from the draft. Potential draftees cited any number of reasons why they should be excused. Isaac Bush of Colquitt asked for exemption on account of "my ankles swelling." For B. J. Smith of Cuthbert, leaving home would mean leaving his "large warehouse" with 3,000 bales of cotton unattended. Those who could not get exemptions outright tried to avoid military service by other means. When the Confederacy made county officials exempt from the draft, such positions became the focus of heated campaigns. In Early County thirty-seven candidates vied for five seats on the Inferior Court. "But there were no politics in the race," said one county resident. "The candidate just wanted the office to keep him out of the war." M. W. Johnson of Oglethorpe County, a soldier of the 6th Georgia Regiment, went home on furlough and had himself elected justice of the peace to keep from going back to the front....

Even among those who stuck with the Confederacy to its painful end, most did so half-heartedly. What loyalty they still felt was more for their commanders and comrades than the government in Richmond. William Andrews of Clay County had joined the army in February 1861 and remained through the entire war. Few could match his record of service to the cause of Southern independence. Still, in May of 1865 he wrote: "While it is a bitter pill to have to come back into the Union, don't think there is much regret for the loss of the Confederacy. The treatment the soldiers have received from the government in various ways put them against it." That attitude on the part of Johnny Rebs throughout the ranks, brought on largely by class antagonism, was among the major reasons for Confederate defeat.

Wilson's Raid through Georgia[10]

James P. Jones

Rain, rain, rain! Thirteen thousand four hundred and eighty Union cavalrymen stood on the north bank of the Tennessee River mounted, armed, and ready to cut a path of destruction through the heart of Alabama and Georgia. If the rain would only stop, the troopers could cross the river, but day after day it fell in sheets. It was March 1865 and Maj. Gen. James Harrison Wilson ached to hear his buglers blare "Boots and Saddles" through the camps. If the horsemen did not ride soon, Nathan Bedford Forrest might organize an effective Confederate force out of the stragglers, deserters, and irregulars in Mississippi and Alabama. It was also possible that continued Union victories might end the war and leave untested the fine force honed to an edge by its young commander. Piqued at the delay, Wilson wrote to his friend Adam Badeau, Gen. Ulysses S. Grant's military secretary, "Isn't it unfortunate that the rain cannot be controlled by General Grant."

Not even the general-in-chief could halt the deluge, and Wilson paced the floor and watched the skies and the muddy Tennessee. By the fifteenth the rain slackened, the river began to fall, and bugles rang. Seven days later advance units of the largest cavalry force of the Civil War swung south. Wilson's raid had begun....

Columbus, like Selma, was a certain target for Wilson. The general called the city "the key" and "the door" to Georgia. The campaign aimed at destroying the Confederacy's ability to make war from the Southwest. Selma's factories had been destroyed; Columbus's equally important facilities were to meet the same fate. Columbus, on the Chattahoochee River, was a major railroad and shipping center. A spur of the Montgomery and West Point crossed the river from the west, and the Muscogee Railroad moved eastward into Central Georgia. Union capture of Apalachicola, Florida, had forced wider use of the Chattahoochee after 1863. In 1865 five steamers moved goods up and down the river.

Even more valuable to the Confederate war effort were the city's factories and mills. Rifles, cannon, cotton and woolen cloth, shoes, and knapsacks were made there. The Eagle Mills produced 2,000 yards of gray tweed and 1,500 yards of cotton duck daily. The Columbus Factory, north of the city, had once

[10] From James Pickett Jones, *Yankee Blitzkrieg: Wilson's Raid through Alabama and Georgia* (Louisville: University Press of Kentucky, 1976). Used with permission of the University Press of Kentucky.

produced 300,000 yards of cotton cloth, 75,000 yards of woolens, and 40,000 pounds of yarn and thread a year. Tents and shoes produced in Columbus added their value to the Confederate cause. The Columbus Factory ran a tannery worked by thirty slaves. The shop produced 12,000 pairs of shoes a year. There were also flour mills capable of producing 250 barrels a day for transportation to Confederates in Virginia.

Of more direct value to the Confederate military were the products of the factory of L. Haiman and Brother and of the Columbus Arsenal and Armory. Haiman and Brother made swords, saddles, and eventually revolvers at the Muscogee Iron Works. Confederate troops also used Haiman's belts, buckles, bayonets, and cartridge boxes. The Columbus Arsenal supplied the Confederacy with rifles and pistols. When Sherman marched into Georgia everything movable in the Atlanta Arsenal was sent to Columbus. Therefore, in the war's last year the Columbus facility's capacity had increased.

Thousands of gray-clad soldiers owed what comfort they enjoyed to the Confederate Quartermaster Depot in Columbus. The principal output of the factory was uniforms and shoes. In June 1862 Richmond received fourteen railroad cars filled with uniforms from the depot. Even more significant is the estimate that more than 300,000 pairs of shoes were produced there. The depot also contributed saddle and harness to the Confederate cavalry.

Since Columbus was a river city its works had been turned to casting cannon, building gunboats, and repairing steamboats. The Confederate Naval Iron Works cast eighty 6-pound brass cannon during the war and made the boilers for a majority of the steamboats constructed in the South. Most famous products of the city's naval yards were the gunboats *Chattahoochee*, *Jackson*, and *Muscogee*. Union control over the river outlets had kept the gunboats out of action and the *Jackson* still lay at Columbus. In addition to these more obvious aids to the Confederate cause, many specialized workshops produced smaller items for both civilian and military consumption. One Georgia historian has boasted that Columbus sent more goods to the Confederate Quartermasters Department than any city in the South except Richmond. It was toward this arsenal that Wilson's horsemen trotted in the second week of April 1865....

When Wilson entered Columbus he gave Gen. Winslow command of the city and charged him with destroying all property deemed of use to the rebels in what the major general regarded as the last great Confederate storehouse. The corps commander established his headquarters in the home of Col. Randolph L. Mott, an opponent of secession who reportedly had flown the Union flag from his home throughout the war. Mott boasted that his home was the only spot in Georgia that had never seceded. Wilson remembered that Mott had flown the flag but kept it "inside but substantially over the part of the house used as a dwelling."

Wilson wrote in his memoirs, "I resolved to destroy everything within reach that could be made useful for further continuance of the Rebellion." Under Winslow's supervision the seventeenth was a day of doom for the Georgia factory city. Explosions rocked Columbus, and a pall of smoke hung in the air. The gunboat *Jackson* was destroyed along with L. Haiman and Brother, the Arsenal, and the Confederate Naval Iron Works. The Confederate Quartermaster Depot, a paper mill, and all textile and flour mills in the city were put to the torch. When the rest of Wilson's corps had crossed the Chattahoochee, both remaining bridges were destroyed. All the railroad rolling stock, including 15 locomotives and about 200 cars, were wrecked. New explosions rocked the city as 5,000 rounds of ammunition and 74 cannon went up....

With hostilities at an end Wilson's veterans "sat about fires, or lay down, in silence. If they spoke it was in subdued tones.... Officers and men alike seemed to have forgotten their smaller duties. All were absorbed in their thoughts and hopes." For the most part, troops used to hard riding, enemy fire, fording streams, and days of destroying railroads and factories had suddenly become an occupation force with few duties and growing boredom. But for some of Wilson's raiders, active service was not over. As Wilson had long ago anticipated, the area into which his troops had ridden was the land toward which most of the Confederacy's leaders would flee. Jefferson Davis, Alexander H. Stephens, Judah P. Benjamin, and a legion of lesser figures were rumored making for Georgia, on their way to escape through Florida or to continue resistance in Texas. Patrols were organized, and many of Wilson's raiders scattered across the state to pursue the fugitives. Wilson also dispatched forces in all directions to accept the surrender of isolated Confederate garrisons and begin the transition from war to peace.

The corps' principal duty remained the capture of Jefferson Davis.... Wilson was convinced that the Rebel fugitives would make their way through the pine forests of southwestern Georgia. He ordered guards placed on ferries on the Ocmulgee River and prepared to dispatch fresh troops toward the area Davis was believed to be traversing. On May 6 [Gen. John] Croxton and [Col. Robert] Minty were ordered to send their best regiments toward Dublin on the Ocmulgee. Croxton picked Henry Harnden's 1st Wisconsin and Minty Benjamin Pritchard's 4th Michigan. The corps commander had set a network of Union troops over the entire state. [Gen. Emory] Upton was at Augusta and [Gen. Edward] Winslow at Atlanta. [Gen. Andrew] Alexander had veered northward from Augusta and was ranging into extreme North Georgia. Small detachments were fixed at Columbus and West Point, and [Gen. Edward] McCook was ordered to lead a force due south to Albany and on toward Thomasville and Tallahassee to look for fugitives. With the departure of the 1st Wisconsin and 4th Michigan, only a fraction of the corps remained at Wilson's Macon headquarters.

While he rested in Washington, Davis learned of the presence of Upton's men in Augusta. He decided to dismiss the bulk of his accompanying troops and ride on southward with a small escort. Of great concern to the harried president was the safety of his wife and children, traveling just ahead of his own group. Shortly after leaving Washington he caught up with Mrs. Davis's party. Slowed by poor roads and concern for his family, Davis covered about 150 miles in the four days after his departure from Washington....

While Pritchard moved into position [in Irwinville on May 10], Col. Harnden rested his men. They were roused just before dawn and moved at daylight toward Davis's camp. After a short march the Wisconsin troopers encountered a detachment that opened fire. Harnden immediately assumed he had struck Davis's escort, and he dismounted the bulk of his men to fight on foot. A small force was sent on horseback to prevent the fugitives' escape. A sharp skirmish rolled through the pines. Two men were killed and one officer and three men were wounded before it was discovered that the combatants were the two Union units. Pritchard left his men posted on the edge of the Davis camp to ride toward the sound of the firing and there encountered Harnden, riding from the opposite direction. The two commanders quickly discovered the truth and brought the tragic melee between friends to an end.

The noise of Union firing aroused Davis and his party. The Confederate president, fully clothed in a gray suit, jumped up, at first convinced the attackers were Southern marauders rumored to have been along the party's flanks for several days. Davis opened the tent flaps and saw Pritchard's blue-clad troops swarming over the camp. Mrs. Davis urged immediate flight, but Davis, fearing for his family, hesitated a few minutes. Finally, grabbing his wife's waterproof, he left the tent. At the last moment, Mrs. Davis took off her shawl and put it around her husband's shoulders.

Davis had not moved far when troopers commanded by Lt. Julian Dickinson, adjutant of the 4th Michigan, ordered him to halt and surrender. Instead of surrendering, Davis advanced toward a mounted trooper, intending to hurl him out of the saddle and vault into the saddle and escape. It was an old Indian trick known to Davis since his early days as a frontier lieutenant. As he advanced, the cavalryman lowered his carbine, and Mrs. Davis, fearing for her husband's life, rushed forward and embraced him. The act probably saved the president's life, but it surely doomed his escape attempt. "God's will be done" was all he could say as he sat down under guard.

Additional Sources

Bailey, Anne J. *War and Ruin: William T. Sherman and the Savannah Campaign.* Wilmington DE: Scholarly Resources, 2002.

Boney, F. N. *Rebel Georgia.* Macon GA: Mercer University Press, 1997.

Bragg, William. *Joe Brown's Army.* Macon GA: Mercer University Press, 1987.

DeBats, Donald. *Elites and Masses: Political Structure, Communication, and Behavior in Ante-bellum Georgia.* New York: Garland Publishing Company, 1990.

Eckert, Ralph L. *John Brown Gordon: Soldier, Southerner, American.* Baton Rouge: Louisiana State University Press, 1989.

Evans, David. *Sherman's Horsemen: Union Cavalry Operations in the Atlanta Campaign.* Bloomington: Indiana University Press, 1996.

Freehling, William W. and Craig M. Simpson, editors. *Secession Debated: Georgia's Showdown in 1860.* New York: Oxford University Press, 1992.

Iobst, Richard. *Civil War Macon: The History of a Confederate City.* Macon GA: Mercer University Press, 1999.

Johnson, Michael P. *Toward a Patriarchal Republic: The Secession of Georgia.* Baton Rouge: Louisiana State University Press, 1977.

Jones, James P. *Yankee Blitzkrieg: Wilson's Raid through Alabama and Georgia.* Athens: University of Georgia Press, 1976.

Marvel, William. *Andersonville: The Last Depot.* Chapel Hill: University of North Carolina Press, 1994.

Morgan, Chad. *Planters' Progress: Modernizing Confederate Georgia.* Gainesville: University Press of Florida, 2005.

Parks, Joseph H. *Joseph E. Brown of Georgia.* Baton Rouge: Louisiana State University Press, 1977.

Schott, Thomas E. *Alexander H. Stephens of Georgia: A Biography.* Baton Rouge: Louisiana State University Press, 1988.

Williams, David. *Johnny Reb's War: Battlefield and Homefront.* Abilene TX: McWhiney Foundation Press, 2000.

Williams, David, Teresa C. Williams, and David Carlson. *Plain Folk in a Rich Man's War: Class and Dissent in Confederate Georgia.* Gainesville: University Press of Florida, 2002.

Chapter 8

WOMEN IN GEORGIA

Throughout much of Georgia's history women have struggled to achieve social and political rights and equality with men. From the founding of the colony in 1733 Georgia's women were relegated to almost second-class status and only slowly gained some rights. The most obvious example from the Trustee period is the colony's land policy. Only men could receive land grants and this land could be inherited only by males. Male colonists who died without a male heir could not pass their land on to their wives or daughters; the land reverted back to the colony to be granted to yet another male. Gradually the Trustees began to change their policy to allow women to possess land. When the Trustee period ended and the colony came under royal authority, the number of women who owned land increased drastically. The most prominent women landowners in early Georgia history were Mary Musgrove Bosomworth, who owned some 6,200 acres, and Elizabeth Butler, who possessed 5,230 acres.

Outside of the home many Georgia women found personal satisfaction by participating in reform movements; one of those was the Temperance Movement. The Georgia State Temperance Society was created in 1828 but only lasted until 1836. Georgia women continued their interest in temperance in the years after the Civil War. A state chapter of the Women's Christian Temperance Union was formed in 1880, and in 1906 a Georgia chapter of the Anti-Saloon League was organized. The lobbying efforts of these organizations helped the General Assembly pass a prohibition bill in 1907.

Undoubtedly the most important reform movement for women was the drive for suffrage. The granting of women's suffrage began in the West with Wyoming in 1890. As in the case of prohibition, organizations were formed in Georgia to promote women's suffrage; the first was the Georgia Woman Suffrage Association (GWSA), formed in Columbus in 1890. Over the next fifteen years, splinter organizations were created and competed with the GWSA for members, including the Georgia Woman Equal Suffrage League, Georgia Men's League for Woman Suffrage, and the Equal Suffrage Party of Georgia. The General Assembly first held hearings on women's suffrage in 1914 but the hearings failed to produce a suffrage bill. Future hearings in 1915 and 1917 were equally unsuccessful. In the meantime the cities of Waycross and Atlanta permitted women to vote in municipal elections in 1917 and 1919, respectively. Although Georgia's General Assembly did not act on women's suffrage, the US Congress did—in June 1919 it passed the 19th Amendment to the Constitution, which provided for women's suffrage. Georgia was the first state to reject the amendment; on July 24, 1919, both houses of the General Assembly passed resolutions against the amendment. Despite Georgia's rejection of the 19th Amendment it won ratification in August 1920. As a symbolic gesture Georgia finally ratified the 19th Amendment in 1970.

The state of Georgia has had its share of prominent women. The first was probably Mary Musgrove Bosomworth, who served as an interpreter for James Oglethorpe after the colony was founded. Ellen Craft was a slave who escaped with her husband in 1848 and became prominent when her owner attempted to capture her in 1850, an event that became national news. Juliette Gordon Low founded the Girl Scouts in Savannah in 1912. Rebecca Latimer Felton was Georgia's most well-known woman activist; in fact, in 1922 she became the first woman to serve in the US Senate. Flannery O'Connor and Margaret Mitchell were two of the state's best writers. More recently, Coretta Scott King participated in the Civil Rights Movement in Georgia and Rosalyn Carter served as the First Lady of the United States.

DOCUMENTS

The first document to follow is the 1748 land deed to Mary Musgrove Bosomworth. The second document contains newspaper articles on women's riots in Georgia during the Civil War. Document 3 is a summary of the activities of Georgia's chapter of the Women's Christian Temperance Union. The fourth document is an essay by Rebecca Latimer Felton on the needs of farmer's wives. Document 5 is a 1915 open letter calling for women's suffrage. The sixth document is Georgia's 1921 law permitting women to vote. Document 7 is the 1922 Senate speech of Rebecca L. Felton, the first woman to serve in the US Senate. The eighth document contains Eleanor Roosevelt's 1941 speech at Georgia State Woman's College in Valdosta and her newspaper column describing that visit. Document 9 is the 1953 law that allowed women to serve on juries.

1. Mary Musgrove Bosomworth's Land Acquisition[1]

January 4, 1748

To all People to whom these presents shall come be seen or be made known Malatchi Opiya Mico Emperour of the Upper and Lower Creek Nations sendeth Greeting. Know ye That the said Malatchi Opiya Mico for and in consideration of Ten Peices of strouds twelve Peices of Duffles two Hundred weight of Powder two Hundred weight of Bulletts twenty Guns twelve Pair of Pistols One Hundred weight of Vermillion and thirty Head of Breeding Cattle to him given and delivered by Thomas and Mary Bosomworth of the Colony of Georgia the Receipt whereof is hereby acknowledged hath for himself Subjects and Vassals Granted Bargained sold enfeoffed [transferred] and confirmed and by these presents doth Grant Bargain Sell enfeoffed and confirm to the said Thomas Bosomworth and Mary his Wife their Heirs and Assigns for ever all that Tract or Tracts of Land Island or Islands known or distinguished by the names of Hussope or Hussabaw [Ossabaw] Island Cowlegee or Saint Catherine's Island and Sappala Island bounded on the North east by Husaba sound on the south west by Doeboy [Doboy] sound and divided by the sounds of St. Catherines and Sappalo on the South East by the Sea and on the North west by several Rivers and Creeks having no particular names which divide the said several Islands from the Continent and through which Boats and other small Vessels are Navigated to and from the Town of Frederica and to and from the Northern parts of Georgia aforesaid and South Carolina Together with all Rights Priviledges and Appurtenances unto the said Island and Islands in any ways belonging or appertaining and also all Woods Timber and Timber Trees thereon growing and all Mines Fossils Minerals precious Stones or Metals which are or may be digged opened or discovered within the same. To have and to hold all and Singular the said Lands Islands Hereditaments and premises and every part and parcel thereof unto the said Thomas Bosomworth and Mary his Wife their Heires and Assigns as long as the Sun shall shine or the Waters run in the Rivers for ever. In Witness whereof the said Malatchi Opiya Mico hath hereunto set his hand and Seal this fourth day of the Windy Moon called the Month of January by the English in the Year of their Saviour by their account and reckoning 1747 and in the twenty first Year of the Reign of George the Second the Great King.

---

[1] From John T. Juricek, ed., *Early American Indian Documents: Treaties and Laws, 1607–1789*, vol. 11, Georgia Treaties, 1733–1763 (Washington, DC: University Publications of America, 1989).

2. Women's Riots during the Civil War[2]

Columbus Daily Sun
April 11, 1863

A MOB IN COLUMBUS

An event we have been long expecting transpired in this city on this morning. A company of women led on and encouraged by a few vagabonds whose presence is a pestilence in any community, and especially so in ours, congregated near the new bridge in the upper part of the city, organized themselves into a "seizing" party and proceeded down Broad street for the purpose of making impressments of private property on their own account.

The company numbered about sixty-five viragos, some of whom were armed with pistols and knives, all cursing and swearing, and threatening what they intended to do in case the "speculators" or merchants refused to grant their reasonable requests. They proceeded down nearly the whole length of the business part of the street, when they came to a halt in front of Mr. Geo. A. Norris' dry goods store, entered it and commenced helping themselves to whatever they wanted, when the police was called in and the mob dispersed. A competent guard has since been furnished by Maj. Humphreys, of the Ordnance Department, and no further apprehension is felt.

Macon Daily Telegraph
April 22, 1863

SUSTAIN LAW AND ORDER

An ugly piece of work was done in Monroe County, last Friday, which impresses us with lively ideas of the dangers threatening all classes from the spirit of lawlessness which is abroad, and the necessity of invoking our whole people to rebuke and discountenance in every possible way all infractions of private rights.

A Factory at Seven Islands, in Butts County, had loaded a wagon with seven bales of manufactured goods, and dispatched it by their customary driver, a trusty old negro, to Forsyth, for transportation upon the Macon & Western Rail Road. The wagon arrived at Forsyth in due time with only three bales, and the driver's story, (which there is no reason to doubt as he identified many of the parties, and it is also confirmed by circumstantial evidence,) is as follows: When the wagon had progressed about seven miles on its journey, it was stopped by a line of twenty-eight women, drawn up across the road—the most

---

[2] From *Columbus Daily Sun*, April 11, 1863; *Macon Daily Telegraph*, April 22, 1863; and *Savannah Daily Constitutionalist*, April 22, 1864.

of them armed with knives and pistols, and in the thicket close to the scene of action sat a man upon a stump, also armed with a double-barrelled gun. The women called upon the negro to halt upon peril of his life, and then immediately commenced discharging the load of the wagon—cutting open the bales, and so soon as they had taken as many pieces of cloth as they could carry away, made off, leaving Jim to proceed on his journey with the three bales left....

Savannah Daily Constitutionalist
April 22, 1864

A LAWLESS PROCEEDING

Yesterday forenoon a combination of women, numbering from fifty to one hundred, suddenly appeared at the grocery store of Br. A. F. Mira, on Whitaker street, near Broughton. While several of them entered the store, the balance remained outside. Those inside stated to Mr. Mira that they wished something to eat, and would have it. The proprietor of the store seeing from their number that he was at their mercy, told them that he would give them some bacon, and while in the act of so doing, those outside rushed into the store and forced Mr. Mira into one corner, when each of the party commenced helping herself to whatever came within reach. After having done this they retired.

The same party also went to the store of Mr. William McIntyre, on Market Square, and demanded provisions. Mr. McIntyre told them that if they actually stood in need of food he would supply them with a small quantity. He then distributed to them a quantity of bacon, &c. From this store they took nothing forcibly.

The store of Mr. John Gilliland, on the same block, was also visited by the same party. Here they entered commenced to help themselves to a small lot of bacon....

3. Activities of the Georgia WCTU[3]

On January 11, 1883 representatives of the five rather large Unions of the state met in the basement of the First Baptist Church in Atlanta and organized the Georgia WCTU Convention with Mrs. W. C. Sibley of Augusta as president. Miss Frances Willard, National President, was present and guided

---

[3] From Georgia WCTU Records, Manuscript, Archives, and Rare Book Library, Emory University, Atlanta, Georgia.

the group as they set up their organization. Also Mrs. Sallie F. Chapin of South Carolina was present and rendered valuable service.

The WCTU induced the Legislature to keep local option, which provided that each county could have the privilege of saying whether they would have liquor sold legally or not.

The WCTU was responsible for getting the Convict Lease system done away. They found that women and men convicts were boarded together. In one place they found 25 children under three years of age were born there and the guards who were supposed to punish all offenders had forced some of the women to yield to their beastly desires.

At their seventh annual convention in 1889 the state WCTU passed a resolution memorializing the next Legislature to appropriate a fund for the establishing of an Industrial School for Girls. The different women wrote articles for the papers and wrote to and talked with the different Legislators, with the result that the next Legislature passed the bill and later the Industrial College for Girls was founded in Milledgeville.

The WCTU was largely responsible for getting unfermented wine served in the churches on communion.

The WCTU succeeded in getting a law passed to observe two hours a year (the fourth Friday in March) for the teachers to teach temperance in the schools.

Close to a dozen films have been placed in the library of the State University showing the evils of the alcoholic beverage. The librarian tells us that our films are called for more than any others in the library.

Last but not least our state gave to the nation and world a brilliant lecturer for our Temperance cause. She lectured in every state in the United States and in many different countries over the world. She was the great leader of the WCTU in Georgia who led us to victory in this state in 1907, Mrs. Mary Harris Armor.

4. Farmers Wives and Their Needs[4]

By Rebecca L. Felton [undated, probably 1890s]
...I now call your attention to the value or woman's work on the farm. You know the old saying,

---

[4] From Rebecca Latimer Felton Papers, Hargrett Rare Book and Manuscript Library, University of Georgia Libraries.

"Man's work is from sun to sun,
But woman's work is never done."
...Now gentlemen, I would like to ask, if you can pay tithes to church state cheerfully—why shouldn't you give your wife a crop, small of course, to be sold when she so decides, and the money to be used as she pleases?—Did it ever occur to you, that she is like other laborers, worthy of her hire?—Suppose you go into the market to hire help—what would you pay for such services as she gives you so willingly? Ah! But you will say, we are joint owners. Is that true? If you chance to die while that crop is on hand, would she be the sole owner, if you have children?

If you plant twenty acres in cotton—and hire the help to plow hoe and pick it, while she cooks their food—and waits on you and the crowd—would you consider one acre or two to be extravagant pay for her services?

5. An Open Letter for Woman Suffrage[5]

An Open Letter
To members of the Georgia Legislature,
To the Members of the press and to
You, sir. Greeting:
The equal suffrage party of Georgia, believing "that the right of citizens of this state to vote shall not be denied or abridged on account of sex," desire to place before you our plan for our own enfranchisement.

We feel that you cannot justly deprive us of our voice in the administration of the affairs of the government, which we are taxed to maintain, and to whose laws we are held amenable. In respectfully asking your favorable consideration of this question, which we are not permitted to decide for ourselves, we are not asking for the adoption of any partisan issue, nor for any untried experiment.

In twelve states, women are enjoying the free use of the ballot and from each of these states, through her press, her legislatures, her governors, senators, clergymen, judges, representatives and chief educators, the statement is sent forth that only good has accrued to the people and state from the enfranchisement of women.

There have been anonymous writers who have distributed misrepresentations of the facts, but no two men or women in all these states will assert over their own names and addresses, that equal suffrage has produced any bad

---

[5] From *Columbus Enquirer*, May 2, 1915.

results. The evils predicted have not come to pass, the benefits claimed, for it have been secured or are in process of development.

Every person knows that the enfranchisement of the women of the south will enormously increase white supremacy. Quoting the United States census of 1914, we find the proportion of white women to negro women and of white women to the whole negro population as follows: There are 8,788,961 white women in the south and 4,316,565 negro women, less than half—and the white women of the south out number the entire negro population by 494,627. In Georgia there are 110,590 more white women than negro women.

Every person knows that the enfranchisement of women in inevitable. Everybody realizes that the progress of woman suffrage, like all the great movements in the advancement of the human race, profound, irresistible and virtual—is seemingly beyond the power of any human agency to retard or control.

By order of the legislative committee of the equal suffrage party of Georgia. Emily C. McDougald, President

6. Woman's Suffrage Bill[6]

Section 1. Be it enacted by the General Assembly of the State of Georgia, and it is hereby enacted by the authority of the same, That Section 2167 of the Civil Code of Georgia of 1910, which is in the following language: "2167, (No. 1910) Females. Females are not entitled to the privilege of the elective franchise, nor can they hold any civil office, or perform any civil function, unless specially authorized by law, nor are they required to discharge any military, jury, police, patrol or road duty. Provided, nothing contained herein prevent a woman, a resident of the State for four years, and who has attained the age of twenty-one years, from being eligible to the position of State Librarian by appointment by the Governor, under the provisions of force regulating appointment by the Governor. A woman is eligible to the office of assistant physician at the Georgia State Sanitarium; and females, residents of the county for four years preceding, may be appointed to hold any office in the children's courts," be, and the same is, hereby repealed.

Sec. 2. Be it further enacted by the authority aforesaid, That in lieu of said section the following shall be, and is, hereby adopted, and shall be known and numbered as Section 2167 of the Civil Code of Georgia, from and after the

---

[6] From *Acts and Resolutions of the General Assembly of the State of Georgia*, 1921.

passage of this Act, to-wit: "Section 2167 . Females. Females are entitled to the privilege of the elective franchise, to hold any civil office or perform any civil functions in as full and complete a manner as the same can be enjoyed by any male citizen of this State; provided, however, females shall not be liable to discharge any military, jury, police, patrol or road duty."

Sec. 3. Be it further enacted by the authority aforesaid, That all laws and parts of laws in conflict with this Act be, and the same are, hereby repealed.

Approved August 13, 1921.

7. Rebecca Latimer Felton's Senate Speech[7]

November 22, 1922

Mr. President, in my very remarkable campaign in Georgia, which, contrary to precedent, all came along after I was selected, one of the very amusing things that came to me by mail was a cartoon from San Antonio, Tex. The cartoon represented the United States Senate in session. The seats seemed to be fully occupied, and there appeared in the picture the figure of a woman who had evidently entered without sending in her card. The gentlemen in the Senate took the situation variously. Some seemed to be a little bit hysterical, but most of them occupied their time looking at the ceiling. Over the cartoon was written the wonderful words: "Will they ask the lady to take a chair?" [Laughter] I want to return my thanks to-day for the beautiful, hospitable welcome that you have accorded the lady when you gave her a chair.

I also want to return thanks to the noble men of Georgia. Georgia was very slow in her promises with reference to woman suffrage. She has been rapid to perform, for Georgia is the first State in the Federal Union composed of the 48 States, where one chivalric governor went to the front and said: "Send that old lady there and let her look at the Senate for even day."

The Senator elect from Georgia, Mr. George, said, "She shall have her day there," and I want to thank him in their presence. He is a worthy successor. I want to plead for your gracious attention to him. He has been most chivalric. The sitting Senator from Georgia [Mr. Harris] has been most obliging. Indeed, I feel that I am the happiest woman in the United States. I am at home in the Senate for a day. I appreciate the wonderful hospitality and beautiful attention thus accorded to me.

---

[7] From *Congressional Record: Proceedings and Debates of the Third Session of the Sixty-Seventh Congress of the United States of America* (Washington, DC: Government Printing office, 1922).

I want to say further that I commend to your attention the 10,000,000 women voters who are watching this incident. It is a romantic incident, Senators, but it is also a historical event. If Lady Astor, from the State of Virginia, can go to London and be accepted as a member of the British House of Commons, you can take this remnant of the old South that has never flickered in her patriotism to her country and be very well assured that she is not going to discredit her commission.

Let me say, Mr. President, that when the women of the country come in and sit with you, though there may be but very few in the next few years, I pledge you that you will get ability, you will get integrity of purpose, you will get exalted patriotism, and you will get unstinted usefulness.

Mr. President and Senators, I thank you very much for this hearing. [Applause on the floor and in the galleries]

8. Eleanor Roosevelt Visits and Speaks at Georgia State Woman's College[8]

March 27, 1941

I am very happy to be here today. It's been a delightful trip. I drove over yesterday from Charleston and enjoyed every minute through this interesting country....

I am also very much interested in seeing this college. Beautifully situated it offers so many advantages and I think that the girls themselves who I had the pleasure of dining with last night are a very delightful group of girls. They asked a few questions after I had talked and I wish that we could have spent a great deal longer having a real interchange of thought. Because in these days it really matters a great deal what the younger generation is thinking.

But one of the rather sad things that has come to light is the fact that a great many of our young people do not enjoy or really know how to read. And perhaps the movies are to blame, perhaps the radio is to blame I don't know. But the fact remains that unless our young people enjoy books and learn to use them while they are still in school and college they are losing one of the great joys of life. And also they are losing an opportunity to prepare themselves for

---

[8] From Eleanor Roosevelt, speech, March 27, 1941, Valdosta State University Archives, Odum Library, Valdosta State University; and *Atlanta Constitution*, March 31, 1941.

many of the questions which are going to come before them for decisions as they take their place in the world.

A woman today has just as great a responsibility to carry as men have. She shares the responsibility of citizenship. It is quite true that in some ways her responsibility is greater because in the home she really has the greatest influence over the early years of the life of her children. And you know that many great educators feel that it is the early years that count the most. And therefore the woman's responsibility intellectually, morally, spiritually, and physically for the young people of the nation is a very great responsibility. And I think that colleges such as this one give something to our young people which will mean much in the way the future generation shapes the life of this nation.

And it is the young people who are going to decide what is going to happen to our country and perhaps to the world in the future. So it is important what young girls and young men think and do today. And above everything else I think it is important that we older people should give them the help to actually prepare for the responsibility of being citizens in one of the most critical periods of history.

Probably never since our earliest days have we faced as critical a period in the world as we are facing today. The question before us seems to be shall a rule of force dominate the world or shall a rule of reason as represented by the democracies dominate in the future? And that our young people probably will have to decide. They will have to care enough about democracy, they will have to know what they mean by democracy. They will have to really make democracy succeed. And that's no small charge that lies before them.

Eleanor Roosevelt's "My Day" Column:
Education Builds Happy Marriages

Yesterday morning we drove around the grounds of the Georgia State Woman's College, where the students certainly have every opportunity for a healthy and happy outdoor life. Available are tennis courts, horses to ride, a beautiful swimming pool, archery and a delightful student activity house, where meals can be served and entertainment of every kind given by the students.

I wish very much that I had had more opportunity to talk with the faculty. They seemed young and progressive. When we finally ended up at the library, which was being dedicated, I felt that one could be justly enthusiastic about the opportunities offered here to girls for a rounded education.

I was told there was a great difference between the size of the freshman class and the number of graduates, for a good many girls leave to get married. Because the Georgia law allows girls to teach after two years of college, those facing economic difficulties go to earn a living.

From the way people talk, I get the impression occasionally that it is not considered important for girls to be really well educated, if they are going to marry and bring up a family. I would like to register here my thought that marriage and the upbringing of children in the home, require as well trained a mind and as well disciplined a character as any other occupation that might be considered a career.

I think we ought to impress on both our girls and boys that successful marriages require just as much work, just as much intelligence and just as much unselfish devotion, as they give to any position they undertake to fill on a paid basis.

The principles of democratic citizenship are taught in the home and the example is given there of the responsibility assured to the individual under a democratic form of government. Every man and woman's college should have that objective in view as part of the education process. Without it no education is complete.

We left Valdosta, Ga., about 11 o'clock and drove through a sudden heavy rainstorm on the way to Albany, Ga. Just at its height, one of my tires went flat, luckily, another car was with us and we drove with Mr. Horace Caldwell, leaving our two chauffeurs to change the tire when the rain stopped and then to follow us. After a very pleasant lunch given by the Rotarians, we proceeded to Tuskegee, where we arrived about 5 o'clock.

9. Women to Serve as Jurors[9]

Be it enacted by the General Assembly of Georgia as follows:
Section 1. Section 59–106 of the Code of Georgia of 1933, relating to the revision of jury lists and the selection of grand and traverse jurors, is hereby amended by striking the word "men" from line five and inserting in lieu thereof the word "citizen", and by striking the word "men" from line eight and inserting in lieu thereof the word "citizen"....

Section 3. Section 59–201 of the Code of Georgia of 1933, relating to the qualification of grand jurors, is hereby amended by striking the word "male" in the first line....

Section 4. Any woman of this State who does not desire to serve upon juries shall notify the jury commissioners of the county in which she resides in writing

---

[9] From *Acts and Resolutions of the General Assembly of the State of Georgia*, 1953.

to that effect, and thereupon the jury commissioners shall not place the name of such woman in the jury box for said county.

Section 5. All laws and parts of laws in conflict with this Act are hereby repealed.

Approved December 21, 1953.

ESSAYS

Land Grants to Georgia Women, 1755–1775[10]

Lee Ann Caldwell Swann

In the twenty years of Trustees rule, hampered by an impractical land policy, ownership of land by women was a rarity. Under the initial Trustee land policy recipients of grants had to be male and the land granted had to be held in tail male. Thus women could not acquire land by grant or inheritance. In spite of this policy, the Trustees often demonstrated laxness in enforcement and women did obtain land, but this remained the exception to the rule. Gradually, under criticism and pressure from the colonists, and in view of the decline of the colony, the Trustees relaxed their restrictive policies altogether in 1750. When the crown actually took over the government of the colony in 1754, Georgia's women owned several thousand acres of land. The number of women controlling land under the royal government from 1755 to 1775 increased dramatically.

Land in royal Georgia was granted free utilizing the headright system whereby the head of a family, male or female, was eligible for 100 acres for himself and 50 acres for each dependent including indentured servants and slaves. This system attempted to give each grantee the amount of land he could feasibly cultivate. Applicants petitioned for land to the Governor and his Council describing the size, location, and intended utilization of the requested grant. If the applicant appeared capable of using more land than he could claim under the headright system, the Governor and Council sometimes allowed purchase of land for 1shilling per 10 acres. After receiving their initial

---

[10] From Lee Ann Caldwell Swann, "Land Grants to Georgia Women, 1755–1775," *Georgia Historical Quarterly* 61/1 (Spring 1977). Courtesy of the Georgia Historical Society.

headright grant, several of Georgia's women were permitted to purchase land, an indication of their success and ability.

Interesting statistics concerning facts and trends of land ownership by women emerge from the data gleaned from the *Proceedings of the Governor and Council*, which contain the petitions made by applicants for grants. In the period from 1755 to 1775 a total of 248 grants were made to 164 individual women in the colony for a total of approximately 67,000 acres. Forty-two of these women received grants referred to in the petitions as town lots that were usually town, garden, and farm lot combinations totaling 50 acres. In the early years of the royal period, as in the Trustee period, a majority of the grants to women were for town lots; in fact, 64 percent of all town lots granted during this twenty-year period were granted from 1755 to 1765....

As the colonial period progressed, fewer women remained content to stay within the towns and requests for farm acreage increased. Of the 164 women in royal Georgia who received land grants, 122 women got farm acreage. In the first ten years of the royal period, large women landowners, those who owned 500 acres or more, received proportionately more grants than the moderate and smaller landowners. But the number of small and medium-sized farms owned by women increased steadily throughout the two decades of royal government; farms of less than 500 acres constituted 60 percent of all farms granted in the five years preceding the Revolution, as compared with only 41 percent in the first five years of the period. As the colony became more settled, increasing numbers of women of the middle class began to take their place among the landowners of Georgia.

The majority of women in royal Georgia who received grants of land for farm acreage owned modest farms of less than 500 acres. Seventy-five women, or 61.5 percent (this excludes those owning town lots) fell into this category. The number of women with grants of less than 250 acres came within one grant of equaling the women owning town lots. The number of grants for town lots steadily decreased while grants in the less than 250-acre category increased after 1765, particularly in the five years preceding the American Revolution, when more than 52 percent of women in this category received their grants. The number of women with grants of between 250 and 490 acres also peaked between 1771 and 1775. As the colonial period progressed, women of modest means began to venture beyond the relative shelter and security of Georgia's towns to own and cultivate their own farms. The women who owned tracts of this size received a total of eighty-six grants. Most cultivated their single grants with their children and perhaps a few slaves. The deeds and conveyances of the royal period contain little evidence of these women purchasing additional slaves or additional lands as did the larger landowners. The lives of these humble women landowners can be only partially reconstructed....

Thirty-one Georgia women received a total of fifty-three grants that ranged from 500 to 999 acres. These figures indicate that these women received subsequent grants after successful management of their initial grant, although not with the frequency of the wealthier landowners. The number of grants given in this category remained relatively uniform throughout the period with no concentration of grants occurring in one particular span. In December 1771 Hannah Bradwell had been in the Georgia province for two months. Having four children and thirty-eight Negroes, she desired 500 acres in St. Andrew parish for cultivation, which the Governor granted. Six months later, on the basis of having Negroes for which she had obtained no land, she requested and received an additional 300 acres to adjoin her initial grant. Her will, dated July 22, 1775, bequeathed both of these tracts to her son Thomas, with the remainder of her estate divided between her other children and grandchildren.

In the royal period sixteen women accumulated tracts of 1,000 or more acres. The fact that these women received a total of sixty-one separate grants indicates that in most cases their operations were quite successful; the accumulation of several grants over a ten to fifteen year span indicates a steady growth in their farms and often an increase in the number of slaves owned. (Under the headright system each slave entitled all landowners to another 50 acres.) By 1765 ten of the sixteen women landowners in this category had already received their initial grant of land. The majority of grants in the second decade of the royal period were subsequent grants to the same women. Thirty-eight grants were conferred from 1766 to 1775 compared to twenty-one from 1755 to 1765. As these statistics indicate, the larger landowners successfully operated and increased their holdings throughout the period. The following illustrations demonstrate this more graphically.

The most prominent woman landowner in colonial Georgia was Mary Musgrove Matthews Bosomworth. She provided invaluable assistance on innumerable occasions as an interpreter and adviser on Indian affairs, constantly aiding in the maintenance of amicable relations between the British and the Creeks. Mary's influence on the Georgia colony began with its founding in 1733 and ended after a prolonged conflict with both Georgia and imperial authorities over her land claims. With the conclusion of this conflict in 1760, Mary became one of Georgia's largest women landowners, receiving St. Catherine's Island, the most sizable single grant conferred upon a woman in the colonial period—6,200 acres....

A study of the marital status of women landowners gives some insight into what type of women received land and why. In those cases where it was possible to determine marital status, widows formed the majority of women who received grants. Sixty-eight widows obtained grants compared to twenty-seven spinsters and twenty-two married women. In the category of large women landowners, 75 percent were widows; although the percentage was not as high in the remaining categories, in each case widows formed the majority. The practicality of widows owning land is obvious, for widows with land to cultivate could provide for themselves and their often large families, relieving the government of the necessity of providing some form of aid. In many of the petitions for land to the Governor and Council widows stated that they desired the land in order to provide for their families. This same rationale applied to spinsters; they could provide for their own maintenance if they owned land. Upon studying the petitions for grants from married women, it was found in many cases a woman petitioned for land she had inherited from a previous husband, parents, or other relatives. This grant established clear title to the land, especially in cases where the deceased had petitioned for a grant, had it surveyed, but had not received final title. Mary Arthur, formerly Mary Stevens, told the Council that her late husband, John Stevens, obtained a warrant for 200 acres of land on Herron's Island intentionally for the petitioner in case of his death. He had died so soon after his warrant that he had not taken out the grant. Her son John, also his father's heir, convinced of his father's intentions had renounced any claim and given her the right to the land. The Governor and Council granted her petition.

In addition to the married women who received grants in their own name, another group of women received grants jointly with associates, sisters, brothers, and husbands. These joint grants have been excluded from previous statistical analyses. In the royal period thirty-two joint grants involved women; eleven of these were for town lots, the remaining twenty-one in farm lands....

In recapitulation, several conclusions emerge from a study of women landowners in royal Georgia. During this twenty-year period, 164 women received a total of approximately 67,000 acres in individual grants. A majority of these grants went to widows, allowing them to support themselves and their families. As the royal period progressed more women sought farm acreage and the number of town lots granted steadily decreased. Women were moving from the towns to the country. The number of women granted small and medium-sized farms steadily increased throughout the royal period, indicating that landowning was no longer a characteristic of wealthy women only but was increasingly prevalent among women of modest means. Toward the end of the royal period, in the years immediately preceding the American Revolution, more of the modest women landowners moved into the rapidly expanding upcountry to own and cultivate land. Thus by 1775 women landowners formed and established and accepted part of Georgia society, playing an increasingly significant role in the colony's economic and social life.

The Last Phase of the Woman Suffrage Movement in Georgia[11]

A. Elizabeth Taylor

In 1914, for the first time, the question of enfranchising women received serious consideration in a Georgia legislative session. On June 25th of that year Representative Barry Wright introduced a proposal to grant equal suffrage through an amendment to the State Constitution. The House referred this proposal to the committee on constitutional amendments. A few days later, on July 6th, the House heard its first suffrage speech delivered by a woman. This was an address by Mrs. Frances Smith Whiteside, president of the Georgia Woman Suffrage League. Mrs. Whiteside said that the Georgia suffragists were not militant agitators but that they did want the right to vote. She considered woman suffrage beneficial to society and cited California as an example of a progressive woman suffrage state. She claimed that the enfranchisement of women was inevitable and predicted that the suffrage states soon would hold a balance of power in the electoral college. To her address the members of the House listened with "much interest and attention" and at its conclusion they applauded Mrs. Whiteside heartily.

The following day the House committee conducted a hearing on Wright's suffrage proposal. About 200 women and about 50 men attended. Mrs. Mary Latimer McLendon, Leonard J. Grossman, Mrs. Elliott Cheatham, James L. Anderson, and Mrs. Rebecca Latimer Felton spoke in favor of the measure, while Mrs. Dolly Blount Lamar and Miss Mildred Rutherford spoke against it. Mrs. McLendon reported that the number of women suffrage states was increasing and maintained that white women had as much right to vote as negro men. She said: "The negro men, our former slaves, have been given the right to vote and why should not we Southern women have the same right?" Mr. Grossman argued that woman suffrage would insure white supremacy in the South because negro women would not be allowed to vote in white primaries.

---

[11] Reprinted from A. Elizabeth Taylor, "The Last Phase of the Woman Suffrage Movement in Georgia," *Georgia Historical Quarterly* 43/1 (March 1959). Courtesy of the Georgia Historical Society.

Mrs. Cheatham asked why women should not help conduct public affairs, since government was "only public housekeeping." Mr. Anderson said that women were only asking for what belonged to them and denied that their enfranchisement would increase the negro vote. Mrs. Felton, a sister of Mrs. McLendon, concluded the speeches by stating: "Why should our women not have the right to vote? Why can't they help you make the laws the same as they help you run your homes and your churches? I do not want to see a negro man walk to the polls and vote on who should handle my tax money while I myself can not vote at all. Is this fair?"

In opposing the measure Mrs. Lamar said that the majority of the women of Georgia did not want to vote and that "the bulk of those who are for suffrage form a fungus growth of misguided women." She thought that women should stay out of politics and that woman suffrage was a threat to state rights. Miss Rutherford agreed with Mrs. Lamar as follows: "The women who are working for this measure are striking at the principle for which their fathers fought during the Civil War. Woman's suffrage comes from the north and west and from women who do not believe in state rights and wish to see negro women using the ballot. I do not believe that the State of Georgia has sunk so low that her good men can not legislate for the woman. If this time ever comes then it will be time enough for women to claim the ballot." After listening to these arguments the committee voted five to four against the proposal and recommended to the House that it not pass.

On June 30, 1914, W. J. Bush introduced in the Senate a woman suffrage measure, which was referred to the general judiciary committee. When the committee conducted its hearing, Mrs. Cheatham and Mrs. Felton spoke for suffrage and Mrs. Lamar spoke in opposition. Mrs. Cheatham said that the leaders of the National Democratic Party were for votes-for-women and that voting was within woman's sphere. She explained that the main reason women wanted the ballot was "to get back the control of the home," which had been "taken from them by industrial progress." She explained: "Officers selected by the vote of the people are in charge of the inspection of food and milk and the water supply. And the only way in which women can see to it that this works, which is her work, is properly done by the use of the ballot." Mrs. Felton told the committee: "I have no knowledge of any law that gives you liberty to deny any right of citizenship to your mother who loves you. You will grant that she is as good as you are."

Speaking in opposition, Mrs. Lamar maintained that votes-for-women was contrary to the conservatism of the South and that the majority of women did not want to vote. She stated: "It is my belief that when it is proved that a majority of the women want the ballot—then men will gladly give it. It is up to the suffragists to show that majority." She denied the validity of the "taxation without representation" argument and said that if all taxpayers should be allowed to vote, then negroes would be allowed to vote. At the close of these addresses the committee voted five to two against the issue and on July 16 recommended to the Senate that it not pass....

During the 1915 legislative session the women were allowed to place in the corridor between the House and Senate chambers a table of suffrage literature. They were permitted to put on the wall a map showing the states that had enfranchised women. In this way they distributed much literature and advertised their cause, but as subsequent events showed, this activity had little influence on the legislators.

When the legislature assembled in June, woman suffrage measures were introduced in both houses. On July 29 the House committee on constitutional amendments conducted hearings. The first speaker, Mrs. Frances Smith Whiteside, said that women could be depended upon to vote right on all questions affecting the advancement of the human race and that they should work side by side with men "not only in domestic life but political life as well." The second speaker, Mrs. Elliott Cheatham, said that women should vote on questions affecting the home and the school system and that they wanted to be enfranchised by the men of Georgia, not by an amendment to the Federal Constitution. Another speaker, Mrs. Rebecca Latimer Felton, told the committee: "I have heard it said that women are too hysterical to enter politics. What do you think of the way men behave at national conventions? I have heard it said that the ballots were a substitute for muskets. Who makes a soldier but the women? I call upon you men to make the women your equal in politics."

Speaking against the measure, Mrs. Mildred Rutherford said she did not want "to see women unsexed and thrown into politics." Also she did not think it "wise to tamper with the Georgia constitution on the question of suffrage when the negro question was unsettled." In support of Miss Rutherford, Mrs. Dolly Blount Lamar urged the committee "not to let the women leave their homes and firesides and enter into a sphere for which they are neither fitted nor educated." At the conclusion of the hearing the committee took no action, but a few days later, on August 3, it voted unanimously against woman suffrage.

On August 3, 1915, the Senate Committee on Constitutional Amendments conducted its hearing. No one spoke in opposition, but Mrs. Mary Latimer McLendon and several other women spoke in favor of the issue. Mrs. McLendon stated that under existing laws Georgia women are placed in the class with lunatics, idiots, paupers, criminals, and aliens and that they should be removed from that category through enfranchisement. After the hearings the committee deliberated for less than five minutes and then voted unanimously against the measure. The following day this action was reported to the Senate, and the suffragists, therefore, failed to win any concessions from the 1915 legislature.

When the legislature assembled in 1916, the suffragists were "greatly disappointed" to find opposition "as strong as ever." Nevertheless, equal suffrage measures were introduced in both houses. In the House of Representatives the matter was referred to the committee on constitutional amendments, which reported it unfavorably. Ed Wohlwender of Muscogee County, one of its chief supporters, tried to have it placed on the calendar in the hope that the House would disagree with the committee report, but he was voted down. In the Senate the suffrage measure met with less success than in the House. When it seemed that that body would ignore it entirely, a delegation appealed to the committee on constitutional amendments for a hearing. The committee scheduled one for August 18, but as the legislature adjourned on August 17, the hearing never took place.

Once again in 1917, suffrage measures were introduced in both houses. On July 19, the House committee on constitutional amendments conducted hearings. As she had in the past, Mrs. Mary Latimer McLendon spoke for suffrage. She told the committee: "All we ask of you is to make us, the other half of humanity, the equal of yourselves. Before we go abroad to teach democracy to other nations, we should first give liberty to our women at home. Miss Rose Ashby, an organizer for the Georgia Woman Suffrage Association, reported that there were 9 million women in the United States and that they needed the protection of the ballot. Mrs. Beatrice Carleton, chairman of the Georgia division of the National Woman's Party, argued that a democracy that barred one-half of its population from a share in governmental affairs was no true democracy.

Miss Caroline Patterson maintained that the majority of the women of Georgia did not want to vote and that it would be undemocratic to force on the majority something that they did not want. Miss Mildred Rutherford stated that the movement originated with the pre-Civil War abolitionists and that it was contrary to Southern ideals. She said that woman suffrage stood no chance in Georgia and that the issue had been raised merely as propaganda for the pending Susan B. Anthony Amendment. After listening to these arguments the committee ruled against the measure and recommended to the House that it not pass.

A few days later the Senate Committee on Constitutional Amendments considered the suffrage question. Among the speakers before the committee was Professor E. L. Martin, who said that women had played an important part in the establishment of the government and that in all justice the franchise should be extended to them. Mrs. Mary Latimer McLendon stated that women suffrage was in accord with the ideals for which the United States was fighting the World War. Mrs. Frances Smith Whiteside said that President Wilson wanted it and called upon the committee to honor him with a favorable report. By a vote of eight to four the committee approved the measure and recommended its passage to the Senate. The suffragists were delighted with this encouraging development, but their victory proved a hollow one, for the Senate adjourned without taking further action....

Additional Sources

Alexander, Adele, *Ambiguous Lives: Free Women of Color in Rural Georgia, 1789–1879*. Fayetteville: University of Arkansas Press, 1991.

Davis, Robert Scott, editor. *Requiem for a Lost City: A Memoir of Civil War Atlanta and the Old South*. Macon GA: Mercer University press, 1999.

Felton, Rebecca L. *My Memoirs of Georgia Politics*. Atlanta: Index Printing Company, 1911.

Marsh, Ben. *Georgia's Frontier Women: Female Fortunes in a Southern Colony*. Athens: University of Georgia Press, 2007.

Spalding, Phinizy, editor. *Women on the Colonial Frontier: A Study of Frederica and Early Georgia*. St. Simons: Fort Frederica Association and National Park Service, 1995.

Talmadge, John E. *Rebecca Latimer Felton: Nine Stormy Decades*. Athens: University of Georgia Press, 1960.

Whites, LeeAnn. *The Civil War as a Crisis in Gender: Augusta, Georgia, 1860–1890*. Athens: University of Georgia Press, 1995.

Chapter 9

RECONSTRUCTION, 1865–1871

Following the Civil War those Southern states that seceded had to be readmitted to the Union, which meant having their representation in Congress returned. The Reconstruction Era was one of the most complex—and at times confusing, chaotic, and violent—periods in American history, and Georgia was no exception. This process of reconstruction in Georgia lasted from 1865 until 1871. Between 1865 and 1871 Georgia seemingly met the requirements of Reconstruction not once, not twice, but three times; rewrote its state constitution twice; ratified the 13th, 14th, and 15th Amendments to the US Constitution; saw the emergence of the Ku Klux Klan with its racial violence; enacted Black Codes; elected black legislators to the General Assembly, expelled them, and reinstated them; moved the capital from Milledgeville to Atlanta; elected a Republican governor and a Republican-controlled General Assembly; had Reconstruction ended; and "redeemed" itself for the Democratic Party. Whew.

The politics of Reconstruction was perhaps the most complex issue. Under the initial plan of reconstruction, commonly called Johnson's Plan of Reconstruction, Georgia rewrote its constitution in 1865, ratified the 13th Amendment, and duly elected senators and representatives to represent the state in Congress. The notable provisions of the Constitution of 1865 were the prohibition of slavery and the voting provision, which gave the right to vote to "free white male citizens of this State." Georgia had seemingly met all the requirements of Reconstruction and fully expected to be represented in Congress when it convened in December 1865.

The Republican-controlled Congress, however, did not seat the Southern senators and representatives and embarked on a course that led to new requirements for readmission into the Union. These new requirements were outlined in the First Reconstruction Act, which passed Congress over President Johnson's veto in March 1867 and included ratification of the 14th Amendment, the registration of voters, and the rewriting of the state constitution yet again. In the summer of 1867 registration boards consisting of three men were formed to register Georgia's voters. The outstanding feature of the registration boards was that they were biracial; one of the three members was an African American man. During winter 1867–1868 the state rewrote its constitution; there were several significant changes in this document. The voting provision was changed from the 1865 constitution to read "male persons born in the United States," the capital was moved to Atlanta, and the constitution assured citizenship and equal protection of the law for blacks. The document did not, however, include a specific statement about the right of blacks to hold office. In July 1868 Georgia ratified the 14th Amendment, completing the requirements of Reconstruction. On July 25, 1868, Congress approved the state's readmission to the Union; Georgia was once again a member of the Union in good standing.

Membership in good standing did not last. Two events took place in September 1868 that earned Georgia the distinction of being kicked out of the Union. The first was the expulsion of the black legislators from the General Assembly. When the General Assembly met in 1868, there were twenty-nine blacks in the House and three in the Senate. Once the state was readmitted to the Union and no longer had the federal government supervising its activities, the white conservative members of the General Assembly began discussing the expulsion of the black legislators. Since there was no provision in the Constitution of 1868 guaranteeing blacks the right to hold office, there was nothing preventing their expulsion. In early September 1868 they were expelled. The second event was perhaps the worst act of racial violence in Georgia during Reconstruction, the Camilla Massacre. On September 19, 1868, a Republican political rally/meeting was scheduled for Camilla, located about 25 miles south of Albany in Mitchell County. Numerous black Republicans traveled from Albany to Camilla. As they reached the town limits they were ambushed by some fifty armed white residents of Camilla, leaving about twelve killed. As a result of these two events, military rule was reinstituted in Georgia; the state was essentially ejected from the Union.

A new set of requirements was established for Georgia's readmission to the Union. In January 1870 the black legislators who were expelled were reinstated, and in February 1870 the state ratified the 15th Amendment. With these acts Georgia had, for the third time, met the requirements of Reconstruction; in July 1870 Congress passed legislation readmitting the state. Georgia was once again, and for the last time, a member of the Union in good standing. The final episode of the politics of the Reconstruction Era took place in 1871. With the removal of federal supervision, Democrats regained control of the state government. A Democratic-controlled General Assembly was elected in December 1870 and a Democratic governor was elected in December 1871. Georgia had been "redeemed."

The social aspects of the Reconstruction Era involve the transition from slavery to freedom. When the 13th Amendment was ratified, the freedmen did not have much going for them in Georgia—a hostile white population and a weak federal agency created to assist them. In 1865 Congress created the Bureau of Refugees, Freedmen, and Abandoned Lands to assist in this transition from slavery to freedom. Unfortunately for the freedmen, the agency did not have a strong presence in Georgia. The most significant accomplishments included the education of the freedmen and temporary possession of lands along the Georgia coast. True social progress for the freedmen in Georgia was inhibited by several agents such as the creation of Black Codes that restricted the activities of the freedpeople, the inherent racism among white Georgians, and the presence of the Ku Klux Klan. Intimidation at the polls and systematic violence were the hallmarks of Klan activity in Georgia.

DOCUMENTS

The first document below is an order from General William T. Sherman that set aside land along the Georgia coast for the freedpeople. Documents 2 and 3 are important provisions in the constitutions of 1865 and 1868. The fourth document is a formal protest from black legislators after their expulsion from the General Assembly. Document 5 is a report from Colonel O. H. Howard on the Camilla Massacre. The sixth document is the Congressional resolution that admitted Georgia into the Union for the last time. The final document is an excerpt from the Congressional testimony of John B. Gordon, long recognized as the leader of the Ku Klux Klan in Georgia.

1. Sherman's Special Field Orders, No. 15[1]

In the Field, Savannah, Ga., January 16, 1865
Special Field Orders, No. 15
I. The islands from Charleston south, the abandoned rice-fields along the rivers for thirty miles back from the sea, and the country bordering the Saint John's River, Fla., are reserved and set apart for the settlement of the negroes

---

[1] From *War of the Rebellion: A Compilation of the Official Records of the Union and Confederate Armies*, ser. 1, pt. 2, vol. 47 (Washington, DC: Government Printing Office, 1880–1901).

now made free by the acts of war and the proclamation of the President of the United States.

II. At Beaufort, Hilton Head, Savannah, Fernandina, Saint Augustine, and Jacksonville the blacks may remain in their chosen or accustomed vocations; but on the islands, and in the settlements hereafter to be established, no white person whatever, unless military officers and soldiers detailed for duty, will be permitted to reside; and the sole and exclusive management of affairs will be left to the freed people themselves, subject only to the United States military authority and the acts of Congress. By the laws of war and orders of the President of the United States the negro is free, and must be dealt with as such....

III. Whenever three respectable negroes, heads of families, shall desire to settle on land, and shall have selected for that purpose an island, or a locality clearly defined within the limits above designated, the inspector of settlements and plantations will himself, or by such subordinate officer as he may appoint, give them a license to settle such island or district, and afford them such assistance as he can to enable them to establish a peaceable agricultural settlement. The three parties named will subdivide the land, under the supervision of the inspector, among themselves and such others as may choose to settle near them, so that each family shall have a plot of not more than forty acres of tillable ground, and when it borders on some water channel with not more than 800 feet water front, in the possession of which land the military authorities will afford them protection until such time as they can protect themselves or until Congress shall regulate their title....

V. In order to carry out this system of settlement a general officer will be detailed as inspector of settlements and plantations, whose duty it shall be to visit the settlements, to regulate their police and general management, and who will furnish personally to each head of a family, subject to the approval of the President of the United States, a possessory title in writing, giving as near as possible the description of boundaries, and who shall adjust all claims or conflicts that may arise under the same, subject to the like approval, treating such titles altogether as possessory....

VI. Brig. Gen. R. Saxton is hereby appointed inspector of settlements and plantations and will at once enter on the performance of his duties....

By order of Maj. Gen. W. T. Sherman

2. Constitution of 1865[2]

Preamble

We, the people of the State of Georgia, in order to form a permanent Government, establish justice, insure domestic tranquility, and secure the blessings of liberty to ourselves and our posterity, acknowledging and invoking the guidance of Almighty God, the author of all good government, do ordain and establish this Constitution for the State of Georgia.

Article 1

Declaration of Rights

1. Protection to person and property is the duty of government.

2. No person shall be deprived of life, liberty, or property, except by due process of law.

3. The writ of Habeas Corpus shall not be suspended, unless, in case of rebellion or invasion, the public safety may require it.

...6. Freedom of speech, and freedom of the press, are inherent elements of political liberty. But while every citizen may freely speak or write, or print on any subject, he shall be responsible for the abuse of liberty.

...13. Legislative Acts in violation of the Constitution are void, and the Judiciary shall so declare them.

...20. The Government of the United States having, as a war measure, proclaimed all slaves held or owned in this State, emancipated from slavery, and having carried that proclamation into full practical effect, there shall henceforth be, within the State of Georgia, neither slavery nor involuntary servitude, save as a punishment for crime, after legal conviction thereof; provided, this acquiescence in the action of the Government of the United States is not intended to operate as a relinquishment, waiver, or estoppel of such claim for compensation of loss sustained by reason of the emancipation of his slaves, as any citizen of Georgia may hereafter make upon the justice and magnanimity of that Government.

Article 2

Legislative Department

Section I

1. The Legislative, Executive, and Judicial Departments shall be distinct, and each department shall be confided to a separate body of magistracy....

2. The Legislative power shall be vested in a General Assembly, which shall consist of a Senate and House of Representatives, the members whereof shall be

---

[2] From *Acts of the General Assembly of the State of Georgia*, 1865.

elected, and returns of the election made, in the manner now prescribed by law....

Section II

1. There shall be forty-four Senatorial Districts in the State of Georgia, each composed of three contiguous Counties, from each of which Districts one Senator shall be chosen, until otherwise arranged....

2. No person shall be a Senator who shall not have attained to the age of twenty-five years and be a citizen of the United States, and have been for three years an inhabitant of this State, and for one year a resident of the District from which he is chosen.

Section III

1. The House of Representatives shall be composed as follows: The thirty-seven counties having the largest representative population shall have two Representatives each; every other county shall have one Representative. The designation of the Counties having two representatives shall be made by the General Assembly immediately after the taking of each census.

2. No person shall be a Representative who shall not have attained to the age of twenty-one years, and be a citizen of the United States, and have been for three years an inhabitant of this State, and for one year a resident of the County which he represents.

...5. All bills for raising revenue or appropriating money, shall originate in the House of Representatives, but the Senate may propose or concur in amendments, as in other bills.

Section V

...5. It shall be the duty of the General Assembly at its next session, and thereafter as the public welfare may require, to provide by law for the government of free persons of color, or the protection and security of their persons and property...; for the legalizing of their existing....

Article 3

Executive Department

Section I

1. The Executive power shall be vested in a Governor, the first of whom, under this Constitution, shall hold the office from the time of his inauguration, as by law provided, until the election and qualification of his successor. Each Governor subsequently elected shall hold the office for two years, and until his successor shall be elected and qualified, and shall not be eligible to reselection, after the expiration of a second term, for the period of four years....

3. No person shall be eligible to the office of Governor who shall not have been a citizen of the United States twelve years, and an inhabitant of this State six years, and who hath not attained the age of thirty years.

Section II

...9. The Great Seal of the State shall be deposited in the office of the Secretary of State, and shall not be affixed to any instrument of writing, but by order of the Governor or General Assembly, and that used previously to the year 1861, shall be the Great Seal of the State.

Article 4

Judicial Department

Section I

...2. The Supreme Court shall consist of three judges, who shall be elected by the General Assembly, for such term of years not less than six as shall be prescribed by law....

Article 5

Miscellaneous Provisions

Section I

1. The electors of members of the General Assembly shall be free white male citizens of this State, and shall have attained the age of twenty-one years, and have paid all taxes which may have been required of them...and no person not qualified to vote for members of the General Assembly shall hold any office in this State.

...9. The marriage relation between white persons and persons of African descent, is forever prohibited, and such marriage shall be null and void....

...11. This Constitution shall be altered or amended only by a convention of the people, called for that purpose by act of the General Assembly.

Herschel V. Johnson, President. Signed Nov. 7th, 1865.

3. Constitution of 1868[3]

Preamble

We, the people of Georgia, in order to form a permanent government, establish justice, insure domestic tranquility, and secure the blessings of liberty to ourselves and our posterity, acknowledging and invoking the guidance of Almighty God, the author of all good government, do ordain and establish this constitution for the State of Georgia.

Article 1

Declaration of Fundamental Principles

---

[3] From *Acts of the General Assembly of the State of Georgia*, 1868.

...Section 2. All persons born or naturalized in the United States, and resident in this State, are hereby declared citizens of this State, and no laws shall be made or enforced which shall abridge the privileges or immunities of citizens of the United States, or of this State, or deny to any person within its jurisdiction the equal protection of its laws. And it shall be the duty of the General Assembly, by appropriate legislation, to protect every person in the due enjoyment of the rights, privileges, and immunities guaranteed in this section.

...Section 4. There shall be within the State of Georgia neither slavery nor involuntary servitude, save as a punishment for crime after legal conviction thereof.

...Section 9. Freedom of speech and freedom of the press are inherent elements of political liberty. But while every citizen may freely speak, write, or print on any subject, he shall be responsible for the abuse of the liberty.

...Section 11. The social status of the citizen shall never be the subject of legislation....

...Section 22. Whipping, as a punishment for crime, is prohibited.

Section 23. No lottery shall be authorized, or sale of lottery-ticket allowed, in this State, and adequate penalties for such sale shall be provided by law.

...Section 33. The State of Georgia shall ever remain a member of the American Union; the people thereof are a part of the American nation; every citizen thereof owes paramount allegiance to the Constitution and Government of the United States, and no law or ordinance of this State, in contravention or subversion thereof, shall ever have any binding force.

Article 2

Franchise and Elections

...Section 2. Every male person born in the United States and every male person who has been naturalized, or who has legally declared his intention to become a citizen of the United States, twenty-one years old or upward, who shall have resided in this State six months next preceding the election, and shall have resided thirty days in the county in which he offers to vote, and shall have paid all taxes which may have been required of him, and which he may have had an opportunity of paying, agreeably to law, for the year next preceding the election (except as herein provided), shall be deemed an elector....

Section 5. No person who, after the adoption of this constitution, being a resident of this State, shall engage in a duel in this State, or elsewhere, or shall send or accept a challenge, or be aider or abetter to such duel, shall vote or hold office in this State, and every such person shall also be subject to such punishment as the law may prescribe.

...Section 8. The sale of intoxicating liquors on days of election is prohibited.

Article 3

Legislative Department

Section 1. One. The legislative power shall be vested in a general assembly, which shall consist of a senate and house of representatives....

Section 1. Two. The members of the senate shall be elected for four years, except that the members elected at the first election from the twenty-two senatorial districts numbered in this constitution with odd numbers, shall only hold their office for two years....

Section 2. One. There shall be forty-four senatorial districts in this State, composed each of three contiguous counties, from each of which districts one senator shall be chosen....

Section 3. One. The house of representatives shall consist of one hundred and seventy-five representatives, apportioned as follows: to the six largest counties, to wit, Chatham, Richmond, Fulton, Bibb, Houston, and Burke, three representatives each; to the thirty-one next largest, to wit, Bartow, Columbia, Cobb, Coweta, Clarke, Decatur, Dougherty, Floyd, Gwinnett, Greene, Hancock, Harris, Jefferson, Lee, Muscogee, Monroe, Meriwether, Morgan, Macon, Newton, Oglethorpe, Pulaski, Randolph, Sumter, Stewart, Troup, Thomas, Talbot, Washington, Wilkes, and Warren, two representatives each; and to the remaining ninety-five counties, one representatives each.

Section 4. One. Each house shall be the judge of the election, returns, and qualifications of its members, and shall have power to punish them for disorderly behavior, or misconduct by censure, fine, imprisonment, or expulsion; but no member shall be expelled except by a vote of two-thirds of the house from which he is expelled....

Section 4. Ten. Every senator, or representative, before taking his seat, shall take an oath, or affirmation, to support the Constitution of the United States, and of this State....

Article 4

Executive Department

Section 1. One. The executive power shall be vested in a governor, who shall hold his office during the term of four years, and until such time as a successor shall be chosen and qualified....

Section 1. Two. After the first election, the governor shall be elected quadrennially by the persons qualified to vote for members of the general assembly....

Article 5

Judicial Department

Section 1. The judicial powers of this State shall be vested in a supreme court, superior courts, courts of ordinary, justices of the peace, commissioned notaries public, and such other courts as have been or may be established by law....

Section 2. ...Two. The supreme court shall have no original jurisdiction, but shall be a court alone for the trial and correction of errors from the superior courts and from the city courts of Savannah and Augusta, and such other like courts as may be here after established in other cities....

Section 9. One. The judges of the supreme and the superior courts, the attorney-general, solicitors-general, and the district judges and attorneys, shall be appointed by the governor, with the advice and consent of the senate, and shall be removable by the governor on the address of two-thirds of each branch of the general assembly, or by impeachment and conviction thereon.

...Section 17. ...Two. All contracts made and not executed during the late rebellion, with the intention and for the purpose of aiding and encouraging said rebellion, or where it was the purpose and intention of any one of the parties to such contract to aid or encourage such rebellion, and that fact was known to the other party, whether said contract was made by any person or corporation with the State or Confederate States, or by a corporation with a natural person, or between two or more natural persons, are hereby declared to have been and to be illegal, and all bonds, deeds, promissory notes, bills, or other evidences of debt, made or executed by the parties to such contract or either of them, in connection with such illegal contract, or as the consideration therefore or in furtherance thereof, are hereby declared null and void....

Article 6

Education

One. The general assembly, at its first session after the adoption of this constitution, shall provide a thorough system of general education, to be forever free to all children of the State, the expense of which shall be provided for by taxation or otherwise....

Article 10

Seat of Government

One. The seat of government of this State, from and after the date of the ratification of this constitution, shall be the city of Atlanta, and the general assembly shall provide for the erection of a new capitol, and such other buildings as the public welfare may require....

4. Black Legislators Protest Their Expulsion from General Assembly[4]

House of Representatives, September 3, 1868

To the Speaker and Members of the House of Representatives:

This House having decided by a vote this day, to expel the undersigned members from the seats to which they have been legally elected, from no improper conduct on their part, and for no other legal reason, or pretended cause, except their color, the undersigned ardently desiring the peace of society, and the prosperity of the State, and determined to do all in their power to avoid bloodshed or a war of the races, have decided to suffer wrong for a time, rather than to attempt to redress them in a manner that may, in this time of high political excitement, produce civil strife.

For these considerations the undersigned will *abide* the decision of this House, and will peaceably retire from the seats to which they consider themselves legally elected.

But before doing so, the undersigned, as the representatives of their race, consisting of over five hundred thousand citizens, and over ninety thousand legal electors, of this State, in the State whose peaceful citizens they are, whose laws they have obeyed, and whose white women and children they have supported and protected when their fathers and brothers were upon distant battle-fields, in the service of the Confederate States; in the name of justice and that equality before the laws to which they are entitled; in the name of peace and humanity, without which anarchy and confusion might take the place of good government, stability and protection of life and property, and in the name of that friendship and good understanding, which it is their interest and their ardent desire to cultivate with the white race, do hereby *enter their solemn protest* against the outrage perpetrated upon their race by the action of this House; and they hereby give notice that they will appeal, at the proper time, to the Congress of the United States and the justice of the American people, to redress their grievances, to which they are subjected by the intolerant and oppressive conduct of the dominant party in this House, who, while part of their members were in danger of losing their seats on account of ineligibility under the Fourteenth Constitutional Amendment, were met by the colored members of this House in a spirit of conciliation and kindness during that investigation:

But who, when they had obtained an erroneous decision of the House in their favor, which enabled them to retain seats, to which under the Constitution

---

[4] From *Atlanta Daily New Era*, September 10, 1868.

of the United States, they are not entitled, on account of their participation in the rebellion, forgetting that Congress has power, under said Constitutional Amendment, to pass all laws and establish all courts or tribunals necessary to carry out said Amendment, and that by the judgment of such tribunals they may yet be compelled to vacate seats illegally held by them who now make war on the rights of colored members and drive them from this Hall.

The undersigned respectfully demand that this, their protest, be entered upon the Journal of the House.

Name County Represented

Phillip Joiner	Dougherty
Edwin Belcher	Wilkes
Mat. Davis	Clarke
Thomas P. Beard	Richmond
Thomas M. Allen	Jasper
Alexander Stone	Jefferson
Henry M. Turner	Bibb
Peter O'Neal	Baldwin
Abram Colby	Green
T. H. Fyall	Macon
J. T. Costin	Talbot
James Porter	Chatham
James M. Simms	Chatham
W. L. Houston	Bryan
G. H. Clower	Monroe
W. A. Golding	Liberty
George Linder	Laurens
Robert Lumpkin	Macon
S. Gardner	Warren
A. Richardson	Clarke
A. Smith	Muscogee
Munday Floyd	Morgan
E. C. Barnes	Hancock
John Warren	Burke
M. Claiborne	Burke
Samuel Williams	Harris
W. H. Harrison	Hancock
R. Moore	Columbia

5. Colonel O. H. Howard Reports on
the Camilla Massacre[5]

Sept. 19th, 1868, 7 P.M.

At 6 P.M. Ishmael Lunnon, freed. Reported himself directly from Camilla, Mitchell Co. that he left there at 2 P.M. That in the forenoon of this day he approached Camilla with John Murphy Wm. P. Pierce and F. F. Putney, whites and about seventy five colored persons, all enroute to Camilla, where Messers Pierce and Murphy were to deliver a political address—

Upon approaching Camilla, the relator being in the advance was accosted by an armed and mounted white man who at first stated that he was in search of a "Doctor" to attend to a Freedman who had been injured by the falling of a tree, but who subsequently stated that he was a "Courier" and advised the relator and others of the party who had overtaken him, not to go to Town, that the people there were determined that the Radicals should not speak in Camilla— That not withstanding the warning the party moved on towards Camilla when they were met by the Sheriff and a posse who accosted Capt. Pierce and who was assured by Capt. Pierce that he desired and intended to speak in Camilla on political subjects, the Sheriff endeavored to dissuade him from doing so, telling him that the people would not permit it— That the Sheriff then went back into Camilla and again returned saying that he had done all in his power to dissuade the people from violence, but with no avail— That the party moved on to the Town, that Pierce and Putney entered the Town, dismounted from their Buggy and hitched their horses at the Court House— That as the wagon containing the music of the party entered the Town it was fired upon by the mounted man who had first accosted him, and by several other white men, that the freedmen then started to escape to the woods, that Pierce attempted to rally them calling on them not to fly, that the Colored men being unarmed would not stop. The relator being mounted dashed out of the Town past the freedmen on foot and past the musicians who had abandoned their wagon....

At 6:30 P.M. a large body of freedmen much excited, came to me for advice, expressing their desire to proceed at once on foot to Camilla to the rescue of the Republicans there—I counselled and ordered and directed them to say to all colored men from me that the affair at Camilla should be thoroughly investigated, and if any great wrong has been done the proper legal remedy should be applied— They departed in peace apparently satisfied....

---

[5] From Records of the Assistant Commissioner for Georgia, Bureau of Refugees, Freedmen, and Abandoned Lands, 1865–1870, National Archives, Washington, DC.

At 1 A.M. Charles Rose (freed) from Field & Flaggs plantation— He reports Sewis Davis (freed) wounded & shot

Howard Bruce (freed) shot in the head

Mr. Murphy wounded in the head by the butt of a musket

The man that plays the bass drum William Durand shot

Squire Ace (freed) shot off his horse supposed to be killed

One woman with child killed

Wesley Chatman (freed) one of the drummers was shot in the back, is now in Albany

Wm. P. Pierce (white) candidate for Congress 2nd Dist. Shot in the leg and is at Fish & Flagg plantation

F. F. Putney (white) serious gun shot wounds in arm and shoulders

John Murphy (white) struck over the head with butt of Gun, head badly cut

Howard Bruce (freed) serious gun shot wounds (five) in arms side & head

William Dessand (freed) badly wounded supposed to be killed. Gun shot wound in back & shoulder

A. B. Collins (freed) supposed to be mortally wounded

Severel men (freed) names unknown gun shot wounds

Six (6) men (freed) reported to be left dead at the roadside

One woman with a child in her arms shot (freed)

Four white men of the attacking party seen to fall shot....

I am confident that the preceding pages numbered contain a correct account of the affair at Camilla, and subsequent events so far as known.

Signed

O. H. Howard

6. Reconstruction Ended in Georgia[6]

An Act Relating to the State of Georgia

Whereas great irregularities have been practiced in the organization of the legislature in the State of Georgia, both in its first organization and in the expulsion of certain members, as well, also, as in its reorganization since the act of December last: Therefore,

Sec. 1. *Be it enacted by the Senate and House of Representatives of the United States of America in Congress assembled,* That the State of Georgia having complied with the reconstruction acts, and the fourteenth and fifteenth articles

---

[6] From United States House of Representatives, Resolution 1335 (1870).

of amendments to the Constitution of the United States having been ratified in good faith by a legal legislature of said State, it is hereby declared that the State of Georgia is entitled to representation in the Congress of the United States. But nothing in this act contained shall be construed to deprive the people of Georgia of the right to an election for members of the general assembly of said State as provided for in the constitution thereof and nothing in this or any other act of Congress shall be construed to affect the term to which any officer has been appointed, or any member of the general assembly elected, as prescribed by the constitution of the State of Georgia.

Sec. 2. *And be it further enacted,* That so much of the act entitled 'An act making appropriations for the support of the army for the year ending June thirty, eighteen hundred and sixty-eight, and for other purposes,' approved March two, eighteen hundred and sixty-seven, as prohibits the organization, arming, or calling into service of the militia forces in the States of Georgia, Mississippi, Texas, and Virginia, be, and the same is hereby repealed.

Approved, July 15, 1870

7. John B. Gordon Testifies on the Ku Klux Klan in Georgia[7]

Washington, D.C., July 27, 1871

Question: What do you know of any combinations in Georgia, known as Ku-Klux, or by any other name, who have been violating the law?

Answer: I do not know anything about any Ku-Klux organization, as the papers talk about it. I have never heard of anything of that sort except in the papers and by general report; but I do know that an organization did exist in Georgia at one time. I know that in 1868—I think that was the time—I was approached and asked to attach myself to a secret organization in Georgia. I was approached by some of the very best citizens of the State—some of the most peaceful, law-abiding men, men of large property, who had large interests in the State. The object of this organization was explained to me at the time by these parties; and I want to say that I approved of it most heartily. I would approve again of a similar organization, under the same state of circumstances.

Question: Tell us about what that organization was.

---

[7] From *Report of the Joint Select Committee to Inquire into the Condition of Affairs in the Late Insurrectionary States*, vol. 8 (Washington, DC: Government Printing Office, 1872).

Answer: The organization was simply this—nothing more and nothing less: it was an organization, a brotherhood of the property-holders, the peaceable, law-abiding citizens of the State, for self-protection. The instinct of self-protection prompted that organization; the sense of insecurity and danger, particularly in those neighborhoods where the negro population largely predominated. The reasons which led to this organization were three or four. The first and main reason was the organization of the Union League, as they called it, about which we knew nothing more than this: that the negroes would desert the plantations, and go off at night in large numbers; and on being asked where they had been, would reply, sometimes, "We have been to the muster;" sometimes, "We have been to the lodge;" sometimes, "We have been to the meeting." These things were observed for a great length of time. We knew that the "carpet-baggers," as the people of Georgia called these men who came from a distance and had no interest at all with us; who were unknown to us entirely; who from all we could learn about them did not have any very exalted positions at their homes—these men were organizing the colored people. We knew that beyond all question. We knew of certain instances where great crime had been committed; where overseers had been driven from plantations, and the negroes had asserted their right to hold the property for their own benefit. Apprehension took possession of the entire public mind of the State. Men were in many instances afraid to go away from their homes and leave their wives and children, for fear of outrages. Rapes were already being committed in the country. There was this general organization of the black race on the one hand, and an entire disorganization of the white race on the other hand. We were afraid to have a public organization; because we supposed it would be construed at once, by the authorities at Washington, as an organization antagonistic to the Government of the United States. It was therefore necessary, in order to protect our families from outrage and preserve our own lives, to have something that we could regard as a brotherhood—a combination of the best men of the country, to act purely in self-defense, to repel the attack in case we should be attacked by these people. That was the whole object of this organization. I never heard of any disguises connected with it; we had none, very certainly. This organization, I think, extended nearly all over the State. It was, as I say, as organization purely for self-defense. It had no more politics in it than the organization of the Masons. I never heard the idea of politics suggested in connection with it....

Question: You had no riding about at night?

Answer: None on earth. I have no doubt that such things have occurred in Georgia. It is notoriously stated—I have no personal knowledge of anything of the kind, but I have reason to believe it—that disguised parties have committed outrages in Georgia; but we have discovered in some cases that these disguised parties did not belong to any particular party....

Question: The killing of Ashburn has been alluded to once or twice by witnesses before the committee. State what you know about the circumstances of that case.

Answer: I do not know anything about the killing of Ashburn, except that he was killed by parties in Columbus, and that the general feeling in Columbus is that he was killed by members of his own party, in which there was a division at that time. This I give simply as public rumor; the public rumor is that there had been a split in his party, among some negroes and others; that there was a great deal of bitterness between the two factions; and the general belief was that Ashburn's life was taken by members of his own party....

ESSAYS

Sherman's Reservation in Georgia[8]

Paul A. Cimbala

The Georgia coast was an avenue to freedom even before Sherman completed his famous march from Atlanta to the sea, emerging from the Georgia interior in late 1864. From spring 1862 on, Union naval guns kept the abandoned plantations on the sea islands open to black refugees. Yet Sherman's special field order of January 16, 1865, was important because it held out to the ex-slaves a formal promise that their Yankee allies would recognize their desire for land of their own.

Sherman's order set aside land for the use of former slaves in an exclusively black reservation running along the Atlantic coast south from Charleston, South Carolina, down through the land between the coast and the St. Johns River in the northernmost counties of Florida. Additionally, the order included in the reservation land along the rivers that nurtured the region's rice plantations up to 30 miles inland from the coast. The order specified that freedmen could request permission to settle an island or an area of land within

---

[8] From Paul A. Cimbala, "The Freedmen's Bureau, the Freedmen, and Sherman's Grant in Reconstruction Georgia, 1865–1867," *Journal of Southern History* 45/4 (November 1989): 597–632. Reprinted with permission.

this reservation when "three respectable negroes, heads of families" came together for that purpose. Once the "inspector of plantations and settlements," as Sherman designated the officer in charge of the area and of the process by which the ex-slaves would settle it, approved the request, the freedmen could claim their land and subdivide it among themselves and any other freedmen who wished to settle near them, allotting no more than 40 acres of tillable ground to each family.

Sherman's promise of homesteads for the freedmen, however, was intentionally limited. The freedmen could not claim their land in fee simple, for Sherman ordered his officer-in-charge to give to the claimants "possessory titles," titles that acknowledged their right to work the land and enjoy the products of their labor but fell short of conveying ownership. Consequently, his order made no stipulations about how long the freedmen would be able to stay on the land or how much they would have to pay in order to purchase it. Sherman preferred to allow Congress to deal with such matters while he went about the business of fighting a war, now free of the troublesome train of black refugees who had followed him through the Georgia interior.

Vaguely defined possessory titles would cause problems in the near future. So too would the freedmen's failure to carry out the requirements for claiming land in the neat, orderly fashion prescribed by Sherman—a majority probably presented government officials with a fait accompli, forcing those officials to try to make the records agree with the reality of settlement in the reservation. Nevertheless, no matter what the titles actually conveyed to the freedmen, they undoubtedly encouraged those who held one or hoped to receive one to assume that the government had acknowledged their right to the land. Furthermore, Sherman charged Brigadier General Rufus Saxton with the execution of the provisions of the special field order, an appointment that guaranteed a vigorous commitment to the spirit of the order....

As inspector of plantations and settlements and, after May 20, 1865, Freedmen's Bureau assistant commissioner for South Carolina, Georgia, and, briefly, Florida, Saxton vigorously pursued his charge. Before the summer of 1865 he had placed agents in the Ogeechee district (an area along the Ogeechee and the Little Ogeechee rivers in Chatham County near Savannah), in Savannah, and on St. Catherines and St. Simons islands. In June, when he first reported to General Oliver Otis Howard, commissioner of the Freedmen's Bureau, he estimated that his efforts had settled 40,000 ex-slaves on 400,000 acres within the swath of land subject to Sherman's order. Saxton also hoped to secure abandoned property on mainland Georgia for the freedmen's use, taking his cue from the bureau's enabling legislation that authorized it to rent and to sell abandoned or confiscated property to the freedmen. By all indications Saxton meant to fulfill Sherman's promise.

...during the spring and summer of 1865, the freedmen who took up their Sherman lands, whether duly registered or not, gave their former masters and the federal government sufficient notice by their actions that they intended to stay on the land. Furthermore, the handful of Freedmen's Bureau officials who supervised the transition from slavery to freedom encouraged the ex-slaves to explore the potential of their new status. Consequently, the federal agents strengthened the freedmen's belief that the government would support their cause....

In addition to organizing community affairs, the freedmen established agricultural routines. During spring and summer 1865 the Ogeechee blacks who cultivated the rice plantations in the district continued to farm the land quite productively "in concert" instead of working on the individual plots to which they were entitled. That productivity and the communal approach to labor reflected the freedmen's sense of proprietorship. They were on land, most likely on old plantation homes that they had formerly worked by the task system, that was now under their control....

Even as some refugees completed the construction of their log and tabby dwellings on the islands, there were indications that the freedmen's claim to the reservation was not entirely secure. During spring and summer 1865 Saxton and his officers sparred with the military authorities over the implementation of Sherman's special field order. The assistant commissioner also had no success in expanding the distribution of abandoned and confiscable property to the rest of Georgia in accordance with the provisions of the Freedmen's Bureau law. There simply were no such plantations identifiable by the time the bureau began to establish itself on the mainland outside the reservation.

More important as disturbing omens were the battles being waged in Washington. During the summer, Commissioner Howard engaged President Andrew Johnson in a paper duel over the definition of confiscable and abandoned property. By September 12 the president had effectively nullified the section of the Bureau's enabling law concerning the distribution of land to the freedmen.

Changes were also taking place in the Georgia bureau. During August, Commissioner Howard began to consider giving the state its own assistant commissioner because of the difficulty the agency was experiencing in establishing a respected and effective presence outside the reservation. On September 22 general Davis Tillson, a veteran of the Tennessee bureau and a strong advocate of a free labor system based on contracts, became the Freedmen's Bureau assistant commissioner in Georgia. Until the end of 1865, however, Saxton retained control over the Georgia grant lands, a jurisdictional division that Tillson recognized. In the meantime, Saxton clearly refused to believe that Howard's Circular No. 15 of September 12, which embodied the president's lenient land restoration policy, had anything to do with Sherman's grant.

Not everyone accepted Saxton's interpretation of the signals coming from the nation's capital. Planters who during the war had abandoned lands now in the reservation believed that they were entitled to the same consideration as those who were regaining land that was unencumbered by Sherman's special field orders. Once these planters made their acts of contrition, they expected restoration of their property.

Unfortunately for the freedmen, the numerous applications for the restoration of estates and the uncompromising fealty of Rufus Saxton to Sherman's order did not escape the attention of the ever-absolving President Johnson. In October 1865 he ordered Commissioner Howard to proceed to South Carolina, Georgia, and Florida to bring about "mutually satisfactory" arrangements between planters and freedmen on the Sherman lands. On October 19 Howard issued orders that recognized the right of the pardoned planters to petition for the restoration of their lands in the reservation, providing they pledged the current crop to the freedmen who had raised it and made equitable contracts with the freedmen for the next season. Word of Howard's activities preceded him to Savannah, and by the time he arrived there in mid-October a white resident reported that the freedmen "are all in despair at not having any land....plantations are to be restored at once." "At once," however, was a phrase open to interpretation....

Black Politicians in Reconstruction Georgia[9]

Edmund L. Drago

Like Henry Turner, many of Georgia's black politicians derived much of their influence over the freedmen from their role as religious leaders. Even Aaron Bradley, although he was not a preacher, launched his political career in Savannah churches, and the black church remained the focal point of black political activity throughout Reconstruction. It provided both the political

---

[9] From Edmund L. Drago, *Black Politicians and Reconstruction in Georgia: A Splendid Failure* (Baton Rouge: Louisiana State University Press, 1983). Used with permission from Louisiana State University Press.

leadership and the organization necessary to mobilize black voters. According to conservatives, black preachers "control them [the blacks], and their preaching is often political in character." White Republicans, on the other hand, thought that the preachers retained such popularity among the freedmen because "they are to some extent representative men; there is no doubt about that. They are generally a little better educated than the mass of the negro race."

The relationship between the pulpit and politics was not always harmonious. Some blacks resented their ministers' involvement in politics. After Bryan County Baptist minister Ulysses L. Houston won a seat in the assembly in 1868, his parishioners became angry over his absence from church affairs, as well as apprehensive at the hostility his political activity was engendering among local whites....

Georgia's black politicians also looked to other than religious sources for their political ideology. The Declaration of Independence was especially favored, and black conventions rang with the rhetoric of the American Revolution. In terms reminiscent of Jefferson's indictment of George III, a black gathering in 1868 castigated its political enemies:

> They have expelled our colored legislators in violation to the Constitution and laws....
>
> They then refused to allow their protests to go on the Journals of the House.
>
> They have robbed us of the right to be jurors....
>
> They have inaugurated strife and discord between white and colored citizens.
>
> They have demoralized society....
>
> They have refused to require common carriers to give us respectable accommodations, when we pay equal rates....
>
> They have voted down every measure for the establishment of schools for the education of our children....
>
> They have not only invaded our political rights, but nullified by prejudicial legislation, our civil rights.
>
> They have given indirect countenance to the murdering bands of the KKK....

Similarly, Albany blacks justified federal intervention in Georgia on the grounds that "the State government does not answer for the purpose for which it was established, protection and justice for all."

Most black politicians also adopted the "free soil, free speech, free labor, and free men" ideology of the Northern Republicans. "This is the day of gratitude for the freedom of labor," Henry Turner told Augusta blacks celebrating the Emancipation Proclamation in January, 1866. "Heretofore, our chief study was how to do the least work possible and escape punishment. Labor was not sweetened by reward—it was forced from us then." Three years later, a black labor convention proclaimed "its unqualified admiration of the doctrine which asserts the dignity of labor and holds up an honest laborer as the noblest work of God." It likewise declared that "the laborer is the life of the country" and extolled "the men whose brawny arms and skilled hands feed and clothe humanity."

As radical Reconstruction progressed, black political leaders from other institutions, including the army, the Freedmen's Bureau, and the Union League, began to come into prominence. Edwin Belcher, for example, came to Georgia as an officer in the Union army and later became a bureau agent. In 1868 he developed a sufficient following among Wilkes County blacks to get himself elected to the assembly. Lacking the pulpit, some black leaders used the Union League for their entry into politics. George Wallace, for example, joined the Macon league in 1868 and proceeded to organize similar associations throughout the state. That year he was one of a handful of blacks elected to the state senate. Jefferson Long, the state's only black congressman, was president of the Macon league....

The three most popular black legislators were Tunis Campbell, Sr., Henry Turner, and Aaron Bradley, all of whom spent time in the North. Like Campbell, Turner was a minister-politician. A relentless campaigner, Turner drew thousands of blacks into the AME (African Methodist Episcopal) church and the Republican party. As the organizing force behind most of the black conventions, he became Georgia's leading black reconstructionist. Aaron Bradley was never popular with Turner, Campbell, and the rest of the black political elite, but he established a strong and loyal following among the ex-slaves living on the river plantations outside Savannah. Once, when authorities arrested him, a local newspaper correctly predicted that his imprisonment would only add "the éclat of a successful knight militant to his previous reputation among his followers for serene saintship." In 1870 this "knight militant" split with the regular Republicans of Chatham County; he encouraged 1,500 of his supporters to nominate a predominantly black ticket to oppose the regulars.

All three of these charismatic leaders used the church as a rallying point. "Mr. Campbell's influence is great with the majority of the colored people," a federal army officer observed, "they gaze upon him as...a demigod...and they almost worship him and follow him withersoever he leads." Given the turmoil of the war, emancipation, and Reconstruction, times were ripe for the emergence of such men....

Additional Sources

Cimbala, Paul A. *Under the Guardianship of the Nation: The Freedmen's Bureau and the Reconstruction of Georgia, 1865–1870*. Athens: University of Georgia Press, 1997.

Conway, Alan. *The Reconstruction of Georgia*. Minneapolis: University of Minnesota Press, 1966.

Drago, Edmund L. *Black Politicians and Reconstruction in Georgia: A Splendid Failure*. Athens: University of Georgia Press, 1992.

Duncan, Russell. *Freedom's Shore: Tunis Campbell and the Georgia Freedmen*. Athens: University of Georgia Press, 1986.

Duncan, Russell. *Entrepreneur for Equality: Governor Rufus Bullock, Commerce, and Race in Post-Civil War Georgia*. Athens: University of Georgia Press, 1994.

Jones, Jacqueline. *Soldiers of Light and Love: Northern Teachers and Georgia Blacks, 1865–1873*. Chapel Hill: University of North Carolina Press, 1980.

Nathans, Elizabeth Studley. *Losing the Peace: Georgia Republicans and Reconstruction, 1865–1871*. Baton Rouge: Louisiana State University Press, 1968.

Chapter 10

POSTWAR POLITICS AND ECONOMICS, 1865–1890

Following the Civil War, the state's economy was in shambles. In addition to the physical destruction, Georgia's railroads suffered losses of hundreds of miles of track (Georgia had only 1,400 miles of railroad track in 1860), torn up by both Union and Confederate troops, state bonds were virtually worthless, Georgia had a $20 million debt, and three-quarters of all of Georgia's wealth (about $272 million) vanished with the ratification of the 13th Amendment. In the immediate aftermath of the war Georgia had to rebuild its economy.

Georgia's prewar economy was largely agricultural and would remain so after the war; there was little to no industry in the state and much of what existed in 1860 was destroyed in the war. Perhaps the most important issue facing the state's agricultural economy was replacing the labor of the 462,000 slaves who were emancipated by the war. In Georgia as in most of the Southern states, the tenant system would replace the slave system. Tenant farming, or sharecropping (the terms can be used interchangeably), was designed as a temporary solution to the labor problems in the South. There were two primary labor problems: 1) with the abolition of slavery, who would work the region's farms; and 2) what work would the former slaves perform? The tenant system would resolve both issues. The problems with the tenant system were that it was not temporary but became permanent, and sharecropping, rather than solving the labor problems, became the problem. Rather than decreasing over time, the tenancy rate in Georgia steadily increased as the state moved into the twentieth century, hitting almost 70 percent by 1930. One of the outstanding features of the tenancy was the crop lien system, a system of credit in sharecropping. Georgia passed its first crop lien law in 1866. This law gave the owner of the land a legal lien against the tenant's share of the crops. The only chance a tenant had was to have a good harvest; if there were a bad harvest, the tenant went deeper and deeper into debt every year. Were the tenants angry? Yes. Were they desperate? Yes. Was there anything they could do about it? Unfortunately, no.

In postwar Georgia politics, like in most Southern states, the Democratic party controlled the state government after redemption. There were divisions within the Democratic party in Georgia, though, as politicians disagreed on numerous issues. One of the most divisive was the issue of reconciliation with the North. Those who supported sectional reconciliation were called Bourbons, although a more accurate name is New Departure Democrats. In addition to favoring reconciliation, New Departure Democrats wished to put the issues of the Civil War and Reconstruction behind them and looked toward diversifying the state's economy. The leaders of this faction of the Democratic party were Joseph E. Brown, John B. Gordon, and Alfred H. Colquitt. Along with Henry Grady, who worked behind the scenes, these three were known as the "Bourbon Triumvirate"; between 1873 and 1897 these three men rotated in and out of the offices of governor and US senator. They controlled Georgia politics.

One other political development in Georgia during this period was the rewriting of the state's constitution in 1877; Robert Toombs was the leading advocate for revision. The result was arguably the most conservative constitution in Georgia's history. Among the important provisions were those that prohibited the state from offering tax exemptions to encourage industrial development. Other significant provisions include the cumulative poll tax and minor revisions to state government officials. This constitution would last until 1945.

DOCUMENTS

The first two documents to follow relate to the tenant system in Georgia; one is a sample contract between a tenant farmer and the landowner, the second the state's crop lien law. Document 3 is the law that established the convict-lease system in Georgia. The fourth document is an editorial by Henry Grady that urged the state and the region to industrialize. Document 5 is the creation of the Georgia Department of Agriculture and its responsibilities. The sixth document details important provisions of the Constitution of 1877. Document 7 contains some of the correspondence among the Bourbon Triumvirate in 1880, an exchange that hints at scandal. The eighth and ninth documents give agricultural and industrial statistics for Georgia in 1870, 1880, and 1890.

1. Sample Tenant Farmer Contract[1]

Articles of Agreement Between _____ and the Freedmen, Whose Names are Hereunto Attached.

Article 1. The said freedmen agree to hire themselves as laborers on the plantation of the said _____, from the 1st of January, 1866, to the 1st of January, 1867. They agree to conduct themselves honestly and civilly, and to perform any labor on the said plantation or connected therewith, that may be required by the said _____ or his agents.

Article 2. The said freedmen agree to perform the following daily task per hand, fractional hands in proportion:

Listing
Bedding
Cultivating
Splitting rails
Ditching
Cutting marsh

In all cases where the task cannot be assigned, they agree to labor diligently ten hours per day.

Article 3. The said freedmen agree to forfeit for every day's absence from labor 50 cents per day. If absent voluntarily and without leave, two dollars per day. If absent more than one day without leave, to be dismissed from the plantation, and forfeit their share of the crop.

Article 4. The said freedmen agree to take good care of all utensils with which they may be entrusted, and to pay for the same if lost or destroyed. They agree to be kind and gentle with the animals under their charge, and to pay for any injury they may sustain while in their hands. Damages to be assessed by arbitrators, to be selected by each contracting party.

Article 5. They agree to keep their houses and premises in good repair and order—subject to inspection at any time by their employer or his agents, and liable to a fine of one dollar if found in an improper condition.

Article 6. They agree to furnish from their number a foreman, a nurse and a stock minder—to be selected by their employer.

Article 7. They agree to bear all their own expenses, and to return any advance that may be made during the year from their respective shares in the crop, and to protect their employer's property.

Article 8. The said _____ agrees to treat his employees with kindness and respect, to do all in his power to elevate and improve their condition. He

---

[1] From *Southern Cultivator*, January 1866.

agrees to furnish each family with a comfortable house, and the fourth part of an acre of land for a garden; to allow them to raise poultry and one hog to each laborer, to be kept within their own enclosures. He agrees to divide the crop with them at the end of the year in the following proportions per hand, fractional hands in proportion: One-third of the net proceeds of all the cotton, and one-third of all other crops raised on the plantation, except long forage.

Article 9. The said _____ agrees to be attentive to his employees in sickness; to see that they are supplied with medical attendance, and medicines if required, to be paid for out of their respective shares. He further agrees to supply them with their bread rations, if required, to be paid for in the same manner.

Article 10. The said _____ agrees to furnish work animals at the rate of one animal to every eight full hands; to furnish wagons, carts and plantation utensils, as may be required, such as cannot be made on the plantation.

Article 11. It is agreed that the crop to be cultivated, shall be in the following proportion per hand, fractional hands in proportion:

Cotton	Corn	Rice
Potatoes	Peas	Slips
Turnips		

Article 12. It is agreed that the fines for absence be appropriated to the hiring of other labor to cultivate the absentee's share of the crop, and that the fines for untidiness be appropriated as a premium to the family who keep their premises and garden in the best order.

Article 13. It is agreed that no liquor or firearms be brought on the plantation, except by consent and permission of the employer.

2. Crop Lien Law[2]

An Act to give landlords a lien upon the crops of tenants, for stock, farming utensils and provisions furnished such tenants, for the purpose of making their crops, and to give factors and merchants a lien upon the growing crops of farmers...

Section I. *Be it enacted, etc.*, That from and after the passage of this act, that landlords may have, by special contract in writing, a lien upon the crops of their

---

[2] From *Acts of the General Assembly of the State of Georgia*, 1866.

tenants, for such stock, farming utensils and provisions furnished such tenants for the purpose of making their crops.

Section II. That factors and merchants shall have a lien upon the growing crops of farmers, for provisions furnished and commercial manures furnished, upon such terms as may be agreed upon by the parties.

Section III. That such liens shall be enforced in the same way and manner that liens are now enforced against steamboats in this State.

Section IV. Repeals conflicting laws.

Approved 15th December, 1866.

3. Convict-Lease System Established[3]

An Act to regulate the manner in which the Penitentiary shall be managed, and to provide for farming out the same.

Section I. *Be it enacted, etc.*, That the Governor shall cause to be advertised, for sixty days, in two or more newspapers in the State of Georgia, for proposals to farm out the Penitentiary; and the same shall be farmed out to such persons as shall take it on the best terms, and give such bond as the Governor may require, to secure the comfort and security of the prisoners: *provided*, that the same shall not be leased unless a lease can be made relieving the State from all further expenses, during the term of the lease, in keeping up the same: *and provided, also*, that said lease shall not be for a longer term than five years.

Section II. Repeals conflicting laws.

Assented to 28th December, 1866.

4. Henry Grady's "New South"[4]

Atlanta Daily Herald
March 14, 1874

...For many generations the South got along well enough, with its monopoly of cotton growing, its labor maintained at the simple cost of food and shelter, and its society organized on principles of pure aristocracy. But all that is changed, and it is found that the laws of growth and wealth must be observed there as in all the rest of the world. Something has been done in Georgia and two or three other States toward building up manufactures with very favorable

---

[3] From *Acts of the General Assembly of the State of Georgia*, 1866.
[4] From *Atlanta Daily Herald*, March 14, 1874.

results. The water power of the Chattahoochee River above Columbus now keeps in operation several mills, which, besides paying good wages to a large number of operatives, pay also handsome profits to their owners. The operatives in the mills are chiefly the white people of the neighborhood, who have been educated to the work, and have been ready and willing to learn. Cotton is cheaper than it is out of the cotton growing region, labor is thirty percent cheaper than in New England, the climate is adapted to economical and profitable manufacture, and new machinery and new mills are exempted by law from all taxes for ten years after the introduction. Only a small part of the power of the river is yet used for manufacturing purposes, and new mills are already contracted for. The sagacious and enterprising men who control it look forward confidently to the time when the villages now springing into new life under their care will become to Georgia what Lowell and Lawrence are to Massachusetts.

But they must have help from abroad, or their hopes will not be realized in their generation. They must have labor already trained and educated as well as capital, and these the South does not now afford, and cannot for a long time to come. They must make it safe and attractive for strangers to unite with them in developing their resources. The pioneers in manufacturing are not the only men who would profit by such co-operation. The land-owners whose unsaleble estates are now a burden to them, would either find it profitable to cultivate them, or would be able to dispose of them at something like their value. Labor would be in greater demand and of greater value, and the whole State would feel the stimulating influence of the new life infused into it....

5. Creation of the Georgia Department of Agriculture[5]

Section I. *Be it enacted by the General Assembly of the State of Georgia*, That the Governor of this State is hereby authorized and required to establish a Department of Agriculture for the State of Georgia.

Section II. That said Department shall be under the control and management of one officer, who shall be known as the Commissioner of Agriculture. He shall be appointed by the Governor, by and with the advice and consent of the Senate....

...Section IV. That the duties of said Commissioner shall be:

---

[5] From *Acts and Resolutions of the General Assembly of the State of Georgia*, 1874.

1. He shall prepare, under his own direction, a hand-book describing the geological formation of the various counties of this State, with information as to the general adaptation of the soil of said counties for the various products of the temperate zone, and for the purpose of giving a more general and careful estimate of the capacity and character of the soil of the counties of this State.... Information upon the above subjects, and others of interest to those who till the soil of this State, shall be given in circular or pamphlet form, to the Ordinaries and to the Agricultural Associations of the various counties in this State, for distribution at such times as the Commissioner may be prepared to do so.

2. Said Commissioner shall provide for the proper and careful distribution of any seeds that the Government of these United States may desire to introduce into the State of Georgia, and he shall make arrangements for the importation of seeds that he may deem of value to this State, and for the proper, careful and judicious distribution of the same; also, for the exchange of seeds with foreign countries or adjoining States, for seed from this State; and their distribution in a proper manner shall be entirely under his supervision and control.

3. Said Commissioner shall have under his especial charge the study of the various insects that are injurious to the crops, plants and fruits of this State, their habits and propagation; and he shall, at various times, as he may deem proper, issue circulars for distribution as aforesaid in this State, as to the proper mode for their destruction, and any information upon said subject that he may deem of interest to the planters, farmers and horticulturalists of this State.

4. Said Commissioner shall examine into any question that may be of interest to the horticulturist and fruit-growers of this State, and in all endeavors that he may deem proper toward encouraging these important industries.

...6. Said Commissioner shall have under his especial charge the analysis of fertilizers. A fair sample of all fertilizers sold in this State shall be first submitted to said Commissioner, and the same shall be thoroughly tested by him, and if any brand of fertilizers so tested by said Commissioner is pronounced of no practical value, the sale of the same shall be prohibited in this State....

Section VII. That the office of said Commissioner shall continue for four years from the date of his appointment; and he shall perform the duties of the same for said length of time, unless removed in the manner now prescribed by law for the removal of officers of the State Government.

Approved February 28, 1874.

6. Constitution of 1877[6]

Preamble

To perpetuate the principles insure justice to all, preserve peace, promote the interest and happiness of the citizen and transmit to prosperity the enjoyment of liberty, we, the people of Georgia, relying upon the protection and guidance of Almighty God, do ordain and establish this Constitution.

Article 1

Bill of Rights

Section I

Paragraph I. All government, of right, originates with the people, is founded upon their will only, and is instituted solely for the good of the whole. Public officers are the trustees and servants of the people, and, at all times, amenable to them.

...Par. VII. Neither banishment beyond the limits of the State, nor whipping, as a punishment for crime, shall be allowed.

...Par. XI. The writ of habeas corpus shall not be suspended.

...Par. XVII. There shall be within the State of Georgia neither slavery nor involuntary servitude, save as a punishment for crime after legal conviction thereof.

Par. XVIII. The social status of the citizen shall never be the subject of legislation.

...Par. XXI. There shall be no imprisonment for debt.

Section II

...Paragraph IV. All lotteries, and the sale of lottery tickets, are hereby prohibited; and this prohibition shall be enforced by penal law.

Par. V. Lobbying is declared to be a crime, and the General Assembly shall enforce this provision by suitable penalties.

Article 2

Elective Franchise

Section I

...Paragraph II. Every male citizen of the United States (except as hereinafter provided) twenty-one years of age, who shall have resided in this State one year preceding the election, and shall have resided six months in the county in which he offers to vote, and shall have paid all taxes which may hereafter be required of him, and which he may have had an opportunity of paying, agreeably to law, except for the year of the election, shall be deemed an elector....

---

[6] From *Acts and Resolutions of the General Assembly of the State of Georgia*, 1877.

Section V

Paragraph I. The General Assembly shall, by law, forbid the sale, distribution, or furnishing of intoxicating drinks within two miles of election precincts, on days of election State, county or municipal and prescribe punishment for any violation of the same.

Article 3

Legislative Department

Section I

Paragraph I. The legislative powers of the State shall be vested in a General Assembly which shall consist of a Senate and House of Representatives.

Section II

Paragraph I. The Senate shall consist of forty-four members. There shall be forty-four Senatorial Districts, as now arranged by counties. Each District shall have one Senator.

Section III

Paragraph I. The House of Representatives shall consist of one hundred and seventy-five Representatives, apportioned among the several counties as follows, to wit: To the six counties having the largest population, viz: Chatham, Richmond, Burke, Houston, Bibb and Fulton, three Representatives each; to the twenty-six counties having the next largest population, viz: Bartow, Coweta, Decatur, Floyd, Greene, Gwinnett, Harris, Jefferson, Meriwether, Monroe, Muscogee, Newton, Stewart, Sumter, Thomas, Troup, Washington, Hancock, Carroll, Cobb, Jackson, Dougherty, Oglethorpe, Macon, Talbot and Wilkes, two Representatives each; and to the remaining one hundred and five counties, one Representative each....

Section IV

Paragraph I. The members of the General Assembly shall be elected for two years, and shall serve until their successors are elected.

...Par. VI. No session of the General Assembly shall continue longer than forty days, unless by a two-thirds vote of the whole number of each house.

Section VII

...Paragraph XVIII. The General Assembly shall have no power to grant corporate powers and privileges to private companies, except banking, insurance, railroad, canal, navigation, express and telegraph companies....

Article 5

Executive Department

Section I

Paragraph I. The officers of the Executive Department shall consist of a Governor, Secretary of State, Comptroller General, and Treasurer.

Par. II. The Executive power shall be vested in a Governor, who shall hold his office during the term of two years, and until his successor shall be chosen and qualified. He shall not be eligible to reelection, after the expiration of a second term, for the period of four years....

Par. VII. No person shall be eligible to the office of Governor who shall not have been a citizen of the United States fifteen years, and a citizen of the State six years, and who shall not have attained the age of thirty years.

...Par. XVI. The Governor shall have the revision of all bills passed by the General Assembly, before the same shall become laws, but two-thirds of each House may pass a law, notwithstanding his dissent; and if any bill should not be returned by the Governor within five days (Sunday excepted) after it has been presented to him, the same shall be law; unless the General Assembly, by their adjournment, shall prevent its return....

Article 6

Judiciary

Section I

Paragraph I. The judicial powers of this State shall be vested in a Supreme Court, Superior Courts, Courts of Ordinary, Justices of the Peace, commissioned Notaries Public, and such other courts as have been, or may be, established by law.

Section II

Paragraph I. The Supreme Court shall consist of a Chief Justice and two Associate Justices. A majority of the court shall constitute a quorum.

...Par. IV. The Chief Justice and Associate Justices shall hold their offices for six years, and until their successors are qualified....

Section XII

Paragraph I. The Judges of the Supreme and Superior Courts, and Solicitor General, shall be elected by the General Assembly, in joint session, on such day, or days, as shall be fixed by joint resolution of both Houses....

Article 8

Education

Section I

Paragraph I. There shall be a thorough system of common schools for the education of children in the elementary branches of an English education only, as nearly uniform as practicable, the expenses of which shall be provided for by taxation, or otherwise. The schools shall be free to all children of the State, but separate schools shall be provided for the white and colored races.

7. 1880 Resignation-Appointment Controversy[7]

Henry Grady to Joseph E. Brown, early May 1880:
These words are to be used in reverse, that is Jones means Newcomb—
State road—neck
Jones—Newcomb
Smith—Brown
Agrees—shoots
Gordon—Williams
Senatorship—wash
Presidency—wood
Attorney—more
Thousand—slow
Refuses—poor
Year—proud
Colquitt—Jim
Appointment—break
Resignation—play
Send in—pass
Where a word not included in this list is used it stands for itself.
HWG
I will telegraph as soon as I know.

Henry Grady to Joseph E. Brown, May 15, 1880:
Williams will pass play certain [Translation: Gordon will send in resignation certain]. Jones highly pleased with Smith's assurances & anxious to do all wanted [Translation: Newcomb highly pleased with Brown's assurances & anxious to do all wanted].... It fixes everything precisely as wanted. Answer.

Henry Grady to Joseph E. Brown, May 17, 1880:
Everything is fixed. Williams play pass to Jim & Jones shoots that Smith shall hold wood and wash but says in adjusting Williams salary four thousand should come from Smith's road [Translation: Gordon's resignation sent in to Colquitt & Newcomb agrees that Brown shall hold presidency and senatorship but says in adjusting Gordon's salary four thousand should come from Brown's road]....

---

[7] From Joseph E. Brown Papers, Hargrett Rare Book and Manuscript Library, University of Georgia.

Governor Alfred Colquitt to Joseph E. Brown, May 19, 1880 [not in code]:
Gen. Gordon has resigned his seat in U.S. Senate. If you can accept appointment to vacancy please notify me & return immediately.

Joseph E. Brown to Governor Alfred Colquitt, May 19, 1880 [not in code]:
I accept the appointment. Will return Friday.

8. General Agricultural Statistics[8]

	1870	1880	1890
Number of farms	69,956	138,626	171,071
Acres in farms	23,647,941	26,043,282	25,200,435
Average acres/farm	338.0	187.9	147.3
Value of farms	$75,647,574	$111,910,540	$152,006,230
Cotton (bales)	473,934	814,441	1,191,846
Tobacco (pounds)	288,596	228,590	960,000 (1899)
Rice (pounds)	22,277,380	25,369,687	945,000 (1895)
Corn (bushels)	17,646,459	23,202,018	29,261,422
Wheat (bushels)	2,127,017	3,159,771	1,096,312
Oats (bushels)	1,904,601	5,548,743	4,767,821

9. General Industrial Statistics[9]

	1870	1880	1890
Establishments	3,836	3,593	4,285
Number of workers	17,871	24,875	52,298
Value of products	$31,196,115	$36,440,948	$68,917,020

---

[8] US Bureau of the Census, 1870, 1880, 1890.
[9] US Bureau of the Census, 1870, 1880, 1890.

ESSAYS

The New Departure Democrats in Georgia[10]

Judson Clements Ward, Jr.

...During these nineteen years [1872–1890] the Democratic party was dominated by a group of leaders who were branded by contemporary opponents with the epithet "Bourbon." Because of its confusing usages the term will not be used in this paper. Instead the phrase "New Departure" will be used to describe the conservative leadership that dominated the Democratic party. The New Departure leaders were far too realistic to advocate a return to the status quo ante bellum. They acquiesced in the defeat of the right of secession, in the abolition of the institution of slavery, and in the legal enfranchisement of the Negro. They paid their most eloquent tributes to the "lost cause" and to the "heroes in gray." They were determined, however, to maintain white supremacy at all costs. They were confirmed anew in their devotion to the principle of state rights as opposed to the growing tendency toward centralization in the national government, hoping to be permitted to work out the readjustment with the Negro without federal interference.

Likewise the realism and the opportunism of the New Departure leaders inspired them to advocate the development of Georgia along the lines of the national pattern. They promoted business and industry; they encouraged immigration; and they invited the exploitation of mineral resources, water and power, and timberlands in an attempt to diversify the economy of the state. Their watchwords were "youth," "progress," "reconciliation," "material prosperity," and "the new era." Their economic ideas have been popularized in the concept "the New South." The New Departure Democrats were sufficiently clever to exploit the emotional devotion to the past and the basic fear of racial equality to help secure election to political office, where once ensconced they were able to direct in their own fashion and therefore to their own personal and

---

[10] From Judson Clements Ward, Jr., "The New Departure Democrats of Georgia: An Interpretation," *Georgia Historical Quarterly* 41/3 (September 1957). Courtesy of the Georgia Historical Society.

class interests the changes that were to make the new Georgia. They nullified the liberal revolution the egalitarians sought to accomplish; yet they themselves promoted an economic revolution the benefits of which they were able to restrict largely to an oligarchy of businessmen, industrialists, and big farmers.

The first problem of the New Departure leaders was to establish themselves in a position of political power. This they did by uniting the great majority of the native whites under the banner of the Democratic party in opposition to the Republican party, which they pictured as a party of carpetbaggers, scalawags, and Negroes. The Republican administration of Governor Rufus B. Bullock was vulnerable to charges of fraud, corruption, favoritism, and outside support. The Democratic leadership was quick to seize upon these weaknesses and play upon the emotions of fear, hate, and provincialism to establish a white man's party. They used threats, fraud, intimidation, trickery, and other devices to prevent the Negroes from effectively employing the franchise against them; while at the same time, Democrats were able in many cases to win and use the support of Negro voters, thus dividing this solid and most important bloc of Republican voters. Despite Georgia's two-party tradition, and the basic economic, social, and geographic cleavage in the body politic, it was not long before effective Republican opposition was crushed. The last Republican congressmen were defeated in 1874, and the last outright Republican candidate for governor was nominated in 1876.

Thereafter, the principal opposition to the New Departure-dominated Democracy came from Independent Democratic candidates. By 1878 these individual dissidents threatened to organize an effective indigenous second party in Georgia. Although there was an element of economic discontent among the Independents, the movement was chiefly a political protest against ring rule and undemocratic methods of nomination within the Democratic party....

The preoccupation of the New Departure Democrats with business and industry has generally blinded investigators to their interests in agriculture. Despite the rapid growth of business, Georgia continued to be primarily an agricultural state. New Departure leaders were sufficiently shrewd to recognize the necessity of appeasing farmers in order to insure political victories. They established a state department of agriculture and a railroad commission, authorized a geological survey, and enacted fertilizer inspection laws, lien laws, and usury laws. They debated but refused to enact fence laws, dog laws, and appropriations for agricultural education, farmers institutes, and wagon roads. Most of the legislation enacted, however, was designed to help the large landowners. The agencies that were established were little more than sops thrown to the small farmers who paid for them out of inspection fees or disproportionately high taxes on land.

It must be admitted that in general agriculture made impressive gains during this era. Land values rose; the production of money crops and foodstuffs increased; crop diversification and soil conservation were widely practiced. The profits, however, went principally to the big farmers. The revolution in landholding presaged by the decline of the plantation failed to materialize. Shiftless, poor, ignorant tenants displaced the sturdy, independent landowners who might have possessed the land had the revolution taken place. In 1881 Henry W. Grady expressed apprehension over the rapid concentration of ownership in the hands of large operators. New Departure policies also failed to provide for such basic agricultural needs as credit, improved marketing facilities, and cheap and improved methods of transportation. They also failed to halt the rapid growth of tenancy.

The New Departure leadership was thus more than an oligarchy of businessmen and industrialists. It admitted to membership many agriculturalists. The New Departure leaders themselves continued to pursue agricultural interests along with their business ventures, and they played an important part in the leadership of the State Agricultural Society, the Grange, and the Alliance. The agriculture represented in these organizations, however, was of a new type. The post bellum farmer was no agrarian planter. He was a capitalistic promoter who directed his activities from an office in a town or in a city. He made as much money from advances of supplies to tenants and from time prices as he did from planting itself. The New Departure Democrats retained the political support of the small farmer by appeals to race prejudice and by sops thrown to him, but they largely ignored him in their agricultural legislation. The violent nature of the discontent of the small farmer group is evidenced by the explosive force with which their protests broke forth in the Populist Revolt of the 1890s....

The inevitable conclusion is that the Democratic regime was a mixture of liberalism and conservatism. The New Departure leaders were progressive in the sense that they sought realistically to live in the new era. They increased the wealth of the state by promoting business, industry, and agriculture. At the same time by moving Georgia in the direction of the national economic pattern, they hastened sectional reconciliation. They were conservative if not reactionary, however in the sense that they constituted an oligarchy who were unwilling to entertain suggestions for a more equitable distribution or taxation of the wealth that was without question created. They adhered to a theory of extreme individualism and freedom of enterprise in which they claimed financial success to be the reward of hard work, initiative, and good judgment, while failure was attributed to a lack of these qualities. The New Departure leaders also had a narrow concept of the appropriate functions of government. They increased the number of state services very little and supported those already in existence with inadequate funds. At first glance it might appear that they would have been willing to spend the taxes collected from land with some degree of liberality, but they were apprehensive that large appropriations might necessitate additional taxation that would eventually reach the newly created business and industrial wealth. It should also be pointed out that despite their parsimony many of the New Departure leaders held more liberal views on spending than did the representatives of many of the small rural counties. Together, however, these advocates of economy kept the expenses of government low. This enabled the state to emerge free of the burden of debt from a period in which many of her people were relatively poor. Meanwhile public services languished. Despite the general poverty, however, more money could have been made available for services if the tax burden had been distributed more equitably.

When the Democrats assumed office in 1872 they were confronted with a difficult task. They inherited a great burden of debt; the general economic condition of the people was poor; yet government was called upon to bear a greater burden than ever before with the admission of the Negro to participation in the state's services. In addition to this, the Negro was not financially able to bear his share of the additional burden. With costs great and income low, the difficulties were increased many times. The record of the Democratic administration, however, is one of efficiency. The leaders slowly improved services over what they had been in 1872, reduced taxes, and left the state in sound financial condition. The record of Democratic efficiency and honesty in administration is not without blemishes, but it was infinitely superior to that of their Republican predecessors.

On the other hand, the New Departure Democrats became an oligarchy who used their political power selfishly to enrich themselves. They profited personally from the barbarous and benighted convict lease system. They made money from the lease of the state-owned Western and Atlantic Railroad. They refused to shift the burden of taxation from the already overburdened farmer or provide other measures of relief. They increased appropriations somewhat, but even so they failed to provide adequately for schools, roads, charitable institutions, and other public services. They saddled the one-party system on the state. They used white supremacy to crush political differences and prevent the free discussion of public questions. They segregated and discriminated against the Negro. Without question they were the strong men who rose to positions of power during a turbulent era of change. There is little doubt that they directed the problem of adjustment to the new scene better than the irreconcilables and the unreconstructed would have done, but it is equally certain that they failed to do as good a job as many of their more liberal critics would have been able to accomplish. Perhaps the greatest condemnation of the advocates of the New Departure is the heritage they left Georgia of intolerant, bigoted, one-party control and a weal parsimonious government unwilling to support in adequate fashion the state's public services.

The Farmers' Alliance in Georgia[11]

William F. Holmes

When the Alliance came to Georgia, farmers were ripe for an organization that promised to improve their status. In the antebellum era they had enjoyed self-sufficiency and sold staple crops at good prices, but since the Civil War conditions had deteriorated. The South's poor credit facilities contributed greatly to the problem. Since Georgia's few banks extended loans mainly to well-to-do landowners, many farmers became involved in the crop lien system under which they mortgaged their crops to merchants in return for advances in agricultural supplies and household items. Merchants viewed those transactions as risky, and they imposed annual interest charges ranging from 25 percent to over 100 percent. The system proved debilitating. To insure a maximum return from customers, merchants insisted that farmers produce only cotton; that, in turn, contributed to overproduction and drove down cotton process. The high interest charges, coupled with low commodity prices, left many farmers deeply in debt. As a farmer's indebtedness mounted year after year, he mortgaged his land to obtain additional credit. When the merchant eventually foreclosed the mortgage, the farmer became a tenant.

The economic problem that farmers confronted certainly contributed to the acceptance of the Alliance. In the summer of 1888, when the order made its initial appearance in Greene County, one resident declared that if "there is a set of men at the mercy of everybody and everything, it is the farmers. They haven't got a say about anything and have to do just what is told them to do or get nothing." But that attitude did not represent anything new because farmers had faced those problems long before the Alliance's arrival, just as they would

---

[11] From William F. Holmes, "The Southern Farmers' Alliance: The Georgia Experience," *Georgia Historical Quarterly* 72/4 (Winter 1988). Courtesy of the Georgia Historical Society.

contend with them long after its demise. The Alliance succeeded in Georgia because it effectively mobilized country people and gave hope for revitalization.

In trying to understand rural life in post-Reconstruction Georgia, we should not romanticize farming, for it required hard work and long hours while leaving many of its practitioners with meager incomes. Even with its problems, farming encompassed a way of life that had prevailed for over a century and that many wanted to maintain. Most country people liked the old ways, for example, and did not subscribe to the latest farming techniques that agricultural experts recommended. Some still planted and harvested crops in accordance with the stages of the moon. Outsiders might have difficulty identifying rural neighborhoods, but country people knew exactly where they were because their social life revolved around small churches and one-room schools. Farmers realized that cities offered many attractions, and they expected some of their children to become urban residents. Still, most farm people remained in the country out of choice. For them farming represented the basic occupation on which others depended. To understand why the Alliance became a powerful organization, therefore, we must examine how it worked within the prevailing rural culture.

Alliance lecturers conducted the important work of introducing people to the new order and organizing suballiances in country neighborhoods. Initially the Texas Alliance selected J. B. Wilkes, a native Georgian, to return to his former home in Heard County and establish the Alliance. As Wilkes traveled through western Georgia during summer 1887, he persuaded others to help him in establishing the Alliance by serving as lecturers. Having been farmers, the lecturers knew well the ways of rural Georgia and could communicate effectively with country people. Like Methodist circuit riders, they traveled through the rural regions expounding the benefits the Alliance could bring. Of the lecturers Wilkes recruited, J. H. Turner, a Troup County schoolteacher, became one of the most active. Whenever possible, Turner appealed for help from sympathetic country newspaper editors. Several weeks before he visited a county, the local editor touted the Alliance and published an itinerary of Turner's schedule. When Turner arrived, he canvassed the country, meeting with small groups of farmers in rural churches and schools. He received no salary for that work, but earned 50 cents from the dues of each suballiance he organized. Lecturers like Turner quickly became part of an extensive network that established an effective way of communicating with the Alliance membership scattered throughout the lonely countryside....

From the outset Alliance leaders realized that it would take more than self-determination and hard work to resolve farm problems. While Alliance members wanted to increase self-sufficiency by growing more foodstuffs, they had no intention of abandoning commercial agriculture. Instead, they wanted to escape the high costs imposed by the crop lien system and thereby compete more effectively within the prevailing economic system. Some Alliances initially attempted to achieve that goal by working with established merchants. The Heard County Alliance became one of the first to do that in fall 1887 when it appointed a trade committee to ask merchants in the county seat to bid for the order's business. Unaware of the Alliance's strength, most merchants refused to negotiate. Of those who did, the Alliance accepted the bids of two who agreed to sell selected items 25 percent below prevailing prices and to allow the Alliance trade committee to insure the reasonableness of the charges by inspecting their bills. That agreement resulted in startling changes as farmers who had done business with other merchants for years abandoned them in favor of those stores that offered lower prices. Stung by economic losses, many merchants quickly made concessions to regain former customers.

Alliances throughout Georgia followed the practice of making arrangements with specific stores. In the South Georgia county of Terrell the Alliance designated one store for groceries, one for dry goods, and one for drugs. The Franklin County Alliance, which boasted one of the largest memberships in the state, selected six stores in Northeast Georgia to handle its business. By arranging for merchants to buy a large supply of fertilizer that they could sell below the prevailing price, Jackson County Alliance members saved 6 dollars per ton. Alliances also promoted bulk sales of their members' crops. The Greene County Alliance arranged for cotton buyers in the region to gather at Greensboro on a day in the fall of 1888. By selling that year's crop at one time and one place, the Alliance members hoped to get better prices than they could when conducting business individually.

As the Alliance became stronger, it tried to strengthen its cooperative programs by forming its own stores, cotton warehouses, and gins. When merchants in Putnam County presented a united front and refused the Alliance's request to grant lower prices, the Alliance formed its own store. Members bought stock, elected a board of directors, and employed a manager to supervise the store's operations. Some of the more substantial Alliance members supported the enterprise by using their farms as collateral to secure loans from the local bank; with those funds they purchased supplies from the Alliance store. Initially the store did well, selling $30,000 worth of goods during its first six months. How long it operated successfully is unknown, but as with many Alliance operations its members probably came to realize that local cooperatives could not compete successfully without help from a larger agency—a state exchange that could provide assistance in making wholesale purchases and in selling crops on a bulk basis....

When the Georgia Alliance held its state meeting in October 1888, the delegates knew that the Texas Exchange faced serious problems. Also knowing that farmers in their own state currently paid interest rates averaging 78 percent, they were determined to establish an exchange. They took the initial step by electing a board of directors headed by Felix Corput, a vineyard owner with extensive mercantile experience. To avoid mistakes that had proved so harmful in Texas, the directors decided that the Georgia Exchange would not open until the suballiances had purchased at least $60,000 in stock. To protect their resources, they limited inventory to farm implements and fertilizer while leaving to local Alliance stores responsibility for offering members the opportunity to buy clothing, food, and household items. They also provide suballiances with lists of reasonable prices for a wide range of items. Where Alliance stores either had limited inventories or did not exist, the suballiances could use those lists to bargain with merchants for better prices....

During its brief life, the Southern Alliance became the most vigorous farm organization in post-Reconstruction Georgia. It achieved that by appealing to the large class of landowning farmers who had become concerned with the mounting problems that for over twenty years had weakened their way of making a living as well as their way of life. By instilling a sense of unity, the Alliance enabled its members to develop a better collective understanding of their plight while offering them hope for improvement. Through its local cooperatives and state exchange it tried to provide farmers with the means to compete more successfully and not to fall into tenancy. Along with its economic programs, the Alliance helped country people gain a new sense of autonomy at a time when cities and towns had begun to eclipse the rural order. Toward that goal it worked to vitalize country schools, churches, and benevolent associations.

The organization's brief heyday ended in 1891, when it became apparent that the cooperatives could not reverse economic problems. With the demise of the Alliance, some of its members joined the People's Party. Indeed the Alliance helped prepare the way for Populism, but the two organizations were distinct. In Georgia the People's Party never developed the vitality the Alliance had enjoyed in its heyday, because loyalty to the Democratic party and white supremacy represented beliefs too strong for most whites to challenge. In addition, Populism was a political movement embracing issues that went beyond the concerns of rural people. The Alliance always remained a farmers' movement that worked for the revitalization of rural America. Today, a century after its appearance, we can see that the Alliance tried to maintain a way of life that a more modernized culture eventually replaced.

Additional Sources

Davis, Harold E. *Henry Grady's New South*. Tuscaloosa: University of Alabama Press, 1990.

Eckert, Ralph L. *John Brown Gordon, Soldier, Southerner, American*. Baton Rouge: Louisiana State University Press, 1989.

Ferald, J. Bryan. *Henry Grady or Tom Watson? The Rhetorical Struggle for the New South, 1880–1890*. Macon GA: Mercer University Press, 1994.

Hahn, Steven. *The Roots of Southern Populism: Yeoman Farmers and the Transformation of the Georgia Upcountry, 1850–1890*. Updated Edition. New York: Oxford University Press, 2006.

Outland, Robert B. *Tapping the Pines: The Naval Stores Industry in the American South*. Baton Rouge: Louisiana State University Press, 2004.

Parks, Joseph. *Joseph E. Brown of Georgia*. Baton Rouge: Louisiana State University Press, 1977.

Reidy, Joseph P. *From Slavery to Agrarian Capitalism in the Cotton Plantation South: Central Georgia, 1800–1880*. Chapel Hill: University of North Carolina Press, 1992.

Wallenstein, Peter. *From Slave South to New South: Public Policy in Nineteenth-Century Georgia*. Chapel Hill: University of North Carolina Press, 1987.

Woodward, C. Vann. *Tom Watson, Agrarian Rebel*. New York: Oxford University Press, 1938.

Chapter 11

JIM CROW GEORGIA, 1890–1920

The last decade of the nineteenth century and the first few decades of the twentieth century are collectively known as the Jim Crow Era. It is ironic that this period coincides with the Progressive Era, a time notable for its spirit of reform. In the South, however, that reform did not extend to all citizens; historian John Dittmer has suggested that the Progressive Era was "for whites only."[1] The Jim Crow Era in Georgia was the low point in race relations; it was marked by race violence, economic exploitation, political and social oppression, lynchings, and the reappearance of the Ku Klux Klan.

Social oppression was carried out through Jim Crow laws and local ordinances and practices that institutionalized segregation. The first Jim Crow law passed by the Georgia General Assembly, in 1891, provided for separate railway cars for white and black passengers. Additional actions made the separation of the races almost complete. Political oppression in Georgia was carried out by both the General Assembly and the Democratic party. In 1900 the Democratic party adopted the white primary, a practice that permitted blacks to vote only in the general election. During the administration of Governor Hoke Smith, who is generally regarded as the state's most progressive chief executive, the General Assembly passed legislation that essentially disfranchised black voters completely. These provisions passed the legislature in 1907 and were then added to the state constitution in 1908. The registration of black voters dropped precipitously, from 28 percent in 1904 to 4 percent in 1910.

Race violence was prevalent in this era, and examples abound. One of the worst examples of race violence in Georgia was the Atlanta Race Riot of 1906, in which mobs of whites indiscriminately attacked and killed numerous blacks over a span of three days in September. The lynching of black Georgians was yet another example of race violence; mob violence was so prevalent in this era that it was called a national pastime, and Georgia was a national leader in this phenomenon. Historian Fitzhugh Brundage counted 460 victims of mob

---

[1] See "Black Georgia in the Progressive Era" in the essays section of this chapter.

violence in Georgia between 1880 and 1930; 441 of those victims were African Americans. Violence against blacks in Georgia knew no bounds.

Perhaps the most sinister development during the Jim Crow Era in Georgia was the reappearance of the Ku Klux Klan in 1915. William Simmons, who grew up in Atlanta hearing stories of the Reconstruction-era Klan from his father, led a group of men onto Stone Mountain on Thanksgiving night and, in an act of misguided symbolism, burned a cross. This version of the Ku Klux Klan peaked in the mid-1920s and declined just as quickly as it rose.

DOCUMENTS

The first document to follow is Booker T. Washington's famed Atlanta Compromise Speech of 1895. The second document is the Democratic party's white primary, adopted in 1900. Document 3 is a statement from the Georgia Equal Rights Convention from 1906. The fourth document contains two newspaper reports of the 1906 race riot in Atlanta. Document 5 is the legislation that disfranchised black voters, which was passed in 1907 and added to the state constitution in 1908. The sixth document is a report from the NAACP's Walter White to Georgia governor Hugh Dorsey regarding a 1918 lynching spree in South Georgia. Document 7 is a 1921 statement from Governor Dorsey on the status of blacks in Georgia.

1. Atlanta Compromise Speech[2]

Atlanta, Georgia, September 18, 1895
Mr. President and Gentlemen of the Board of Directors and Citizens:

One-third of the population of the South is of the Negro race. No enterprise seeking the material, civil, or moral welfare of this section can disregard this element of our population and reach the highest success....

...To those of my race who depend on bettering their condition in a foreign land or who underestimate the importance of cultivating friendly relations with the Southern white man, who is their next-door neighbour, I would say: "Cast down your bucket where you are"—cast it down in making friends in every manly way of the people of all races by whom we are surrounded.

Cast it down in agriculture, in mechanics, in commerce, in domestic service, and in the professions. And in this connection it is well to bear in mind that

---

[2] From *The Booker T. Washington Papers* (Urbana: University of Illinois Press, 1974).

whatever other sins the South may be called to bear, when it comes to business, pure and simple, it is in the South that the negro is given a man's chance in the commercial world, and in nothing is this exposition more eloquent than in emphasizing this chance. Our greatest danger is that in the great leap from slavery to freedom we may overlook the fact that the masses of us are to live by the production of our hands, and fail to keep in mind that we shall prosper in proportion as we learn to dignify and glorify common labour, and put brains and skill into the common occupations of life....

To those of the white race who look to the incoming of those of foreign birth and strange tongue and habits for the prosperity of the South, were I permitted I would repeat what I say to my own race, "Cast down your bucket where you are." Cast it down among the eight millions of Negroes whose habits you know, whose fidelity and love you have tested in days when to have proved treacherous meant the ruin of your firesides. Cast down your bucket among these people who have, without strikes and labour wars, tilled your fields, cleared your forests, builded your railroads and cities, and brought forth treasures from the bowels of the earth, and helped make possible this magnificent representation of the progress of the South. Casting down your bucket among my people, helping and encouraging them as you are doing on these grounds, and to educate of head, hand, and heart, you will find that they will buy your surplus land, make blossom the waste places in your fields, and run your factories. While doing this, you can be sure in the future, as in the past, that you and your families will be surrounded by the most patient, faithful, law-abiding, and unresentful people that the world has seen. As we have proved our loyalty to you in the past, in nursing your children, watching by the sick-bed of your mothers and fathers, and often following them with tear-dimmed eyes to their graves, so in the future, in our humble way, we shall stand by you with a devotion that no foreigner can approach, ready to lay down our lives, if need be, in defense of yours, interlacing our industrial, commercial, civil, and religious life with yours in a way that shall make the interests of both races one. In all things that are purely social we can be as separate as the fingers, yet one as the hand in all things essential to mutual progress....

2. White Primary[3]

State Democratic Executive Committee Resolutions

At a meeting of the state democratic executive committee, held in the city of Atlanta this 16th day of March, 1900, called for the purpose of taking action whereby the white democrats of this state may give expression of their choice for state offices to be filled by the vote of the people at the ensuing elections, it is ordered:

1. That a general primary election be held on the 15th day of May in every county in the state, at which all qualified white democratic voters (who have registered in 1900 within ten days before said primary) shall be given an opportunity to cast their votes for the following officers, to-wit: governor, attorney general, secretary of state, comptroller general, treasurer, commissioner of agriculture, state school commissioner, two justices of the supreme court, two prison commissioners; and the democratic executive committee in each county are hereby directed to prepare and furnish to the managers of such primary a list of such qualified registered voters under the terms herein provided for....

3. The Georgia Equal Rights Convention, 1906[4]

We, colored men of Georgia, representing every district in the State and speaking for more than a million human souls send this statement and plea to the world:

Two races came to Georgia in the early eighteenth century and lived as master and slave. In that long hard apprenticeship we learned to work, to speak the tongue of the land, and better to know God. We learned this but we learned it at the cost of self-respect, self-reliance, knowledge, and the honor of our women.

This training left us above all ignorant. We are still ignorant, partly by our own fault in not striving more doggedly after knowledge, but chiefly because of the wretched educational opportunities given us in this state. The white and black school populations are nearly equal and yet out of every dollar of the state school money eighty cents go to the white child and twenty cents to the Negro child; each white child receives $5.92 a year, while the Negro child receives $2.27; white teachers receive over a million dollars a year, Negro teachers less

---

[3] From *Atlanta Constitution*, March 17, 1900.
[4] From *The Voice of the Negro*, March 1906.

than three hundred thousand. Less than half our children have school facilities furnished them and not a cent is given by the state to the higher training of Negro teachers and professional men. Of more than a million dollars given by the United States government for agricultural training, we who are preeminently the farmers of this state have received only $264,000, and the fund is at present being divided at the rate of $34,000 to the whites and $8,000 to the Negroes. We are a poor people. Poor in wealth and habit. We are not as efficient laborers as we might be. Yet the accumulated wealth of this great state has been built upon our bowed backs, and its present prosperity depends largely upon us. No portion of the community is giving more of its labor and money to support the public burdens than we; and yet we are not receiving just wages for our toil; we are too often cheated out of our scanty earnings; while the laws that govern our economic life and the rules of their administration are cunning with injustice toward us....

To stand up thus in our own defense, we must earn a decent living. We must work hard. We must buy land and homes. We must encourage Negro business men. And at the same time we must agitate, complain, protest and keep protesting against the invasion of our manhood rights; we must besiege the legislature, carry our cases to the courts and above all organize these million brothers of ours into one great fist which shall never cease to pound at the gates of opportunity until they fly open. Brethren of the white race, living together as we do, let us be friends and not enemies. Let us not stir up the darker, fiercer passions. Let us strive together, not as master and slave, but as man and man, equal in the sight of God and in the eyes of the law, eager to make this historic state a land of peace, a place of plenty and an abode of Jesus Christ.

4. Atlanta Race Riot[5]

Atlanta Constitution
September 23, 1906
Facts of Last Night's Reign of Terror
Mob of 10,000 ruled city for five hours, police powerless, and troops not on scene until worst was over.

Sixteen negroes and one white man known to be dead. Thought list of dead negroes may reach thirty.

Trouble started at corner of Decatur and Pryor Streets.

---

[5] From *Atlanta Constitution*, September 23, 24, 1906.

Mob pulled negroes from cars and chased them on streets whenever one was seen.

Number of injured unknown. About twenty cases taken to Grady Hospital.

All troops called out and entire police force kept on continuous duty. Civil and military authorities working together.

Trolley cars smashed and many show windows broken and property destroyed.

Rioting caused by assaults on white women during past few months and four attempts yesterday.

Atlanta Constitution
September 24, 1906
What Kind of Mob Ruled in the City

People are asking what kind of a mob was it that caused so much trouble Saturday night. How large was it and of what class of citizens was it composed of?

When the disorder first started there was no mob, but simply a crowd of turbulent, noisy men and youths. This seemed to be so apparent that the police did not realize there would be any serious developments.

The mob was composed mostly of youths, from 16 to 20 years of age. To these were added several men who were well-known to the police as persons who would rather have trouble than not. There were also in the crowd men who were ready for lawless deprivations. There were some, of course, who were angry because of the way in which white women of this county had recently been treated by negro brutes.

It is admitted by all who saw the mob that the large majority of those in it were minors. It was Saturday night and the boys had their week's wages and a few drinks. They started in for a night of negro chasing and this was all that was done for nearly two hours.

The first disorder was at the corner of Pryor and Decatur streets, when some of the youths attacked a negro bicycle messenger. The police had to rescue the boy. From that time on the mob chased negroes along Decatur and Pryor streets and Central avenue until the fire department produced an artificial rain storm. The mob at that time numbered about 2,000....

5. Disfranchisement Legislation[6]

Amendment to Constitution

An Act to amend the Constitution of the State of Georgia by repealing section I of article 2 of the Constitution of this State and inserting in lieu thereof a new section, consisting of nine paragraphs, prescribing the qualifications for electors, providing for the registration of voters, and for other purposes.

...Par. 3. To entitle a person to register and vote at any election by the people, he shall have resided in the State one year next preceding the election, and in the county in which he offers to vote six months next preceding the election, and shall have paid all taxes which may have been required of him since the adoption of the Constitution of Georgia of 1877 that he may have had an opportunity of paying agreeably to law. Such payment must have been made at least six months prior to the election at which he offers to vote, except when such elections are held within six months from the expiration of the time fixed by law for the payment of such taxes.

Par. 4. Every male citizen of this State shall be entitled to register as an elector and to vote in all elections of said State who is not disqualified under the provisions of section 2 of article 2 of this Constitution, and who possesses the qualifications prescribed in paragraphs 2 and 3 of this section or who will possess them at the date of the election occurring next after his registration, and who in addition thereto comes within either of the classes provided for in the five following sub-divisions of this paragraph.

1. All persons who have honorably served in the land or naval forces of the United States in the Revolutionary war, or in the War of 1812, or in the war with Mexico, or in any war with the Indians or in the War between the States, or in the war with Spain, or who honorably served in the land or naval forces of the Confederate States, or of the State of Georgia in the War between the States, or

2. All persons lawfully descended from those embraced in the classes enumerated in the sub-division next above, or

3. All persons who are of good character, and understand the duties and obligations of citizenship under a republican form of government, or

4. All persons who can correctly read in the English language any paragraph of the Constitution of the United States or of this State and correctly write the same in the English language when read to them by any one of the registrars, and all persons who solely because of physical disability are unable to comply

---

[6] From *Acts and Resolutions of the General Assembly of the State of Georgia*, 1907.

with the above requirements, but who can understand and give a reasonable interpretation of any paragraph of the Constitution of the United States or of this State, that may be read to them by any one of the registrars; or

5. Any person who is the owner in good faith in his own right of at least forty acres of land situated in this State, upon which he resides, or is the owner in good faith in his own right of property, situated in this State and assessed for taxation at the value of five hundred dollars.

Approved August 21, 1907.

6. A Lynching Rampage in South Georgia[7]

Submitted in person
July 10, 1918
Memorandum for Governor Dorsey from Walter F. White

Below are given some of the facts discovered during a recent visit to Brooks and Lowndes Counties, with reference to the recent lynchings in these two counties:

It was learned that the following Negroes are known to have been lynched, the first six of these having been reported in the daily press:

Will Head,
Will Thompson,
Hayes Turner,
Mary Turner,
Eugene Rice,
Sidney Johnson.

In addition to these, a Negro by the name of Chime Riley was lynched and turpentine cups (these being clay cups used to catch turpentine gum when the trees are cut to obtain gum) were tied to his body, and the body was thrown into the Little River near Barney Georgia.... Another Negro by the name of Simon Schuman was called out of his house near Berlin on the Moultrie Road between eight and nine o'clock at night and has not been seen since.... In addition to the eight mentioned above, bodies of three unidentified Negroes whose names I have been unable to learn but which I expect to receive at an early date, were taken from the Little River just below Quitman. I was informed by a minister that eighteen Negroes have been killed. I discovered only the eleven mentioned above.

---

[7] From "Memorandum for Governor Dorsey from Walter F. White," July 10, 1918, Papers of the NAACP, Library of Congress.

As stated above, Will Head and Will Thompson were lynched on Friday night, May 17th. Hayes Turner was taken from the jail at Quitman by Sheriff Wade and the Clerk of the County Court, Roland Knight by name, for the purpose of being carried to Moultrie for safe-keeping. Turner was taken from these officers about three and a half miles from Quitman near a bridge on the Okapilco Creek. He was hanged with his hands hand-cuffed behind him. He hung on the tree between Saturday and Monday and was then cut down by the county convicts and buried about five feet from the tree on which he was lynched. Mary Turner, his wife, made the remark that the lynching of her husband was unjust, that he knew nothing of the crime, and that if she knew the parties who were in the mob she would have warrants sworn out against them. For this she was captured on Sunday and carried to a place a few yards from Folsom's Bridge on Little River and there lynched. The method of execution in this case, was most brutal. At the time she was lynched Mary Turner was in her eight month of pregnancy. Her ankles were tied together and she was hung to the tree head down. Gasoline was taken from the cars and poured on her clothing which was then fired. When her clothes had burned off, a sharp instrument was taken and she was cut open in the middle, her stomach being entirely opened. Her unborn child fell from her womb, gave two cries, and was then crushed by the heel of a member of the mob. Her body was then riddled with bullets from high-powered rifles until it was no longer possible to recognize it as the body of a human being....

A spirit of unrest exists in both Brooks and Lowndes Counties which will undoubtedly affect the labor situation in that community. It is my information that over five hundred Negroes have left the community since the lynching. Many more, because of property which they own and crops which they have now in process of cultivation, are unable to do so at the present time, but are planning to leave as soon as they can dispose of their land and gather their crops.

7. A Statement from Governor Hugh M. Dorsey as to the Negro in Georgia[8]

Atlanta, Ga., April 22, 1921
To the Conference of Citizens
Called to Meet this Day in Atlanta:

---

[8] From "A Statement from Governor Hugh Dorsey as to the Negro in Georgia," Rare Pamphlets, Georgia Archives.

A. The negro Lynched—

B. The negro held in peonage—

C. The negro driven out by organized lawlessness—

D. The negro subject to individual acts of cruelty—

Under these four headings, in the following pages I have grouped 135 examples of the alleged mistreatment of negroes in Georgia in the last two years. Without design, or the knowledge of each other, Georgians, with one exception, have called these cases to my attention as Governor of Georgia....

In some counties the negro is being driven out as though he were a wild beast. In others he is being held as a slave. In others, no negroes remain.

In only two of the 135 cases cited is the "usual crime" against white women involved.

As Governor of Georgia, I have asked you, as citizens having the best interests of the State at heart, to meet here today to confer with me as to the best course to be taken. To me it seems that we stand indicted as a people before the world. If the conditions indicated by these charges should continue, both God and man would justly condemn Georgia more severely than man and God have condemned Belgium and Leopold for the Congo atrocities. But worse than that condemnation would be the destruction of our civilization by the continued toleration of such cruelties in Georgia....

The Remedy

To end these conditions I would suggest

1. Publicity, namely the careful gathering and investigation by Georgians, and not by outsiders, of facts as to the treatment of the negro throughout the State and the publication of these facts to the people of Georgia.

...4. The organization of State Committees on race relations, one Committee composed of leading white citizens, another of leaders among the negroes, and local committees made up in the same manner in each county of the State, the committees to confer together when necessary concerning matters vital to the welfare of both races.

...6. The enactment of laws—

... (b) Imposing a financial penalty upon any County in which a lynching may occur, when the officials of that county have failed in their duty.

(c) Authorizing the Governor of the State to appoint at any time three judges of the Superior Court to act as a commission to investigate any lynching occurring in any County of the State and empowering the Governor to remove from office any public official found by such commission to have failed to enforce or uphold the law.

ESSAYS

Black Georgia in the Progressive Era[9]

John Dittmer

Protests failed to stop the march of Jim Crow through Georgia. Although blacks had never shared equal access to public accommodations, laws separating the races had not appeared with any frequency until the 1890s. The *Plessy v. Ferguson* decision of 1896 gave federal sanction to "separate but equal" facilities. Whether by law or custom, urban blacks in the early twentieth century found themselves increasingly segregated. Canton, with less than a thousand inhabitants, prohibited any blacks except nurses in charge of white children from "passing upon or loitering in the park of the town." Violators were subject to a hundred-dollar fine or sixty days on the chain gang, or both. Other towns excluded blacks from most parks, either legally or through intimidation. In the early twentieth century Savannah had five playgrounds for white children, none for blacks. These recreational areas had facilities and equipment for baseball, basketball, tennis, soccer, volleyball, and gymnastics, all paid for in part by black Savannahans who could not even set foot on the playgrounds as spectators.

By the second decade of the twentieth century, nearly all larger cities required racial separation in restaurants, usually by partition. Theatres, lectures, concerts, and athletic events were either closed to blacks or open only on a Jim Crow basis. Swimming pools were exclusively for whites. When the Southern Bank of Savannah established separate deposit windows in 1903, most black patrons withdrew their accounts—but the separate windows remained.

Despite its "New South" image, Atlanta was also a Jim Crow city. Bars and restaurants were open to only one race, and barber shops also had to designate whether they served black or white patrons. Jim Crow trains were becoming the rule in the South, yet Atlanta even refused blacks permission to enter and leave by the front door of the terminal. The city council passed an ordinance in 1903 prohibiting black college athletes from playing football games in Brisbane Park, black prisoners rode to the stockade in separate vehicles, and black witnesses swore on Jim Crow Bibles in Atlanta courts. As in other cities, black customers received shabby treatment in Atlanta stores. A clerk in a local haberdashery told a college graduate that he might "buy but not try on" a hat, while clerks in

---

[9] Reprinted with permission of John Dittmer, professor emeritus of History, Depauw University.

other stores would not fit gloves or shoes on black women. By the 1900s nearly all office building elevators were labeled "For White People Only," or "For Colored People, Freight, Etc." All of Atlanta's twenty parks were segregated, including the zoo area in Grant Park. There each race followed its separate passage through the grounds. Separation of the races became so complete that when a black man first bought an automobile a white Atlantan asked him, "Whose road are you going to drive it on?"

Blacks could not even visit public libraries. Du Bois led an Atlanta delegation into the newly dedicated Carnegie Library in 1902 to ask trustees to open the building to all people, arguing that a public library should benefit both races and pointing out the illegality of using tax money to support library facilities for whites only. The chairman responded: "Do you not think that allowing whites and negroes to use this library would be fatal to its usefulness?" As the delegation left, the trustees promised a separate library for blacks would soon be forthcoming. Nineteen years later the Negro public library branch opened its doors. The officials who denied intellectual opportunities to blacks could not have been unaware that the decision was yet another step toward a permanent caste system.

During the first two decades of the twentieth century, segregation in Georgia reached a new plateau: the color line gave way to a color wall, thick, high, almost impenetrable. Whether *de jure* or *de facto*, blacks found themselves Jim Crowed at every turn. Separation of the races was essential to white supremacy, and white supremacy was necessary for survival of the white Southern way of life. Belief that theirs was the superior race no doubt caused some whites to demand segregation. W.E.B. Du Bois maintained that Jim Crow laws and other segregationist practices were not designed primarily to brand blacks as inferior but to "flatter white labor to accept public testimony of its superiority instead of higher wages and social legislation."

As for Georgia blacks, they dealt with the caste system in different ways. Theoretically, many forms of protest were open, but in fact choices were few, limited by the very system they were fighting. Petitions to the city council, court suits, lobbying influential whites, and selective boycotts were tactics endorsed by most leaders. Later many would accept the status quo as a necessary evil. Fathers who never rode streetcars or sat in Jim Crow theatres looked on as their children boarded the segregated trolley en route to the "peanut gallery" of the local white moviehouse. Other blacks "arranged their lives so that they touched as few raw edges as possible," avoiding contact with the white world by withdrawing into their own society. Yet some men and women saw potential for racial advancement in Jim Crow Georgia, and they dreamed of a separate and independent community built on the bedrock of a self-sustaining black economy....

The Great Migration began as early as 1914, with the departure from Savannah of five Pennsylvania Railroad trains packed full of black laborers bound for work on railroad lines. It marked the onset of a movement which would relocate a half-million Southern blacks during the war years, the most important event in black America since emancipation. Its cause was the demand for skilled and unskilled labor in the North, brought on by decreasing migration from Europe. Blacks went north to obtain higher wages and to escape Southern repression. In 1915 farm laborers were earning less than a dollar a day in Georgia, while shops and factories paid only $1.25. Northern wages were from two to four times as high. Blacks also wanted to escape white violence, and an investigation in South Georgia showed a direct correlation between lynching and migration. The denial of legal rights, which affected almost all blacks, caused many to leave the South. In short, emigrating blacks hoped to leave the caste system behind.

Long subject to social, economic, and political inequities in the South, blacks had endured these conditions because of limited opportunities elsewhere. Reports that the North was the "promised land" spread through black communities. Labor agents first brought the news, but their presence declined after white authorities made recruiting conditions unpleasant. The Chicago *Defender*, a radical black weekly edited by native Georgian Robert S. Abbott, urged its growing Southern constituency to move north; the newspaper was so persuasive that several Southern towns banned both its sale and possession. The most effective emigration agent was the United States mail, which brought encouraging letters from friends and relatives in the North, often accompanied by money for train tickets to Philadelphia, Chicago, and other Northern centers.

Blacks migrated from all parts of Georgia, but the exodus was greatest in southwestern areas where the boll weevil, "a cross between a termite and a tank," had entered and badly damaged cotton crops in twenty counties. For farmers ruined by the boll weevil, Northern employment was a godsend. Over 4,500 people left the Albany area in a ten-month period beginning in June 1916. Americus reported that 3,000 blacks had migrated and that thousands of acres of land were abandoned. Thomasville, Bainbridge, and other small towns were affected. Early in 1917 the Southwest Georgia Conference of the AME Church reported its offerings sharply down, attributing the decrease "to the fact that within the past few months more than a thousand of our best paying members had migrated to the North."

On the coast, Savannah's good rail and ship connections made it the South's leading migration center. Georgia migrants settled in the New York-Newark area, in Pennsylvania, Ohio, Michigan, and as far west as Chicago. They worked in Connecticut tobacco fields, on railroads, in foundries, steel mills, slaughterhouses, and later in munitions plants. All sorts of people joined the exodus. Skilled tradesmen quickly found jobs, and black professionals followed their clients north. Factories furnished transportation for the unemployed and unskilled; wealthier blacks paid their own fares. Migration was light in North Georgia, where black population was sparse. Few blacks left the Black Belt, partly because whites had them bound by contract or indebtedness; those in peonage were even more tied to the soil. Some did escape, stealing away from their cabins at night while leaving lights burning.

The Geography of Lynching in Georgia, 1880–1930[10]

W. Fitzhugh Brundage

Many, if not most, white Southerners either acquiesced to or openly celebrated mob violence, and yet white residents of different regions did not share the same proclivity to take the law into their own hands. Virtually all observers and scholars of lynching suggest that whites resorted to mob violence to shore up caste lines in the face of some perceived threat, or, more simply, to "keep blacks in their place." If, as the Tuskegee Institute claimed, the frequency of mob violence is a barometer of race relations, then white fears about maintaining racial hierarchy varied considerably from region to region in the South.

In reconstructing the forces that generated mob violence, it is crucial to recognize that the boundaries defining black behavior and keeping blacks "in their place" were products of historical developments that varied from region to region. To be sure, virulent racism and white economic and political dominance shaped race relations throughout the South, but significant variations existed in the tone of race relations and the status of blacks from region to region. The inherent ambiguities in racial lines allowed whites ample opportunities to define and redefine the code of racial etiquette to suit local circumstances. Thus, forms of black behavior that might spark white retribution in one region went unnoticed in another. In some areas of Georgia, for example, whites perceived

---

[10] From W. Fitzhugh Brundage, *Lynching in the New South: Georgia and Virginia, 1880–1930* (Urbana: University of Illinois Press). Used with permission of the University of Illinois Press.

black landholding and economic autonomy, however modest, to be serious challenges to the racial hierarchy....

Although mob violence in Georgia left no region of the state untouched, it occurred at different rates in the state's different regions. In the six counties that comprise coastal Georgia, thirteen lynchings occurred between 1880 and 1930. In neighboring southern Georgia, mobs executed 182 victims. In the Cotton Belt, which stretched across roughly the middle of the state, mobs claimed 202 lives. In the Upper Piedmont region, along the northern border of the Cotton Belt, forty-two people died at the hands of mobs, while in northern Georgia, nineteen victims were lynched. By 1930, mobs had claimed lives in 119 of the 159 counties in Georgia.

The Cotton Belt underwent little noticeable change during the late nineteenth and early twentieth centuries and became a byword for economic stagnation and social stasis. Bordered to the north by the rolling, red-clay hills of the Upper Piedmont and to the south by the vast plains of wire grass and stands of long-leaf pine of southern Georgia, the Cotton Belt was the heart of cotton cultivation in the state, both before and after the Civil War. Abolition initially unsettled plantation agriculture, but by the 1880s whites had established virtually unchallenged control over the resources of the region. Through a combination of subtle intimidation and outright violence, whites seized political power in spite of the very large black majorities in most counties. Extremely limited access to landownership consigned most blacks to tenantry. Rural laborers with aspirations beyond plowing, hoeing, and picking could find little satisfaction in a region largely bereft of either industrial or urban growth. Beyond the corporate limits of Augusta, Columbus, and Macon, which have been described aptly as "oversized towns," only small towns and hamlets interrupted the rural landscape. Finally, whites, suspicious of any innovation that might threaten their dominance, created a system of public schools that challenged blacks to derive any benefit from education.

For the small white population of the Black Belt that was dependent on black labor, mob violence, as the sociologist Oliver C. Cox observed, was "the culminating act of continuing white aggression against the Negro." Despite a secure grip on the Cotton Belt, whites felt the need to reassert dominance repeatedly with whipping sprees and lynchings. Violence was as central to the maintenance of white domination in the region as disfranchisement and black poverty. Not only were there more lynchings in the Cotton Belt than anywhere else in the state, but mob violence also became more frequent over time, increasing from an average of fewer than two incidents a year during the decade from 1880 to 1889, to four a year during the subsequent two decades, and seven a year between 1910 and 1919.

Virtually every county in the Cotton Belt experienced at least one lynching, many more in most counties. Oglethorpe County, with three lynchings scattered over four decades, represented the average. In other more mob-prone counties, lynchers claimed upwards of ten lives, and in the case of Early County, eighteen lives, between 1880 and 1930. The pervasiveness of lynching ensured that most people in the region had some personal exposure to mob violence, if only through the stories of bystanders or participants. That generation after generation of whites and blacks witnessed lynchings is borne out by the fact that 44 percent of the Cotton Belt counties had at least one lynching in each of three or more decades. What these statistics cannot convey adequately is the cumulative psychological toll that such commonplace extralegal violence took on the entire community.

The atmosphere of violence, so pronounced in Cotton Belt race relations, also was evident in the alleged crimes that provoked lynchings. Murder or violent assault, not rape, was the allegation most often leveled against mob victims in the region. Before 1900, alleged sexual offenses prompted the largest number of lynchings, but in the subsequent three decades, murder topped the list of causes of mob violence. Between 1910 and 1919, for example, lynchers executed fifty-five victims for violent attacks and murders, nine for a variety of lesser affronts, and eight for sexual transgressions. Although it is impossible to know how common intraracial homicide was, it is clear that whites in the Cotton Belt chose to make the punishment of blacks charged with offenses against whites an object lesson for the entire black community.

The racial violence of the Cotton Belt was nearly duplicated in southern Georgia, a region that was incorporated rapidly into the cotton kingdom following the Civil War. Southern Georgia, which includes the comparatively fertile lands of the southwestern corner of the state, the unrelieved expanse of the pine barrens, and the irreclaimable Okefenokee Swamp, escaped the antebellum era with only scattered incursions of the plantation agriculture that flourished along the tidal inlets and plains of the coastal region to the east and the Cotton Belt to the north. During the late nineteenth century, however, southern Georgia underwent a succession of rapid settlement and rural industrialization before taking on the familiar character of the Cotton Belt. The fluid, frontier-like conditions in the region attracted large numbers of upcountry whites, who envisioned better prospects in the wire-grass frontier, and blacks, who hoped to secure a foothold in the region's economy. Predictably, many whites viewed the ambitions of blacks as a direct threat to their own aspirations and to the fragile racial hierarchy. This tension between blacks' aspirations and whites' determination to replicate the social relations of the Cotton Belt fostered brittle race relations and fueled a half-century of violence.

The mob violence that claimed 182 lives in southern Georgia, then, was in part an expression of the deeply rooted tensions produced by the rapid settlement and development of the region. The most rapidly developing counties were the most prone to mob violence. Those in southern Georgia, where lynchings occurred, were more densely populated and (excepting the decade from 1880 to 1889) grew faster than did the region as a whole. The most mob-prone counties also had larger black populations than did the region as a whole. Finally, mob violence occurred in virtually all of the major towns, the most striking symbols of "progress and prosperity" in the region, as well as in smaller crossroad hamlets and industrial villages.

Virtually every county in the region hosted at least one lynching; the four in Toombs County represented the average. Brooks County, with twenty-two, earned the unenviable reputation as the most mob-prone county in both the region and the state—and possibly even in the South. Forty-three percent of the counties in the region experienced at least one lynching in each of three or more decades; in the case of Emmanuel County, mobs claimed lives in each decade between 1880 and 1930.

The crimes that provoked mob violence in southern Georgia also mirrored those in the Cotton Belt. Murders and violent assaults accounted for the majority, a trait that became especially pronounced between 1900 and 1920. During these two decades mobs murdered forty victims for alleged murders and only twenty-nine for all other crimes combined.

It would be a grave error to assume that persistent racial strife and mob violence were inherent to staple-crop agriculture. The postbellum history of the Upper Piedmont underscores that not all portions of the cotton kingdom were hotbeds. The comparatively low levels of mob violence in the region, at least when compared to those of the Cotton Belt and southern Georgia, also demonstrate that rapid change did not inherently generate chronic mob violence. Certainly, few regions of the South underwent more rapid change than did the Upper Piedmont of Georgia during the late nineteenth century. While farmers in the region were drawn into market-driven cotton cultivation, a period of sustained urban and industrial transformations had far-reaching and unforeseen consequences. But while these jarring changes produced serious social strains, including violence, they failed to produce a bloody record of mob violence as in other parts of Georgia.

Racial tensions did flare in the region but seldom in the context of white landlord-black tenant relations. Rather, some of the violence expressed the rage and frustration of white tenants and sharecroppers. Landless whites, who chafed when they found themselves caught in a system of labor they believed fit only for blacks, insisted that they be in loftier positions on the agricultural ladder. But the evolution of Upper Piedmont agriculture almost certainly stripped most embattled poor whites of any hope of acquiring land. They were left with the token advantages they received from white landlords—modestly better land to till and a degree of latitude denied blacks. Their pent-up discontent periodically surfaced in terrorist racial violence.

To be sure, the bulk of lynchings in the Upper Piedmont were not carried out by terrorist mobs of whitecappers. Serious alleged crimes prompted most of the mob murders in the region. Attempted rape or rape was the allegation leveled against seventeen of the thirty-five black victims of mob violence between 1880 and 1919. Lesser infractions comprised the next most common cause for mob violence. Twelve blacks and one white were lynched for overstepping the boundaries of acceptable conduct by arguing with an employer, informing revenue agents, or committing sundry affronts so obscure that they were not recorded. The remaining nine lynchings of three whites and six blacks were prompted by alleged attempted murders and murders. What these statistics reveal is that the alleged crimes that prompted violence in the Upper Piedmont differed markedly from the crimes that produced mob violence in the Cotton Belt and southern Georgia....

The social tensions played out to their violent conclusions in the Upper Piedmont had their counterparts in northern Georgia. During the late nineteenth century, northern Georgians were drawn simultaneously into the market economy and subjected to a new and intrusive imposition of federal authority when federal revenue agents set out to suppress illegal alcohol distilling. Whites in the region, like so many Southerners, reacted to unwelcome change with resentment and outbursts of violence. The violence in northern Georgia, like the bloodshed in the Upper Piedmont, flared only sporadically, however. The social crisis that these deeply divisive innovations sparked left as its imprint on generations of mountain folk festering tensions that bred feuds, murders, and personal violence of all kinds, but not mob violence.

Whitecapping violence was most pronounced in the western corner of northern Georgia, which had experienced rapid and complete economic transformation since the Civil War. The region also hosted the largest number of lynchings in northern Georgia. Eleven occurred between 1880 and 1930, and of these, nine took place between 1880 and 1894. The spate of lynchings, not coincidentally, occurred at the same time that the changes in the region had given rise to mounting concerns over the passing of the old order. Newspaper editors worried that indolence and lasciviousness would invade the budding towns of the region, and many locals resented surrendering local autonomy to the whims of the market economy. Finally, some whites were troubled by the vexing problem of blacks who did not always abide by the tenets of white supremacy. Thus, the spasm of lynchings and whitecappings against prostitutes, wife-beaters, petty criminals, "uppity" blacks, and revenue informers were all part of a futile rear-guard action to restore much-valued traditions and mores.

Six lynchings occurred in the region after the flurry of violence during the early 1890s. Even after the crisis of the 1890s eased, whites still harbored many of the same fears of black criminality that whites did elsewhere in the state. The diffuse racial fears surfaced in communal responses to heinous crimes allegedly committed by blacks. Whites reacted to alleged sexual assaults and murders by blacks according to the brutal etiquette of race relations that justified lynching black rapists and murderers....

If there was any region of Georgia where whites seemingly should have felt a constant need to keep places, it should have been coastal Georgia. Before the Civil War, white planters, with armies of black slaves, had carved out vast, lucrative rice and cotton plantations. With the war and Reconstruction, however, came social and economic upheavals as wrenching as any endured elsewhere. Yet comparatively tranquil race relations prevailed in coastal Georgia during the late nineteenth and early twentieth centuries. Although conditions for blacks were something less than the "black paradise" that the British traveler Sir George Campbell thought he found in neighboring coastal South Carolina, blacks in coastal Georgia escaped the furious bloodletting that characterized neighboring southern Georgia and the Cotton Belt. With only thirteen lynchings between 1880 and 1930, the low country had fewer lynchings than any other portion of the state.

Despite the abundant signs of black strivings for autonomy, racial violence never became the preferred weapon of whites intent upon bullying. Although coastal Georgia was not free from lynchings, mob violence occurred only sporadically. Of the thirteen lynchings in the region, nine took place between 1880 and 1902. Twenty years passed until a small private mob from southern Georgia waylaid the Dodge County sheriff in 1922, seized the two prisoners he was moving to Savannah for safekeeping, and lynched them in Liberty County. The final lynchings in the region occurred in 1930, when the murder of the sheriff of McIntosh County led to the lynching of two black men. Lynchings in the Low Country were scattered between five of the six coastal counties, and only in Camden County, which borders on Florida, did no lynchings occur. If there was a portion of the Low Country that was mob-prone, it was the western part of Bryan and Liberty counties, where the low country gave way to the piney woods and the predominantly white population cultivated a reputation for hostility to blacks. Between 1888 and 1902, mobs claimed the lives of five blacks in this area.

In most regards, little distinguished individual lynchings in coastal Georgia from lynchings elsewhere in the state. The alleged causes of lynchings in the low country were apportioned among alleged murders, sexual offenses, and various "other crimes." Private mobs and mass mobs carried out the bulk of the lynchings, while posses and terrorist mobs practically never surfaced in the region. Thus, what is distinctive about mob violence in coastal Georgia is not where it occurred or the form it took, but that it took place so infrequently....

However considerable the regional variations in mob violence, blacks recognized that its potential threatened every black in the South. Blacks in coastal Georgia almost certainly felt safer than blacks living in the Cotton Belt of Georgia, but newspaper accounts and oral testimonies of persistent violence elsewhere were vivid reminders of their oppressed status. Lynching was a powerful tool of intimidation that gripped blacks' imaginations, whether blacks lived in a mob-prone county or in the relative safety of coastal Georgia. Neither W.E.B. DuBois, from the shelter of the campus of Atlanta University, nor the author Richard Wright in Mississippi could escape the fear, insecurity, and rage provoked by distant racial violence. As Wright later observed about his youth in the Deep South during the 1920s, "The things that influenced my conduct as a Negro did not have to happen to me directly; I needed but to hear of them to feel their full effects in the deepest layers of my consciousness. Indeed, the white brutality that I had not seen was a more effective control of my behavior than that which I knew."

Additional Sources

Brundage, W. Fitzhugh. *Lynching in the New South: Georgia and Virginia, 1880–1930.* Urbana: University of Illinois Press, 1993.

Dittmer, John. *Black Georgia in the Progressive Era, 1900–1920.* Urbana: University of Illinois Press, 1977.

Godshalk, David F. *Veiled Visions: The 1906 Atlanta Race Riot and the Reshaping of American Race Relations.* Chapel Hill: University of North Carolina Press, 2005.

Inscoe, John, editor. *Georgia in Black and White: Explorations in the Race Relations of a Southern State, 1865–1950.* Athens: University of Georgia Press, 1994.

Mixon, Gregory. *The Atlanta Riot: Race, Class, and Violence in a New South City.* Gainesville: University Press of Florida, 2005.

Chapter 12

THE PROGRESSIVE ERA, 1890–1920

The Progressive Era, defined here as 1890–1920, was a reform movement in the United States. Nationally the goals of the Progressives included government regulation, democratization of government, and social justice. In Georgia Progressive goals included such issues as prohibition, regulation of the railroads, education reform, and penal reform, but Progressives in the state did not unite on a single issue. The first phase of this period was the time of the farmers' revolt as they mounted a challenge to Democratic party policies. In several notable instances the Progressives in Georgia seemed to make some progress, but then they regressed; they took one step forward and two steps back. This period was also marked by worsening race relations (as discussed previously in chapter 11).

The era began in the midst of a farmers' revolt. Georgia farmers, like those in many parts of the country, were suffering economically. Commodities were not commanding high prices and farmers were distressed and disorganized; generally the plight of the farmers was worsening. Organizations formed to assist the farmers, and these groups had an impact in Georgia. The Grangers first made an appearance in the state in 1872 but soon died out and gave way to the Farmers' Alliance. Founded in Texas in 1887, it reached Georgia in 1888. The Alliance had a significant impact on Georgia and was a serious challenge to the power of the New Departure Democrats. Politicians associated with the Alliance dominated the 1890 election in the state, choosing the governor, William J. Northen, and a majority in both houses of the General Assembly (sometimes called the Farmers' Legislature). Yet this legislature failed to enact reforms beneficial to farmers, and by 1891 the Alliance lost most of its strength and influence and gave way to the People's party. The Populists, as the party was more commonly called, had some truly progressive goals in Georgia, and the most visible and powerful Populist figure in the state was Tom Watson. The Populists gained strength as the economy turned sour in 1893. The 1894 election marked the high point of Populism in Georgia, as the party captured fifty-two seats in the General Assembly. The Georgia Democratic party adopted the Populist position on several issues, undercutting their strength. The Populists declined as quickly as they rose.

Georgia's most progressive governors were without a doubt Joseph M. Terrell, elected in 1902 and 1904, and Hoke Smith, elected in 1906 and 1910. Terrell and Smith were also Georgia's only Progressive governors during this era. The reform legislation passed during the administrations of Governors Terrell and Smith includes increased appropriations for public schools, generous support of higher education, a statewide pure food and drug act, the regulation of child labor, the creation of state boards of education and labor, the strengthening of the state Railroad Commission, greater regulation of lobbyists, and statewide prohibition. Another reform measure was the abolition of the convict-lease system. This is probably the best example of taking a step forward and two back; to replace the convict-lease system, the state created the infamous chain gang to control its criminals.

DOCUMENTS

The first document below is an 1888 speech in which Tom Watson encouraged farmers to unite behind a boycott of jute. Document 2 outlines the platform of the state's Populist party in 1892. The third document contains an 1897 piece of legislation banning the playing of football in Georgia and Governor Atkinson's veto of that bill. In Document 4 University of Georgia chemist Charles H. Herty describes his new tree-saving method of collecting pine resin. The fifth document is Governor Slaton's 1915 commutation of Leo Frank's death sentence in the state's most famous court case. Document 6 is a US Supreme Court case involving the ingredients in Georgia's most famous soft drink, Coca-Cola. The seventh document is 1917 legislation that created the county unit system of election in Georgia.

1. Tom Watson Urges a Boycott on Jute[1]

Taxation, other than for the legitimate expenses of the government is unconstitutional, has been, and is yet, held by the ablest and wisest lawyers and statesmen; that taxation, as enforced by the existing tariff, is unjust, unfair and criminally wrong does not admit of successful contradiction.

But there is no tariff on cotton, and when they began to advance the price of the staple, telegrams to Europe, ordering shiploads of cotton back to the United States, annihilated the cotton trust and forced the speculators to compromise on

---

[1] From *Atlanta Constitution*, September 14, 1888.

reasonable terms. So it would be with the bagging trust if bagging was not excluded by a high tariff. While under a low tariff, or no tariff at all, a pool or combination to control the price of any article of limited productions, such as coffee, might be possible, yet when such a combination must embrace a number of nations, with all of their jealousies and prejudices, and requires almost unlimited capital, such a trust would not only be improbable, but practically impossible. For instance, cotton goods of all kinds, woolen goods, cotton bagging, etc., would afford little or no inducement for the formation of trusts.

But this bagging trust has been formed. They control all of the jute bagging on the market, and have advanced the price more than one hundred per cent. Knowing that a reduction of the present tariff is inevitable, they are determined to rob the planter of every dollar which they possibly can while the high tariff remains to protect them, and they have given us no notice that the price shall continue to advance. The southern man who can contemplate this outrage and not get mad hasn't enough blood to fatten a mosquito. This, as well as all other combinations of the kind, is clearly illegal, and ought to be promptly and effectually crushed by congress. But we know that it is folly to expect aid from that direction. ...when the farmers of the south, who are being robbed by this bagging trust, ask relief, congress returns as an answer that they will begin to prepare to get ready to consider to matter in October.... It is useless to ask congress to help us, just as it was folly for our forefathers to ask relief from the tea tax; and, as they revolted at the injustice of the mother country and dumped the obnoxious tea into Boston harbor, so should we resent this great wrong that is being forced upon us, by boycotting the bagging trust....

We have the advantage, let us use it. They say to us, "You must have bagging!" Our answer is, "You must have cotton." They may have the frying pan, but we've got the stuff to fry in it. Let us say to our merchants, "We boycott jute; get us something else," and we believe that they will promptly comply. If not, then they must wait until we can get it for ourselves.

Let the southern farmers band together and make the agricultural influence felt. Demand of your representatives that your views and your interest be consulted. Gather to yourselves the power of unity. Sink all personal differences in the common danger and the common purpose. Good news comes to us from Wilkes and Hancock; let good news go from us to them. Let us keep it up and speed it on. Listen to no man who croaks "Too late, we must submit." Leave that yawp to the laggard or the dastard. True manhood, which dares and does, never yet stooped to such a motto.

2. Georgia's People's Party Platform in 1892[2]

State Platform, Adopted at Atlanta, July 20th, 1892

We <u>endorse</u> and reaffirm the preamble, resolutions and platform adopted by the People's Party in national convention assembled at Omaha, July 4, 1892. We indorse the ticket nominated and pledge the party when it shall come into power in the State to frame and administer the laws in the spirit of the Omaha platform, which is equal justice to all, and special privileges to none.

We condemn the convict lease system.

We demand rigid economy in all public matters and insist on every possible reduction of taxation during the present impoverished condition of the people.

And we call public attention to the fact that the producing interest in both city and country is bearing more than its fair share of taxation.

National Platform, Adopted at Omaha, July 4th, 1892

We declare therefore:

We demand a national currency, safe sound and flexible, issued by the general government only, a full legal tender for all debts, public and private, and that without the use of banking corporations; a just, equitable and efficient means of distribution direct to the people at a tax not to exceed 2 per cent per annum be provided as set forth in the sub-treasury plan of the Farmers' Alliance, or some better system, also by payment in discharge of its obligations for public improvements.

We demand the free and unlimited coinage of silver and gold at the present legal ratio of 16 to 1.

We demand that the amount of the circulating medium be speedily increased to not less than fifty dollars per capita.

We demand a graduated income tax.

We believe that the money of the country should be kept as much as possible in the hands of the people, and hence we demand, that all state and national revenues shall be limited to the necessary expenses of the government economically and honestly administered.

We demand that postal savings banks be established by the government for the safe deposit of the earnings of the people and to facilitate change.

Transportation being a means of exchange and a public necessity, the government should own and operate the railroads in the interest of the people. The telegraph and telephone, like the postal system, being a necessity for the

---

[2] From *The People's Party Paper*, July 29, 1892.

transmission of news, should be owned and operated by the government in the interest of the people.

3. Banning Football in Georgia?[3]

A bill to be entitled an act, to prohibit the playing of prize or match games of foot-ball in this state and to prescribe a penalty for the same.

Sec. 1. Be it enacted by the General Assembly of the state of Georgia, and it is hereby enacted by the authority aforesaid, that from and after the passage of this act, it shall be unlawful for any person or persons to engage in any prize or match game of foot ball or other game.

Sec. 2. Be it further enacted by the authority aforesaid, that it shall be unlawful for any person or persons to come together and play a prize or match game of foot ball in any park or place in this state, where an admission fee is charged for admission to the same.

Sec. 3. Be it further enacted by the authority aforesaid, that each and every person violating the provisions of this act shall be guilty of a misdemeanor and on conviction therefore shall be punished as prescribed in section 1039 of Vol. 3 of the Code of Georgia of 1895.

Sec. 4. Be it further enacted by the authority aforesaid, that all laws and parts of laws in conflict with this act be and the same are hereby repealed.

November 17, 1897.

[Governor Atkinson's] Veto Message
To the House of Representatives:

I hereby return to the House, in which it originated, bill No. 309, entitled "An Act to prohibit the playing of prize or match games of Foot Ball, and for other purposes," which I have declined to approve. It is with great reluctance that I affix my official disapproval to a measure which has received the sanction of the people's representatives, but believing that this one goes beyond the proper limits of legislation, ignores the rights of parents, violates a sound legislative policy and opposes a fundamental principle of our government, I have been constrained to withhold my approval....

I was not unmoved by the sad occurrence which, in my opinion, was the immediate cause of the passage of this bill, but under all circumstances the law making power of a people should adhere to a sound policy and fixed principles.

---

[3] House Bill 309; from House and Senate Bills and Resolutions of the General Assembly, Georgia Archives; Executive Minutes, December 8, 1897, Georgia Archives.

The game as played under existing rules can be made, and is often too rough, but if it can be admitted that the abuses of the game call for legislative action, it could only justify the enactment of a statute sufficiently far reaching to require a modification of the rules and correct the abuses which were deemed a public evil. It would not authorize a statute so severing in its provisions as the one now under consideration....

If the game of football seriously interferes with the welfare of society and inflicts injuries upon others of a character which public opinion will not obviate or correct, legislation should then go just so far as may be necessary to remedy the wrong, but no farther. The right of a parent to say what games his boy shall play should not be questioned nor disturbed until demanded by imperative necessity. The humblest citizen of this state should be secure in his right to control his own child and say in what games he may be permitted to engage. Football causes less deaths than hunting, boating, fishing, horseback riding, bathing or bicycling. If we are to engage in legislation of this character now under discussion, the state should assume the position of parent, forbid all these sports to boys, make it a penal offense for a boy to engage in any of them, and for any parent to permit his child to engage in them. The government should not usurp all the authority of the parent, yet this legislation is a long stride in that direction....

December 8, 1897.

4. Charles Herty Describes His Cup and Gutter System of Turpentine Collection[4]

Herty to Mr. Robert Johnston
Ocilla, Ga., November 17, 1902
Concerning the method of turpentining, about which you wrote me, I beg to say that we have been conducting experiments during this whole season, on a more conservative method of gathering turpentine from pine trees, the main ideas in this method being, 1st—To protect the timber better by not cutting the deep boxes in the face of the tree. 2nd—To avoid waste of spirits of turpentine, by using a receptacle, which catches the crude turpentine in every year, just as soon as it leaves the tree. 3rd—To improve the grade of rosin, by not allowing the fresh turpentine to pass over the colored surface of the previous year's work.

---

[4] From Charles Herty to Mr. Robert Johnston, November 17, 1902, Charles H. Herty Papers, Manuscript, Archives, and Rare Book Library, Emory University, Atlanta, Georgia.

I enclose a clipping from The Atlanta Constitution, which contains an illustration, showing the equipment, which we use. This equipment consists simply of an ordinary clay cup with a hole in the rim, the cup resembling very much an ordinary flower pot, thought the form is narrower and the cup is not porous. The two gutters used to conduct the gum to the cup are simply strips of galvanized iron, #29 gauge, cut in desired lengths and bent along their lengths at a slight angle to form a gutter. These gutters are inserted in the face of the tree in a shallow cut about 1/4 of an inch deep made by a common broad-ax, the gutters being placed about one inch apart at the center, the lower gutter projecting about 1 1/2 " beyond the center of the face and forming a spout. The cup is hung just below the spout on a 6 D. Nail. The result obtained this season show conclusively that timber, which has not been "Boxed" is capable of producing about 23 1/2 % more crude turpentine than timber that has been "Boxed". The saving in the later years of working run as high as 65 %, while the net sales of the rosin from the old trees bring from three to four times as much profit to the operator at present market prices, as trees of similar age, working under the box system.

5. Commutation of Leo Frank's Sentence[5]

June 21st, 1915
            In Re Leo M. Frank, Fulton Superior Court.
            Sentenced to be executed, June 22nd, 1915.
Saturday, April 26th, 1913, was Memorial Day in Georgia and a general holiday. At that time Mary Phagan, a white girl, of about 14 years of age was in the employ of the National Pencil Company located near the corner of Forsyth & Hunter Sts. in the City of Atlanta. She came to the Pencil Factory a little after noon to obtain the money due her for her work on the preceding Monday, and Leo M. Frank, the defendant, paid her $1.20, the amount due her and this was the last time she was seen alive.

Frank was tried for the offense and found guilty the succeeding August. Application is now made for clemency....

In the Frank case three matters have developed since the trial which did not come before the jury, to wit: the Carter notes, the testimony of Becker, indicating that the death notes were written in the basement, and the testimony of Dr. Harris, that he was under the impression that the hair on the lathe was

---

[5] Courtesy of the Georgia Archives.

not that of Mary Phagan, and thus tending to show that the crime was not committed on the floor of Frank's office.

While made the subject of an extraording motion for a new trial, it is well known that it is almost a practical impossibility to have a verdict set aside by this procedure.

The evidence might not have changed the verdict, but it might have caused the jury to render a verdict with the recommendation to mercy.

In any event, the performance of my duty under the Constitution is a matter of my conscience. The responsibility rests where the power is reposed. Judge Roan, with that awful sense of responsibility, which probably came over him as he thought of that Judge before whom he would shortly appear, calls to me from another world to request that I do that which he should have done. I can endure misconstruction, abuse and condemnation, but I cannot stand the constant companionship of an accusing conscience, which would remind me in every thought that I, as Governor of Georgia, failed to do what I thought to be right. There is a territory "beyond A REASONABLE DOUBT and absolute certainty," for which the law provides in allowing life imprisonment instead of execution. This case has been marked by doubt. The trial Judge doubted. Two Judges of the Supreme Court of Georgia doubted. Two Judges of the Supreme Court of the United States doubted. One of the three Prison Commissioners doubted.

In my judgment, by granting a commutation in this case, I am sustaining the jury, the judge, and the appellate tribunals, and at the same time am discharging that duty which is placed on me by the Constitution of the State.

Acting, therefore, in accordance with what I believe to be my duty under the circumstances of this case, it is

ORDERED: That the sentence in the case of Leo M. Frank is commuted from the death penalty to imprisonment for life.

This 21st day of June, 1915.

John M. Slaton

6. *U.S. v. Forty Barrels and Twenty Kegs of Coca Cola*[6]

Argued February 29, 1916
Decided May 22, 1916
Mr. Justice Hughes delivered the opinion of the court:

---

[6] From *U.S. v. Forty Barrels and Twenty Kegs of Coca Cola*, 241 US 265.

This is a libel for condemnation under the food and drug acts, of a certain quantity of a food product known as "Coca Cola" transported for sale, from Atlanta, Georgia, to Chattanooga, Tennessee. It was alleged that the product was adulterated and misbranded. The allegation of adulteration was, in substance, that the product contained an added poisonous or added deleterious ingredient, caffeine which might render the product injurious to health. It was alleged to be misbranded in that the name "Coca Cola" was a representation of the presence of the substances coca and cola; that the product "contained no coca and little if any cola" and thus was an "imitation" of these substances and was offered for sale under their "distinctive name." We omit other charges which the government subsequently withdrew. The claimant answered, admitting that the product contained as one of its ingredients "a small portion of caffeine," but denying that it was either an "added" ingredient, or a poisonous or a deleterious ingredient which might make the product injurious. It was also denied that there were substances known as coca and cola "under their own distinctive names," and it was averred that the product did contain "certain elements or substances derived from coca leaves and cola nuts." The answer also set forth, in substance, that "Coca Cola" was the "distinctive name" of the product under which it had been known and sold for more than twenty years as an article of food, with other averments negativing adulteration and misbranding under the provisions of the act.

Jury trial was demanded, and voluminous testimony was taken. The district judge directed a verdict for the claimant, and judgment entered accordingly was affirmed on writ of error by the circuit court of appeals. And the government now prosecutes this writ....

In the present case, the article belongs to a familiar group; it is a syrup. It was originally called "Coca-Cola Syrup and Extract." It is produced by melting sugar,—the analysis showing that 52.64 per cent of the product is sugar and 42.63 per cent is water. Into the syrup thus formed by boiling the sugar, there are introduced coloring, flavoring, and other ingredients, in order to give the syrup a distinctive character. The caffeine, as has been said, is introduced in the second or third "melting." We see no escape from the conclusion that it is an "added" ingredient within the meaning of the statute....

In the present case we are of opinion that it could not be said as matter of law that the name was not primarily descriptive of a compound with coca and cola ingredients, as charged. Nor is there basis for the conclusion that the designation had attained a secondary meaning as the name of a compound from which either coca or cola ingredients were known to be absent; the claimant had always insisted, and now insists, that its product contains both. But if the name was found to be descriptive, as charged, there was clearly a conflict of evidence with respect to the presence of any coca ingredient.

The judgment is reversed and the cause is remanded for further proceedings in conformity with this opinion.

It is so ordered.

7. Neill Primary Act[7]

An Act to provide for nominations by political parties in this State of candidates for United States Senator, Governor, State House officers, Justices of the Supreme Court and Judges of the Court of Appeals at primary elections, by the county unit system....

Section 1. Whenever any political party in this State shall hold primary elections for nominations of candidates for United States Senator, Governor, State House Officers, Justices of the Supreme Court, and Judges of the Court of Appeals, such party or its authorities shall cause all candidates for nominations for said offices to be voted for on one and the same day throughout the State, which is hereby fixed on the second Wednesday in September of each year in which there is a regular general election. Candidates for nominations to above named offices who receive, respectively, the highest number of popular votes in any given county shall be considered to have carried such county, and shall be entitled to the full vote of such county on the county unit basis, that is to say, two votes for each representative to which such county is entitled in the Lower House of the General Assembly. If in any county any two or more candidates should tie for the highest number of popular votes received, then the county unit vote of such county shall be equally divided between the candidates so tying....

---

[7] From *Acts and Resolutions of the General Assembly of the State of Georgia*, 1917.

ESSAYS

The Populist Party in Georgia[8]

Barton C. Shaw

The time was right for the arrival of the Populists. Between 1892 and 1897, the People's party held ninety-nine seats in the Georgia General Assembly. At no time did it have a majority in either chamber, and at the height of its strength in 1894, the party claimed only 21 percent of the house and senate membership. Consequently, it could influence legislation only when the majority divided—something Democratic leaders strove to prevent. To add to their difficulties, Populist legislators were confused about how their doctrine was to influence state government. The People's party had been founded as an answer to national and international problems, and the St. Louis and Omaha platforms addressed themselves only to these issues. Both documents were silent about the role of Populist legislators. The Georgia General Assembly could do little to bring about federal ownership of the railroads, the subtreasury plan, the free and unlimited coinage of silver, or an end to the national banks of issue. Thus the question remained: What did Populism mean on the state level?

At first the Georgia People's party seemed baffled by the problem, its platform in 1892 containing only two vague demands: an end to convict lease (without saying what was to replace it) and, when feasible, lower taxes. But by 1894 the party seemed to be attaining an identity. Its new platform supported the secret ballot, the election of all government officials, and the monthly payment of schoolteachers. In an attack on Georgia's notorious fee system, it also demanded that whenever possible public servants receive salaries. The platform ended with a plank calling for the state control of prisoners and a resolution denouncing the whitecaps. The proposals of 1896 were similar to those of 1894, except that the Populists replaced the whitecap resolution with an antilynching plank. In addition, they called for the construction of a state reform school. Only two of their demands during this period went beyond a desire for honest government and less mob rule. In 1894 the platform argued that the state, rather than parents, should pay for primary school textbooks, and two years later it came out in favor of prohibition.

---

[8] From Barton Shaw, *The Wool Hat Boys: Georgia's Populist Party* (Baton Rouge: Louisiana State University Press, 1984). Used with permission of Louisiana State University Press.

Democrats constantly charged that Georgia Populism and socialism were synonymous. But a careful reading of the third-party's state platforms would have caused little alarm. Most surprising was the absence of any challenge to the economic order in Georgia. As much as farmers strained under the lien system and the South's seemingly feudal notions of land tenure, there was no demand for reform. Whatever the real nature of Georgia Populism, it was not the bomb-throwing radicalism that so many Democrats feared.

Indeed, in 1892 the danger of Populism appeared slight. "The Third party organization will not last in Georgia. In fact it is practically dead already," wrote the Atlanta *Journal* two days before the first Populists took their legislative seats. In the house there were 15 third-party men out of a membership of 175; in the senate, 1 out of 45. It looked, indeed, as if the *Journal*'s prediction would come true. But two years later, with the near victory of James K. Hines in the gubernatorial election, Populist membership swelled to 43 members in the house and 7 in the senate.

As usual Tom Watson's influence was evident. His *People's Party Paper* printed numerous suggestions to legislators, and two of his lieutenants ruled the Populists in each chamber. In the house, Mell Branch's cheerful disposition made it difficult to believe that this watermelon farmer was known as "hell-raising" Mell and that he had once chaired the committee that had written the Omaha platform of 1892. Branch's knowledge of parliamentary procedures, his understanding of national and state politics, and his ability to remain on pleasant terms with Democrats made him an able minority leader. In the senate the Populist chief was Major Charles E. McGregor, the man who had both defended and angered black delegates at the third-party convention in 1894 and had gruffly rebuked a black man for trying to speak to Tom Watson. McGregor was well known in Georgia….

But Major McGregor was only one of seventy-seven third-party men who served in the General Assembly between 1892 and 1898. As a group they possessed less wealth, less status, less education, less political experience, and more limited prospects that their democratic colleagues. Although information about their schooling is sketchy, it is possible that only two received any formal education beyond the common school level. Nevertheless, their ranks included two lawyers (who apparently read law as young men), a director of a cotton mill, a physician, and a minister. But most were engaged in agriculture. In the 1880s fifty-three were farmers or, in a few cases, men who combined farming with some other business. It is likely that most continued in this field in the 1890s. Besides McGregor, none was a large or even a medium-sized planter; indeed, in 1886 only ten (18.8 percent) were small planters—that is, men who employed tenants and who were worth between $5,000 and $10,000. The remaining forty-two held property valued at less than $5,000, and of these, twenty-two (41.5 percent) fell into the $1,000 to $2,000 range. A few of these were men of modest means, five being worth only $500 to $1,000. It is not known how these men fared in the 1890s, but it is unlikely that many prospered. None, however, was a tenant, a sharecropper, or a black. Only nine (11.6 percent) had previously served in the legislature.

By almost every index the Populists differed from Democratic legislators. At forty-two years of age, the average Democrat was almost five years younger than the average Populist. He was also better educated—65.4 percent having attended college, law school, or some other institution of higher education. Two-thirds were professionals, of which 56.0 percent were lawyers and 10.6 percent were physicians. In the 1880s only one in five was engaged in agriculture, and of these 45.4 percent were planters. Nearly a third (29.2 percent) had previously sat in the legislature. Many were up-and-coming young men who would one day rule the state. Indeed, a random sample of just a fourth of their number turned up a future governor, United States senator, congressman, state commissioner of agriculture, public service commissioner, judge of the federal court of appeals, and seven future judges of the superior court. Among all of the Populists, there were only a future state pension commissioner (Charles McGregor, who served from 1923 until his death in 1924) and a state superior court judge.

Despite their inexperience, Populist legislators labored diligently to master the workings of the General Assembly. At first, the demand for honest elections was a secondary concern. But after the questionable defeats of Watson, Hines, and Felton, election reform became a passion with them. Soon they were submitting bills favoring the Australian ballot, the initiative, the referendum, and the election of all public officials. Most of these proposals died in committee. One exception was the Populist demand for the election of superior court judges and solicitors-general. Countless Georgians had been disgusted by the tawdry actions that preceded appointments to the superior court bench. Even Democrats in the legislature were beginning to grouse about the cost of these affairs. Other politicos, and especially the supporters of Clement Evans, complained that the judiciary had fallen into the hands of their enemies. Thus by 1897 numerous legislators favored the measure. With Populist support, it easily passed through both chambers and was signed by the governor. Although Democrats proudly claimed the bill as their own, the third party had been crusading for it since 1894. This was the only important election reform bill that was enacted during these years.

But Populists had other legislative interests. In particular, they seemed driven by a desire to reduce waste. In the house they tried to reduce the salaries of the governor, the members of the legislature, and all state judges; in the senate they attempted to lower the salaries of almost every other state employee. A few Populists even objected to paving the street in front of the governor's mansion, and some grumbled when the lower chamber hired an extra page. W. F. Goldin, a third-party senator from the Thirty-Eighth District, was especially famous as a legislative miser. "He watches the expenditure of every dollar with the scrutiny [of]...a hawk eye[ing] a chicken with which it has prospective business," wrote the Atlanta *Constitution*....

When explaining their tightfistedness, Populists made it plain that they took seriously the conventional wisdom of the day: in times of depression the government, like the citizen, should reduce expenses. Yet on some matters, People's party legislators were not entirely frugal. They usually favored adequate appropriations for the common school fund, but they objected to professionals or a select group of citizens controlling educational institutions. Instead, they called for the election of all school commissioners and boards of education....

Thinking back over their years in the General Assembly, former third-party legislators probably remembered their Democratic colleagues with some fondness. On most bills there had existed surprising unanimity. When dispute flared, as in the case of the election of superior court judges, a considerable number of Democrats had voted with the Populists. The third-party demand for free textbooks, the Democrats' intransigence on election reform, and the battle over convict lease produced the appearance of great struggle. But for the most part, this was an illusion. Indeed, one is struck by the similarity rather than dissimilarity of the views of these men.

With such harmony, some citizens wondered why the Populist party ever appeared in Georgia. They forgot the Populists had been founded as an answer to national issues. The People's party needed an organization in the state only to turn out the vote in federal races and to elect legislators who in turn would appoint United States senators. On many state questions there was little reason for the party's existence. Democratic reformers already sat in the legislature, and because the Farmers' Alliance had elected some of these Democrats to office in 1890, many possessed ideas similar to those of the Populists. They differed from third-party legislators only in that they failed to renounce the Democratic party and could not accept every provision of the Omaha platform. Indeed, the real legislative battles of these years were usually between reformers and Bourbons rather than Democrats and Populists. Such battles foretold the struggles of the Progressive Era.

Governor Hoke Smith's Reform Program[9]

Dewey W. Grantham, Jr.

The day of Hoke Smith's inauguration—June 29, 1907—was an occasion to remember. There had been nothing like it, asserted an Atlanta newspaper, since "colonial patriots gathered at Savannah to declare Georgia a sovereign state." Since early morning the streets had been lined with people eager to greet the marching soldiers, the brass bands, and the political clubs. Almost every building was decked with masses of bunting and flags, and festoons of flowers encircled portraits of the state's leading politician. At noon the center of attention became the improvised pavilion on the capitol grounds, where a tall, somewhat ponderous figure attired in a light silk coat and a plain straw hat was preparing to take the oath of office as governor of Georgia. A few minutes later the new governor began to read his inaugural address.

Smith said little that was new to his audience; his address was a comprehensive summary of the familiar reform proposals. "I accept office," he declared, "under solemn direction by the people to carry out the platform pledges." Foreseeing, perhaps, the temptations of reformers to follow the siren calls of other movements, he warned that "We must not be led away to other tasks until our specific pledges to the people have been performed." In a one-two-three fashion he outlined his plans to prohibit lobbying, outlaw free passes, ensure clean election, regulate the primaries by state law, amend the constitution by adopting a literacy test and a "grandfather clause," extend the Western and Atlantic Railroad, and strengthen the railroad commission and regulate public-service companies. Georgia must move forward, declared Smith, and "constantly broaden opportunities for mental, moral and financial growth to [the] less fortunate....

Smith had hoped to force his program rapidly through the legislature in 1907. But no sooner had the General Assembly met than an unexpected issue—prohibition—emerged to complicate the situation. It had played no part in the campaign of 1906, but after Smith's term began, it assumed an importance that made it impossible to evade. Under the local-option law of 1883, approximately 125 of Georgia's 145 counties had adopted prohibition by 1907, but most of the large urban centers remained wet. Prohibition advocates like Fred Loring Seely, editor of the Atlanta *Georgian and News*, now saw in the

---

[9] From Dewey W. Grantham, *Hoke Smith and the Politics of the New South* (Baton Rouge: Louisiana State University Press, 1958). Used with permission of Louisiana State University Press.

new reform administration a golden opportunity to secure statewide prohibition. Smith was a long-time proponent of local option, but he was careful not to make an issue of the prohibition proposal. To take a stand either way would divide his followers in the General Assembly and jeopardize the chances of enacting his reforms.

The prohibition bill encountered strong opposition and long filibustering tactics before its supporters managed to get it through the legislature early in August, making Georgia the first Southern state to adopt statewide prohibition during this era. Despite Smith's efforts to effect a compromise and hasten the disposal of the issue by the embattled legislators, it largely consumed thirty of the fifty days of the annual session. On the evening of the bill's passage by the house, prohibition champions led 1,500 cheering people to the executive mansion, where the governor promised to sign the measure and pledged himself to do all he could to enforce it....

Meanwhile, Smith had tried to accomplish certain other reforms. When the General Assembly convened in June 1908, he had presented a series of proposals calling for closer regulation of primary elections and a "pure ballot." A major complaint of Georgia Progressives was the influence exerted by money, liquor, free passes, and corporation contributions in elections, particularly in the all-important primary elections. Numerous testimonials of these years tell of the corruption and dishonesty that characterized the election process. Most of the rules governing the primary were party rather than state regulations. This meant that the executive committee of the party possessed great latitude in determining how the system would operate. Furthermore, state primaries used the county-unit system, which allowed the candidate with a plurality of votes in each county to receive the county's unit votes and gave the rural counties a disproportionately large voice in the outcome of statewide primaries....

In response to Smith's detailed recommendations in 1908, the General Assembly enacted a primary regulatory act, a registration law, a measure requiring candidates to submit a sworn statement of their campaign expenses, and a corrupt-practices act designed to prohibit corporation contributions to any political campaign or through contributions to influence political action. The registration plan defined the duties of the registrars and tax collectors and laid down detailed requirements for the payment of taxes before registering, the taking of a special oath by every voter, and the right of appeal from the action of the registrars. The primary act stipulated that statewide primaries must be held on the same day for candidates for governor, state house officers, congressmen, members of the General Assembly, and state judicial officials, the date to be fixed by the state executive committee. Primaries could not be held earlier than sixty days before the regular elections, and electors must vote in the militia districts in which they resided.

In addition to the election laws enacted by the legislature in 1908, several other measures of a reform nature were passed. A pure food and drug act extended the provisions of a law of 1906 by providing for a food inspector and a drug inspector. Another act limited the interest rate on loans made in the state, and other legislation provided for the regulation of telegraphic service and for the establishment of a tuberculosis sanitarium.

By the time the legislature met in 1908, the Atlanta *Georgian and News* and such reformers as Dr. John E. White, an Atlanta minister, had launched a vigorous crusade against the convict-lease system in Georgia. The leasing system had long been criticized. "Every one knows that the question of the convict lease system is so rotten that it smells to heaven," exclaimed Senator Thomas S. Felder. Yet many legislators, worried by the loss of revenue its abolition would entail, urged that it be continued when the current leases expired April 1, 1909.

In his initial message to the General Assembly in 1908, Hoke Smith called the "whole [penal] system…unsound in that it too nearly stamps all criminals alike and provides no plan for their reformation." Yet he offered no solution to the leasing problem. The disclosures resulting from an investigation of the leasing practice by a joint legislative committee stimulated the demand for reform, and on July 30, 1908, the governor announced that he believed the leases could be ended without damage to the state's finances. He soon fell in line with lease reformers and let it be known late in the session that he would veto any bill to continue convict leasing. The question was "too important to the people of Georgia" and involved too greatly the future of the state, he declared, "for us to hesitate about spending a few thousand dollars to handle it in the most intelligent and best manner possible." When it became apparent that the problem could not be dealt with in the regular session, he decided to call an extra session to end the leasing system.

When the legislature convened in extra session near the end of August 1908, Smith recommended a plan to abolish the leasing system by constitutional amendment and to use the convicts "to complete and perfect public highways and other internal improvements, using the farm as a basis of operation." He suggested that the convicts might also be used to extend the Western and Atlantic Railroad. "Good roads and common schools go together," he reminded the legislators. He also urged them to adopt the parole system, and to improve the prison farm and the reformatory.

Given a committee report that fairly bristled with evidences of the leasing system's abuses and with charges of "grave neglect of duty," and faced with an increasingly indignant public, the General Assembly abolished the leasing system in September 1908, after numerous disagreements between the two houses. The legislature provided for the use of the convicts on the public works and roads in the counties, created a parole system, established juvenile courts as branches of the superior courts, provided for improved treatment of women prisoners, and set up a commission to investigate the possibility of using the convicts to extend the Western and Atlantic Railroad....

No fundamental changes in the state's tax laws were made during Smith's tenure as governor, but his administration witnessed the largest appropriations that had been made in the state's history. The public schools were among the chief beneficiaries of the increased appropriations, receiving about 30 per cent more money from the state in 1909 than in 1907.... He recommended larger appropriations for the district agricultural and mechanical schools, whose establishment he had supported in earlier years, and he suggested the reorganization of the state colleges and experiment stations. He gave his support to the special education train sponsored by the state college of agriculture, accompanying the train on a number of occasions....

Hoke Smith proved to be one of the most successful of the Southern anti-machine governors of his day. His administration achieved a number of its objectives, in spite of certain unfortunate circumstances and the bitter factionalism that rent the party. Smith was an excellent administrator, and much of the success of his administration was the result of some good appointments and his own vigorous supervision of the affairs of the state, including the work of such agencies as the railroad commission. Except in matters of race, Smith was a genuine reform governor.

Additional Sources

Brundage, W. Fitzhugh. *A Socialist Utopia in the New South: The Ruskin Colonies in Tennessee and Georgia, 1894–1901.* Urbana: University of Illinois Press, 1996.

Dinnerstein, Leonard. *The Leo Frank Case.* Athens: University of Georgia Press, 1966.

Kemp, Kathryn W. *God's Capitalist: Asa Candler of Coca-Cola.* Macon GA: Mercer University Press, 2002.

Grantham, Dewey. *Hoke Smith and the Politics of the New South.* Baton Rouge: Louisiana State University Press, 1958.

Oney, Steve. *And the Dead Shall Rise: The Murder of Mary Phagan and the Lynching of Leo Frank.* New York: Random House, 2003.

Shaw, Barton. *The Wool Hat Boys.* Baton Rouge: Louisiana State University Press, 1984.

Woodward, C. Vann. *Tom Watson, Agrarian Rebel.* New York: Oxford University Press, 1938.

Chapter 13

DEPRESSION AND NEW DEAL
ERA, 1920–1939

The era between World War I and World War II was one of the most turbulent in Georgia's history. The state's agricultural economy was hit with a series of crises that began a decline from which it almost did not recover. Georgia's cotton farmers were hit particularly hard. The first crisis was the precipitous drop in cotton prices from 35 cents per pound in 1919 to 17 cents in 1920 and 7 cents in 1932. A more serious problem for cotton farmers hit the state with a vengeance during this period; the boll weevil made its appearance in Georgia. Moving eastward from Texas at a rate of about 75 miles a year, this "winged demon" arrived in Georgia in 1913. Leaving a path of devoured cotton in its wake, the initial loss in Georgia was not heavy, but by 1919 the damage to the cotton crop was serious. By 1923 the boll weevil became a disaster; Georgia's entire cotton production in 1923 amounted to 588,000 bales. The consolation for cotton farmers was that many diversified their crops and made far more money. Among the new cash crops grown in the state was the peanut; Georgia is currently the leading peanut-producing state in the nation.

It was during this era that New Yorker Franklin D. Roosevelt discovered the therapeutic and recuperative value of Georgia's Warm Springs, located 60 miles south of Atlanta in Meriwether County. In that location the spring water from Pine Mountain poured into a pool at a constant 88 degrees. Having contracted polio in 1921, which led to infantile paralysis, Roosevelt needed warm water to soothe his aching legs. He first learned of Warm Springs in 1924 and in 1927 he created the Warm Springs Foundation; Roosevelt spent two-thirds of his personal wealth on the foundation. After being elected President in 1932 Roosevelt's residence at Warm Springs was called the "Little White House." He spent a considerable amount of time Warm Springs; he visited 41 times for a total of 797 days. President Roosevelt died there on April 12, 1945.

This era also witnessed the emergence of Eugene Talmadge, arguably Georgia's most colorful and controversial governor. Talmadge was not terribly successful as a lawyer and fared only marginally better as a farmer, but he was mesmerized by politics. His first attempts at statewide public office, running for the General Assembly in 1920 and 1922, were not successful. Talmadge finally broke through in 1926 when he won election as agriculture commissioner, a post to which he was reelected in 1928 and 1930. After three terms as agriculture commissioner, Talmadge was elected governor in 1932 and 1934. Gene Talmadge excelled on the campaign trail; he was a master campaigner. He was a showman and has been described as "a prancing, dancing, arm-waving, holy-roller, circus barker, medicine man." Although highly educated (Talmadge had both a bachelor's degree and law degree from the University of Georgia), he tailored his speeches and language to the small dirt farmer, something that brought back memories of Tom Watson. This campaign style made Talmadge popular with Georgia's small farmers. His gubernatorial administration was controversial. His actions as governor included the suspension of all state taxes in 1933, the declaration of martial law in 1934 to break a textile strike, and outspoken opposition to President Roosevelt's New Deal; and, after the General Assembly failed to pass an appropriations bill in 1935, Talmadge discovered an old law that permitted the governor to make appropriations if the General Assembly failed to pass an appropriations bill.

President Roosevelt's New Deal had a positive impact on Georgia despite Governor Talmadge's opposition to it. When Eurith D. Rivers was elected governor in 1936 and inaugurated in 1937, he was determined to bring the New Deal to Georgia; what he brought to the state was called the "Little New Deal." Arguably the legislation with the greatest influence on the state was the Agricultural Adjustment Act, Roosevelt's farm relief program. Designed to restore farm prices by voluntary cutbacks in production, Georgia's cotton farmers needed the most assistance. By 1934, 1 million acres of cotton in Georgia had been diverted, the state's farmers received $10 million in benefit payments, and the price of cotton rose to 12 cents a pound. A New Deal agency that had an important impact on the state was the Civilian Conservation Corps (CCC). One of the most popular agencies, the CCC was also the most blatantly racist, so white Georgians benefited more from it than African Americans. Whites in need of assistance easily enrolled in the CCC while black Georgians found it nearly impossible. This problem was addressed in 1935 when a system of quotas was put in place. Other agencies that impacted Georgia included the Federal Emergency Relief Administration, which contributed over $45 million to the state's economy; the Civil Works Administration, which added another $14 million to the state's relief; and the Works Progress Administration, which employed 67,000 at its peak in Georgia in December 1938.

DOCUMENTS

The first document to follow charts cotton production following the boll weevil's arrival in Georgia. In the second document, the State Board of Entomology explains how to grow cotton in spite of the boll weevil. Document 3 is a speech by Governor Clifford Walker to a Ku Klux Klan meeting in Kansas City in 1924. The fourth document is a chart of Franklin D. Roosevelt's visits to Warm Springs. Document 5 is Governor Richard Russell's address to the state's reorganization committee in 1931. The sixth document describes the work performed by Georgia's chain gang. Document 7 is a campaign song written for Eugene Talmadge in 1932. The eighth document is Governor Talmadge's declaration of martial law in 1934. Document 9 is the emergency appropriation action Governor Talmadge took after the General Assembly did not pass an appropriations bill in 1935. The tenth document charts New Deal assistance to Georgia. Document 11 outlines the progress made in rural electrification in Georgia.

1. Cotton Production during the Flight of the Boll Weevil[1]

YEAR	NUMBER OF BALES PRODUCED
1914	2.718 million bales
1915	1.909 million bales
1916	1.821 million bales
1917	1.884 million bales
1918	2.122 million bales
1919	1.659 million bales
1920	1.415 million bales
1921	787,000 bales
1922	715,000 bales
1923	588,000 bales
1924	1.004 million bales
1925	1.164 million bales
1926	1.496 million bales

---

[1] From National Agricultural Statistics Services.

2. How to Grow Cotton in Spite of the Boll Weevil[2]

Georgia State Board of Entomology

It is necessary to have a perfect stand of cotton. In order to secure this the seed must be properly taken care of in the fall of the year.

The destruction of stalks is very important, as it reduces the number of weevils that go through the winter. The weevils do not live long without cotton for food unless they are in hibernation. Destroying the stalks before frost causes them to leave the premises and large numbers of them die. Those that do not die go into winter quarters very much weakened.

Ground should be thoroughly prepared in the fall of the year, if possible harrowed two or three times during the winter. No cover crop should be planted before cotton.

The cotton acreage should be reduced. The high, dry land as far removed from good hibernating quarters for the weevil as possible should be planted in cotton.

Seed should be pedigreed and free from diseases. How to secure this is fully discussed [elsewhere in the document]. The varieties should be locally adapted, and if the seed are not bred by the farmer himself enough seed should be bought from some man who produces pedigreed seed to plant the entire crop the second year. If the soil and location are very much changed, seed will do better the second year.

Fertilizer should be applied very early in order that the seed bed may become firm before time for planting. All the fertilizer should be applied before planting with the possible exception of some nitrate of soda just before the cotton comes up, or a small amount of fertilizer with the seed not in close contact with them. It has been claimed that the application of nitrate of soda just as the cotton starts to bloom is beneficial. This might be tried as an experiment.

---

[2] From Georgia State Board of Entomology, "How to Grow Cotton in Spite of the Boll Weevil," bulletin 47, February 1917.

3. Governor Clifford Walker
Addresses Ku Klux Klan[3]

Under the caption "Georgia Governor crusader for Klan" the *New York World* prints the following dispatch from its Kansas City Correspondent:

What was described as a spiritual message of utmost importance to all Klansmen was delivered by Gov. C. M. Walker of Georgia, who made one of the opening addresses of the National Klonvokation of the Ku Klux Klan which adjourned last Friday after a four-day session.

The Publicity Committee, official news source of the Klonvokation, did not disclose the Governor's identity in its reports. The orator was described as a Governor of a great State.

The Governor, said the publicity men, made an eloquent plea for Klansmen to get a clearer vision of Christ and Christ's teachings and to make Him their leader in the battle for Klan supremacy.

It was said by the Klan's publicity men again that the Governor made forceful arguments against the hierarchy of the Catholic Church and the threatened destruction of America and Americanism by encroachment of Jewish, Celtic and Mediterranean races.

A reporter who had been admitted to the state suite of a Kansas City hotel to interview Dr. Hiram W. Evans, Imperial Wizard, was introduced to Gov. Walker, who had been in conference with the Imperial Wizard after his speech.

4. Franklin D. Roosevelt's Visits to Warm Springs[4]

DATES OF VISIT	LENGTH OF VISIT
Friday, October 3–Sunday, October 20, 1924	18 days
Wednesday, April 1–Friday, May 15, 1925	45 days
Saturday, March 27–Wednesday, May 5, 1926	50 days
Wednesday, September 29–	
Wednesday, November 10, 1926	43 days
Friday, February 11–Thursday, March 12, 1927	30 days
Friday, May 24–Saturday, June 11, 1927	19 days
Friday, July 29–Wednesday, August 3, 1927	6 days

---

[3] From *Columbus Enquirer-Sun*, October 1, 1924.

[4] From Trip Files, Franklin D. Roosevelt Presidential Library, Hyde Park, New York. Compiled by the Franklin D. Roosevelt Library staff based upon a chronology compiled by Rexford E. Tugwell and James Curry in 1938.

Tuesday, September 27–Monday, December 5, 1927	70 days
Friday, January 20–Saturday, February 11, 1928	23 days
Wednesday, February 29–Thursday, May 3, 1928	65 days
Wednesday, June 20, 1928	1 day
Saturday, June 30–Monday, July 3, 1928	4 days
Wednesday, September 19–Friday, October 5, 1928	17 days
Thursday, November 8–Monday, December 10, 1928	33 days
Monday, April 22–Tuesday, June 4, 1929	44 days
Thursday, October 3–Monday, October 14, 1929	12 days
Tuesday, November 27–Tuesday, December 4, 1929	8 days
Thursday, May 1–Friday, May 30, 1930	30 days
Monday, November 17–Wednesday, December 10, 1930	24 days
Thursday, October 1–Wednesday, October 14, 1931	14 days
Friday, November 20–Thursday, December 10, 1931	21 days
Saturday, April 30–Friday, May 27, 1932	28 days
Sunday, October 23, 1932	1 day
Wednesday, November 23–Tuesday, December 6, 1932	14 days
Tuesday, January 24–Saturday, February 4, 1933	12 days
Friday, November 17–Wednesday, December 6, 1933	20 days
Sunday, November 18–Wednesday, December 5, 1934	18 days
Thursday, November 21–Sunday, December 8, 1935	18 days
Thursday, April 9, 1936	1 day
Thursday, March 12–Friday, March 26, 1937	15 days
Wednesday, March 23–Saturday, April 2, 1938	11 days
Wednesday, August 10, 1938	1 day
Monday, November 21–Sunday, December 4, 1938	14 days
Thursday, March 30–Sunday, April 9, 1939	11 days
Wednesday, November 22–Wednesday, November 29, 1939	8 days
Thursday, April 19–Saturday, April 27, 1940	9 days
Sunday, December 15, 1940	1 day
Saturday, November 29, 1941	1 day
Thursday, April 15–Friday, April 16, 1943	2 days
Tuesday, November 28–Sunday, December 17, 1944	20 days
Friday, March 30–Friday, April 13, 1945	15 days
TOTAL	797 DAYS

5. Governor Richard Russell Address
to Reorganization Committee[5]

The creation of these different boards, departments and agencies were usually the result of some legislation which had a definite objective in view but which did not consider the effect that the creation of such agencies would have upon the general structure of government, and its economical administration. As a result the administrative machinery of our state government has become top-heavy, cumbersome, and expensive and in many cases there are two or more of such departments and agencies which are performing similar duties, resulting in overlapping and duplication of effort and additional burdens on the taxpayers who pay the expense of our state....

Those who are interested in public affairs in Georgia have long recognized the necessity for reorganizing and simplifying the administrative machinery of our state government and there has been agitation in this direction which has served to crystallize public opinion throughout the state in favor of such legislation in Georgia in order that the people of this state may obtain the benefits of increased efficiency and financial savings.

The recent extra session of the legislature acceded to this feeling on the part of the people by the passage of a resolution creating the committee which is meeting here today. Its duty is to make a thorough and complete investigation of our state government to ascertain the needs of the departments and the benefits which are accruing to the people of the state by reason of their existence and to recommend to the next general assembly legislation which will give the people of Georgia a government in keeping with modern times and conditions....

There are many reasons why this committee in its labor should have the support of every public-spirited citizen of the state. In the first place, few states have a more unwieldy, haphazard and complicated departmental system than has Georgia. Our departments are so numerous and our machinery of government is so complex that the average citizen who is paying taxes to support this government cannot understand all of its various details. The machinery of government should be so simple that the humblest citizen can understand it. In many instances there is such an overlapping of effort and

---

[5] "Address to the Reorganization Committee," April 28, 1931, Speech File, Georgia Gubernatorial Papers, Richard B. Russell Jr. Collection, Richard B. Russell Library for Political Research and Studies, University of Georgia.

division of duties that it is difficult to fix responsibility for the proper operation of the government....

Here in Georgia we have more than 100 different agencies to carry on the state's business and I venture to say there are very few who can sit down with pen and paper and name them all and outline the duties that each is supposed to perform.

I am confident that practically every citizen of Georgia who has no personal interest in the matter favors a reorganization of our government. When we face the fact that the State of Georgia has a large casual deficiency which is increasing year by year as governmental expenditures continue to exceed the amount of income derived from taxes—despite the fact that the burden of taxation on our people has been increased from time to time—and when we further know that there is urgent necessity for a decrease in expenditures, it would seem that it should be a relatively easy matter to secure this much desired reform....

The task that is before us is Herculean in proportion. But there can be no more exalted service than public service. No greater public service can be rendered the people of Georgia than to accomplish this reform. No undertaking in this state within the past few years will be watched more closely. Those who dedicate themselves whole-heartedly and unselfishly in this endeavor will make a substantial contribution to the welfare and progress of Georgia. They may be assured that their labors will not be forgotten but will receive due reward in the approval of those whose interests they seek to serve as well as that of their own consciences.

6. "Keeping the Lick" on the Georgia Chain Gang[6]

Robert Burns, 1932

In the chain gangs, human labor had been synchronized as the goose step was in the German Army. When using pickaxes, all picks hit the ground at the same time, all are raised and steadied for the next blow with uncanny mechanical precision. So it is with all work, shoveling, hammering, drilling. The convict bodies and muscles move in time and unison as one man. The tempo and speed is regulated by the chanting of Negro bondage songs, led by a toil-hardened Negro of years of servitude as follows:

"A long steel rail," croons the leader.

---

[6] From Robert Burns, *I Am a Fugitive from a Georgia Chain Gang* (New York: Vanguard Press, 1932).

"Ump!" grunts all the rest in chorus as pickaxes come down.
"An' a short cross tie," croons the leader.
"Ump!" grunts all the rest in chorus as pickaxes come up.
"It rings lik' sil-vah," croons the leader.
"Ump!" goes the chorus as the picks come down.
"It shin's lik' go-old," croons the leader.
"Ump!" and all the picks come up.

And so it goes all day long, with the torrid rays of the blazing monarch of the skies adding their touch of additional misery.

This work in unison is called "Keeping the lick."

7. The Three Dollar Tag Song[7]

I got a Talmadge dog, I got a Eugene cat;
I'm a Talmadge man from my shoes to my hat.
Tell me how long must I wait;
Before he gets old Georgia into shape.
Farmer in the cornfield hollering "whoa, gee haw";
Can't put a thirty dollar tag on a ten dollar car.
Tell me how long must I wait;
Before he gets old Georgia into shape.
Got chickens in the coop, eggs in the bag;
Eugene's got us our three-dollar tag!
Tell me how long must I wait;
Before he gets old Georgia into shape.
I got a Talmadge dog, I got a Eugene cat;
I'm a Talmadge man from my shoes to my hat.
Tell me how long must I wait;
Before he gets old Georgia into shape.

8. Martial Law Declaration[8]

A Proclamation

Whereas: Under Article I, Section 8, paragraph 14, of the Constitution of the United States it is provided that "Congress shall have the power and

---

[7] From "The Three Dollar Tag Song," by Fiddlin' John Carson. Traditional arranged Carson.

[8] From Executive Minutes, September 14, 1934, Georgia Archives.

authority to provide for calling forth the Militia and execute the laws of the Union, to suppress insurrection and repel invasion," and

Whereas: In accordance with the above provision of the Federal Constitution, the Constitution of this State, Article No. 5, section No. 1, paragraph 11, provides "The Governor shall be Commander-in-Chief of the Army and Navy of this State, and of the Militia thereof," and....

Whereas: There now exists organized and open insurrection, rioting and rebellion against the laws and Constitution of this State; and, such acts of violence and insurrection against the laws of the State are beyond the control of the Sheriffs and Civil Officers of the counties affected, and

Whereas: Insurrection, rebellion, rioting and deeds of violence are being agitated, fermented and incited by armies of insurrectionists imported and coming in to the affected areas from other counties and from other States....

Now, Therefore, I, Eugene Talmadge, Governor of the State of Georgia, do hereby under authority of the Constitution and laws of the United States, and of this State, exercise the supreme executive power as Chief Executive of the State of Georgia, and do hereby declare martial law over all the territory embraced in—

An area including each and every textile mill and manufactory of cotton and rayon products, also an area of five hundred feet distance from and around each and every such textile mill and manufactory of cotton and rayon products in each and every direction; also an area including all highways and public roads in the State of Georgia, also all jails and prisons in the State in which military prisoners and persons confined by the Military, operating under this proclamation are confined; also all camps, guard houses, military encampments and other places where persons are confined by the military in operating under this proclamation; also each and every area constituted by drawing a circle around each military company, regiment, guard and picket within a radius of five hundred feet, wherever they may be found, posted or stationed, and when on the march and when being transported.

The writ of habeas corpus is hereby suspended within all areas embraced in this proclamation and in any areas which may hereafter, by amendment, be put under martial law under this proclamation, as well as persons arrested by the Military authorities....

Done at the State Capitol, Atlanta, Georgia,

On this 14th day of September, 1934.

By the Governor of the State of Georgia:

Eugene Talmadge.

9. Emergency Appropriations Action[9]

A Proclamation
By the Governor:

Whereas: The General Assembly, at its session of 1935, failed to enact a general appropriations bill making appropriations for the operation of the State Government for the year 1936; and

Whereas: Such failure to enact a general appropriations act creates an emergency which renders executive action necessary in order that the Government of the State may function, that the executive and judicial branches of the State may continue to operate, that the public schools and institutions of higher education of the State may continue....

Whereas: There being no legislative enactment making appropriations for such departments, boards, bureaus, and agencies of the State for the year 1936, any revenue coming into the State Treasury after January 1, 1936, not otherwise appropriated to one of the objects hereinbefore mentioned, is revenues available for the payment of such appropriations within the meaning of the Acts of the General assembly making such appropriations....

Now, Therefore, in order that the essential functions of the State Government may be continued, and in order that the interests and welfare of the people of the State of Georgia may be protected, I Eugene Talmadge, Governor of the State of Georgia, do hereby order and proclaim as follows:

1. That the amounts of the several special funds herein referred to, and heretofore provided by the General Assembly, by legislative enactment for the support of the various departments, boards, bureaus, and agencies of the State, and continuously appropriated for such purposes, be made available, for and during the year 1936, as such funds are collected, for the purposes herein referred to for which sum appropriations are made.

2. That the sum of the salaries of the various public officers of this State, including the officers of the Executive and Judicial Departments, whose salaries are fixed by law, be made available for the purpose of paying such salaries as the same become due and payable.

4. That the State Treasurer and Comptroller General set up on their books, to the credit of the various departments, boards, bureaus, institutions, and agencies of the State for the year 1936, the amount of the special allocations and appropriations hereinbefore referred to, where any such department, board, bureaus, institutions, or agency is supported by special funds provided by

[9] Executive Proclamation, February 17, 1936, Governor's Press Releases, Georgia Archives.

legislative enactment for such purpose, and that said funds be disbursed to such departments, boards, bureaus, institutions, and agencies of the State upon warrants of the Governor issued pursuant to approved budgets as now provided by law....

In Witness Whereof, I, Eugene Talmadge, Governor of the State of Georgia, have hereunto set my hand and caused the Great Seal of the State of Georgia to be hereunto affixed, at the State Capitol, in the City of Atlanta, Georgia, this 17th day of February, in the year of our Lord One Thousand Nine Hundred and Thirty Six.

Eugene Talmadge,
Governor.

10. New Deal Relief Assistance to Georgia[10]

FERA Assistance to Georgia

YEAR	FEDERAL $	LOCAL $
1933	$5,692,732	$170,773
1934	$18,861,648	$962,266
1935	$20,323,117	$1,630,020
1936	$964,391	$1,412,479
1937	$91,088	$276,267
TOTAL	$45,932,976	$4,451,805

CWA Assistance to Georgia

Federal Funds	$14,092,128.00
State Funds	$57.60
Local Funds	$1,314,025.80

Georgians Employed by the WPA, 1935–1942

December 1935	53,724
June 1936	34,469
December 1936	33,602
June 1937	25,447
December 1937	24,272
June 1938	47,187

[10] Adapted and modified from Michael S. Holmes, *The New Deal in Georgia: An Administrative History* (Westport CT: Greenwood Press, 1975).

December 1938	67,203
June 1939	57,367
December 1939	47,707
June 1940	35,388
December 1940	41,995
June 1941	30,061
December 1941	24,430
June 1942	16,376

Farm Income from Government Assistance, 1933–1940

1933	$7.932 million
1934	$14.209 million
1935	$12.615 million
1936	$6.787 million
1937	$10.030 million
1938	$20.218 million
1939	$25.794 million
1940	$24.419 million
TOTAL	$122.004 million

11. Rural Electrification in Georgia[11]

January, 1941

We are proud of our progress in Rural Electrification in Georgia during the past four years. Since the potential return on investments necessary to provide electric service in rural sections was not sufficient to fully attract private capital the necessity for the formation of a purely cooperative plan of construction of lines into rural sections resulted in the creation of the Federal Rural Electrification Administration....

The advancement of this program by my administration has been accomplished without a penny's expense to the taxpayers of the State, while other States, as for example our sister State of South Carolina, have expended considerable State funds out of tax receipts for the furtherance of rural electrification with a great deal less accomplished. Georgia with only 2 1/2% of the nations total population has received 5% of the total allotments in the amount of $17,274,845.00 up to January 1, 1941. As of September 30, 1940, 37

---

[11] From Eurith Rivers, "Final Message to the General Assembly of Georgia," Georgia Archives.

cooperatives had energized 15,716 miles of line serving 43,888 customers. Six newly formed cooperatives and extensions of present lines of the others will provide for a total construction of 18,000 miles of lines including that already in operation and will make electricity available to over 70,000 rural families....

ESSAYS

Georgia Faces the Great Depression[12]

Michael S. Holmes

Georgia's farmers rejoiced in the prosperity of the century's second decade, but their joy was to be shortlived. Cotton remained at the core of Georgia's economy. But it was the state's dependency upon this one crop that was the most important factor leading to the agricultural depression of the 1920s. Continuous cotton planting sapped the soil's strength, and fertilizers were either too expensive, or, for many, simply unknown. Poor farming practices eventually caused irreversible damage by erosion.

The state's agricultural establishment long had operated under these conditions, and it might have continued to do so with a reasonable amount of profit, if three factors had not combined at this time to destroy that prosperity. The first of these developments was the maturation of the cotton culture in Texas and Oklahoma. Although soil conditions in these two states were not particularly good, they were comparable to Georgia's more depleted areas. Furthermore, the flat lands of the West lent themselves to a nascent cotton farming technology that reduced the cost of growing and harvesting. The uneven ground of the South Atlantic states and the traditional use of farm labor by the tenancy system kept such technology from making inroads into that area.

The second factor that led to the immediate collapse of the cotton market was a slump in cotton prices following the First World War. From a record high 36 cents a pound in 1919, the price of cotton dropped to 17 cents a pound in 1920, causing the value of Georgia's crop to fall by $176,470,000. Georgia's farmers might have ridden out the slump, but a small "winged demon," the boll

---

[12] Reprinted from Michael S. Holmes, "From Euphoria to Cataclysm: Georgia Confronts the Great Depression," *Georgia Historical Quarterly* 58/3 (Fall 1974). Courtesy of the Georgia Historical Society.

weevil, administered the *coup de grace* which sent the state tumbling into an agricultural depression.

Spreading eastward from Texas, the boll weevil reached Georgia's borders about 1913. It did not affect all areas at once, however, and because of this and the persistent dreams of prosperity prevailing in the state, farmers refused to take the weevil seriously. By 1916 it had caused only a 3 percent loss to the cotton crop, and by 1918 only a 10 percent loss. Some counties were hit before others. Greene County received a three-year respite. Laurens County was not affected until 1921, and Tift County "enjoyed for a while the 'hang over' of war-time prosperity," even though its financial structure began to totter in 1920. Tift County continued its building program almost until 1929, but it was evident to at least one local prophet in 1923 that "1922 was marked by more than the average of business worries, industrial distress, and financial uncertainty."

Whether out of disbelief, ignorance, or staunch individualism, Georgia's farmers were unable or unwilling to accept aid offered by the federal and state governments. One commentator suggested that the farmers became complacent when the federal government announced that it had developed effective boll weevil controls. By 1923, however, the state was blanketed by the weevil, and apathy turned to panic as Georgia's cotton yield was reduced by 30 to 45 percent below "normal" each year.

The value of cotton lint fell from $296,261,000 in 1919 to $29,782,000 in 1932, as total production dropped from 1,659 bales (of 500 pounds gross weight) to 853 bales. Farmers were at an additional disadvantage, for by the time the weevil struck in full force, the Texas and Oklahoma yields were again increasing. This meant that the nation's total production was not going down and forcing prices up. To the contrary, total cotton production was increasing so that prices declined from 36 cents a pound in 1919 to 7 cents a pound in 1932.

The low point for Georgia cotton production actually had been in 1923, when only 588 bales had been harvested. From that time to 1929, farmers grew more cotton and received more money, as the weevil slowly succumbed to various arsenate insecticides and eradication process. Meanwhile, however, foreign markets (which also had been recovering from a post-war slump) began to crumble, causing a severe drop in cotton prices in 1930. Georgia's farmers did not reach 1929 income levels again until 1948, and they never again attained the heights achieved in 1919.

The unbridled gaiety of the golden years now appeared to Georgians as an hysterical echo that was to haunt them through the days of the Great Depression. No rural citizen escaped the effects of the boll weevil and the depression. Large landowners still had their property, but it was often mortgaged and its worth was not equal to the owner's debts, especially as land values began to drop. From 1920 to 1925 the average value per farm declined by $1,304, while the total value of all farms plummeted nearly 50 percent. Although the rate of loss slackened after 1925, the value of farms still dropped steadily to 1935....

Individual experiences and responses to the depression varied across the state as a bewildered populace struggled against the forces that had taken them by surprise and left them numb. Americus reported that most of its wealthy citizens were able to "get by with a little retrenchment," but the lower-middle class suffered greatly. The poor "were able to accept their status by virtue of long conditioning." Soup kitchens were set up for this latter group in the Americus business district where they operated continuously. As money became scarce, the city began to issue "city bills" accepted as currency in local stores. Thomasville used scrip to pay its city employees. When a merchant received or paid out a "dollar certificate," he put a stamp on it. After fifty-two stamps were affixed to the scrip, it could be redeemed. Thomasville hoped, by this device, to accomplish three goals: put more "money" into circulation, underwrite the worth of that money by making it redeemable, and encourage local trade by including it in the redemption process.

In Tift County "everyone was depression conscious," and the financial situation was the main topic of discussion at all social gatherings. Citizens of the county attempted to improve their spirits by raising "depression plants" grown from a mixture of salt, soda, water, and mercurochrome.[13] The county's social life did not diminish, perhaps because people sharing in this terrible experience needed the comfort of each other's presence. The focus of these events, however, was upon simplicity of decorations, entertainment, and dress. Penniless housewives strove to make use of excess energy by finding substitutes for non-essentials. Homeowners planted gallberry bushes and other wild plants in their yards—"depression shrubbery." "Democrats" put automobile wheels on carts, "signifying that people had no use for cars," and Sumter County residents added a new twist by using old model "T" bodies, naming the result "Hoover wagons." Jobs everywhere were scarce.

Atlanta did not feel the full weight of the depression until the crash of 1929, but when it came, the effects were harsh. By 1932, the situation had become so acute that a mass demonstration of both Negroes and whites occurred. Over a thousand people marched on City Hall protesting the inadequacy of relief

---

[13] Depression plants were inexpensive plants grown for home decoration by those who could not afford store-bought plants.

measures. The Atlanta *Constitution*, attempting to "inspire more purchasing," began a "Jinky" contest—cutting designs in folded paper. To enter the contest one had to submit ten Jinky receipts with his Jinky. These receipts could be obtained at local stores with every purchase of 25 cents or the payment of a like amount on any account.

Many occurrences seemed hysterical or even foolish. People became fascinated with their own brand of flagpole sitting and goldfish swallowing. One of the most notable depression events in Tift County, for example, was the appearance of one of its citizens, Smokey Joe Cravy, on the Robert L. Ripley show in New York. The county's citizens were justifiably proud of Smokey Joe's ability to play a harmonica while blowing a police siren through his ear. This was the type of neurotic behavior that grew from almost total despair. The people of Georgia were willing to grasp at almost anything that might relax the depression's grip, or, at least, take their minds off of their hopeless situation.

Governor Eugene Talmadge vs. President Roosevelt and the New Deal[14]

William Anderson

...In 1934 Gene [Talmadge] was privately becoming critical of the Roosevelt administration and its policies. Publicly, he was promising FDR's administration Georgia's "undivided and unstinting faith." The increasing social activism and growing federal involvement of the New Deal was positioning itself at the opposite pole of Gene's governmental and social philosophies. He wrote in the January 15 issue of the *Statesman*, "If you have a rich government, you have a poor people, and a depressed people. If you have a poor government, you will have a rich and happy people."

For all of his pro-Roosevelt talk during the campaign, Talmadge had been firmly, but rather quietly, jousting FDR and his department heads for a year. Since the rush of the first New Deal programs Gene had sent a steady stream of telegrams to Washington, complaining and advising about the AAA cotton-reduction program, processing taxes on corn, tobacco prices, and disbursement of road money. Ironically Gene had also beseeched the president to offer some

---

[14] From William Anderson, *The Wild Man From Sugar Creek: The Political Career of Eugene Talmadge* (Louisiana State University Press, 1975). Used with permission of Louisiana State University Press.

immediate help. In August 1933 he had written, "The very foundation of this section is the farmer. The farmer must receive some help." To discuss the programs, particularly the huge federal road grants scheduled to come to Georgia, the governor had met FDR at the White House that September. Gene had become so concerned by that time with Roosevelt's impact that he had sent Atlanta's Fulton National Bank president, Ryburn Clay, to Washington, asking for a letter from FDR saying that he was not against Gene Talmadge in the 1934 gubernatorial races—a veiled attempt at getting a presidential endorsement. The request was refused. Talmadge's position through the 1934 campaign, then, appeared to be one of respect for the president, growing concern, if not hostility, toward his programs, but a keen interest in Washington doing something to help the states. Talmadge was insisting, however, that the states have control over the federal money and its disbursement, and that they have the right to ignore any programs of which they disapproved. A split was emerging along states-rights' lines....

Gene was actually having a great struggle within himself on FDR. He told a friend, "I really want to be for the man, but I can't accept his socialistic programs." The crux of the "Roosevelt problem" with Gene and other Georgia politicians was that they felt they had been fooled by the president. Gene had voted for him in 1932 when the man sounded conservative. But the emerging social activism and expanding government had "scared the hell" out of the Talmadge crowd. Gene feared socialism and its big government as he feared nothing else. He loathed welfare as corrupt and saw in it the destruction of the independent man. Philosophy began to clash with Gene's admiration for FDR, and the contradiction showed through 1933 and 1934. By late fall 1934, however, hatred of the New Deal began to shift to the man who had created it. His praise for FDR in the 1934 campaign and later were no more than attempts to keep things smooth until the General Assembly met and to garner votes from FDR's popularity. It was highly out of character for Gene to be riding coattails. But he was. In November the split was opened for all to see when FDR visited Atlanta and Gene went to Savannah. In December Georgians were asked to vote for the New Deal's Bankhead Cotton Control Act, and Gene went on a heavy speaking tour to fight it. They voted it in by six to one. Georgians appeared to be making a profound turn-around in their attitudes toward the function of government and reconsidering which government they would relinquish their power to. Had they, in a sudden societal reversal, discarded the foundation stones of their heritage? Were they now willing to embrace big government, with its intrusions and restrictions? Yes and no. It was a time of ambiguity, dual loyalties, and two consciousness levels. But it did seem that in Georgia's attitudinal structure, pragmatism was overcoming romanticism and delusion as a base for decision-making. The roots of the past could be heard breaking with undeniable clarity.

Many factors served to split Gene from Roosevelt. The governor knew that when the populace relinquished power to Washington they also weakened the power of their states. Also, his close circle of friends and many state politicians who detested FDR and the New Deal constantly told Gene so, and many of his banker friends who had hated FDR since he closed the banks pressured him. Equally influential was the growing number of pro-Roosevelt politicians who were joining forces behind the name of the Democratic party in opposition to Gene. And finally, there was Gene's inbred fear of liberalism and socialism, his dogmatic belief that the country was being blindly swept up into a spiritually and economically destructive movement. A man of Talmadge's intensity of belief could not continue publicly to "like" FDR while hating his programs. In Gene's eyes, man and program soon became one. Gene's turn from FDR had involved a two-year process, but once made, it was complete. The incongruities of the 1934 public and private statements were resolved by 1935.

The Georgia farmer in 1934 voted for radical conservative Talmadge on the one hand and radical liberal New Deal on the other. It must be remembered that during the summer campaign of 1934 ideology was not an issue, though [Claude] Pittman tried to make it one. The voter was not forced to choose between FDR and Gene, for Gene had constantly assured voters that he was backing the president. Of those who were aware of the opening chasm between the two, the contradiction was not particularly disturbing, because the votes were made for totally different reasons. The farmer voted for Talmadge because of his personality; he voted for the New Deal, not because he was a budding socialist, but because he was desperate and this seemed the only viable escape from hard times. Gene lifted his spirits; the New Deal filled his stomach....

The powerful voices in the house, [Roy] Harris, [E. D.] Rivers, and Ellis Arnall, wanted to give Georgia some of the benefits of the New Deal legislation. But out of deference to the governor they waited until his program had passed. A six-man committee was then sent to study the possibility of Georgia's participating in federal work-relief programs and to see that federal posts in Georgia be staffed by Georgians. The group returned bubbling with enthusiasm. Arriving on Sunday night, they went straight to the governor's mansion. Rivers later recounted what happened. He said their recitation of the millions available was met with a stony silence from Gene. After they had finished, the governor said there wasn't going to be any New Deal legislation passed. He said it would destroy the country with its giveaway programs. Furthermore, in the election year of 1936, there wasn't going to be any more talk about "Roosevelt and Talmadge"; there was only going to be talk about "Roosevelt *or* Talmadge." He told the startled group that they might as well make up their minds right there in that room which side of the line they were going to be on. The men did not fully comprehend all that had been said in those few minutes, and their silence goaded Gene to say that he wanted them to be in his office early the next morning to sign a report that would tell Washington not to send any more federal aid to Georgia. The group filed out into the night, dazed by the governor's remarks. Gene was apparently going to openly oppose Roosevelt for party allegiance and, at the same time, he was asking the legislature to close down and go home! The battle lines were drawn very quietly but firmly that night, and Gene's influence with certain legislative leaders started a precipitous decline....

The members of the legislature began to split badly in February [1935] along pro- and anti-New Deal lines. Rivers and Harris knew Gene was holding the veto over their heads, but they moved ahead pushing for a sales tax, old age pension, free texts, and a seven-month school year. They also wanted a slum-clearance program, a child labor amendment, and cooperation with the national employment system. But Gene was having none of it, and those bills that his strong influence could not hold back, he vetoed. He later told a staff worker, W. O. Brooks, that he threw every New Deal bill in the trash can without even reading it. Rivers was particularly angered over Gene's refusal to let the old age pension and the sales tax pass.

For the moment, the forces of conservatism held; in fact, a backlash against the New Deal developed, and a states' rights movement and consciousness swept the legislature. As the session neared its close, not one piece of New Deal legislation had passed....

Gene's emergence from the 1935 session as the symbol of total resistance to the new way spotlighted the new way (or the New Deal) as the dominant voter consideration for the 1936 state elections. Gene had also fostered an increase in voter consciousness by making an issue of the New Deal, whereas his previous successes had thrived on a constricted consciousness....

Additional Sources

William Anderson. *The Wild Man from Sugar Creek: The Political Career of Eugene Talmadge*. Baton Rouge: Louisiana State University Press, 1975.

Ferguson, Karen. *Black Politics in New Deal Atlanta*. Chapel Hill: University of North Carolina Press, 2002.

Fite, Gilbert. *Richard B. Russell, Jr., Senator from Georgia.* Chapel Hill:
    University of North Carolina Press, 1991.
Holmes, Michael S. *The New Deal in Georgia: An Administrative History.*
    Westport CT: Greenwood Press, 1974.

Chapter 14

THE WORLD WAR II ERA, 1939–1945

The era of World War II wrought many significant changes in Georgia, politically, socially, and economically. One of the more important political events was the revision of the state constitution in 1945, something that had not been done since 1877. Among other changes, this constitution set the governor's term of office at four years, permitted 18-year-olds to vote, and created the office of lieutenant governor, to be filled for the first time in the 1946 election. Governor Ellis Arnall, who was governor from 1943 until 1947, oversaw one of the most extensive reform programs the state had seen since the administration of Hoke Smith. Arnall made education a top priority and immediately after taking office worked to remove politics from education in the state. The governor also filed suit in federal court to end discriminatory freight rates among the country's railroads; when the case made it to the US Supreme Court, Governor Arnall appeared in person to represent the state of Georgia.

The war signaled many changes in the state and among the most important were the number of military instillations and war-related industries. The war plants succeeded in ending the Great Depression in Georgia. Some 320,000 Georgia men and women served their country, with 6,754 making the ultimate sacrifice. A frequently neglected aspect of Georgia history during the war years was the incarceration of 11,800 Axis prisoners of war at forty locations throughout the state.

This era also marked the passing of both Eugene Talmadge and President Franklin D. Roosevelt. The death of Talmadge led to one of the state's most embarrassing episodes. Talmadge was elected governor in the 1946 election but died before he could take the oath of office. This created a scenario in which three men claimed to be the rightful and legal governor of the state, an event known as the Three Governors Controversy. Those who claimed the governorship included the lieutenant governor-elect, Melvin E. Thompson; the candidate selected by the General Assembly, Herman Talmadge; and the sitting governor, Ellis Arnall. A series of lawsuits later, on March 19, 1947, the Georgia Supreme Court ruled that Thompson was the legal governor, but it ordered a special election for governor in 1948.

DOCUMENTS

In the first document to follow, a 1941 proclamation by Governor Talmadge suspended the collection of taxes on fuel, a war measure. Document 2 is a report from the Southern Association of Colleges and Schools that removed accreditation from all of the colleges and universities in the state university system in 1941. The third document is a memoir by a German prisoner of war who was incarcerated in Georgia. Document 4 is the US Supreme Court's decision in a suit Governor Arnall filed to end discriminatory freight rates. The fifth document is the Constitution of 1945. Document 6 contains two newspaper accounts of the death of President Roosevelt at his "Little White House" in Warm Springs, Georgia. The seventh document relates the decision of the Georgia Supreme Court that settled the Three Governors Controversy.

1. Emergency Wartime Measures[1]

A Proclamation

By the Governor:

Whereas: The nations of Europe are now engaged in war, and

Whereas: As a result of the said war in Europe our country is enlarging its army, navy, and air force; and

Whereas: The State of Georgia desired to lend its assistance in every possible manner to aid in a program for national preparedness, and

Whereas: Certain sections of Georgia have been selected as an ideal place for the training of air pilots to defend our country,

It Is, Therefore, Ordered: by me as Governor of the State of Georgia that the tax levied by the State of Georgia on all gasoline, motor fuel and lubricants by the State of Georgia be suspended on such motor fuels herein described which are used in planes owned by the Federal Government in which planes cadets in the service of the United States Government are trained whether the motor fuels herein described be purchased by either a governmental agency or private agency.

This suspension shall become effective immediately and is made under the provisions of Section 40–205 of the 1933 Code of Georgia.

It Is Further Ordered that the persons or agencies who may be due the taxes herein suspended shall purchase and use said motor fuels herein described in

---

[1] Executive Proclamation, May 16, 1941, Messages of Governor to General Assembly, Georgia Archives.

accordance with this order of suspension and in accordance with the rules and regulations of the Commissioner of Revenue of the State of Georgia who shall have full authority to require reports and such other information as he may in his opinion think proper in connection with such taxes herein suspended to avoid any abuse of this suspension.

Now, Therefore, I, Eugene Talmadge, as Governor of Georgia, do hereby promulgate and make effective this my executive order suspending the collection of the taxes above described falling within the group described and upon such purposes as are specifically enumerated above. Effective this the 16th day of May 1941, and subject, however, to the conditions and limitations provided herein.

Eugene Talmadge,
Governor.

2. State University System Controversy[2]

Report on University System of Georgia

The Committee of the Southern Association of Colleges and Secondary Schools appointed to investigate the situation in the University System of Georgia, had a preliminary meeting in Birmingham, Alabama, on September 29, 1941, for the purpose of considering the evidence then in hand, and to consider what steps should be taken to insure full and accurate information on the problem. At this meeting it was decided to hold a hearing in Atlanta on November 3 and 4 to which all members of the Board of Regents and all presidents of colleges belonging to the Association would be invited. The Committee further agreed that other organizations wishing to investigate the matter would be welcome to sit in with the committee and participate in the hearing. The hearing began at the Ansley Hotel, Atlanta, at 9 A.M., November 3, 1941....

After considering all the data the committee respectfully submits the following findings:

1. That Governor Talmadge requested the Board of Regents to dismiss Dean Walter D. Cocking, head of the Department of Education at the University of Georgia on May 30, 1941, though he was recommended for reappointment by President Caldwell and Chancellor Sanford. Upon the refusal of the Board to do so, he gave notice that he would prefer charges, and the date of the trial was set for June 16. After a trial lasting five hours, Dean Cocking

---

[2] From *The Southern Association Quarterly*, February 1942.

was exonerated of all charges by a vote of 8 to 7, and appointed for another year, effective September 1, 1941.

2. The Governor immediately thereafter denounced the action of the Board of Regents, gave notice of a rehearing, and set about to change its personnel. Three of his own appointees who voted against his wishes were asked to resign on the ground of illegal appointment. Failing to secure the resignations of these men he turned to others who opposed his wishes, and finally obtained three resignations. He then appointed three new members. Thus the Board of Regents was reconstituted for the specific purpose of serving the Governor's will.

3. He then notified Dean Cocking that he would be tried again despite the fact that he had been exonerated on June 16, and that the trial was set for July 14. President Marvin Pittman of Statesboro, who was recommended for reappointment by Chancellor Sanford, was also summoned to appear on this date for his trial, which had been postponed from June 16.

4. From the record it is clear that these trials were a mockery of democratic procedure. As if to crown this act of injustice the motion to vote on the validity of the evidence submitted was lost by a vote of 10 to 5, and Dean Cocking and President Pittman were dismissed by the same vote.

After examining a great body of evidence the committee is convinced that the charges preferred against Dean Cocking and President Pittman were either spurious or entirely unsupported by the evidence....

7. Another feature of the situation in the University System of Georgia which adds seriously to the difficulty of insuring proper educational administration is the fact that the Governor under the statutes of the State has the authority to modify in any way he sees fit the budget as adopted by the Board of Regents. He can delete or modify any item of expenditure or remove any individual from the pay roll without the Board's approval. It is thus possible for one man to nullify the Board's action by refusing to approve any individual or item. Arbitrary power of this kind in the hands of any individual or agency is a threat to sound procedure in the operation of an educational system....

Conclusion

In light of all the evidence the Committee is forced to conclude that the University System of Georgia has been the victim of unprecedented and unjustifiable political interference; that the Governor of the State has violated not only sound educational policy, but proper democratic procedure in insisting upon the resignation of members of the Board of Regents in order to appoint to that body men who would do his bidding; that the Board of Regents has flagrantly violated sound educational procedure in dismissals and appointments of staff members; that every institution in the System is profoundly affected by the precedents established and by the actions already taken whether any of its staff has been dismissed to date or not; can be no effective educational program where this condition exists; that in view of the actions of the Board of Regents of the University System of Georgia which brought about this condition, and in view of its dependence upon the concurrence of the Governor in matters vital to the operation of the System, the Board of Regents does not appear to be an independent and effective educational board of control.

The Committee, therefore, recommends that the following institutions be dropped from membership in the Southern Association of Colleges and Secondary Schools:

Georgia School of Technology, Atlanta, Ga.
Georgia State College for Women, Milledgeville, Ga.
Georgia State Woman's College, Valdosta, Ga.
University of Georgia, Athens, Ga.
Georgia Teachers College, Collegeboro, Ga.
Georgia Southwestern College, Americus, Ga.
Middle Georgia College, Cochran, Ga.
North Georgia College, Dahlonega, Ga.
South Georgia College, Douglas, Ga.
West Georgia College, Carrollton, Ga.

It recommends further that this suspension take effect September 1, 1942, and continue until removed by vote of this Association at its next or later annual meeting on recommendation of the Executive Committee and of the Commission on Institutions of Higher Education.

December 3, 1941

3. A German Prisoner of War Recalls His Time at Camp Fargo[3]

...From November 5, 1944 to March 10, 1946 Fort Benning—side camp Fargo. In a clearing in the Fargo wood forest several tents were set up. They were built of wood flooring and side walls about 1 m high. After that was screen wire to keep the flies out this was topped by a tent cloth top which could be let down to cover the top part of the tent walls if needed. The whole area was forest. I estimated about 250 to 300 German POWs in the camp. The camp was secured with a gate, watch houses and barbed wire toward the street. The work assignment went fast.

---

[3] From manuscript memoirs, private collection.

South Georgia consists of mostly forest—which means we will be cutting trees for the Paper mill and the turpentine industry. The trees are cut with a handsaw, two men per saw. The underbrush, the palmetto, is sometimes so tall one can't see the lumber.

To get Turpentine, the trees are scratched at the upper end with a knife. This is repeated after two weeks so the turpentine will flow again due to the new cuts then it is collected flowing over metal pieces into a cup at the bottom. The cups are emptied by our Turpentine crew. The lumberjacks were supposed to stack 1 cord of wood. I am unsure if the amount was to be accomplished by one or two men. After the shift the wood stack was marked with chalk. It should be clear to anyone who knows the South Georgia climate, that we often removed the marked pieces and replaced them with unmarked one. This way our daily quota was accomplished quickly. Besides the minimal guarding we were supervised by an American civilian. He and I got along good which would pay off later. Even though it was a small camp, camp life was entertaining. Jochen Rehfeld was our translator and musician, then there were two ballet dancers, who also knew how to step dance, and a clown from Heidelberg....

For clarification I need to add that our workplace was located toward Homerville and beyond. We were transported by truck from Camp Fargo to Homerville where we waited between the wooden church and the train station for being assigned and transported.

The mood in the Camp was getting tenser the closer we got to May 1945. Through press and radio we were kept well informed. Then—the big relief—the war had ended. Now what? All the sacrifices for nothing! Feeling sorrow for the comrades that will never come home again. The days after the capitulation we all had to attend movies showing the horrid conditions the occupation forces were discovering in the Concentration camps. We all were shocked at such deeds and had not expected anything like that to happen behind our fighting backs.

Now our rations were cut severely. The 1945 summer was extremely hot. In order to fill our daily quotas we had to leave in the dark of the morning and came back in the dark of the evening to the camp....

Back to Camp Fargo. Because of the scarce rations hunger was growing.... Our supervisor was managing a little store for a small negro settlement. We made an agreement to buy stuff like toothpaste, soap and such with our POW money and exchange the items for food with him. That's how we solved the hunger problem in our tent. One of the tent mates had a sister living in the U.S. who came to visit and brought a radio....

Around 10 March 1946 we left Camp Fargo by train—destination home....

4. *State of Georgia v. Pennsylvania Railroad Company*[4]

Argued January 2, 1945

Decided March 26, 1945

Mr. Justice Douglas delivered the opinion of the Court.

The state of Georgia by this motion for leave to file a bill of complaint seeks to invoke the original jurisdiction of this Court under Art. III, Sec. 2 of the Constitution. The defendants are some twenty railroad companies. On November 6, 1944, we issued a rule to show cause why Georgia should not be permitted to file its bill of complaint. Returns to the rule have been made and oral arguments had.

Georgia sues in four capacities only two of which we need mention: (1) In her capacity as a quasi-sovereign or as agent and protector of her people against a continuing wrong done to them; and (2) in her capacity as a proprietor to redress wrongs suffered by the State as the owner of a railroad and as the owner and operator of various institutions of the State.

The essence of the complaint is a charge of a conspiracy among the defendants in restraint of trade and commerce among the States. It alleges that they have fixed arbitrary and noncompetitive rates and charges for transportation of freight by railroad to and from Georgia so as to prefer the ports of other States over the ports of Georgia. It charges that some sixty rate bureaus, committees, conferences, associations and other private rate-fixing agencies have been utilized by defendants to fix these rates; that no road can change joint through rates without the approval of these private agencies; that this private rate-fixing machinery which is not sanctioned by the Interstate Commerce Act, 49 U.S.C.A. 1 et seq., and which is prohibited by the anti-trust Acts has put the effective control of rates to and from Georgia in the hands of the defendants. The complaint alleges that these practices in purpose and effect give manufacturers, sellers, and other shippers in the North an advantage over manufacturers, shippers and others in Georgia. It alleges that the rates so fixed are approximately 39 per cent higher than the rates and charges for transportation of like commodities for like distances between points in the North. It alleges that the defendants who have lines wholly or principally in the South are generally dominated and coerced by the defendants who have northern roads and therefore that even when the southern defendants desire, they cannot publish joint through rates between Georgia and the North when the northern carriers refuse to join in such rates. It is alleged that the rates as a result of the conspiracy are so fixed as

---

[4] From *State of Georgia v. Pennsylvania Railroad Company*, 324 US 439.

(a) to deny to many of Georgia's products equal access with those of other States to the national market;

(b) to limit in a general way the Georgia economy to staple agricultural products, to restrict and curtail opportunity in manufacturing, shipping and commerce, and to prevent the full and complete utilization of the natural wealth of the State;

(c) to frustrate and counteract the measures taken by the State to promote a well-rounded agricultural program, encourage manufacture and shipping, provide full employment, and promote the general progress and welfare of its people; and

(d) to hold the Georgia economy in a state of arrested development.

The complaint alleges that the defendants are not citizens of Georgia; that Georgia is without remedy in her own courts, as the defendants are outside her jurisdiction; that she has no administrative remedy, the Interstate Commerce Commission having no power to afford relief against such a conspiracy; that the issues presented constitute a justiciable question.

The prayer is for damages and for injunctive relief....

It follows that we should not in the exercise of our discretion remit Georgia to the federal district courts for relief against the injuries of which she complains.

The motion for leave to file the amended bill of complaint is granted.

It is so ordered.

Motion for leave to file bill of complaint granted.

5. Constitution of 1945[5]

Preamble

To perpetuate the principles of free government, insure justice to all, preserve peace, promote the interest and happiness of the citizens, and transmit to prosperity the enjoyment of liberty, we, the people of Georgia, relying upon the protection and guidance of Almighty God, do ordain and establish this Constitution.

Article I

Bill of Rights

Section I

---

[5] From *Acts and Resolutions of the General Assembly of the State of Georgia*, 1945.

Paragraph I. All government, of right, originates with the people, is founded upon their will, and is instituted solely for the good of the whole. Public officers are the trustees and servants of the people, and at all times, amenable to them.

Paragraph II. Protection to person and property is the paramount duty of government, and shall be impartial and complete.

Paragraph III. No person shall be deprived of life, liberty, or property, except by due process of law.

...Paragraph XVII. The social status of the citizen shall never be the subject of legislation.

...Paragraph XIX. The civil authority shall be superior to the military, and no soldier shall, in time of peace, be quartered in any house, without the consent of the owner, nor in time of war, except by the civil magistrate, in such manner as may be provided by law.

...Paragraph XXII. The legislative, judicial and executive powers shall forever remain separate and distinct, and no person discharging the duties of one, shall, at the same time, exercise the functions of either of the others, except as herein provided.

Section II

...Paragraph IV. All lotteries, and the sale of lottery tickets, are hereby prohibited; and this prohibition shall be enforced by penal laws....

Article II

Elective Franchise

Section I

...Paragraph II. Every citizen of this State who is a citizen of the United States, eighteen years old or upwards, not laboring under any of the disabilities named in this Article, and possessing the qualifications provided by it, shall be an elector and entitled to register and vote at any election by the people: provided, that no soldier, sailor or marine in the military or naval services of the United States shall acquire the rights of an elector by reason of being stationed on duty in this State.

...Paragraph IV. Every citizen of this State shall be entitled to register as an elector, and to vote in all elections in said State, who is not disqualified under the provisions of Section II of Article II of this Constitution, and who possesses the qualifications prescribed in Paragraphs II and III of this Section or who will possess them at the date of the election occurring next after his registration, and who in addition thereto comes within either of the classes provided for in the two following subdivisions of this paragraph.

1. All persons who are of good character and understand the duties and obligations of citizenship under a republican form of government; or,

2. All persons who can correctly read in the English language any paragraph of the Constitution of the United States or of this State and correctly write the same in the English language when read to them by any one of the registrars, and all persons who solely because of physical disability are unable to comply with the above requirements but who can understand and give a reasonable interpretation of any paragraph of the Constitution of the United States or of this State that may be read to them by any one of the registrars.

Article III

Legislative Department

Section I

Paragraph I. The legislative power of the State shall be vested in a General Assembly which shall consist of a Senate and House of Representatives.

Section II

Paragraph I. The Senate shall consist of not more than fifty-four members and there shall be not more than fifty-four Senatorial Districts with one Senator from each District as now constituted, or as hereafter created. The various Senatorial Districts shall be comprised of the Counties as now provided, and the General Assembly shall have authority to create, rearrange and change these Districts within the limits herein stated....

Section III

Paragraph I. The House of Representatives shall consist of representatives apportioned among the several counties of the State as follows: To the eight counties having the largest population, three representatives each; to the thirty counties having the next largest population, two representatives each; and to the remaining counties, one representative each....

Section IV

Paragraph I. The members of the General Assembly shall be elected for two years, and shall serve until the time fixed by law for the convening of the next General Assembly.

...Paragraph III. The General Assembly shall meet in regular session on the second Monday in January 1947, and biennially thereafter on the same day until the date shall be changed by law....

Article V

Executive Department

Section I

Paragraph I. The executive power shall be vested in a Governor, who shall hold his office during the term of four years, and until his successor shall be chosen and qualified. The Governor serving at the time of the adoption of this constitution and future Governors shall not be eligible to succeed themselves and shall not be eligible to hold the office until after the expiration of four years from the conclusion of his term of office....

Paragraph VII. There shall be a Lieutenant Governor, who shall be elected at the same time, for the same term, and in the same manner as the Governor. He shall be President of the Senate, and shall receive $2,000.00 per annum. In case of the death, resignation, or disability of the Governor, the Lieutenant Governor shall exercise the executive power and receive the compensation of the Governor until the next general election for members of the General Assembly, at which a successor to the Governor shall be elected for the unexpired term.... In case of the death, resignation, or disability of both the Governor and the Lieutenant Governor, the Speaker of the House of Representatives shall exercise the executive power until the removal of the disability or the election and qualification of a Governor at a special election, which shall be held within sixty days from the date on which the Speaker of the House of Representatives shall assume the executive power. A Lieutenant Governor shall be elected at the general election in 1946 and shall qualify at the same time as the Governor....

Paragraph XV. The Governor shall have the revision of all bills passed by the General Assembly before the same shall become laws, but two-thirds of each house may pass a law notwithstanding his dissent; and if any bill should not be returned by the Governor within five days (Sunday excepted) after it has been presented to him, the same shall be law; unless the General Assembly, by their adjournment, shall prevent its return....

Section II

Other Executive Officers

Paragraph I. The Secretary of State, Attorney General, State School Superintendent, Comptroller General, Treasurer, Commissioner of Agriculture, and Commissioner of Labor shall be elected by the persons qualified to vote for members of the General Assembly at the same time, and in the same manner as the Governor....

Article VI

Judiciary

Section I

Paragraph I. The judicial powers of this State shall be vested in a Supreme Court, a Court of Appeals, Superior Courts, Courts of Ordinary, Justices of the Peace, Notaries Public who are ex-officio Justices of the Peace, and such other Courts as have been or may be established by law....

Article VII

Finance, Taxation and Public Debt

...Section IX

Appropriation Control

Paragraph I. The Governor shall submit to the General Assembly within fifteen days after its organization, a budget message accompanied by a draft of a General Appropriations Bill, which shall provide for the appropriation of the funds necessary to operate all the various departments and agencies, and to meet the current expenses of the State for the ensuing fiscal year....

Article VIII

Education

Section I

Paragraph I. The provision of an adequate education for the citizens shall be a primary obligation of the State of Georgia, the expense of which shall be provided for by taxation. Separate schools shall be provided for the white and colored races.

Section II

Paragraph I. There shall be a State Board of Education, composed of one member from each Congressional District in the State, who shall be appointed by the Governor, by and with the consent of the Senate. The Governor shall not be a member of the State Board of Education.

Section IV

Paragraph I. There shall be a Board of Regents of the University System of Georgia, and the government, control, and management of the University System of Georgia and all of its institutions in said system shall be vested in said Board of Regents of the University System of Georgia. Said Board of Regents of the University System of Georgia shall consist of one member from each Congressional District in the State, and five additional members from the State-at-large, appointed by the Governor and confirmed by the Senate. The Governor shall not be a member of the said Board....

Article XII

The Laws of General Operation in Force in this State

Section I

Paragraph I. The laws of general operation in this State are, first: As the Supreme Law: The Constitution of the United States, the laws of the United States in pursuance thereof and all treaties made under the authority of the United States.

Paragraph II. Second. As next in authority thereto: This Constitution.

Paragraph III. Third. In subordination to the foregoing: All laws now in force in this State, not inconsistent with this Constitution shall remain of force until the same are modified or repealed by the General Assembly.

6. President Roosevelt Dies at Home in Warm Springs[6]

The people of Warm Springs and the nation were stunned when the word came late Thursday evening (April 12) that President Roosevelt died suddenly at the Little White House, in Warm Springs, where he came, two weeks previous, for rest.

President Roosevelt's last words were: "I have a terrific headache," spoken to Commander Harold Bruenn, naval physician. He then passed out without regaining consciousness.

President Roosevelt was 63, on January 30, and was serving his fourth term as President of the United States—longest ever held by any president.

Mayor Frank W. Allcorn had invited President Roosevelt to a barbecue at his Shaker Heights home overlooking Warm Springs at 4 p.m., and a number of newsmen and secret servicemen were there awaiting the President when the news came that he had died suddenly. The President was also planning to view a minstrel given by the patients following the barbecue.

Mrs. Roosevelt, who was in Washington, came by plane to Ft. Benning and rushed to Warm Springs from there by automobile.

On Friday morning a Guard of Honor from Ft. Benning lined the road from the Foundation entrance to the Southern Railway station as the funeral procession left from the White House. Approximately two regiments of troops were on hand as guard, and in the procession.

The funeral train pulled out silently at eleven o'clock Friday morning and arrived in Washington at 10 o'clock Saturday morning. The funeral was held there in the famous East Room of the White House at 4 p.m., with burial at his home in Hyde Park, N.Y. Sunday afternoon.

Lumber cut from Georgia pine and grown on the Warm Springs Foundation was used for making the bier on which rested the casket of President Roosevelt to Washington.

The sudden passing of President Roosevelt, at the very hour of victory in Europe, closed a great chapter in American history. He died, as he had lived, a good soldier for his country. The effect of his death on the future of American life and especially politics, cannot be measured.

---

[6] From *Warm Springs Mirror*, April 20, 1945.

7. *Thompson, Lieutenant Governor v. Talmadge*[7]

1. While the courts have no jurisdiction of purely political matters, or to review actions of the General Assembly done within the powers conferred by the Constitution, yet courts have jurisdiction of all justiciable matters; and questions made in the present cases as to whether the General Assembly had the power to elect a Governor, and as to who has title to that office, are justiciable, and the courts have jurisdiction, which is neither ousted nor impaired by reason of the fact that involved therein are political questions and actions by the General Assembly.

2. In 1824 by constitutional provision the General Assembly was divested of its general power to elect a Governor, and that power was retained by the people, where it remains today. The General Assembly was given the conditional power to elect a Governor. A condition precedent to such an election by the General Assembly is a failure of the people to case a majority of their votes for any person, in which event the General Assembly is given the power to elect one of the two persons having the highest number of votes who are in life and willing to accept election at the time appointed for the General Assembly to elect.

(a) The death of the Honorable Eugene Talmadge after his election by the people and before publication of the returns by the General Assembly did not change the duty of that body to declare his election nor authorize the General Assembly to declare his resolution that because of his death no person had a majority of the votes and to elect a Governor.

(b) Accordingly, where in such circumstances the General Assembly undertook to elect another person as Governor, name the Honorable Herman Talmadge, such an attempted election was a void act, which did not confer upon him any right or title to the office of Governor.

(c) It follows that upon the resignation of Governor Arnall on January 18, 1947, M. E. Thompson, the duly qualified Lieutenant Governor, became vested with full executive powers of this State.

March 19, 1947

---

[7] From *Reports of Cases Decided in the Supreme Court of the State of Georgia*, vol. 201 (Atlanta: Harrison Company, 1947).

ESSAYS

Governor Ellis Arnall's Reform Program[8]

Harold Paulk Henderson

Arnall realized that the success of his administration depended on the cooperation his program received from the legislature. Unlike Talmadge, Arnall had served in the General Assembly. His two terms in the House had given him firsthand experience of the workings of the legislative process. Talmadge had usually had an adversarial relationship with the legislature; Arnall desired cooperation. The governor traditionally handpicked the presiding officers of the two houses of the legislature. Arnall continued that practice. He chose former speaker Roy V. Harris, who played a crucial role in his election, as his candidate for speaker of the House. He picked another close supporter, Frank C. Gross, as his candidate for president of the Senate, the presiding officer of the Senate. Both were elected unanimously. The reform-minded governor, totally rejecting the idea of an independent legislature, continued the practice of governors picking the standing committee chairmen. Willingness on the part of the lawmakers led by Harris and Gross to enact Arnall's reform program characterized the spirit of the 1943 legislative session. In contrast, Talmadge could not even obtain permission to deliver a farewell address to the legislature.

The lawmakers quickly began consideration of Arnall's reform program. At his request, the legislature unanimously adopted a resolution of support for President Roosevelt's conduct of the war. The legislature then considered the major plank in Arnall's platform, which called for the abolition of the Talmadge-controlled Board of Regents, the creation of a new board, and the proposal of an amendment changing the board to a constitutional body. The governor insisted that the regents could be insulated from future political interference only by placing the board under the protection of the constitution. Arnall emphasized that such action was needed in order to hasten the reaccreditation of the university system. Both houses unanimously supported House Bill One, which created a new board and removed the governor as a member. The legislation retained the power of the governor to nominate regents subject to senatorial confirmation. The legislature also unanimously

---

[8] From Harold Paulk Henderson, *The Politics of Change in Georgia: A Political Biography of Ellis Arnall* (Athens: University of Georgia Press, 1991). Used with permission of the University of Georgia Press.

voted to submit to the voters an amendment making the board a constitutional body.

On January 22, 1943, Arnall proudly signed House Bill One into law and proclaimed it to be a major victory for education. Shortly thereafter Arnall nominated fifteen members—all white and all male—to the newly created Board of Regents. Although the governor received praise for his nominations, the Atlanta *Daily World* criticized him for not nominating any blacks. The Senate unanimously approved the nominations the governor had made. Eight days after Arnall had signed House Bill One into law, the Executive Committee of the Southern Association of Colleges and Secondary Schools notified Arnall that accreditation had been restored to the University System of Georgia. Arnall quickly expressed gratitude for the action and praised the legislature for its role in the restoration of accreditation. As he promised in the campaign, Arnall also requested the legislature to reorganize the state Board of Education and to make it a constitutional body as well. The legislature unanimously created a new board and proposed a constitutional amendment changing the board to a constitutional body. A proud Arnall praised the legislature for its actions and pledged to continue to champion education because it was "the cure for ignorance, poverty, prejudice, hatred, and demagoguery."

Arnall's reform program called for the legislature to remove from the governor the power to suspend the state treasurer and the state comptroller-general. Under existing statutes, the governor had the power to suspend the two state officials under certain conditions. Arnall recommended that the grant of such power be repealed, and the legislature unanimously agreed. He also requested that the power of the governor to appoint the state auditor be transferred to the legislature. Again the legislature unanimously complied. The lawmakers further agreed without dissent to remove the governor as a member of the governing board of all state agencies. The legislature also unanimously agreed to Arnall's request to remove the power of the governor to arbitrarily strike state employees from the budget....

After obtaining the passage of his reform program, Arnall urged the legislature to consider several other legislative requests. These included creating a teachers retirement system, limiting gubernatorial campaign expenditures, increasing the investigative powers of the state attorney general, creating a "non-political" game and fish commission, and lowering the state's voting age to eighteen. Arnall called for the creation of a teachers retirement system because teachers "certainly deserve special consideration at the hands of the state." With only two dissenting votes, the legislature created the state Teachers Retirement System with the provision that the system would become operational only when the governor or legislature provided funding. Because of the state's financial difficulties, Arnall made no request in the 1943 session for state funds to implement the system. In order to have a teachers retirement system, the legislature had to propose two constitutional amendments. One provided that the taxing power of the state and local governments could be used for the purpose of paying pensions to teachers. The other authorized the payments of benefits under the retirement system. Both passed with little opposition.

Arnall also asked the legislature to strengthen an office he had previously held—the attorney generalship. Arnall pointed to a "glaring defect" in the operation of the attorney generalship in that investigations by that office had to be authorized by the governor. Arnall called for the attorney general to have the authority to initiate investigations of alleged irregularities in state agencies. Arnall accused Talmadge in the primary of having a similar bill defeated in the 1941 legislative session. This time the bill received a more favorable reception with only four dissenting votes. The governor still retained the right to order the attorney general to conduct investigations.

This far in the legislative session, Arnall's requests had met little resistance. His effort to make Georgia the first state to lower the voting age to eighteen, however, provoked strong opposition. Arnall told the lawmakers that Georgians should be allowed to vote if they were old enough to fight for their country and asked for a constitutional amendment lowering the voting age. The proposal quickly met opposition. Senator W. W. Stark charged that the proposed amendment would enfranchise young blacks and "mix politics up in every high school and college in Georgia." Senator Stark asserted that Arnall never would have been elected if he had advocated such a proposal in the primary. Another senator, Herschel Lovett, warned that "this is a university system bill, and they want the children to control their parents." Despite such criticism, the Senate passed the amendment with three more votes than was needed in order to propose a constitutional amendment.

In the House, however, the amendment encountered stronger resistance. Representative J. Robert Elliott, Talmadge's former House floor leader, led the attack. He denounced the amendment, charging that it had the support of the Communist party. He warned that their amendment would enfranchise all of the state's young people, "regardless of their race or whether they had paid their poll taxes." Another representative feared the amendment would allow the state to become a "hotbed for every subversive influence." Talmadge even came to the legislature to lobby against the amendment. At first the opposition forces prevailed. The proposed amendment fell short by thirteen votes of the required two-thirds majority needed to propose a constitutional amendment. Although

Arnall had suffered his first defeat in the 1943 session, the setback proved to be temporary.

The House voted to reconsider the proposal, which it did the following day. Again Representative Elliott led the opposition. He accused the governor of breaking a campaign promise of never dictating to the legislature. "During the past twenty hours, the contrary has taken place," Elliott charged. To ensure approval of the amendment when it was reconsidered by the House, Arnall engaged in a vigorous lobbying campaign. He also arranged for the Veterans Hospital to send to the capitol many busloads of wounded young veterans. Some were in wheelchairs, some were maimed, some were minus arms or legs. These disabled veterans filled the capitol. Arnall then addressed the legislature and said it was unconscionable to tell these young men under twenty-one that although they had fought for our country and were maimed for life, Georgia would deny them the right to vote at eighteen. The stratagem worked. He prevailed on the second House vote with six votes more than needed to propose the amendment. A pleased Arnall promised to speak in every county if needed to obtain popular approval of the amendment. Several months later, Arnall carried the fight to lower the voting age before a House subcommittee, where he spoke in favor of an amendment to the US Constitution lowering the voting age....

After seventy days of productive work, the 1943 legislative session adjourned. Arnall had thoroughly dominated the session with every bill that he requested being passed—many of them without any change. The Atlanta *Journal* declared that Arnall had "received the most wholehearted cooperation ever given any chief executive by a Georgia legislature." Arnall agreed and praised the 1943 legislature as "the finest that had ever assembled under the dome of the State Capitol." Certainly Arnall had every reason to praise the legislature. A writer in an article in *Collier's* magazine dubbed the governor "Unanimous Arnall" because of his astounding success with the legislature. He called the passage of Arnall's reform platform in twenty-four days a "political record breaker anywhere and a miracle in Georgia." One historian even compared Arnall's success with the general Assembly to President Roosevelt's success in getting the Congress to pass legislation in the first "100 days" of the 1933 congressional session.

The 1943 legislative session received praise from the state press. The Atlanta *Journal* commended the lawmakers for establishing "a new standard for efficiency" and restoring democratic government to the state. The Atlanta *Constitution* applauded the legislature for its record of accomplishment "that has rarely if ever, been equalled by a previous assembly session." Even the pro-Talmadge Savannah *Morning News* conceded that the record of the session was commendable. The editor of the Calhoun *Times* stated, "No governor ever had smoother sailing in translating his campaign promises into law than Ellis Arnall," while the Augusta *Chronicle* praised the legislature for its "outstandingly progressive work." One out-of-state newspaper, the Cleveland (Ohio) *Plain Dealer*, commented that "both Talmadge's abuses of power and the speedy correction of those abuses are unique in state affairs."

WAVES at Georgia State College for Women[9]

Lisa A. Ennis

On the first Navy Day after the attack on Pearl Harbor in 1941, the newspaper in Milledgeville, Georgia, reported the town's "cooperation with the Navy is 100 per cent." The city was the proud home of a naval ordnance plant as well as United States congressman Carl Vinson, chairman of the Naval Affairs Committee. The local college, Georgia State College for Women (GSCW), also participated in the war effort. For instance, student activity fees were used to purchase war bonds, and students and faculty volunteered to roll Red Cross bandages and work in the Civilian Morale Service's Key Center. The most significant contribution, however, came on January 29, 1943, when GSCW opened its doors to a new branch of the United States Navy, Women Accepted for Volunteer Emergency Service, or WAVES.

The navy inspected the school for "possible use" in August 1942. Largely through the efforts of Congressman Vinson, the college became one of seven locations in the nation selected to be a Naval Training School and the only one in the South. College president Guy Wells enthusiastically welcomed this opportunity. The WAVES's school not only meant GSCW could take an active part in helping the country, but the WAVES also brought needed financial support to the college. GSCW was undergoing a period of declining enrollment due to "wartime slippage." While coeducational colleges suffered sharper declines, the GSCW enrollment numbers were low enough to cause financial woes for Wells. The navy's use of GSCW facilities provided a much-needed source of income.

The agreement between the navy and the college stipulated that the government would pay rent for the use of the facilities. Furthermore, the contract also authorized the navy to make repairs and improvements to the

---

[9] From Lisa A. Ennis, "The WAVES and GSCW: 'Good Enough for Each Other,'" *Georgia Historical Quarterly* 85/3 (Fall 2001). Courtesy of the Georgia Historical Society.

buildings they used, benefits that would revert back to the college. Wells stated in the *Alumnae Journal* that a "great deal of money has been put into repairs and improvements in the buildings they are using for the Naval Training School." Sanford Hall, for instance, was equipped with a kitchen and dining hall at the navy's expense. Despite the declining enrollment of regular students, the WAVES's occupation of GSCW allowed Wells to report in the *Alumnae Journal* that all buildings were in use, maintained, and some were receiving improvements.

Approximately 15,000 WAVES, in groups varying in size from 2 to 800 trainees, received instruction at GSCW from January 1943 to May 1945. The navy occupied four dormitories: Ennis Hall, Mansion Annex, Mayfair Hall, and Sanford Hall. The Arts Hall, now Lanier, was used for WAVES classes. The women kept a strict military schedule resembling "a naval vessel at anchor." They also marched in formation, had limited free time, and roomed with at least double the usual number of women in dorm rooms, using bunk beds to simulate military life. WAVES even referred to the buildings as ships; Ennis Hall, for example, became the USS Ennis.

Each group of WAVES normally spent one month of general navy training learning the correct navy terminology, traditions, regulations, and drills, and then three months of specialized training learning the job skills the recruits would need. Recruits sent to GSCW graduated as yeomen and served in office and clerical positions, relieving men for active combat duty. WAVES at other schools received training as radio operators and storekeepers. As the war progressed WAVES also became involved in finance, chemical warfare, aviation ordnance, and other special fields traditionally held by men.

Contact between WAVES and GSCW students ("Jessies") was infrequent, but when the two groups did meet they usually got along. One of the main complaints concerned male companionship; the WAVES were competition for the already low number of eligible men in Milledgeville. An especially sore point was the curfew; WAVES were allowed to stay out later than Jessies. Another area of conflict was purely cultural. The navy women came from all over the country and had varied educational backgrounds—some had college degrees while others were high school dropouts. Occasionally a recruit ridiculed what she viewed as "antiquated" Southern customs and "laughable" accents. One example of Jessie humor can be found in the numerous cartoons author Flannery O'Connor drew for campus publications depicting the WAVES in an unflattering light.

While the WAVES and Jessies may not have voluntarily socialized, there were some events that brought them together. One such occasion was the 1943 "Clean-Up Campaign." This cooperative effort to clean the community brought GSCW, GMC (Georgia Military College), the Baldwin County Health Office, and WAVES together in an effort to bring both campuses and the city "far above government requirements." WAVES and Jessies also shared some areas such as a recreation center donated by a community member. The recreation building included a kitchen, library, laundry, and more. One of the most famous wartime events was comedian Bob Hope's visit in May 1943. Hope aired his coast-to-coast NBC weekly radio show from GSCW's Russell Auditorium in front of an audience of WAVES and Jessies.

Overall, between 1943 and 1945 15,000 WAVES underwent training at GSCW, the last group graduating in May 1945. For the navy, the benefits were use of an already constructed facility where women could be efficiently trained to allow male sailors to move into combat positions. The impact the navy had on the college was significant. The institution received national recognition and honor for being selected as a WAVES school (as well as monetary assistance). Navy funds enabled the college to maintain buildings, keep its faculty without lowering salaries, as well as launch plans for the construction of at least one new building. As the last WAVES class graduated and the war drew to a close, the *Alumnae Journal* could confidently state that GSCW was "in a great many respects, much better than before the Navy dropped anchor" and "entirely aside from the service rendered mutually, the Wave [sic] School and GSCW have been good for each other."

Additional Sources

Ball, Lamar Q. *Georgia in World War II: A Study of the Military and Civilian Effort.* Atlanta: Department of Archives and History, 1946.

Henderson, Harold P. *The Politics of Change in Georgia: A Political Biography of Ellis Arnall.* Athens: University of Georgia Press, 1991.

Henderson, Harold P., and Gary L. Roberts, editors. *Georgia Governors in an Age of Change: From Ellis Arnall to George Busbee.* Athens: University of Georgia Press, 1988.

Lee, Dallas. *The Cotton Patch Evidence: The Story of Clarence Jordan and the Koinonia Farm Experiment.* New York: Harper and Row, 1971.

Chapter 15

THE CIVIL RIGHTS ERA

The separation of the races and the oppression of African Americans have had a long history in Georgia, and by the 1940s there were numerous challenges to this social structure. During World War II there were demonstrations of dissatisfaction with the status of race relations. Many Northern black soldiers posted to Georgia for training did not accept the seating arrangements in public transportation. In 1944 students at Savannah State College occupied all of the seats on a city bus and refused to give them up to white passengers, leading to the arrest of two of the protesters. The next challenge was to the state's white primary, also in 1944. Primus E. King, a black registered voter in Columbus, attempted to vote in the Democratic primary in July 1944. After being turned away, King went immediately to his attorney's office to prepare a legal challenge to the white primary. In the resulting court case, *King v. Chapman*, King argued that his right to vote under the 14th, 15th, and 17th Amendments had been violated. The federal courts ruled in King's favor, much as they had in the 1944 Texas case *Smith v. Allwright*. The end result was that the white primary in Georgia was invalidated.

Public education was a major battleground during the Civil Rights Era in 1950s Georgia. The state's political leaders were determined to prevent the desegregation of Georgia's schools, and as early as 1951 the General Assembly considered several proposals. One such piece of legislation was an appropriations bill that included a clause prohibiting the expenditure of public funds on desegregated schools. Another proposal, which the General Assembly passed in 1954, was a constitutional amendment to abolish the state's public schools in favor of a system of private schools. The Private School Amendment, as it was called, authorized the payment of tuition grants directly to parents, who would then use the funds to send their children to a private school. In this way the state could not be accused of denying equal protection. The General Assembly passed this bill and Georgia's voters approved it in the general election in November 1954, six months *after* the US Supreme Court's Brown decision. Georgia's legislators apparently did not recognize, or ignored, the simple fact that tuition grants from the state would make the school a public institution, not a private school.

One of the most important catalysts behind Georgia's response to the Brown decision was Governor Marvin Griffin. Elected in 1954, Griffin promised during the campaign to protect the state's segregated schools "come hell or high water." He reiterated this statement in his inaugural address in January 1955 and he kept his promise—no schools were desegregated during his administration. Governor Griffin had great influence with the General Assembly and got most of what he wanted. His basic response to Brown was interposition, to interpose the state's authority between the federal government and the state's citizens. The legislation that most accurately represented this philosophy was the Interposition Resolution that the General Assembly passed on March 9, 1956, which declared the Brown decision "null and void and of no effect." Governor Griffin was so committed to segregation that in December 1955 he announced that he would not allow the Georgia Tech football team to play in the 1956 Sugar Bowl. The reason: the opposing team, the University of Pittsburgh, included a black player. Griffin relented after a storm of protest on the Georgia Tech campus (and the University of Georgia campus) and a protest march to the capitol that ended with the governor being hanged in effigy.

Real progress in civil rights took place only after Griffin left office and Ernest Vandiver took office. Although he campaigned to maintain segregation, Vandiver was not nearly as obstructionist as Griffin; desegregation of public schools occurred while he was in office. Two committees, one created by the General Assembly and one a group of concerned citizens, helped ease the state into desegregating public schools. Help Our Public Education, or HOPE, was created in December 1958 by parents of Atlanta schoolchildren to campaign to keep the state's schools open. The General Assembly Committee on Schools, better known as the Sibley Commission, was formed in 1960 to investigate the public's opinion on current school policies. In early 1961 federal courts ordered the desegregation of the University of Georgia and Charlayne Hunter and Hamilton Holmes were enrolled. Real progress was being made in Georgia.

Martin Luther King, Jr., born in Georgia in 1929, made his mark in the fight for civil rights in the state. In 1960 King returned to Georgia from Alabama and took a position at Ebenezer Baptist Church. Later that year, on October 19, 1960, Dr. King joined a student sit-in at Rich's Department Store to desegregate the lunch counter. Along with the students, King was arrested for trespassing. King also appeared in Albany in 1961 and 1962 to assist the Albany Movement in the fight for civil rights there but was less than successful.

Documents

The first document below is legislation that repealed the poll tax in the state, making Georgia the fourth state to do so. Document 2 relates the court's decision in the case that outlawed the white primary. The third document is the list of questions that made up the literacy test for voting in 1949. Document 4 is the petition to desegregate the public schools in Valdosta in 1955, a response to the state NAACP's "Atlanta Declaration." The fifth document is the General Assembly's 1956 Interposition Resolution, the state's attempt to insulate itself from the federal government regarding civil rights issues. Document 6 is the 1960 report of the Sibley Commission, created by the General Assembly to investigate desegregation of the public schools. The seventh document is the US Supreme Court's decision to integrate the University of Georgia. Document 8 is a letter Martin Luther King, Jr., wrote while in a jail cell in Albany. The ninth document is a speech by Senator Richard Russell on the Civil Rights Act of 1964, in which he stated that he opposed the bill but that Georgians would have to accept it.

1. Poll Tax Repealed[1]

Be it enacted by the General Assembly of Georgia:

Section 1. That Section 92–108 of the Code of Georgia of 1933, relating to the levy and collection of a poll tax for educational purposes, which reads as follows:

"There shall be levied and collected each year upon every inhabitant of the State between the ages of 21 and 60 years, on the day fixed for the return of property for taxation, a poll tax of $1, which shall be used for educational purposes in instructing children in the elementary branches of an English education only: provided, that this tax shall not be demanded of blind persons, or female inhabitants of the State who do not register for voting."

be, and it is, hereby repealed in its entirety.

Section 2. That the payment of a poll tax shall not hereafter be a requisite for the exercise of the privilege of voting in any primary or election by the people.

Approved February 5, 1945.

---

[1] From *Acts and Resolutions of the General Assembly of the State of Georgia*, 1945.

2. *King v. Chapman*[2]

March 6, 1946

The appellee King, a citizen of the United States and of the state of Georgia and a qualified and registered voter in Muscogee County according to the laws of Georgia, offered to vote in a Democratic Primary in that County in which nominees for the United States Senate and House of Representatives as well as for State offices were being chosen, and was denied the right by the appellants, who were in charge of the primary as the County Democratic Executive Committee, solely because he was of the colored or negro race. He sued for damages under the Civil Rights Act, 8 U.S.C.A. ss 31 and 43, for the deprivation of a right secured by the Constitution of the United States, and especially by the Fifteenth Amendment. The facts were stipulated, including the amount of damages, if any are recoverable. The District Judge made an exhaustive review of the Georgia statutes touching party primary elections and concluded as a matter of law that this primary election "was by law an integral part of the electoral process of the State of Georgia" and the holding of it "was action by the State of Georgia" and the holding of it "was action by the State of Georgia acting through the Democratic Party as its instrumentality," and that King's right to vote was withheld in violation of the Fourteenth, Fifteenth and Seventeenth Amendment of the Constitution, and thereupon entered judgment for the stipulated damages. The defendants have appealed....

We think these provisions show that the State, through the managers it requires, collaborates in the conduct of the primary, and puts its power behind the rules of the party. It adopts the primary as a part of the public election machinery. The exclusions of voters made by the party by the primary rules become exclusions enforced by the State and when these exclusions enforced by the State and when these exclusions are prohibited by the Fifteenth Amendment because based on race or color, the persons making them effective violate under color of State law a right secured by the Constitution and laws of the United States within the meaning of the statute which is here sued on.

The judgment is accordingly affirmed.

---

[2] From *Chapman et al. v. King. King v. Chapman et al.*, 154 F.2d 460.

3. 1949 Literacy Test[3]

In order to ascertain whether an applicant is eligible for qualification as a voter in this classification, the registrars shall orally propound to him the thirty questions on the standardized list set forth in the following section. If the applicant can give factually correct answers to ten of the thirty questions as they are propounded to him, then the registrars shall enter an order declaring him to be prima facie qualified. If he cannot correctly answer ten out of the thirty questions propounded to him, then an order shall be entered rejecting his application.

Standard List of Questions

(To be propounded to those seeking to register and qualify as voters under Article II, Section I, Paragraph IV, Sub-Paragraph I of the Constitution.)

1. Who is the President of the United States?
2. What is the term of office of the President of the United States?
3. May the President of the United States be legally elected for a second term?
4. If the President of the United States dies in office who succeeds him?
5. How many groups compose the Congress of the United States?
6. How many United States Senators are there from Georgia?
7. What is the term of office of a United States Senator?
8. Who are the United States Senators from Georgia?
9. Who is Governor of Georgia?
10. Who is Lieutenant Governor of Georgia?
11. Who is Chief Justice of the Supreme Court of Georgia?
12. Who is Chief Judge of the Court of Appeals of Georgia?
13. Into what two groups is the General Assembly of Georgia divided?
14. Does each Georgia County have at least one representative in the Georgia House of Representatives?
15. Do all Georgia counties have the same number of representatives in the Georgia House of Representatives?
16. In what city are the laws of the United States made?
17. How old do you have to be to vote in Georgia?
18. What city is the capitol of the United States?
19. How many states are there in the United States?
20. Who is the Commander-in-Chief of the United States Army?

(The following questions requiring a different answer according to the localities in which the applicant lives....)

---

[3] From *Acts and Resolutions of the General Assembly of the State of Georgia*, 1949.

21. In what Congressional District do you live?
22. Who represents your Congressional District in the National House of Representatives?
23. In what State Senatorial District do you live?
24. Who is the State Senator that represents your Senatorial District?
25. In what County do you live?
26. Who represents your County in the House of Representatives of Georgia. If there are more than one representative, name them.
27. What is the name of the County seat of your County?
28. Who is the Ordinary of your County?
29. Who is the Judge of the Superior Court of your circuit? If there are more than one, name one additional judge.
30. Who is the Solicitor General of your circuit?

4. Valdosta NAACP's Petition
to Integrate Schools[4]

To School Board Governing Valdosta Schools
[and] Superintendent of Schools of Valdosta, Georgia, W. G. Nunn.

We, the undersigned, are the parents of children of school age entitled to attend and attending the public elementary and secondary high schools under your jurisdiction. As you undoubtedly know, the United States Supreme Court on May 17, 1954, ruled that the maintenance of racially segregated public schools is a violation of the Constitution of the United States and on May 31, 1955 reaffirmed that principle and requires "good faith compliance at the earliest practicable date" with the federal courts authorized to determine whether local officials are proceeding in good faith.

We, therefore, call upon you to take immediate steps to reorganize the public schools under your jurisdiction on a nondiscriminatory basis. As we understand it, you have the responsibility to reorganize the school systems under your control so that the children of public school age attending and entitled to attend public schools cannot be denied admissions to any school or be required to attend any school solely because of race and color.

The May 31st decision of the Supreme Court, to us, means that the time for delay, evasion or procrastination is past. Whatever the difficulties in according our children their constitutional rights, it is clear that the school board must

---

[4] From *Valdosta Daily Times*, August 10, 1955.

meet and seek a solution to that question in accordance with the law of the land. As we interpret the decision, you are duty bound to take immediate concrete steps leading to early elimination of segregation in the public schools. Please rest assured of our willingness to serve in any way we can to aid you in dealing with this question.

5. Interposition Resolution[5]

Be it resolved by the House of Representatives, the Senate concurring....

That the General Assembly of Georgia denies that the Supreme Court of the United States had the right which it asserted in the school cases, decided by it on May 17, 1954, to enlarge the language and meaning of the compact by the States in an effort to withdraw from the States powers reserved to them and as daily exercised by them for almost a century;...

That the General Assembly of Georgia asserts that whenever the General Government attempts to engage in the deliberate, palpable and dangerous exercise of powers not granted to it, the States who are parties to the compact have the right, and are duty bound, to interpose for arresting the progress of the evil, and for maintaining, within their respective limits, the authorities, rights and liberties appertaining to them;

That failure on the part of this State thus to assert its clear rights would be construed as acquiescence in the surrender thereof; and that such submissive acquiescence to the seizure of one right would in the end lead to the surrender of all rights, and inevitably to the consolidation of the States into one sovereignty, contrary to the sacred compact by which this Union of States was created;...

That implementing its decision of May 17, 1954, said court on May 31, 1955, upon further consideration of said cases, said: "All provisions of Federal, State, or local law...must yield" to said decision of May 17, 1954; said court thereby presuming arrogantly to give orders to the State of Georgia;...

That the State of Georgia has the right to operate and maintain a public school system utilizing such educational methods therein as in her judgment are conducive to the welfare of those to be educated and the people of the State generally, this being a governmental responsibility which the State has assumed lawfully, and her rights in this respect have not in any wise been delegated to the Central Government, but, on the contrary, she and the other States have reserved such matters to themselves by the terms of the Tenth Amendment.

---

[5] From *Acts and Resolutions of the General Assembly of the State of Georgia*, 1956.

Being possessed of this lawful right, the State of Georgia is possessed of power to repel every unlawful interference therewith;...

Therefore, be it further resolved by the House of Representatives, the Senate concurring:

First: That said decisions and orders of the Supreme Court of the United States relating to separation of the races in the public institutions of a State as announced and promulgated by said court on May 17, 1954, and May 31, 1955, are null, void and of no force or effect;

Second: That hereby there is declared the firm intention of this State to take all appropriate measures honorably and constitutionally available to the State, to avoid this illegal encroachment upon the rights of her people;

Third: That we urge upon our sister States firm and deliberate efforts upon their part to check this and further encroachment on the part of the General Government, and on the part of said court through judicial legislation, upon the reserved powers of all the States, that by united efforts the States may be preserved;

Fourth: That a copy of this resolution be transmitted by His Excellency The Governor to the Governor and legislatures of each of the other States, to the President of the United States, to each of the Houses of Congress, to Georgia's Representatives and Senators in the Congress, and to the Supreme Court of the United States for its information.

Approved March 9, 1956.

6. Sibley Commission Report[6]

Recommendation

The Committee recognizes, as has been heretofore stated, that the people of Georgia, though overwhelmingly in favor of both segregation and public schools, are widely divided as to the best means of meeting the situation that confronts them; that the question profoundly affects every phase of the future life and activities of the people of the State; that the question should be considered in an atmosphere of calmness and far-sighted wisdom; that the question should be decided only after the most careful deliberation and the most thoughtful consideration of all the issues involved; and that the public school system is of such transcendent importance that its fate ought to be

---

[6] From "The Report of the General Assembly Committee on Schools," April 28, 1960, John Sibley Papers, Manuscript, Archives, and Rare Book Library, Emory University.

decided by a direct vote of the people. The people of Georgia have never been called upon to make a more important decision.

The Committee further recognizes that the primary concern of each Georgia citizen is the welfare of his own children and that regardless of the fate of the public schools, each parent should be protected by the Georgia Constitution from being forced to allow his child to attend a school under what the parent considers intolerable circumstances.

The Committee further recognizes that the situation before it is one subject to unforeseen future developments and that the Legislature should have the maximum latitude in meeting such developments, including certain constitutional powers which it does not now possess.

We, Therefore, Recommend:

1. That the General Assembly propose to the people of Georgia an amendment to the Constitution, reading substantially as follows:

"Not withstanding any other provision in this Constitution, no child of this state should be compelled against the will of his or her parent or guardian, to attend the public schools with a child of the opposite race; that any child whose parent or guardian objects to his attending an integrated school, shall be entitled to reassignment, if practicable, to another public school, or shall be entitled to a direct tuition grant or scholarship aid, as provided by this Constitution and as may be authorized by the General Assembly."

2. That the General Assembly propose to the people of Georgia a further amendment to the Constitution substantially as follows:

"Notwithstanding any other provision of this Constitution, the General Assembly may provide for a uniform system of local units for the administration of the schools and authorize any such local administration unit, as defined by the General Assembly, to close schools within the unit or to reopen the schools in accordance with the wishes of a majority of the qualified voters of the unit as expressed in a formal election called for the purpose of ascertaining the wishes of the voters."

3. That the General Assembly forthwith enact legislation providing for tuition grants or scholarships for the benefit of any child whose parents chooses to withdraw said child from an integrated school and for the benefit of any child whose school has been closed, whether as a result of existing or future Georgia laws or as a result of a court order.

4. That the General Assembly forthwith enact legislation making the existing teacher retirement system available to teachers in private schools in the same manner and on the same basis as it now extends to teachers in public schools.

5. That the General Assembly consider whether, in view of the urgency created by the Atlanta case and other cases which may be brought, it will propose to close the public schools in order to maintain total segregation throughout the state or whether it will choose a course designed to keep the schools open with as much freedom of choice to each parent and community as possible; and, if it chooses the latter course, that it enact legislation enabling each school board or other local body to establish a pupil assignment plan; empowering the people of each community to vote whether to close their schools in the event of integration or to continue the operation of said schools; and enabling each parent to withdraw his child from an integrated school and have the child reassigned to a segregated school or receive a tuition grant or scholarship for private education.

7. Holmes v. Danner[7]

On September 2, 1960, Hamilton E. Holmes and Charlayne A. Hunter, minors, by their next friends, filed in the Athens division of this court, on behalf of themselves and others similarly situated, their complaint against Walter N. Danner, Registrar of the University of Georgia, seeking a preliminary and permanent injunction enjoining him from refusing to consider their applications and those of other Negro residents of Georgia for admission to the University of Georgia upon the same terms and conditions applicable to white applicants; from failing and refusing to act expeditiously upon applications received from Negro residents of the State of Georgia; from refusing to approve the applications of Negro residents of the State of Georgia for admission into the University of Georgia solely because of race and color of the Negro applicants; from subjecting Negro applicants to requirements, prerequisites, interviews and tests not required of white applicants for admission; from making the attendance of Negroes to the University of Georgia and other schools subject to terms and conditions not applicable to white persons; and, from continuing to pursue the policy, practice, customs and usage of limiting admissions to certain schools in the University System of Georgia to white persons and limiting admissions to certain schools in the University System of Georgia to Negro persons....

Pursuant to the foregoing findings of fact and conclusions of law, it is

---

[7] From *Holmes v. Danner*, 191 F. Supp. 385, September 25, 1960; 191 F. Supp. 394, January 6, 1961.

Ordered, Adjudged and Decreed that the defendant, Walter N. Danner, his agents, employees, successors, associates and all persons in active concert and participation with him are hereby permanently enjoined as follows:

From refusing to consider the applications of the plaintiffs and other Negro residents of Georgia for admission to the University of Georgia upon the same terms and conditions applicable to white applicants seeking admission to said University; and from failing and refusing to act expeditiously upon applications received from Negro residents of Georgia; and from refusing to approve the applications of qualified Negro residents of Georgia for admission to said University solely because of the race and color of the Negro applicants; and from subjecting Negro applicants to requirements, prerequisites, interviews, delays and tests not required of white applicants for admission; and from making the attendance of Negroes at said University subject to terms and conditions not applicable to white persons; and from failing and refusing to advise Negro applicants promptly and fully regarding their applications, admission requirements and status as is done by the defendant and his associates in the case of white applicants; and from continuing to pursue the policy, practice, custom and usage of limiting admissions to said University to white persons.

The court recognizes that the primary right and duty of fixing admission requirements and passing upon the qualifications of applicants for admission to the University of Georgia rests upon those in authority at that institution, and nothing in this order, judgment and decree shall be construed to restrict the proper exercise of that right and duty. The intent of this injunction herein granted is only to restrict the exercise of that right and duty so as to forbid admission requirements which will deny to Negroes equal protection or due process of law and to forbid denial of admission to Negroes, who are qualified for such admission, solely on the ground of their race or color.

Inasmuch, however, as it has been made to appear, and is found by the court, that the two plaintiffs are fully qualified for immediate admission to said University and would already have been admitted had it not been for their race and color, it is a further intent of this injunction that the defendant and other persons above indicated be and they are hereby enjoined from refusing to permit the plaintiffs to enroll in and enter said University as students therein immediately for the now beginning Winter Quarter, 1961, or at the appropriate time for the approaching Spring, Summer or Fall Quarter, 1961, as each plaintiff may elect, provided only that, if either plaintiff is, at the time he or she elects to enroll in and enter said University, then pursuing in any other institution a course or courses of study then not completed, such student shall furnish to defendant a letter or statement from such other institution that such student is then doing passing work in such uncompleted course or courses, and in any event such student shall furnish evidence of having satisfactorily passed all completed work taken by such student at such institution...doing so on or before January 9, 1961, if practicable, in the event present Winter Quarter enrollment is desired, and notifying the defendant with reasonable promptness in the event a later enrollment is desired. The plaintiffs are entitled to this leeway as to choice of enrollment date because of the fact that they are now attending semester basis institutions and might have to give up claim for credits for the work done during the Fall of 1960, their present semesters not having been completed. It is further the intention and purpose of this decree that the defendant and all other persons above indicated shall do whatever is necessary to be done to permit the plaintiffs to enroll in and enter said University as students therein in accordance with this decree.

8. Letter from an Albany Jail[8]

Martin Luther King, Jr.

I am writing this column from the Albany city jail. Perhaps you have already learned that Ralph Abernathy and I were found guilty last Tuesday of "parading without a license" and sentenced to either fines of $178.00 each or the alternative of serving 45-day sentences on the city street force. We chose the latter and willingly deferred bond and waived appeal.

Our course of action was decided after very careful soul searching. There was consideration of our wives and families, our respective pulpits, our official responsibility as chief officers of SCLC and many long standing commitments. However, in the face of all these, we were overwhelmed by some other primary concerns that could be resolved in no other way.

We chose to serve our time because we feel so deeply about the plight of more than 700 others who have yet to be tried. The fine and appeal for this number of people would make the cost astronomical. We have experienced the racist tactics of attempting to bankrupt the movement in the South through excessive bail and extended court fights. The time has now come when we must practice civil disobedience in a true sense or delay our freedom thrust for long years.

Albany, Georgia, as you know, has been the site of the largest mass demonstrations and jail-ins in the non-violent movement in the South. Last

---

[8] From *New York Amsterdam News*, July 21, 1962.

December, in a series of "prayer marches," 735 citizens from every quarter of the community made their moral witness against the system of segregation.

Needless to say, a complete victory was not achieved, but some gains were made which have since been clouded by city officials who refused to keep their word. The Negro community has never faltered in making its wishes known, and from December to the present they have suffered sporadic harassment during a city-wide boycott and picketing activities.

Ralph and I were called to trial along with two other Albany citizens in February. Recorder's Court Judge, A. N. Durden, deferred judgment until Tuesday and no further trials were held. The Albany movement headed by a young osteopath, Dr. W. G. Anderson, interpreted this move as a sword of Damocles "to keep Negroes in their place."

It is by this set of several circumstances that Ralph and I presently serve 45-day sentences.

This is the heart of civil disobedience. Some of our critics complain that our non-violent method fosters disrespect of the law and encourages "lawlessness." Nothing could be further from the truth. Civil disobedience precludes that the non-violent resistor in the face of unjust and/or immoral law cannot in all good conscience obey that law.

His decision to break that law and willingly pay the penalty evidences the highest respect for the law. In so doing, he distinguishes himself from the racist who practices uncivil disobedience; he breaks, circumvents, flouts, and evades the law but is unwilling to pay the penalty.

Thus it is, when the non-violent resistor refuses to cooperate with a law that is out of harmony with the laws of God and the laws of morality, he must break the law—but in so doing he practices civil disobedience and accepts the penalty, thereby practicing moral obedience and transforms the jail into a haven of liberty and freedom.

This is why Ralph and I must serve the remaining 41 days of our sentences in the Albany city jail.

9. Senator Richard Russell on
the Civil Rights Act of 1964[9]

...I cannot close my remarks without making some reference to the biggest and most intense legislative conflict of our history that resulted in the passage by the Senate of the so-called civil rights statute. This statute is now on the books despite the last-ditch opposition of our small group of Senators. We put everything we had into the fight, but the odds against us mounted from day to day until we were finally gagged and overwhelmed.

The signature of President [Lyndon B.] Johnson has placed it on the statute books of our country. This enactment is the most far-reaching federal force bill that the central power of the federal government has ever sought to impose upon the people of this land.

It is the understatement of the year to say that I do not like these statutes. There are hundreds of thousands of people in this country who feel as I do about them. However, they are now on the books and it becomes our duty as good citizens to learn to live with them for as long as they are there. The constitutionality of some of the provisions will be tested immediately in the courts. While it is being adjudicated, all good citizens will learn to live with the statute and abide by its final adjudication, even though we reserve the right to advocate by legal means its repeal or modification.

Time after time during the three-and-a-half months of the agonizing legislative struggle, I was highly critical of the growing disrespect for law and order generated by the campaign of civil disobedience by extremist groups. Time and again, I was shocked to hear persons in high authority not only condone but urge the breaking of established laws because someone had decided that they were either immoral or personally repugnant.

Most shocking of all, our ambassador to the United Nations in a commencement address, claimed it to be a "proud achievement" to spend time in jail for violating local laws with which the violator did not agree.

This strange doctrine that a citizen may pick and choose the laws he will obey and ignore those he does not like is, to me, totally reprehensible. It is a form of anarchy to say that a person need not comply with a particular statute with which he disagrees. Ours is a government of laws, not of men, and our system cannot tolerate the philosophy that obedience to law rests upon the

---

[9] Speech to Coosa Valley Area Planning and Development Commission, 15 July 1964, Speech/Media Files, United States Senatorial Papers, Richard B. Russell Jr. Collection, Richard B. Russell Library for Political Research and Studies, University of Georgia.

person likes or dislikes of any individual citizen, whether he supports or opposes the statute in question. This is true even if the body which now passes as our Supreme Court gives tacit approval to mass violations of local laws in one section of the country while enforcing them ruthlessly in others, as their predilections and preconceptions may dictate.

It is therefore our duty as good and patriotic citizens, in a period that will undoubtedly be marked by tension and unrest as this statute is implemented, to avoid all violence.

Violence and law violation will only compound our difficulties and increase our troubles. I am sure that the vast majority of the people of Georgia were shocked and outraged by the brutal and senseless murder of a Negro Reserve officer upon our public highways a few days ago. I am convinced that this cowardly act was generated by a demented mind and I trust that the guilty party will soon be apprehended so that we may demonstrate to the world that assassins, even if demented, will not be tolerated in Georgia. If our highways are not safe for all, they are not safe for any of us.

I have no apologies to anyone for the fight that I made against the federal force bill. I only regret that we did not prevail. I oppose it because of a profound conviction that, in the long run, this measure could only prove harmful to the country and curtail and destroy the rights of all Americans of every race. I still have faith in the soundness of our free institutions and in the inherent good judgment of the American people. I can but believe that in time the people of this nation will turn back the trend toward statism and enforced conformity in every activity of life.

Violence and defiance are no substitute for the long campaign of reason and logic we must wage to overcome the prejudices and misconceptions which now influence the majority of the American people in this field.

ESSAYS

The Struggle for Racial Equality in Georgia[10]

Stephen G. N. Tuck

The election of Eugene Talmadge in 1946 marked the end of the upsurge in black activism, but it was the election of Herman Talmadge as governor in the special election of 1948 that ushered in a further decade of aggressive white supremacy in the state. As *Harper's* magazine reporter Calvin Kytle predicted, the 1948 election represented a "long, dark night for Georgia." "Poor Ol' Georgia," one voter told a *Time* reporter, "first Sherman, then Herman."

In many ways the gubernatorial election of 1948 proved to be an accurate portent for the ensuing decade of white supremacist politics. First, the election demonstrated that under the county-unit system, the rural portion of the state retained political predominance. Georgia's governmental structure was "created in another era," the *New South* observed in 1949, and "bears little relation to the state's present-day economy and outlook." Therefore, the more moderate race relations in Atlanta and Savannah had no influence on statewide elections. Furthermore, over half of the black voters in the state were in the thirty-eight most populous counties, which were relatively underrepresented by the county-unit apportionment. And as V. O. Key noted, the legislature would never reform the county-unit system because the "legislators themselves are the beneficiaries of the malapportionment that would have to be altered."

Defense of white supremacy and defense of the county-unit system, therefore, became synonymous during the 1950s. Charles Pyles noted that "if Georgia politics has been a history of rural-urban cleavage, it is the attitude toward the position of the Negro that explains the major peculiarities of the cleavage." Racial gains in the major cities fueled the campaigns of rural politicians. Herman Talmadge, for example, circulated over 2 million pieces of segregationist literature, including copies of a photograph of interracial dancing taken at an NAACP meeting in Atlanta. Certainly black activists saw the county-unit system as the major obstacle to black political progress. [Clarence] Bacote called it "the most invidious system that was ever invented." The

---

[10] From Stephen G. N. Tuck, *Beyond Atlanta: The Struggle for Racial Equality in Georgia, 1940–1980* (Athens: University of Georgia Press, 2001). Used with permission of the University of Georgia Press.

Pittsburgh Courier saw the county-unit system as "the last stand of hate-inspired politics in Georgia."

In every respect, Georgia's virulent white supremacist backlash was led from the highest official level. The *New York Times* labeled Herman Talmadge as the "all-time Georgia champion of white supremacy." By his own admission, Talmadge won the 1948 election on "as white a primary as possible" platform and introduced a four-point legislative program to secure white supremacy. Almost immediately, over 12,000 black voters were purged and far more intimidated from exercising their vote in most counties across the state.

Within a year, a new voter registration law reintroduced the poll tax and all voters were required to take a discriminatory test every two years in order to reregister. The fifty questions that could be asked in the test ranged in difficulty from "Name the president of the United States" to "How many judges sit on the state court of Appeals?" While in no doubt that black Georgians would be asked the most difficult questions, a *New York Times* editorial thought the process particularly absurd because Talmadge and "the wool hat group" "could not answer over half a dozen of the fifty proposed questions." Such legislation gave free rein to local officials. In Savannah, 5,000 black voters were sent cards requiring personal information and lost their registration if they did not reply promptly. In Johnson County, where black residents represented a third of the mostly rural population, prospective voters were required to sign a pledge in support of white supremacy.

The voter exclusion bill was flanked by further minor pieces of legislation aimed at obstructing even the most tentative challenge to white supremacy. In the hospitals, all blood from black and white Georgians had to be marked separately. At the behest of Dr. Samuel Green, Georgia's Imperial Wizard of the Ku Klux Klan, Talmadge unsuccessfully sought to ban black baseball stars Jackie Robinson and Roy Campanella when the Dodgers played the Atlanta Crackers.

Talmadge's supremacist stance presaged a decade of staunch defense of segregation by leading state politicians. In Washington, DC, Georgia senator Richard Russell strongly opposed President Harry Truman's call for civil rights legislation. On 27 January 1949, Russell took the offensive against "northern hypocrites" when he introduced a bill in Congress to fund the relocation of black Southerners to Northern states. Minnesota senator Hubert H. Humphrey suggested that the $500 million scheme had been borrowed from the "Hitler-Stalin school of shifting [around] populations one doesn't want." In July 1951, Talmadge asserted that "as long as I am governor in Georgia, Negroes will not be admitted to white schools." Shortly after his inauguration in 1955 as Talmadge's successor, Governor Marvin Griffin prohibited the University of

Georgia from playing sports against any team that included a black player. At the end of September 1958, Governor Ernest Vandiver was elected on the same pledge that "no, not one" black student would ever enter a white public school.

This blatant supremacist rhetoric was backed up by more sophisticated measures in defense of segregation. In 1951, Talmadge introduced a 3 percent sales tax to raise an extra $200 million for education in Georgia. Over half of the initial spending of $30 million was designated for black schools, even though black children represented only one-third of the total enrollment. The state administration also raised the budget to pay for out-of-state college education for black students by almost one-half. Under the heading "Georgia's Last Stand," a *Pittsburgh Courier* editorial jokingly asked, "Has Governor Talmadge sprouted wings and a halo?" Within three years, spending on education had soared from 2.6 to 53 percent of total state revenue.

In reality, such generous spending was a vain attempt to justify the doctrine of separate but equal in advance of the Brown test case. At the same time, Talmadge ushered in an appropriations bill that promised to withhold state funding from any white school in Georgia that admitted a single black child. Instead, the state would reimburse the parents of the schoolchildren concerned and lease the school buildings to a local resident who would then run an independent segregated school. Even leaving aside the other question of Talmadge's motives and moral principles, argued Benjamin Mays, Georgia's state administration needed to spend an exorbitant $175 million on black schools to equalize school standards. Georgia's Department of Education conceded that, if anything, Mays's estimate was slightly conservative. The *Pittsburgh Courier* was less sanguine about the political maneuverings. "The State of Georgia is demonstrating today how one evil man can set back the clock and lower the prestige of an important commonwealth."

The Ku Klux Klan became inextricably linked with the Georgia administration under Talmadge. Gloster Current observed at the end of 1948 that the "election of Talmadge has apparently been a signal to these hooded devils to don their sheets." Grand Dragon Dr. Samuel Green and Talmadge shared the same racial outlook, both men asserting that "God himself segregated the races." In November 1948, Talmadge officially designated Green a lieutenant colonel and his own aid-de-camp. Meanwhile, Green instructed all Georgia Klansmen that the most important task in 1948 was to elect Talmadge. In parallel with the renewed dominance of the Talmadge faction, the Associated Klans of Georgia reemerged from a wartime low of 12 Klaverns to over 110 Klaverns, with an estimated 100,000 members by the summer of 1949. At a time when Klan activity was decreasing across the South and even in Mississippi, Klan membership, therefore, almost equaled the number of black registered voters across the state. "The Ku Klux Klan is surging again in Georgia," the *New York Times* observed.

The growth of the Klan translated into renewed racial violence. During the first six months of 1948, the Southern Regional Council documented an unprecedented dozen reported attacks in Georgia. The following year, Georgia led the South in extralegal racial violence. Typically, Klan activities were targeted at black advocates of racial change, beginning with the election of 1948. In one unusual instance, three investigative white reporters were beaten and stabbed with hypodermic needles for infiltrating an initiation ceremony outside Columbus. Cross-burnings were believed to have been the reason for the minimal turnout of black voters in the southeastern town of Valdosta. In Wrightsville, Johnson County, 300 Klan members marched and then burned a 15-foot cross on the eve of the Democratic primary to remind residents of Dr. Green's warning that "blood will flow in the streets if the Negro votes." It proved to be no idle threat. A turpentine worker, Isaiah Nixon, in Montgomery County and Robert Mallard from Toombs County were both murdered for voting after having been specifically warned not to. Election managers across the state reported that "large numbers of Negroes have been too scared to vote."

After 1948 racial violence was unrestrained and unchecked. After a lynching in Irwinton, Wilkinson County, the local jury deliberated for only twenty minutes before releasing the two local white defendants, not least because two of the jury had already served as character witnesses. Wilkinson County's solicitor expressed relief at the exoneration of the sheriff beyond "any question of doubt." "Most Georgia sheriffs," he explained to reporters, "would have shot the Negro instead of taking him to jail." Angry at the intrusion of the Georgia Bureau of Investigation and particularly the media, the *Wilkinson County News* expressed the hope that "maybe some of these Georgia editors will get the racial tar and rusty feathers they so much deserve for being traitors." White supremacist violence was not confined to the countryside. During 1951–1952, Atlanta experienced almost monthly bombings of houses occupied by middle-class blacks that encroached on all-white residential areas. NAACP branch president C. A. Harper called an emergency meeting with Mayor Hartsfield to express the fears of black homeowners in the tension-filled areas.

The white supremacist backlash succeeded in dismantling the nascent statewide civil rights movement. In 1952, leaders of the registration campaign in Savannah bemoaned the "loss of countless of thousands of registered voters" in the southeast region of the state. In the same year, Hugh Owen concluded that "in state-wide elections Negro voting remains largely only an issue to be held up as a scare by the professional advocates of white supremacy." A 1956

Morehouse College survey found that "the pattern of excluding Negroes as registrants and voters" in the southwest Georgia counties "was virtually the same in each. There is the ever-present threat of racial violence which has erupted on occasions, especially following elections." Except for the atypically high black registration in Atlanta and Savannah, Georgia's proportion of black registered voters by 1952 lagged behind that of every Southern state except Mississippi and Alabama.

The Albany Movement[11]

Clayborne Carson

Albany experienced little protest activity before October 1961, when SNCC field secretaries Charles Sherrod and Cordell Reagon arrived there to open a SNCC office. Students at Albany State College, a restrictive, paternalistic institution that was typical of most black schools in the Deep South, had not taken part in the sit-ins of the spring....

Sherrod and Reagon were experienced activists who had already formulated a strategy for their work in Albany. Both had been freedom riders and were influenced by the religious ideas that pervaded the early student protest movement. Reagon, who was eighteen when he began work in Albany, had been active in the Nashville student movement; Sherrod, who was twenty-two, had led sit-in protests in Richmond, Virginia. Sherrod, the more articulate of the two, was also director of SNCC's Southwest Georgia voter registration project, in which capacity he was able to imprint his own personality and attitudes on the activists in Albany....

Sherrod's experience in the sit-ins and freedom rides led to his decision to use nonviolent protest as a means of prompting Albany blacks to break with previous traditions of accommodation. Initially, however, he found that "the people were afraid, really afraid. Sometimes we'd walk down the street and the little kids would call us freedom riders and the people walking in the same direction would go across the street from us." Sherrod's first objective was to remove "the mental block in the minds of those who wanted to move but were unable for fear that we were not who we said we were."

Sherrod and Reagon sought the support of all segments of the black populace. As Reagon explained, they acted "like neighborhood boys," because

---

[11] From Clayborne Carson, *In Struggle: SNCC and the Black Awakening of the 1960s* (Cambridge: Harvard University Press, 1981). Used with permission of Harvard University Press.

"you don't achieve anything with the preachers, teachers and businessmen until you work with the common people first." Sherrod recalled that they talked to the people "in churches, social meetings, on the streets, in the pool halls, lunch rooms and night clubs," telling them "how it feels to be...in jail for the cause...that there were worse chains than jail and prison. We referred to the system that imprisons men's minds and robs them of creativity. We mocked the system that teaches men to be good Negroes instead of good men. We gave an account of many resistances, of injustice in the courts, in employment, registration and voting...we started to illustrate what had happened to...other cities where people came together and protested against an evil system."

Although Sherrod and Reagon initially focused on "the common people," they later received crucial support from the black middle class, particularly from ministers who allowed their churches to be used for meetings. According to Sherrod, "even the hypocrisy" of the black church bore the "seeds of the ultimate victory of Truth." Rather than attempting to "beat the box," Sherrod advised, one must accept the people "where they are." Sherrod's own religious training helped him to gain the support of the Baptist Ministerial Alliance and the Interdenominational Alliance.

Sherrod and Reagon led nightly workshops in churches in nonviolent tactics. The drew growing numbers of young people from colleges, trade schools, high schools, and the street, who, Sherrod recounted, were "searching for a meaning in life."

On November 1, 1961, their efforts led to a sit-in at a bus station by nine students to test compliance with the Interstate Commerce Commission ruling, which became effective that day, barring segregation in transportation terminals. As Sherrod recalled, many blacks gathered at the bus station, which was located in a prominently black neighborhood, to watch the protesters, who symbolized in their eyes "the expression of years of resentment—for police brutality, for poor housing, for disenfranchisement, for inferior education, for the whole damnable system." Even though the students left as planned when threatened with arrest, in the hearts of black residents "from that moment on, segregation was dead." Later the students filed affidavits with the commission charging that Albany whites were ignoring its ruling.

After the protest at the bus terminal, representatives of civil rights organizations and other black community groups met to discuss their grievances, and they formed the Albany Movement, a coalition of SNCC, NAACP, the ministerial alliances, the Federation of Women's Clubs, the Negro Voters League, and many other groups interested in racial reform. William G. Anderson, a black osteopath, was elected president, and Slater King, a black realtor, became vice president. One of the black leaders of the Albany

Movement commented: "The kids were going to do it anyway…they were holding their own mass meetings and making plans…we didn't want them to have to do it alone."

A few days after the formation of the Albany Movement, three members of the NAACP Youth Council were arrested by Albany police chief Laurie Pritchett as they attempted to use the dining room at the Trailways bus station. Later the same day, Bertha Gober and Blanton Hall, two Albany State students who had been working with SNCC, were arrested after entering the white waiting room at the bus station. These arrests further aroused the black community and set the stage for the first mass meeting of the Albany Movement.

Held on November 25 in Mount Zion Baptist Church, the meeting revealed the depth of pent-up emotions that had been released by the student protest. "The church was packed," Sherrod reported. The students who had been arrested described their experiences in jail, and after the last speaker had finished, "there was nothing left to say. Tears filled the eyes of hard, grown men who had known personally and had seen with their own eyes merciless atrocities committed by small men without conscience."

Then everyone rose to sing "We Shall Overcome," which had recently been adopted as a "freedom song." As Bernice Reagon, one of the Albany student activists, recalled: "When I opened my mouth and began to sing, there was a force and power within myself I had never heard before. Somehow the music…released a kind of power and required a level of concentrated energy I did not know I had." Goldie Jackson, a black woman who had lost her job after allowing SNCC workers to stay in her house, remembered praying and singing in the church for the rest of the night: "Two things we knew held us together: prayer of something good to come and song that tells from the depth of the heart how we feel about our fellow man."

The trial of the five students on November 27 was the scene of a mass rally to protest both their arrests and the expulsion of Gober and Hall from Albany State College. SNCC worker Charles Jones led the demonstrators on a march to a church where 400 people signed a petition demanding the reinstatement of the students. When the *Albany Herald* condemned the march, black residents began a boycott against advertisers in the paper.

On Sunday, December 10, ten activists, including James Forman, Bob Zellner, and Norma Collins of SNCC, arrived from Atlanta to fan the flames of militancy. While several hundred Albany blacks looked on, the integrated group of protesters sat in the waiting room at the Albany train station and were quickly arrested on trespassing charges. Their arrests, which Albany mayor Asa

Kelley later conceded was "our first mistake," ignited a week of mass rallies and demonstrations."

On Monday, Forman addressed a mass meeting where residents planned further protests. On Tuesday, 267 black high school and college students were arrested when they refused to disperse from a protest at the trial of the train station protesters. Most of the students chose to stay in jail rather than paying bail. On Wednesday Slater King, after leading a prayer vigil at the courthouse, was arrested, and later in the day more than 200 demonstrators who had marched to City Hall were jailed for parading without a permit. As Chief Pritchett told newsmen, "We can't tolerate the NAACP or the SNCC or any other nigger organization to take over this town with mass demonstrations." On Thursday, when the number of arrests had exceeded 500, the governor of Georgia sent 150 national guardsmen to Albany.

Local city officials agreed to establish a biracial committee to discuss black demands for the integration of transportation facilities and the release of demonstrators. Anderson invited Martin Luther King to address a rally on Friday, December 15, where King told the largest gathering yet assembled at Shiloh Baptist Church: "Don't stop now. Keep moving. Don't get weary. We will wear them down with our capacity to suffer." The next day after negotiations had broken down, King led a prayer march to City Hall and was arrested along with more than 250 demonstrators. When King announced that he would remain in jail and spend Christmas there, city officials again resumed negotiations in order to resolve the crisis. Two days later, King suddenly announced that he was allowing himself to be released on bail as part of a settlement that included city compliance with the Interstate Commerce Commission ruling and release of the other demonstrators.

The truce marked the end of the first stage of the Albany protests. To the dismay of SNCC workers, the momentum that had developed during December dissipated rapidly. City officials stalled on implementing the concessions they had granted and refused to seek desegregation of the city bus service, which became the target of a black boycott early in 1962. SNCC workers continued to use direct action tactics in attempts to revive the movement, but these protests received little attention. In April 1962, Jones, Reagon, and two others sat in at a lunch counter and were arrested; subsequently they were sentenced to sixty-day jail terms. And in a SNCC-led demonstration at City Hall, twenty-nine persons were arrested while protesting the April shooting by an Albany policeman of a black man for allegedly resisting arrest.

Then on July 10, 1962, the Albany Movement came alive once again when Martin Luther King and his associate, Ralph Abernathy, returned to Albany for sentencing in connection with the December protests. King and Abernathy were given jail terms of forty-five days or a fine of $178. When both announced that they would serve their sentences, Albany Movement leaders announced a mass rally for the following night. The rally was preceded by a march to City Hall, which resulted in the arrest of thirty-two persons, and that evening violent clashes took place between brick-throwing black youngsters and police outside the church where the rally was held. On July 13, the crisis atmosphere eased when King and Abernathy were released from jail after an unidentified black man paid their fines. "I've been thrown out of lots of places in my day," Abernathy later remarked, "but never before have I been thrown out of jail."

Demonstrations, however, continued. Small groups of blacks led by Jones of SNCC and Wyatt T. Walker of SCLC attempted to gain admission to segregated facilities in Albany, and there were mass marches to City Hall demanding civil rights. One of these, on July 24, ended in more rock and brick throwing.

This outbreak of violence brought back national guardsmen to Albany. King responded by calling a "day of penance" while he, Abernathy, and Jones attempted to convince local black residents to remain nonviolent. A few days later King, Abernathy, and Anderson were arrested while leading a prayer pilgrimage to City Hall, and they joined hundreds of protesters already in jail. By this time, the Albany jails had been filled, and prisoners had to be moved to nearby jails....

After repeated requests by Albany black leaders for a statement of support, President Kennedy finally responded by urging Albany officials to negotiate a settlement. At a news conference on August 1 Kennedy noted that the United States government was "involved in sitting down at Geneva with the Soviet Union. I can't understand why the government of Albany, City Council of Albany, cannot do the same for American citizens."

King, Abernathy, and Anderson were convicted on August 10 of disturbing the peace and parading without a permit, but their sentences were suspended. By this time the enthusiasm of Albany blacks had been weakened by the months of fruitless appeals to the conscience of Albany's white residents. According to journalist Pat Watters, "that final despair in Albany—the losing of steam," was perhaps a profound expression "of disappointment at having found and offered so much—and being understood so little." The Albany protests were a turning point for the civil rights movement, after which "activists in the movement to whom, from the beginning, non-violence was merely a sophisticated weapon were to gain in influence over those who were imbued in their personal lives with it as a spiritual quality." Or as SNCC worker Bill Hansen analyzed the situation: "We were naïve enough to think we could fill up the jails...We ran out of people before [Chief Pritchett] ran out of jails." Although the Albany Movement remained in existence through the late 1960s and SNCC continued its activities in Albany for several years, the emotion and sense of hope were never recaptured.

Additional Sources

Bayor, Ronald H. *Race and the Shaping of Twentieth-Century Atlanta.* Chapel Hill: University of North Carolina Press, 2000.

Carson, Clayborne. *In Struggle: SNCC and the Black Awakening of the 1960s.* Cambridge: Harvard University Press, 1981.

Henderson, Harold P. *Ernest Vandiver, Governor of Georgia.* Athens: University of Georgia Press, 2000.

McDonald, Laughlin. *A Voting Rights Odyssey: Black Enfranchisement in Georgia.* New York: Cambridge University Press, 2003.

Roche, Jeff. *Restructured Resistance: The Sibley Commission and the Politics of Desegregation in Georgia.* Athens: University of Georgia Press, 1998.

Short, Bob. *Everything Is Pickrick: The Life of Lester Maddox.* Macon GA: Mercer University Press, 1999.

Tuck, Stephen. *Beyond Atlanta: The Struggle for Racial Equality in Georgia, 1940–1980.* Athens: University of Georgia Press, 2001.

Zinn, Howard. *Albany: A Study in National Responsibility.* Atlanta: Southern Regional Council, 1962.

Chapter 16

MODERN GEORGIA

Modern Georgia can be said to have begun when Carl E. Sanders ran for governor in 1962 on a platform that called for economic growth and progress. Sanders made this call for a "new Georgia" and following his inauguration in 1963 could lay claim to being the state's first true New South governor. Although problems continued in Georgia after Sanders took office, particularly in the area of civil rights, the state seemed to be looking more forward than backward. Governor Sanders emphasized this point in his inaugural address when he said, "This is a new Georgia. This is a new day. This is a new era. A Georgia on the threshold of greatness." Governor Jimmy Carter continued the theme of progress in his 1971 inaugural when he stated, "I say to you quite frankly that the time for racial discrimination is over." Beginning with Governors Sanders and Carter, the state of Georgia was looking ahead and beginning to make progress in all areas of society.

In 1963 the US Supreme Court ended Georgia's antiquated county unit system of electing state officials with the *Gray v. Sanders* case. Following that decision Georgia would elect its state officials based on the popular vote. Another development that could be considered political progress was the formation in the 1960s of a true two-party system in Georgia. Since Reconstruction the state's government had been dominated by the Democratic party, and in many statewide elections there was no Republican opposition. A turning point came in the 1964 presidential election when for the first time in the state's history Georgia's electoral votes went to the Republican candidate, Barry Goldwater. Perhaps building on that momentum, Republican Howard Callaway made a strong run for the governorship in 1966. Although Callaway lost the election, Georgia Democrats were on notice that the Republican party did exist and would contest every election. Republicans in Georgia finally elected a governor in 2002 when voters chose Sonny Perdue; Perdue became the first Republican governor of Georgia since Reconstruction.

Long an agricultural state, economic and industrial development was an important element in modern Georgia. Through the late 1970s and early 1980s Governor George Busbee made economic development a hallmark of his administration. In order to make the state more attractive to industry, Georgia spent tens of millions of dollars to improve its highway system and modernize the ports of Savannah and Brunswick. The city of Atlanta became an important location for industries interested in settling in Georgia. Atlanta became the home for the World Congress Center, which hosted conventions and international trade shows. Coca-Cola, long identified with Georgia and Atlanta, became an international product, probably the most recognized soft drink in the world. With much of the state's industrial growth in Atlanta, the city became the economic center of the state and one of the most spectacular cities in the country. Such was the prestige of Atlanta that the International Olympic Committee awarded the 1996 Olympic Games to the city. For a couple of weeks in July 1996, Atlanta gained the attention of the world.

Since World War II the presence of numerous military installations in Georgia has made them an integral part of the state's culture. Some of the larger installations include Fort Benning in Columbus (Army), Fort Gordon in Augusta (Army), Fort Stewart in Hinesville (Army), Robins Air Force Base in Warner Robins, Moody Air Force Base in Valdosta, and King's Bay Naval Submarine Base north of St. Mary's. Many of these bases make significant contributions to the local economies. With this many military installations in the state, the periodic Base Realignment and Closure (BRAC) reviews conducted by the Department of Defense make for tense times in Georgia. For a variety of reasons Georgia has fared well in the recent BRAC reviews, but in 2005 several bases were closed, including Naval Air Station Atlanta and Fort McPherson. Despite the closures military bases continue to have a significant impact on Georgia communities.

DOCUMENTS

The first document below is the 1963 US Supreme Court decision that invalidated Georgia's county unit system. Document 2 is Governor Jimmy Carter's 1971 inaugural address, in which he called for an end to racial discrimination. The third document is the Constitution of 1983. Document 4 contains two 1990 newspaper articles announcing that Atlanta would host the 1996 Olympic Games. The fifth document is Governor Zell Miller's 1993 comments on changing the state flag. Document 6 is the report that Georgia elected a Republican Governor in 2002, the first Republican governor since Reconstruction. The seventh and eighth documents are charts on agricultural and manufacturing statistics in 2002. Document 9 relates the 2005 BRAC report and how it affected Georgia's military installations.

1. *Gray v. Sanders*[1]

Argued January 17, 1963

Decided March 18, 1963

Appellee, a qualified voter in primary and general elections in Fulton County, Georgia sued in a Federal District Court to restrain appellants, the Secretary of State and officials of the State Democratic Executive Committee, from using Georgia's county-unit system as a basis for counting votes in a Democratic primary election for the nomination of a United States Senator and statewide officers-which was practically equivalent to election. Such primary elections are governed by a Georgia statute, which was amended in 1962 so as to allocate unit votes to counties as follows: Counties with populations not exceeding 15,000, two units; an additional unit for the next 5,000 persons; an additional unit for the next 10,000; an additional unit for each of the next two brackets of 15,000; and, thereafter, two more units for each increase of 30,000. All candidates for statewide office were required to receive a majority of the county-unit votes to be entitled to nomination in the first primary. The practical effect of this system is that the vote of each citizen counts for less and less as the population of his county increases, and a combination of the units from the counties having the smallest population gives counties having one-third of the total population of the State a clear majority of county votes. Held:

1. Since the constitutionality of a state statute was involved and the question was a substantial one, a three-judge court was properly convened to hear this case, as required under 28 U.S.C. 2281.

2. State regulation of these primary elections makes the election process state action within the meaning of the Fourteenth Amendment.

3. Appellee, like any person whose right to vote is impaired, has standing to sue.

4. The case is not moot by reason of the fact that the Democratic Committee voted to hold the 1962 primary election on a popular-vote basis, since the 1962 Act remains in force and it would govern future elections if the complaint were dismissed.

5. The use of this election system in a statewide election violates the Equal Protection Clause of the Fourteenth Amendment....

Mr. Justice Douglas delivered the opinion of the Court.

This suit was instituted by appellee, who is qualified to vote in primary and general elections in Fulton County, Georgia, to restrain appellants from using Georgia's county unit system as a basis for counting votes in a Democratic

---

[1] From *Gray v. Sanders*, 372 US 368.

primary for the nomination of a United States Senator and statewide officers, and for declaratory relief. Appellants are the Chairman and Secretary of the Georgia State Democratic Executive Committee, and the Secretary of State of Georgia. Appellee alleges that the use of the county unit system in counting, tabulating, consolidating, and certifying votes cast in primary elections for statewide offices violates the Equal Protection Clause and the Due Process Clause of the Fourteenth Amendment and the Seventeenth Amendment.

Appellants move to dismiss; and they also file an answer denying that the county unit system was unconstitutional and alleging that it was designed "to achieve a reasonable balance as between urban and rural electoral power."

Appellee asserted that the total population of Georgia in 1960 was 3,943,116; that the population of Fulton County, where he resides, was 556,326; that the residents of Fulton County comprised 14.11% of Georgia's total population; but that, under the county unit system, the six unit votes of Fulton County constituted 1.46% of the total of 410 unit votes, or one-tenth of Fulton County's percentage of statewide population. The complaint further alleges that Echols County, the least populous county in Georgia, had a population in 1960 of 1,876, or .05% of the State's population, but the unit vote of Echols County was .48% of the total unit vote of all counties in Georgia, or 10 times Echols County's statewide percentage of population. One unit vote in Echols represented 938 residents, whereas one unit vote in Fulton County represented 92,721 residents. Thus, one resident in Echols County had an influence in the nomination of candidates equivalent to 99 residents of Fulton County....

The conception of political equality from the Declaration of Independence, to Lincoln's Gettysburg Address, to the Fifteenth, Seventeenth, and Nineteenth Amendments can mean only one thing—one person, one vote.

We agree with the District Court on most phases of the case and think it was right in enjoining the use of the county unit system in tabulating the votes....

It is so ordered.

2. Governor Jimmy Carter's Inaugural Address[2]

January 12, 1971

Governor Maddox and other fellow Georgians:

It is a long way from Plains to Atlanta. I started the trip four and a half years ago and, with a four year detour, I finally made it. I thank you all for making it possible for me to be here on what is certainly the greatest day of my life. But now the election is over, and I realize that the test of a man is not how well he campaigned, but how effectively he meets the challenges and responsibilities of the office.

I shall only take a few minutes today to summarize my feelings about Georgia. Later this week my program will be described in some detail in my State of the State and Budget messages to the House and Senate....

At the end of a long campaign, I believe I know our people as well as anyone. Based on this knowledge of Georgians North and South, Rural and Urban, liberal and conservative, I say to you quite frankly that the time for racial discrimination is over. Our people have already made this major and difficult decision, but we cannot underestimate the challenge of hundreds of minor decisions yet to be made. Our inherent human charity and our religious beliefs will be taxed to the limit. No poor, rural, weak, or black person should ever have to bear the additional burden of being deprived of the opportunity of an education, a job or simple justice. We Georgians are fully capable of making our judgments and managing our own affairs. We who are strong or in positions of leadership must realize that the responsibility for making correct decisions in the future is ours. As Governor, I will never shirk this responsibility....

In Georgia, we are determined that the law shall be enforced. Peace officers must have our appreciation and complete support. We cannot educate a child, build a highway, equalize tax burdens, create harmony among our people, or preserve basic human freedom unless we have an orderly society. Crime and lack of justice are especially cruel to those who are least able to protect themselves. Swift arrest and trial and fair punishment should be expected by those who would break our laws. It is equally important to us that every effort be made to rehabilitate law breakers into useful and productive members of society. We have not yet attained these goals in Georgia, but now we must. The proper function of a government is to make it easy for man to do good and difficult for him to do evil. This responsibility is our own. I will not shirk this responsibility....

---

[2] From *Addresses of Jimmy Carter* (Atlanta: Secretary of State's Office, 1975).

I welcome the challenge and the opportunity of serving as Governor of our State during the next four years. I promise you my best. I ask you for your best.

3. Constitution of 1983[3]

Preamble

To perpetuate the principles of free government, insure justice to all, preserve peace, promote the interest and happiness of the citizen and of the family, and transmit to posterity the enjoyment of liberty, we the people of Georgia, relying upon the protection and guidance of Almighty God, do ordain and establish this Constitution.

Article I

Bill of Rights

Section I

Rights of Persons

...Paragraph VII. All citizens of the United States, resident of this state, are hereby declared citizens of this state; and it shall be the duty of the General Assembly to enact such laws as will protect them in the full enjoyment of the rights, privileges, and immunities due to such citizenship.

...Paragraph IX. The people have the right to assemble peaceably for their common good and to apply by petition or remonstrance to those vested with the powers of government for redress of grievances.

...Paragraph XXVIII. The enumeration of rights herein contained as a part of this Constitution shall not be construed to deny to the people any inherent rights which they may have hitherto enjoyed.

Section II

Origin and Structure of Government

...Paragraph II. The people of this state have the inherent right of regulating their internal government. Government is instituted for the protection, security, and benefit of the people; and at all times they have the right to alter or reform the same whenever the public good may require it.

...Paragraph V. Legislative acts in violation of this Constitution or the Constitution of the United States are void, and the judiciary shall so declare them.

Paragraph VI. The civil authority shall be superior to the military.

---

[3] From *Acts and Resolutions of the General Assembly of the State of Georgia*, 1983.

Paragraph VII. No money shall ever be taken from the public treasury, directly or indirectly, in aid of any church, sect, cult, or religious denomination or of any sectarian institution.

Section III

General Provisions

Paragraph I. (a) Except as otherwise provided in this Paragraph, private property shall not be taken or damaged for public purposes without just and adequate compensation being first paid....

Article II

Voting and Elections

Section I

Paragraph I. Elections by the people shall be by secret ballot and shall be conducted in accordance with procedures provided by law.

Paragraph II. Every person who is a citizen of the United States and a resident of Georgia as defined by law, who is at least 18 years of age and not disfranchised by this article, and who meets minimum residency requirements as provided by law shall be entitled to vote at any election by the people. The General Assembly shall provide by law for the registration of electors.

Section II

General Provisions

...Paragraph IV. The general Assembly is hereby authorized to provide by general law for the recall of public officials who hold elective office. The procedures, grounds, and all other matters relative to such recall shall be provided for in such law.

Article III

Legislative Branch

Section I

Legislative Power

Paragraph I. The legislative power of the state shall be vested in a General Assembly which shall consist of a Senate and a House of Representatives.

Section II

Composition of General Assembly

Paragraph I. (a) The Senate shall consist of not more that 56 Senators, each of whom shall be elected from single-member districts.

(b) The House of Representatives shall consist of not fewer than 180 Representatives apportioned among representative districts of the state.

Paragraph II. The General Assembly shall apportion the Senate and House districts. Such districts shall be composed of contiguous territory. The apportionment of the Senate and of the House of Representatives shall be changed by the General Assembly as necessary after each United States decennial census.

...Paragraph V. The members of the General Assembly shall be elected by the qualified electors of their respective districts for a term of two years and shall serve until the time fixed for the convening of the next General Assembly.

Section IV

Organization and Procedure of the General Assembly

Paragraph I. The Senate and House of Representatives shall organize each odd-numbered year and shall be a different General Assembly for each two-year period. The General Assembly shall meet in regular session on the second Monday in January of each year, or otherwise as provided by law, and may continue in session for a period of no longer than 40 days in the aggregate each year....

...Paragraph XI. The sessions of the General Assembly and all standing committee meetings thereof shall be open to the public. Either house may by rule provide for exceptions to this requirement....

Section VI

Exercise of Powers

Paragraph I. The General Assembly shall have the power to make all laws not inconsistent with this Constitution, and not repugnant to the Constitution of the United States, which it shall deem necessary and proper for the welfare of the state....

Article V

Executive Branch

Section I

Election of Governor and Lieutenant Governor

Paragraph I. There shall be a Governor who shall hold office for a term of four years and until a successor shall be chosen and qualified. Persons holding the office of Governor may succeed themselves for one four-year term of office. Persons who have held the office of Governor and have succeeded themselves as hereinbefore provided shall not again be eligible to be elected to that office until after the expiration of four years from the conclusion of their term as Governor....

...Paragraph III. There shall be a Lieutenant Governor, who shall be elected at the same time, for the same term, and in the same manner as the Governor. The Lieutenant Governor shall be the President of the Senate and shall have such executive duties as prescribed by the Governor and as may be prescribed by law not inconsistent with the powers of the Governor or other provisions of this Constitution....

Section III

Other Elected Executive Officers

Paragraph I. The Secretary of State, Attorney general, State School Superintendent, Commissioner of Insurance, Commissioner of Agriculture, and Commissioner of Labor shall be elected in the manner prescribed for the election of members of the General Assembly and the electors shall be the same. Such executive officers shall be elected at the same time and hold their offices for the same term as the Governor....

Article VI

Judicial Branch

Section VI

Supreme Court

Paragraph I. The Supreme Court shall consist of not more than nine Justices who shall elect from amongst themselves a Chief Justice as the chief presiding and administrative officer of the court and a Presiding Justice to serve if the Chief Justice is absent or is disqualified. A majority shall be necessary to hear and determine cases. If a Justice is disqualified in any case, a substitute judge may be designated by the remaining Justices to serve....

Article VIII

Education

Section I

Public Education

Paragraph I. The provision of an adequate public education for the citizens shall be a primary obligation of the State of Georgia. Public education for the citizens prior to the college or postsecondary level shall be free and shall be provided for by taxation. The expense of other public education shall be provided for in such manner and in such amount as may be provided by law.

Section II

State Board of Education

Paragraph I. (a) There shall be a State Board of Education which shall consist of one member from each congressional district in the state appointed by the Governor and confirmed by the Senate. The Governor shall not be a member of said board....

Section IV

Board of Regents

Paragraph I. (a) There shall be a Board of Regents of the University System of Georgia which shall consist of one member from each congressional district in the state and five additional members from the state at large, appointed by the Governor and confirmed by the Senate. The Governor shall not be a member of said board....

Article IX
Counties and Municipal Corporations
Section I
Counties
Paragraph I. Each county shall be a body corporate and politic with such governing authority and with such powers and limitations as are provided in this Constitution and as provided by law....
Paragraph II. (a) There shall not be more than 159 counties in this state....
Section II
Home Rule for Counties and Municipalities
...Paragraph V. The governing authority of each county and of each municipality may exercise the power of eminent domain for any public purpose.
Article X
Amendments to the Constitution
Section I
Constitution, How Amended
Paragraph I. Amendments to this Constitution or a new Constitution may be proposed by the General Assembly or by a constitutional convention, as provided in this article. Only amendments which are of a general and uniform applicability throughout the state shall be proposed, passed, or submitted to the people....

4. Atlanta to Host 1996 Olympic Games[4]

Atlanta Selected Over Athens for 1996 Olympics
With a powerful display of personal lobbying and financial clout, Atlanta today won the right to hold the 1996 Summer Olympic Games, turning back a strong sentimental appeal by Athens to become the site for the 100th anniversary of the modern Olympic Games.

The dramatic decision by the International Olympic Committee, announced tonight after five rounds of secret balloting, brings the summer Olympics back to the United States only 12 years after the Games were held in Los Angeles.

Atlanta had fashioned a proposal to spend about $1.2 billion in private funds to hold the Games, with the expectation of generating about $1.4 billion in

---

[4] From *New York Times*, September 19, 1990; and *Atlanta Constitution*, September 19, 1990.

revenues from television broadcast rights ($549 million), commercial sponsorships ($331 million), tickets ($337 million) and other promotions.

But to the 300 delirious Georgians in the official delegation here, the Olympics' appeal was less in the profits, which officials said would be used exclusively to fund sports programs, than in the opportunity to display Atlanta as a symbol of racial tolerance and economic progress in the new South....

How the Vote Went

The city with the lowest vote total was eliminated after each round of balloting by members of the International Olympic Committee until the winner was chosen.

First Round: Athens 23, Atlanta 19, Toronto 14, Melbourne 12, Manchester 11 and Belgrade 7.

Second Round: Athens 23, Melbourne 21, Atlanta 20, Toronto 17, Manchester 5.

Third Round: Athens 26, Atlanta 26, Toronto 18, Melbourne 16.

Fourth Round: Atlanta 34, Athens 30, Toronto 22.

Fifth Round: Atlanta 51, Athens 35.

Huge Boost for City's Economy

Atlanta's successful quest for the Olympics could help booster the city's economy, facing its first major downturn in 15 years.

The Games will bring an estimated $3.48 billion into the local economy by 1997, according to an economic impact study prepared for the Atlanta Organizing Committee (AOC). They could mean the difference between Atlanta's economy merely limping along or receiving an unprecedented boost in money and prestige....

While economic impact numbers are preliminary, it is estimated the Olympics will bring nearly 84,000 full-time and part-time jobs into the economy....

The 1996 Games are expected to bring to Georgia a total of $1.16 billion in revenues, including $549 million in television rights and $324 million in corporate sponsorships.

The AOC estimates that it will cost the community $1.01 billion to host the Olympics, including $587 million in organizing and operating costs and $418.4 million to build facilities such as the $145.2 million Olympic Stadium.

Under current estimates, the Games would net a surplus of $157.1 million.

5. Governor Zell Miller on the State Flag[5]

State of the State Address

January 12, 1993

Lieutenant Governor Howard, Speaker Murphy, members of the General Assembly, members of the Consular Corps, members of the Judiciary, ladies and gentlemen.

I thank you for this opportunity to once again come before you and report on the state of this great State of Georgia....

The South is the fastest growing area of the country. And our growing dominance in national leadership reflects our growing prominence in the world economy. Yet at the very time when all southerners may rightly take pride in the region's current success, some Georgians persist in believing that the pride of the South is better defined by a symbol of defiance and intolerance—the Confederate Battle Flag, which was imposed on our state flag in 1956.

Of all the arguments that have been made for keeping this flag, the most infuriating to me is the contention that if we don't, we will somehow forget the sacrifices made by those who fought for the Confederacy. We will not forget. We cannot forget....

But I also cannot forget the many millions of Georgians, my ancestors and yours, who also made sacrifices in other wars both before and after the War Between the States. And in reverence to their memory, I cannot accept the idea that the brief, violent, and tragic period of the Confederacy is the only part—the only part—of our long history that defines our identity and our traditions....

For four brief years—that's 1.5 percent of our state's entire history—Georgia was a member of the Confederate States of America. Yet it is the Confederacy's most inflammatory symbol that dominates our flag today. We all know why. And it has nothing to do with the bravery of the Confederate troops.

You may quibble all you want about who said what in 1956. It is clear the flag was changed in 1956 to identify Georgia with the dark side of the Confederacy—that desire to deprive some Americans of the equal rights that are the birthright of all Americans, and yes, the determination to destroy the United States if necessary to achieve that goal....

Since 1789, Georgia's motto has been: "Wisdom, Justice, Moderation." There is nothing wise, just or moderate in a flag that reopens old wounds and perpetuates old hatreds. Our battlefields, our graveyards, our monuments are

---

[5] From Zell Miller, *"Listen to this Voice": Selected Speeches of Governor Zell Miller* (Macon GA: Mercer University Press, 1998).

important reminders of our history, both the proud and the painful. They will and always should be there. That's history. But our flag is a symbol—a symbol of what we stand for as a state.

I want to see this state live by the words of George Washington to the sexton of the Rhode Island synagogue: "Ours is a government which gives to bigotry no sanction, to persecution no assistance."

If you're truly proud of the South, if you're truly proud of this state, of *all* its 260 years. If you look forward and want to play a significant part in what Georgia can become, then help me now to give bigotry no sanction, and persecution no assistance.

6. Georgia Elects Republican Governor in 2002[6]

Perdue Elected Georgia's First GOP Governor in 130 Years

Gov. Roy Barnes and House Speaker Tom Murphy were swept from office Tuesday, as voters ended 130 years of Democratic domination and created a divided state government that leads Georgia into uncharted territory.

Sonny Perdue, a former state senator from Middle Georgia who was outspent 6-to-1, became the state's first Republican governor since 1872. Georgia was the only state in the nation that didn't elect a Republican governor sometime in the 20th century.

Perdue declared victory at 12:05 a.m. today. He said Barnes had called and "graciously recognized that the people of Georgia had spoken. And you'll have a new governor next January," Perdue told cheering supporters.

"You've stunned Georgia, you've stunned the nation tonight!" Perdue cried....

"We've never seen anything like this in out lifetime," said Charles Bullock, a University of Georgia political scientist. "We really don't have anything to compare this to."

Tuesday's vote sets up an immediate confrontation between the Legislature and Perdue, a former Democratic leader who switched parties in 1998.

---

[6] From *Atlanta Journal Constitution*, November 6, 2002.

7. Agricultural Statistics, 2002[7]

PRODUCT	AMOUNT PRODUCED	NATIONAL RANK
Broilers	1.29 billion head	1
Chicken Eggs	4.96 billion eggs	1
Cucumbers	2.92 million cwt (hundredweight)	1
Peanuts	1.31 billion pounds	1
Pecans	45 million pounds	1
Carrots	1.41 million cwt (hundredweight)	2
Rye	720,000 bushels	2
Snap Beans	753,000 cwt (hundredweight)	2
Cotton	1.578 million bales	3
Peaches	92 million pounds	3
Sorghum Silage	260,000 tons	3
Onions, Spring	1.438 million cwt (hundredweight)	3
Blueberries	17 million pounds	4
Cantaloupe	1.254 million cwt (hundredweight)	4
Squash	1.428 million cwt (hundredweight)	4
Sweet Corn	3.125 million cwt (hundredweight)	4
Watermelons	5.1 million cwt (hundredweight)	4
Bell Peppers	520,000 cwt (hundredweight)	5
Cabbage	2.36 million cwt (hundredweight)	5
Tobacco	55.7 million pounds	6
Tomatoes	750,000 cwt (hundredweight)	9

8. Manufacturing Statistics, 2002[8]

Number of Establishments	8,805
Number of Employees	452,834
Value of Industrial Shipments	$126.16 million
Value Added by Manufacture	$59.66 million

---

[7] From Georgia Agricultural Statistics Service.

[8] Adapted and modified from Selig Center for Economic Growth, *Georgia Statistical Abstract, 2006–2007* (Athens: University of Georgia Press, 2007).

9. Georgia and BRAC 2005[9]

Recommendation: Close Fort Gillem, GA.

Justification: This recommendation closes Fort Gillem, an Army administrative installation and an AAFES distribution center. The recommendation moves the major tenant organizations to Rock Island Arsenal, Redstone Arsenal, Fort Benning, and Fort Campbell. It also moves small components of the Headquarters 3rd US Army and US Army Forces Command to Pope AFB and Shaw AFB. It enhances the Army's military value, is consistent with the Army's Force Structure Plan, and maintains adequate surge capabilities to address future unforeseen requirements. This closure allows the Army to employ excess capacities at installations that can accomplish more than administrative missions.

Economic Impact on Communities: Assuming no economic recovery, this recommendation could result in a maximum potential reduction of 1,824 jobs (1,067 direct and 737 indirect jobs) over the 2006–2011 period in the Atlanta-Sandy Springs-Marietta, GA metropolitan statistical area, which is less than 0.1 percent of the economic area employment.

Recommendation: Close Fort McPherson, GA.

Justification: This recommendation closes Fort McPherson, an administrative installation, and moves the tenant headquarters organizations to Fort Sam Houston, Fort Eustis, Pope AFB and Shaw AFB. It enhances the Army's military value, is consistent with the Army's Force Structure Plan, and maintains adequate surge capabilities to address future unforeseen requirements. This closure allows the Army to employ excess capacities at installations that can accomplish more than administrative missions. The organization relocations in this recommendation also create multifunctional, multi-component and multi-Service installations that provide a better level of service at a reduced cost.

Economic Impact on Communities: Assuming no economic recovery, this recommendation could result in a maximum potential reduction of 7,123 jobs (4,303 direct and 2,820 indirect jobs) over the 2006–2011 period in the Atlanta-Sandy Springs-Marietta, GA metropolitan statistical area, which is 0.3 percent of economic area employment.

Recommendation: Realign Robins Air Force Base, GA. The 19th Air Refueling Group's KC-135R aircraft will be distributed to the 22nd Air Refueling Wing, McConnell Air Force Base, KS (nine aircraft), and to backup aircraft inventory (three aircraft). The 202d Engineering Installation Squadron

---

[9] *Department of Defense Base Closure and Realignment Report*, vol. 1, May 2005.

(ANG), a geographically separated unit at Middle Georgia Regional Airport, will be relocated into available space at Robins Air Force Base.

Justification: This recommendation realigns active duty KC-135R aircraft from Robins (18) to McConnell (15), a base higher in military value for the tanker mission and with available capacity to receive the additional aircraft at no cost.... The vacated infrastructure and capacity resulting from the realignment of the tenant 19th Air Refueling Group will accommodate U.S. Navy aircraft realigning to Robins from Naval Air Station Atlanta. The Navy will pay any costs to reconfigure the AF facility for their use. By realigning geographically separated units onto Robins, the Air Force can use excess capacity and reduce leased facilities in the community. This recommendation does not affect the blended active duty/Air National Guard Air Control Wing at Robins, which remains the major operational flying mission at Robins.

Economic Impact on Communities: Assuming no economic recovery, this recommendation could result in a maximum potential reduction of 795 jobs (471 direct jobs and 324 indirect jobs) over 2006–2011 period in the Warner Robins, GA Metropolitan Statistical economic area, which is 1.2 percent of economic area employment.

ESSAYS

Georgia Republicans and the Election of 1966[10]

Billy B. Hathorn

Since the days of Reconstruction after the Civil War, the Democratic Party nomination for governor of Georgia has been tantamount to election. Only in the colorful and complicated election of 1966 was this Democratic presumption seriously challenged.

Democratic solidarity fragmented in 1966 when health problems kept the frontrunner, former governor Samuel Ernest Vandiver (1959–1963), from the race. Incumbent Carl Edward Sanders (1963–1967) was forbidden by state law from seeking reelection. Serious candidates included flamboyant segregationist Lester Garfield Maddox, former governor Ellis Gibbs Arnall (1943–1947), state senator James Earl Carter, Jr., Albany publisher and former state Democratic

---

[10] Used with permission. Courtesy of the Kenan Research Center at the Atlanta History Center.

chairman James H. Gray, Sr., and former lieutenant governor Garland Turk Byrd. Perennial candidate Hoke O'Kelley was also in the race....

In 1966 the candidacy of Republican Howard H. "Bo" Callaway necessitated the first seriously contested general election in Georgia since the tenure of acting Republican governor Benjamin Conley (1871–1972). Georgians used to having a single Democratic primary produce a winner muddled through three elections in 1966 only to have the state legislature eventually choose the governor.

Because the Republicans held no primary, law required Callaway to obtain 87,000 signatures, or 5 percent of registered voters. He secured 150,765, hand-delivered in a 300-ponud coffin-like box to the secretary of state....

The press continually speculated that Callaway would wage a formidable challenge. *U.S. News and World Report* forecast a Callaway victory resulting from determined business support. Republican optimism soared as municipal elections netted surprising gains, particularly in Savannah, the state's second-largest city, where the GOP won races for mayor and all six council positions....

Georgia primary laws do not require advance registration by party, and prior to the Democratic primary, reports persisted that Callaway backers would vote for Maddox on the theory that Maddox would be more vulnerable than Arnall in the general election. Maddox, who boasted support from unidentified Republicans, joked that Callaway should withdraw. *Time* carried a report that some voters sporting Callaway stickers on their car bumpers voted in the runoff, presumably for Maddox, whom the magazine ridiculed as a "balding bigot." Maddox received 443,055 votes; Arnall, 373,004; one Arnall aide attributed the entire Maddox margin to GOP crossovers. On the other hand, the Marietta *Daily Journal* dismissed the crossovers and speculated that Carter supporters instead made the difference. Callaway denied having urged any Republican to support Maddox; the "losers always blame the other party," he quipped. Years later, Callaway declared that his managers thought that Maddox's nomination might ease fund-raising but that no "formal program" was conceived to subvert Arnall.

Maddox's nomination appalled Southern moderates and liberals. Confessing shame at his native state, King denounced "a corroding cancer in the Georgia body politic. Georgia is a sick state produced by the diseases of a sick nation. This election revealed that Georgia is desperately competing with Mississippi for the bottom." Mayor Allen blamed Arnall's loss on "combined forces of ignorance, prejudice, reactionism and the duplicity of many Republican voters"; he branded Maddox "a totally unqualified individual" who had "tarnished" the state seal....

The Macon *Telegraph* warned Callaway that he must "rise early and work late" to overcome "the little Pickrick warrior." The publication, one of many to endorse Callaway, urged the Republican to woo moderates because he could never outfox Maddox in the "seemingly popular sport of LBJ-cussin'." The Marietta *Daily Journal* depicted Callaway as a "responsible conservative whose weapons are logic and reason" in contrast to the "irresponsible racist" Maddox, whose "weapons are ax handles and intemperate epithets." The *Constitution* asked Callaway to offer specifics shared by "reasonable Georgians in good conscience." While the publication decreed Callaway "better qualified," it withheld any endorsement, a stance evoking criticism from its more conservative competitor, the *Journal*. Callaway refused to edge leftward and declined to label himself a "segregationist" or an "integrationist"; instead he stressed equal treatment, "freedom of choice" desegregation plans, and job opportunity.

Callaway formally launched his campaign on September 30 with a thirty-unit motorcade along Atlanta's Peachtree Street. Few blacks or blue-collar workers were visible in the white-collar crowd numbering 25,000. He discussed such consensus priorities as education, governmental integrity and efficiency, protection of life and property, mental health, industrial development, tourism, highways, and natural resources. Callaway promised to alleviate overcrowded classrooms, build more colleges, and augment teacher salaries by $1,200 per year, but he seemed to contradict himself after criticizing a similar Maddox plan as too costly. Both nominees opposed federal enforcement of segregation guidelines. Callaway sponsored a House amendment that would have barred the US education commissioner from equating "racial imbalance" with segregation in deciding the disposition of federal funds. Callaway emphasized that federal education aid augmented federal authority, but Maddox raised the specter of insensitivity to the needy, a canard which frequently stalked the Republicans....

Enthusiastic crowds and promising opinion polls falsely buoyed Callaway in late October. The Quayle tabulation showed him leading, 42 to 27 percent, with 22 percent undecided and 7 percent for an Arnall write-in. *Newsweek* predicted Georgia Republicans would gain three House seats. Atlanta bookies reduced odds on a Maddox victory to fifty-fifty. When about 5,000 attended his Wheeler County rally, Callaway questioned the existence of "Maddox country." Callaway, who performed well on the stump, was less effective in one-on-one exchanges because his adherence to a strict schedule exuded impatience. Democrats insisted that a Republican governor would clash with an opposition legislature, but Callaway called upon Oklahoma governor Henry Louis Bellmon to refute such claims. Callaway told students in Albany that he would promote industrial development whereas Maddox could undermine their employment possibilities.

Callaway supported higher workmen's compensation benefits but claimed increasing the minimum wage beyond $1.60 would spur inflation, deprive the unskilled of jobs, and damage industrial recruitment. The AFL-CIO remained neutral though some locals made endorsements. Atlanta University president Rufus Clements and the Negro Baptist Convention endorsed Callaway as the best chance to block Maddox. King remained neutral, but after the general election, he said one of the candidates "lives in the nineteenth century and the other...lives in the eighteenth century." He added, "Strangely enough, I think it is Mr. Callaway who lives in the eighteenth century. At least Mr. Maddox...would have sympathized with the poor." Maddox predicted that he would attract blacks "if they are given the truth." He continued to insist that he was never a racist but rather that he was just defending private property rights.

Using early rural returns, the networks forecast a Maddox victory, but the projections failed to gauge Callaway's strength in urban areas. Three days later, Callaway held a slim lead, 453,665 to 450,626. Arnall's historic 52,831 write-in ballots meant no one had a majority. Callaway carried 30 counties, compared to Maddox's 128; Arnall carried Liberty County. Overall, Callaway led by 121,000 in urban areas and trailed by 118,000 in rural precincts....

After certification of the returns, a three-judge federal panel, including Democrat Griffin B. Bell and Republican Elbert Tuttle, struck down the constitutional provision permitting legislative selection. The judges concluded that a malapportioned legislature might "dilute" the votes of the candidate with the plurality. Bell, later President Carter's attorney general, likened legislative selection to the county-unit principle. The judges granted a ten-day suspension of their ruling to permit appeal to the US Supreme Court and stipulated that the state could resolve the deadlock so long as an alternative to legislative selection was found. The American Civil Liberties Union, critical of GOP crossovers in the runoff, opposed legislative intervention or a new general election without write-ins. Instead, the ACLU sought to reopen the primary process, a proposal discarded by the courts. Other citizens' groups asked the courts to authorize a special election. Democratic chairman Gray insisted that anything other than legislative intervention would be "a sad commentary on the decline of constitutional government." The conspiracy-wary Maddox denounced a "Callaway-Tuttle-[Chief Justice Earl] Warren war being waged upon the people."

In the appeal, Georgia attorney general Arthur K. Bolton emphasized that state law permits write-ins in all elections. A general election runoff, which had no precedent, could lead to another deadlock because of write-ins, he reasoned.

Therefore, Bolton argued that the legislature should choose despite malapportionment. And a special election could not be called prior to the tabulation of returns on January 10.

In a five-to-two decision, the high court upheld Bolton's reasoning in *Fortson versus Morris*....

The assembly chose Maddox, 182 to 66, yet more than thirty Democrats defected to Callaway either because he held the statewide plurality or had carried their districts....

So, at 7:18 P.M. on January 10, 1967, Lester Maddox was elected Georgia's eightieth governor, the first Atlantan to hold the position in fifty years. Twelve minutes later he was sworn in during a private ceremony; the next day Supreme Court justice Carlton Mobley administered a public oath....

After his concession, Callaway promised the GOP faithful that they would "meet again on another day in another race," lending to speculation that he would challenge Talmadge in 1968. The *Constitution*, however, painted the departing Callaway as a "lonesome, sad figure." Callaway's "next race" came fourteen years later in Colorado, where he relocated in 1976 after acquiring Crested Butte Mountain Resort. He unsuccessfully sought the 1980 nomination to oppose Democratic senator Gary Hart; he served as Colorado GOP chairman from 1981 to 1987.

Governor Zell Miller, the Lottery, and HOPE[11]

Richard Hyatt

The lottery had helped elect Zell Miller governor. Only when he took office in 1991, his new challenge was guiding a resolution on the lottery through the General Assembly. The resolution would call for a Constitutional Amendment and if voters voiced their approval then Georgia would join thirty-three other states that had gone into the lottery business. Miller hammered on the public demand for a lottery in his State of the State Address that year. "After traveling this state from Blairsville to Brunswick, I can tell you without any doubt that the people of Georgia want a lottery, and they want their lottery to finance new education programs," Miller told the joint session of House and Senate. "I realize the lottery is an issue on which some of us disagree. I know there are strong and deeply held opinions on the subject. I want your input. But at the

---

[11] From Richard Hyatt, *Zell: The Governor Who Gave Georgia HOPE* (Macon GA: Mercer University Press, 1997). Used with permission of Mercer University Press.

same time, I want you to know that I am adamant that the new lottery funds must not supplant existing funds for education. I hope you are, too."

Enter Denmark Groover.

As the final maneuvering continued, both sides figured it was going to be close. Rep. DuBose Porter was handling the bill for Miller. Groover told Miller he would help if it was needed but nothing was decided. When the governor heard Groover was willing he was elated. He was obviously a part of the Old Guard. Having him speak for the resolution would carry a lot of symbolism. He had been a strong supporter of Bubba McDonald's campaign for governor, so it would be apparent that his words weren't partisan. Only when Groover was asked, he said he didn't want merely to speak. "I wanted to pull the last twenty minutes," Groover says. "I wasn't going to get up and talk then have the rest of the world parade up there. By then, whatever I said would be forgotten. Porter needed me, he just didn't know it. Finally he said yes."

Groover explained to his colleagues that he didn't support Miller's campaign for governor because he thought he had a better candidate. "But the Constitution of this state says that all government of right emanates from the people. And this man had the guts to propose a lottery and he was the only one that did. He ran on it and he was elected on it. The people wanted an opportunity to vote on it themselves. Are we going to give them that opportunity and give him the opportunity to sell it, or are we going to take our own personal prejudices and political fears and kill it here?" The enabling legislation was adopted by the House with 126 ayes and 51 nays, only 6 votes more than was needed. The Miller team had predicted it would pass with "about 125 to 130 votes."

On many evenings a city or an organization sponsors a dinner for the legislators. The night after the lottery vote Groover had gone to one of them. The governor was also there and came over to Groover's table and squatted down beside his chair. "I want you to know that you passed the lottery," Miller said. "While you were speaking, I had tears in my eyes." Shirley had been with him in the governor's office as they listened to it. It was one of their most unforgettable moments.

Eight days later the resolution waltzed through the Senate by a vote of 47–9. Resolutions don't require a governor's signature. Usually they go straight to the ballot. In April of that year, Miller held a ceremony, and with reporters all around him he personally signed the lottery resolution. Even the opposition was saying it would pass easily, perhaps by 70 percent. But it was a long way to 1992. Almost too long for Zell Miller.

The 1992 General Assembly created the lottery corporation. Miller's legislation spelled out that 90 percent of all lottery proceeds would be earmarked for three specific programs, college scholarships, and a voluntary Pre-Kindergarten program, tuition grants and public school_outlay. Miller integrated the latter to include technology: satellite dishes and computers. The remaining 10 percent would be set aside in a reserve fund in the event there were fluctuations in lottery ticket sales.

In May of that year, predicting the lottery would generate from $250 to $300 million a year, the governor kicked off a full-scale political campaign to be sure voters understood what was being proposed. Opposition was already marshalling, and one minister compared the dealing of crack cocaine to the promotion of lottery sales. Miller responded by saying, "What I worry about are these four-year-olds who don't even know their colors. Some don't even know the difference between an apple and an orange and they certainly don't know their letters. They are the future dropouts of this state."

Statewide lotteries were not unusual. New Hampshire had adopted the first one in 1964 and thirty-two other states had gone into the lottery business by 1992. More than anything, lotteries were the resurrection of an old idea. They were common in seventeenth-century England and were brought to this country by the early colonists. Many Georgia schools in the nineteenth century were built with lottery money, as were improvements to the state's rivers and harbors. The first hospital in Savannah and the first library at the University of Georgia were built with the game of chance. A state lottery for education was approved in 1866 as a way to provide tuition-free education for Civil War orphans. It was abolished a decade later, following widespread charges of fraud and corruption. Gambling had been illegal in the state until 1977, when Bingo was legalized.

Proponents of the 1992 amendment dwelt on the needs of education. They said passing a lottery would give needed revenue to an outdated, inadequate education system without raising taxes. They also reminded Georgia voters that people in their neighborhoods poured almost $200 million each year into the Florida lottery. "Maintaining the status quo has not worked. Bold steps must be taken if we are to enhance educational opportunities for our children. We have to invest in new ideas and new approaches to education and education funding," said David Garrett III, an Atlanta contractor and the chairman of the governor's Georgians for Better Education, a group created to advocate the passage of the amendment.

Opponents said a lottery was a sucker's game. "It's called a sucker's game for good reason. The odds of winning a typical lottery jackpot are upwards of 14 million to one," said Buddy Crowder, a Marietta advertising executive who was one of the most vocal members of the opposition. "Every legislature that has earmarked lottery money for education has within five years broken that promise...Can anything good be said of a lottery? Yes, indeed. As one California newsman had said when the state's lottery turned to brass: 'This is proof that the lottery does improve education. People get smart and stop playing the lottery.'"

Miller went on the road that year as if he were on the ballot himself, crisscrossing the state week in and week out. Many of his appearances were in schools, where he continually made the connection between the lottery, education, and Georgia's children. It was a disappointing campaign for him since he found little support for his proposal among the state's educational community. "Some education leaders have either tiptoed quietly through the tulips all around the lottery or in some cases strongly opposed it. Did I expect too much from you? Maybe I did," he told a meeting of the Georgia Superintendents Association just a week before the vote. On the other side of the issue, various religious denominations came out against the lottery, and one of the opposition ads featured former Atlanta Brave Dale Murphy. Churches all over Georgia placed anti-lottery statements on their outdoor signs. One of the strongest opponents was the United Methodist Church—and Miller was a lifelong Methodist.

Talk of a 2–1 victory for the amendment was just talk. Voters did vote yes, but it was a narrow 52–48 percent victory. The vote was split among urban and rural Georgians, with city voters being a major factor in the decision along with black voters who went 2–1 in favor of the lottery. The margin was smaller than predicted, but Miller had prevailed. By the end of the year he had a lottery commission in place and by the summer of 1993, the first lottery ticket was sold, appropriately to Zell Miller.

But more rewarding to him were the programs created with the lottery funds. During the campaign for governor, he had been general in his descriptions of what would be done with the lottery dollars. He was more specific as he advocated passage of the amendment. But it would be some time before the scholarship program he had described truly took shape.

Sarah Eby-Ebersole, his longtime speech writer, says she can trace the genesis of the program through his own words, that it was apparent HOPE was being confirmed and his plans were coming together. His chief of staff, Steve Wrigley, knows when it came. "If anybody tells you otherwise—they're wrong. I saw HOPE being born—right on that couch in the governor's office. There had been a lot of memos and papers on the table, but he sat there and described it just as it came to be."

HOPE is an anacronym for Helping Outstanding Pupils Educationally, and it belongs to Miller: "I named it and I conceived it. The paternity rights are mine." He also came up with how it would work. He wanted to keep it simple so it could be easily understood: "free tuition, books and fees—got to keep a 'B' average. I wanted it to be a scholarship program built on merit—not income level. I believe strongly that one can have anything if they are willing to work and pay the price for it. That includes a college education. I also knew what the GI Bill had meant to me. This would be Georgia's GI Bill. You give something, you get something."

In a speech to the Biennial Legislative Institute in 1992 just a month after the lottery amendment was approved at the ballot box, Miller used the name HOPE for the first time in describing the tuition grants. "Today, just seven years before the dawn of the twenty-first century, we are at a critical juncture in our state's history—truly a crossroads. It has never been more important for our student to get a college education, but at the same time, it has never been more difficult for their families to pay for it. HOPE has the potential to touch the lives of 90,000 students in Georgia beginning in the fall of 1993."

Additional Sources

Bayor, Ronald. *Race and the Shaping of Twentieth-Century Atlanta.* Chapel Hill: University of North Carolina Press, 2000.

Cook, James F. *Carl Sanders: Spokesman of the New South.* Macon GA: Mercer University Press, 1993.

Fink, Gary M. *Prelude to the Presidency: The Political Character and Legislative Leadership Style of Governor Jimmy Carter.* Westport CT: Greenwood Press, 1980.

Fleischmann, Arnold and Carol Pierannunzi. *Politics in Georgia.* Athens: University of Georgia Press, 1997.

Harris, Joe Frank. *Joe Frank Harris: Personal Reflections on a Public Life.* Macon GA: Mercer University Press, 1998.

Henderson, Harold P., and Gary L. Roberts, editors. *Georgia Governors in an Age of Change: From Ellis Arnall to George Busbee.* Athens: University of Georgia Press, 1988.

Hyatt, Richard. *Zell: The Governor Who Gave Georgia HOPE.* Macon GA: Mercer University Press, 1997.

Keating, Larry. *Atlanta: Race, Class, and Urban Expansion.* Philadelphia: Temple University Press, 2001.

Kruse, Kevin. *White Flight: Atlanta and the Making of Modern Conservatism.* Princeton: Princeton University Press, 2005.

Martin, Harold. *Atlanta and the Environs: A Chronicle of Its People and Events.* Athens: University of Georgia Press, 1987.

Short, Bob. *Everything is Pickrick: The Life of Lester Maddox.* Macon GA: Mercer University Press, 1999.

Yarbrough, C. Richard. *And They Call Them Games: An Inside View of the 1996 Olympics.* Macon GA: Mercer University Press, 2000.

APPENDIX A—POPULATION OF GEORGIA

YEAR	TOTAL POPULATION	WHITE	BLACK
1790	82,584	52,886	29,662
1800	162,686	102,261	60,425
1810	252,433	145,414	107,019
1820	340,989	189,570	151,419
1830	516,823	296,806	220,017
1840	691,392	407,695	283,697
1850	906,185	521,572	384,613
1860	1,057,286	591,550	465,698
1870	1,184,109	638,926	545,142
1880	1,542,180	816,906	725,133
1890	1,837,353	978,357	858,815
1900	2,216,331	1,181,294	1,034,813
1910	2,609,121	1,431,802	1,176,987
1920	2,895,832	1,689,114	1,206,365
1930	2,908,506	1,837,021	1,071,125
1940	3,123,723	2,038,278	1,084,927
1950	3,444,578	2,380,577	1,062,762
1960	3,943,116	2,817,223	1,122,596
1970	4,590,000	3,391,242	1,187,149
1980	5,464,265	3,948,007	1,465,457
1990	6,478,216	4,600,148	1,746,565
2000	8,186,453	5,327,281	2,349,542

APPENDIX B
GOVERNORS OF GEORGIA

NAME	YEARS OF SERVICE
James Oglethorpe	1733–1743 (Trustee)
William Stephens	1743–1751 (President of the Colony of Georgia)
Henry Parker	1751–1752 (President of the Colony of Georgia)
Patrick Graham	1752–1754 (President of the Colony of Georgia)
John Reynolds	1754–1757
Henry Ellis	1757–1760
James Wright	1760–1776
George Walton	1775–1776 (President of the Council of Safety)
Archibald Bulloch	1776–1777 (President of the Council of Safety)
Button Gwinnett	1777 (President of the Council of Safety)
John Treutlen	1777–1778
John Houstoun	1778–1779
John Wereat	1779–1780 (President of Executive Council)
George Walton	1779–1780
James Prevost	1779 (British military governor)
James Wright	1779–1782 (Restored colonial governor)
Richard Howley	1780
Stephen Heard	1780 (President of Executive Council)
Myrick Davies	1780–1781 (President of Executive Council)
Nathan Brownson	1781–1782
John Martin	1782–1783
Lyman Hall	1783–1784
John Houstoun	1784–1785
Samuel Elbert	1785–1786
Edward Telfair	1786–1787

George Mathews	1787–1788
George Handley	1788–1789
George Walton	1789
Edward Telfair	1789–1793
George Mathews	1793–1796
Jared Irwin	1796–1798
James Jackson	1798–1801
David Emanuel	1801 (President of the Senate)
Josiah Tattnall, Jr.	1801–1802
John Milledge	1802–1806
Jared Irwin	1806–1809 (President of the Senate)
David Mitchell	1809–1813
Peter Early	1813–1815
David Mitchell	1815–1817
William Rabun	1817–1819
Matthew Talbot	1819 (President of the Senate)
John Clark	1819–1823
George Troup	1823–1827
John Forsyth	1827–1829
George Gilmer	1829–1831
Wilson Lumpkin	1831–1835
William Schley	1835–1837
George Gilmer	1837–1839
Charles McDonald	1839–1843
George Crawford	1843–1847
George Towns	1847–1851
Howell Cobb	1851–1853
Herschel Johnson	1853–1857
Joseph E. Brown	1857–1865
James Johnson	1865 (Provisional Governor)
Charles Jenkins	1865–1868
General Thomas Ruger	1868 (Provisional Governor)
Rufus Bullock	1868–1871
Benjamin Conley	1871–1872 (President of the Senate)
James Smith	1872–1877
Alfred Colquitt	1877–1882
Alexander Stephens	1882–1883
James Boynton	1883 (President of the Senate)
Henry McDaniel	1883–1886
John Gordon	1886–1890

William Northen	1890–1894
William Atkinson	1894–1898
Allen Candler	1898–1902
Joseph Terrell	1902–1907
Hoke Smith	1907–1909
Joseph M. Brown	1909–1911
Hoke Smith	1911
John Slaton	1911–1912 (President of the Senate)
Joseph M. Brown	1912–1913
John Slaton	1913–1915
Nathaniel Harris	1915–1917
Hugh Dorsey	1917–1921
Thomas Hardwick	1921–1923
Clifford Walker	1923–1927
Lamartine Hardman	1927–1931
Richard Russell, Jr.	1931–1933
Eugene Talmadge	1933–1937
Eurith Rivers	1937–1941
Eugene Talmadge	1941–1943
Ellis Arnall	1943–1947
Melvin Thompson	1947–1948
Herman Talmadge	1948–1955
Marvin Griffin	1955–1959
Ernest Vandiver	1959–1963
Carl Sanders	1963–1967
Lester Maddox	1967–1971
James Carter	1971–1975
George Busbee	1975–1983
Joe Frank Harris	1983–1991
Zell Miller	1991–1999
Roy Barnes	1999–2003
Sonny Perdue	2003–

APPENDIX C
COUNTIES IN ORDER OF CREATION

1. Wilkes (February 5, 1777)
2. Richmond (February 5, 1777)
3. Burke (February 5, 1777)
4. Effingham (February 5, 1777)
5. Chatham (February 5, 1777)
6. Liberty (February 5, 1777)
7. Glynn (February 5, 1777)
8. Camden (February 5, 1777)
9. Franklin (February 25, 1784)
10. Washington (February 25, 1784)
11. Greene (February 3, 1786)
12. Columbia (December 10, 1790)
13. Elbert (December 10, 1790)
14. Screven (December 14, 1793)
15. Hancock (December 17, 1793)
16. Warren (December 19, 1793)
17. Oglethorpe (December 19, 1793)
18. McIntosh (December 19, 1793)
19. Bryan (December 19, 1793)
20. Montgomery (December 19, 1793)
21. Bulloch (February 8, 1796)
22. Jackson (February 11, 1796)
23. Jefferson (February 20, 1796)
24. Lincoln (February 20, 1796)
25. Tattnall (December 5, 1801)
26. Clarke (December 5, 1801)
27. Wayne (May 11, 1803)
28. Wilkinson (May 11, 1803)
29. Baldwin (May 11, 1803)
30. Morgan (December 10, 1807)
31. Jasper (December 10, 1807)
32. Jones (December 10, 1807)
33. Putnam (December 10, 1807)
34. Laurens (December 10, 1807)
35. Telfair (December 10, 1807)
36. Pulaski (December 13, 1808)
37. Twiggs (December 14, 1809)
38. Madison (December 5, 1811)
39. Emanuel (December 10, 1812)
40. Early (December 15, 1818)
41. Irwin (December 15, 1818)
42. Appling (December 15, 1818)
43. Walton (December 15, 1818)
44. Gwinnett (December 15, 1818)
45. Hall (December 15, 1818)
46. Habersham (December 15, 1818)
47. Rabun (December 21, 1819)
48. Dooly (May 15, 1821)
49. Houston (May 15, 1821)
50. Monroe (May 15, 1821)
51. Fayette (May 15, 1821)
52. Henry (May 15, 1821)
53. Newton (December 24, 1821)
54. DeKalb (December 9, 1822)
55. Bibb (December 9, 1822)
56. Pike (December 9, 1822)
57. Crawford (December 9, 1822)
58. Decatur (December 8, 1823)
59. Upson (December 15, 1824)
60. Ware (December 15, 1824)
61. Lee (June 9, 1825)
62. Muscogee (June 9, 1825)

63. Troup (June 9, 1825)
64. Coweta (June 9, 1825)
65. Carroll (June 9, 1825)
66. Baker (December 12, 1825)
67. Thomas (December 23, 1825)
68. Lowndes (December 23, 1825)
69. Taliaferro (December 24, 1825)
70. Butts (December 24, 1825)
71. Meriwether (December 14, 1827)
72. Harris (December 14, 1827)
73. Talbot (December 14, 1827)
74. Marion (December 14, 1827)
75. Randolph (December 20, 1828)
76. Campbell (December 20, 1828)*
77. Heard (December 22, 1830)
78. Stewart (December 23, 1830)
79. Cherokee (December 26, 1831)
80. Sumter (December 16, 1831)
81. Forsyth (December 3, 1832)
82. Lumpkin (December 3, 1832)
83. Union (December 3, 1832)
84. Cobb (December 3, 1832)
85. Gilmer (December 3, 1832)
86. Murray (December 3, 1832)
87. Bartow (December 3, 1832)
88. Floyd (December 3, 1832)
89. Paulding (December 3, 1832)
90. Walker (December 18, 1833)
91. Macon (December 14, 1837)
92. Dade (December 25, 1837)
93. Chattooga (December 28, 1838)
94. Gordon (February 13, 1850)
95. Clinch (February 14, 1850)
96. Polk (December 20, 1851)
97. Spalding (December 20, 1851)
98. Whitfield (December 30, 1851)
99. Taylor (January 15, 1852)

100. Catoosa (December 5, 1853)
101. Pickens (December 5, 1853)
102. Hart (December 7, 1853)
103. Dougherty (December 15, 1853)
104. Webster (December 16, 1853)
105. Fulton (December 20, 1853)
106. Worth (December 20, 1853)
107. Fannin (January 21, 1854)
108. Coffee (February 9, 1854)
109. Chattahoochee (February 13, 1854)
110. Clay (February 16, 1854)
111. Charlton (February 18, 1854)
112. Calhoun (February 20, 1854)
113. Haralson (January 26, 1856)
114. Terrell (February 16, 1856)
115. Colquitt (February 25, 1856)
116. Berrien (February 25, 1856)
117. Miller (February 26, 1856)
118. Towns (March 6, 1856)
119. Dawson (December 3, 1857)
120. Pierce (December 18, 1857)
121. Milton (December 18, 1857)*
122. Glascock (December 19, 1857)
123. Mitchell (December 21, 1857)
124. Schley (December 22, 1857)
125. White (December 22, 1857)
126. Wilcox (December 22, 1857)
127. Clayton (November 30, 1858)
128. Quitman (December 10, 1858)
129. Banks (December 11, 1858)
130. Johnson (December 11, 1858)
131. Brooks (December 11, 1858)
132. Echols (December 13, 1858)
133. Douglas (October 17, 1870)
134. McDuffie (October 18, 1870)
135. Rockdale (October 18, 1870)
136. Dodge (October 26, 1870)

137. Oconee (February 25, 1875)
138. Crisp (August 17, 1905)
139. Grady (August 17, 1905)
140. Jenkins (August 17, 1905)
141. Tift (August 17, 1905)
142. Jeff Davis (August 18, 1905)
143. Stephens (August 18, 1905)
144. Toombs (August 18, 1905)
145. Turner (August 18, 1905)
146. Ben Hill (November 6, 1906)
147. Bleckley (November 5, 1912)
148. Wheeler (November 5, 1912)
149. Barrow (November 3, 1914)

150. Candler (November 3, 1914)
151. Bacon (November 3, 1914)
152. Evans (November 3, 1914)
153. Atkinson (November 5, 1918)
154. Treutlen (November 5, 1918)
155. Cook (November 5, 1918)
156. Seminole (November 2, 1920)
157. Lanier (November 2, 1920)
158. Brantley (November 2, 1920)
159. Long (November 2, 1920)
160. Lamar (November 2, 1920)
161. Peach (November 4, 1924)

*Milton and Campbell counties merged with Fulton County on January 1, 1932.

APPENDIX D
STATE SYMBOLS

Amphibian	Green Tree Frog
Bird	Brown Thrasher
Butterfly	Tiger Swallowtail
Crop	Peanut
Fish	Largemouth Bass
Flower	Cherokee Rose
Fossil	Shark Tooth
Fruit	Peach
Gem	Quartz
Insect	Honeybee
Marine Mammal	Right Whale
Mineral	Staurolite
Motto	"Wisdom, Justice & Moderation"
Prepared Food	Grits
Reptile	Gopher Tortoise
Song	"Georgia on My Mind"
Tree	Live Oak
Vegetable	Vidalia Sweet Onion
Wildflower	Azalea

INDEX